A regional guide to
FISHING
IN BRITAIN

Marshall Cavendish London & New York

Published by Marshall Cavendish Books Limited.
58 Old Compton Street
London W1V 5PA

© Marshall Cavendish Limited 1977, 1978, 1979

This material was first published by
Marshall Cavendish Limited in the
publication *Fisherman's Handbook*

First printed in 1979

Printed in Great Britain

ISBN 0 85685 696 7

Introduction

With the ease of movement afforded by modern transport, the angler is able to choose from a wider variety of waters when planning a fishing trip. This means that he can now decide upon the species and style of fishing that he prefers and find an area suited to his purpose.

A Regional Guide to Fishing in Britain supplies all the information the angler needs to know about fishing grounds in this country, presented in an interesting and straightforward manner. Each chapter includes several detailed maps of the area concerned and colour photographs to provide a flavour of the surroundings. The book also supplies details of the roads by which access may be gained to the water, the species to be found and information on licences and tickets, local clubs, associations and tackle dealers.

Whether you are planning a whole fishing holiday, a weekend or just a day out, *A Regional Guide to Fishing in Britain* will prove invaluable.

Contents

Bill Howes

North East Scotland

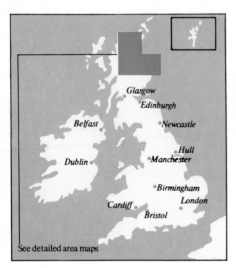

See detailed area maps

The North East of Scotland is one of the most hallowed sanctuaries of the salmon angler. Nursing the rivers Spey and Dee, two of the most prolific salmon rivers, it provides water for the Findhorn, Don, Deveron, Ugie, Nairn, Ness, Conon, Brora, Beauly, Helmsdale and Thurso—not to mention a myriad of smaller tributaries, rivers and lochs too numerous to mention.

Richard Waddington, author of *Salmon Fishing—Philosophy and Practice,* wrote in 1959 of the River Spey: 'This is the king of all the Scottish rivers. Compared to the Spey, the Dee is trivial, the Tay lacking in fish, and the Tweed tedious'. Twenty years later the fortunes of the other rivers may vary, but most salmon anglers of experience would agree with him. The River Spey, from the source to its mouth in Spey Bay, offers challenging fishing, and at a time of the year when other rivers might not be at their best. The Spey does not suffer fools gladly and as a rule will only yield its trophies to those who have served a good apprenticeship to it.

The season opens on 11 February and in a mild winter a few salmon will quickly make good progress into the upper reaches. It is not unusual, for instance, to get odd fresh salmon as far upstream as Grantown during the opening days and weeks. The big build-up of stocks, however, seems to come in late March, April and May—a time when spring fishing might be said to be vaguely allied to spring-like weather. Unfortunately, most of the Spey fishing is in private hands. Some may be had through various estate agents, but usually the best is reserved year upon year by sitting tenants, and it is only rarely that a new let becomes available.

Grantown-on-Spey

A popular centre for the visiting angler is Grantown-on-Spey, where a seven-mile stretch of fishing is made available through the Strathspey Angling Association. The water tends to get heavily fished, but at £5.00 per week plus VAT it must represent about the best value for money in salmon fishing today. There are also, every spring and autumn, angling courses run at the Palace Hotel and the Seafield Lodge Hotel in

Three anglers keeping properly spaced apart on the fabulous River Spey near Cromdale Bridge at Castle Grant.

Arthur Oglesby

Grantown. Visitors can get all the instruction they need, together with a wonderful opportunity to have a few days' fishing on superb private beats.

Generally, the cream of Spey fishing begins at Grantown and thence downstream. Craigellachie and Aberlour make other good centres for the visitor and there is fishing available at the Aberlour and the Lour Hotels at Aberlour, and at the Craigellachie Hotel in Craigellachie, which offers fishing at £30 per week plus VAT.

Interesting tributaries of the Spey include the rivers Avon (pronounced Arn), Dulnain, Feshie, and Truim—the latter noted for excellent brown trout fishing. In a good year the Spey not only abounds with salmon, but has one of the most fantastic runs of sea trout. Only fractionally exploited, there is also excellent brown trout fishing.

The river Dee, rising on the slopes of Ben MacDhui and flowing almost due east through Aberdeenshire, undoubtedly offers some of the finest fly fishing for salmon. It is often referred to as the Royal Dee, and the magnificence of the river and its fishing cannot be disputed. For many miles the river is more intimate than the Spey and from Braemar down there is some legendary fishing for salmon. Unfortunately, much of the river is privately owned and let to long-standing tenants. The casual visitor can seldom find access, although hotels on Deeside may just offer a cancellation.

The premier Dee

For the keen fly fishermen, the Dee is one of the premier rivers in Britain. Beats at Invercauld, Dinnet, Blackhall, Woodend Cairnton (where the late Arthur Wood made his fame) Crathes and Park are almost household words with the salmon fanatic, although it is mainly a question of gaining access before looking for a fish. Some fishing is occasionally available at Mar Lodge in Braemar (Tel: 216) at £24 per day plus VAT which includes gillie and Landrover, and water is sometimes available at £10 a day at the Invercauld Alous Hotel in Braemar (Tel: 605), which has nine miles of fishing on one bank, but no Sunday fishing. One can also try the Banchory Lodge Hotel in Banchory where some rods are available by booking well in advance. Another Hotel is the Cambus O'May Hotel near Ballater (Tel: Ballater 428). Here, fly only is allowed from 15 April to 15 June, with fly and artificial spinner baits at other times. Applications for permits should be made in advance to the Glentanar Estate Office, Aboyne.

Don makes a comeback

Just north of Deeside lies the River Don. Badly hit by pollution, it has recently made a comeback as a salmon river. Among sporting fly fishermen, however, it has a reputation, particularly for its splendid brown trout. Fortunately there are many hotels in the area providing access at modest cost.

Three hotels to mention are the Allargue Arms Hotel in Corgarff, Strathdon (Tel: Corgarff 210), the Kintore Arms Hotel in Kintore, Aberdeenshire, and the Colquhonnie Hotel in Strathdon, which

North East Scotland

(Right) Anglers enjoying expert tuition on part of Arthur Oglesby's famous salmon and trout fishing school at Grantown-on-Spey. Weekly courses are open to anglers from absolute beginners to those anglers having some knowledge of the sport and its techniques.

(Below) Our map of Eastern Scotland's vast and glorious fishing potential.

Arthur Oglesby

offers nine miles of fishing. All hotels offer fishing for both salmon and brown trout.

One can apply for permits to the Municipal Offices in Inverurie (Tel: 891) or to the Inverurie Angling Association which offers day fishing at £1 (February to August) and at £1.50 (September to October), with juniors half price.

Kemnay Fishing

There are also the Kemnay Fishings with permits on application from Kemnay House, (Tel: 2220) and the Kinclune Beat with salmon rods at £3 per day, and trout rods at £1 per day, obtainable from T. Hillary, Stonecircle, Glenkindie, Aberdeenshire. Further information can be obtained from the *Angler's Guide to Scottish Waters* published by the Scottish Tourist Board.

A noted sea trout river is the Ythan, which has excellent runs from June to September. Fishing may sometimes be available from the Udny Arms Hotel at Newburgh, and sometimes, with early booking, from the Ythan Fishery, Udny and District Management Ltd., The Stables, Udny, Ellon, Aberdeenshire. The hotel has a 24-hour self-issuing service for tickets at £3 a day. A boat with a gillie costs £9 a day, and a boat without a gillie £6 a day.

At Banff the River Deveron empties its waters into the Moray Firth. It is a salmon river of modest repute, but also gets runs of large sea trout—not to mention a native population of good brownies. The Banff Springs Hotel can sometimes arrange fishing while at Turriff six weekly permits are available to resident visitors from the Turriff Angling Association at 3 Sunnybrae, Turriff (Tel: 2428). One can also try the Arms Castle Hotel at Huntly (Tel: 2696). The peak season

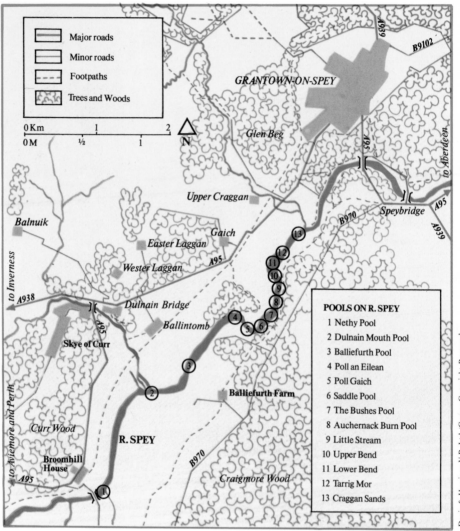

POOLS ON R. SPEY

1 Nethy Pool
2 Dulnain Mouth Pool
3 Balliefurth Pool
4 Poll an Eilean
5 Poll Gaich
6 Saddle Pool
7 The Bushes Pool
8 Auchernack Burn Pool
9 Little Stream
10 Upper Bend
11 Lower Bend
12 Tarrig Mor
13 Craggan Sands

for salmon is from March to October and for sea trout, from June to August.

Moving westwards there are three modest salmon rivers, the Lossie, Findhorn and Nairn. The Findhorn is perhaps the most noted, being a beautiful river and receiving good runs of spring fish. Most of it is in private hands. Forres Angling Association, however, issues weekly tickets to visiting residents at £5 per week (11 February to 31 July) and £7 per week (1 August to 30 September) with prices subject to review, and

Detail map of the Spey area controlled by the Strathspey Angling Association.

there may be good fishing available if a run can be intercepted.

The River Ness at Inverness is readily available, and the tackle shops issue tickets for the Inverness Angling Club stretch which runs from the estuary upstream for nearly three miles. Loch Ness, apart from its monster, also offers good sea trout and brown trout fishing, with a network of

10

feeders and smaller lochs available. The River Moriston is a noted tributary, and it might prove useful to enquire about opportunities at the Glenmoriston Arms Hotel.

Above the Moray Firth

North of the Moray Firth there are such great salmon rivers as the Conon, Brora, Beauly, Shin, Helmsdale, Thurso and Halladale. Technically they should not be dismissed with little more than a mere mention; but in effect most are available only to riparian proprietors or their guests and tenants. On the Thurso though, some salmon fly fishing can be arranged through Thurso Fisheries Ltd at Thurso East (Tel:

3134) or through The River Superintendent at Braal, Halkirk (Tel: 251). Excellent accommodation and fishing may also be available at the Ulbster Arms Hotel in Halkirk provided one books early.

It has been impossible in the space available to give little more than a brief mention to some of the famous rivers in the North-East of Scotland. The price charged gives some clue to the fishing potential, but with migratory fish one must remember another thing. To get the best of salmon fishing on the good rivers needs luck, but to get it on the lesser-known ones requires something approaching a miracle!

INFORMATION

LICENCES

In Scotland, no general licence is needed. . All that is required is a permit for the specific place you wish to fish (often permits cover a number of waters), and this may be obtained from the Angling clubs, tackle dealers and hotels. More local information can be obtained from the Scottish Tourist Board, 23 Ravelston Terr, Edinburgh EH4 3EU.

The Scottish Tourist Board publishes the following useful booklets: *Angler's Guide to Scottish Waters, Where to Stay in Scotland,* listing cottages, chalets, flats and caravans to let, Self-Catering Accommodation in Scotland, and Camping and Caravan Sites in Scotland.

Close season: trout 7 October to 14 March inclusive (although many clubs extend their dates to allow the fish to reach better condition). Trout may not be sold between the end of August and the beginning of April, and not at any time if less than 8in long. For salmon close season, the following dates apply to rod fishing, and different dates apply for net fishing. River Dee 1 October to 31 January, River Deveron 1 October to 10 February, River Don 1 November to 10 February, River Halladale 1 October to 11 January, River Lossie 16 October to 10 February, River Nairn 1 October to 10 February, River Ness 16 October to 4 January, River Spey 1 October to 10 February, River Thurso 6 October to 10 January, River Ythan 1 November to 10 February.

FISHERIES

RIVER SPEY

Palace Hotel, Grantown-on-Spey, Moray.
Seafield Lodge Hotel, Grantown-on-Spey, Moray.
Aberlour Hotel, Aberlour, Banffshire. Tel 287.
Craigellachie Hotel, Craigellachie, Banffshire. Tel 204.

RIVER DEE

Mar Lodge, Braemar, Aberdeenshire AB3 5YJ. Tel 216.
Invercauld Arms Hotel, Braemar, Aberdeenshire. Tel 605.
Banchory Lodge Hotel, Banchory, Kincardineshire. Tel 2625.
Cambus O'May Hotel, near Ballater, Aberdeenshire. 428.
Glentanar Estate Office, Aboyne, Aberdeenshire.

RIVER DEVERON

Clerk to Fishing, Duke St, Huntly, Aberdeenshire. Tel 2291.
Banff Springs Hotel, Goldenknowes Rd, Banff, Banffshire. Telephone 2881.
Arms Castle Hotel, Huntly, Aberdeenshire. Tel 2696.

RIVER DON

Allargue Arms Hotel, Corgarff, Strathdon, Aberdeenshire. Telephone Corgarff 210.

Kintore Arms Hotel, Kintore, Aberdeenshire.
Colquhonnie Hotel, Strathdon, Aberdeenshire. Tel 210.
Municipal Offices, Inverurie, Aberdeenshire AB5 9AQ. Tel 8981.
Kemnay Fishings, Kemnay House, Kemnay, Aberdeenshire AB5 9LH. Tel 2220.
Kinclune Beat, T Hillary, Stonecircle, Glenkindie, Aberdeenshire. Tel 335.

RIVER YTHAN

The Ythan Fishery, Udny and District Management Ltd, The Stables, Udny, Ellon, Aberdeenshire.

RIVER MORISTON

Glenmoriston Estates Office, Glenmoriston, Inverness-shire. Telephone 202.
Glenmoriston Arms Hotel, Glenmoriston, Inverness-shire. Tel 206.

RIVER THURSO

Thurso Fisheries Ltd, Thurso East. Tel 3134.
The River Superintendent, Braal, Halkirk. Tel 251
Ulbster Arms Hotel, Halkirk, Caithness. Tel: Thurso 3134 or Halkirk 641.
Udny Arms Hotel, Newburgh, Aberdeenshire. Tel 273.

LOCAL CLUBS AND ASSOCIATIONS

Elgin Angling Assoc, H B Fleetwood, St Mary's, Dunbar St, Lossiemouth, Moray IV31 6RD. Tel 3142.
Fyvie Angling Assoc, G A Joss, Clydesdale Bank Ltd, Fyvie. Aberdeenshire. Tel: Fyvie 233.
Forres Angling Assoc, P. Garrow, 2 Robertson Place, Forres.
Inverness Angling Club, J Fraser, 33 Hawthorn Drive, Inverness IV3 5RG.
Strathspey Angling Improvement Assoc, G G Mortimer, 81 High Street, Grantown-on-Spey. Tel 2684.
Turriff Angling Assoc, J. Storie, 22 Westbrae Cr. Turriff. Aberdeenshire. Tel 3536.

TACKLE DEALERS

J Munroe, 95 High St, Abelour, Grampian
Abu Fishing Centre, Aviemore
J J Shanks & Son, Sporting Stores, High St, Dingwall, Ross.
The Angling Centre, Moss St, Elgin.
The Tackle Shop, 188 High St, Elgin
The Tackle Shop, Toll Booth St, Forres, Moray.
G G Mortimer, The Tackle Shop, 61 High St, Grantown-on-Spey
Gray & Co, Union St, Inverness
The Sporting Stores, Inglis St, Inverness.
MacDonald's Tackle, Sinclair St, Thurso.
J Ross, Main St, Tomintoul by Ballindalloch

Tyne and Tweed

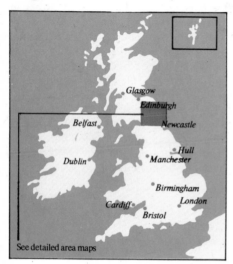

See detailed area maps

Peeblesshire Association waters. Tickets must be booked in advance, however, as only 20 a day are issued. Trout tickets are available for 30 miles of the same water at £1.50 day, £3 Saturday, £6 week and £9 two weeks. Visitors can take out a £15 Monday to Friday Tourist permit bookable from the hotel where they stay. Spinning and maggot fishing are banned.

Kelso is a popular fishing centre. A short 200-yard stretch of free fishing known locally as 'The Cobby' produces good trout and grayling, and Kelso AA offers tickets on both banks at £1 a day, £3 a week, or £6 a season, available from tackle dealers.

At Coldstream, day tickets are available for the Scottish bank only, from the mouth

The rivers Till, Teviot, Aln, Coquet, Wansbeck, Blyth and Rede fall within the Northumbrian Water Authority area, while the River Tweed, which forms the boundary between Scotland and England, is controlled by the Tweed Commissioners. No licence is necessary to fish on the Tweed and its tributaries, and no close season applies for coarse fish.

The Tweed, queen of salmon rivers, also offers good coarse fishing in its deep clear waters. Dace and gudgeon are on the increase, and roach, perch and grayling have long been established species. With over 100 miles of waterway between its source at Tweed Wells to the fortified harbour at Berwick there is plenty of room for fishing along its grassy banks.

Peebles

In the town of Peebles, there is approximately a mile of free fishing for trout, with the odd grayling showing. Other waters are available on ticket. Two miles of town water are available for salmon rods from 14 November to 13 September, Ian Frazer (Sports) in Peebles issues salmon tickets at £3.50 per rod per day for over eight miles of

The River Tweed is famous for its fine salmon fishing. (Below) In the upper reaches, Innerleithen near Peebles.

of the tiny River Leet to the A697 roadbridge downriver. Dace abound in the shallow outlet of the Leet, while grayling to 3lb are found in the downstream shallow. Just above the roadbridge is the 'Big Slack' offering unique sport. Big roach shoals feed in its depths and the late autumn and winter months provide top catches with many fish to 3lb. The river is wide here, so long casting is necessary to reach them except in flood conditions when they close in. Tickets at 25p are sold on the bank.

The Ladykirk and Norham Angling Association water is primarily shallow over a sandy bed, but with five miles of fishing the visitor has a good choice of swims. Norham village, on the English bank, is reached from the A698 from Berwick-on-Tweed, and two hotels in the village, Victoria Hotel (0289 82237) and the Mason Arms (0289 82326), sell Association permits, price 30p day, £1 week, £3 season, excluding salmon.

At Horncliffe the river becomes tidal. Just upstream, the view from high on a cliff overlooking the river takes in a large

Arthur Oglesby

island. This marks the start of free fishing which continues down to the estuary. Deep pools alternate with gravel shallows. The pool immediately below the village offers pleasant mixed fishing sheltered by a natural windbreak, but coarse anglers prefer farther downstream where the Union Bridge, a chainbridge, spans the river. The deep pool just below, on the left bank, runs off into a narrow bend. Big hauls to 60lb of dace and roach are taken from this pool on float-fished maggot drawn or 'tripped' across the river bed. Access to both village and Union Bridge is from the A698.

Tweed and tributaries

The River Tweed has many tributaries. The lower ones are of more interest to anglers, although the small upper streams hold plenty of small trout and in some the fishing is free. Many fine sea trout run up the River Till, lowest tributary into England. Its trout are mainly small, but a good head of grayling provides variety. The huge roach shoals vanished some years ago and few are now caught, but the autumn run of sea trout includes some really large fish.

Ford is the main angling centre for visitors. Downstream of Ford Bridge the river is preserved for match-bookings by angling clubs, while upriver is the Ford and Etal Estates water—a short stretch on the left bank and several miles on the right bank. Permits at 50p day, £1.50 week (no Sunday fishing) are issued by the Estates Office at Ford, the Post Office, the Head Keeper at Ford Kennels, or on Saturday mornings only from the bailiff who is on the roadbridge between 8am and 10am. Telephone bookings can be made to Crookham 224. The permit allows fly, worm, spinning and maggot fishing, and includes historic Flodden Field ford. Access is from the Wooler-Coldstream road.

In its lower reaches, two miles of the river are controlled by Tillmouth Park Hotel which also controls three miles of the River Tweed. Permits are issued for both game and coarse fishing, including Sunday fishing, with priority to residents. The Hotel is on the

Arthur Oglesby

A698 from Berwick-on-Tweed, and the traveller crosses the Till just before the hotel entrance. The deep valley curves here offering shelter on even the most windy day.

The River Teviot rises on the Roxburgh-Dumfries border and tumbles its way two-thirds of the way across the country, with the main Carlisle-Berwick road along most of its length.

In its upper reaches, it is a bubbling river with numerous rock pools and gravel runs. Hawick Angling Club controls many miles, good for trout and grayling, and offers day tickets at 50p, or a Monday to Friday permit for £1. Saturday fishing is limited to the small upriver streams only.

Jedburgh

At Jedburgh, midway between Kelso and Hawick, the river is wider and caters for salmon rods, trout and grayling seekers, and coarse anglers. Fine roach inhabit the deeper pools. Day tickets available on the bank from the Jed Forest AA bailiff. Roach, dace, grayling, trout and salmon inhabit the lower reaches and tickets can be obtained in Kelso for Kelso AA waters.

The River Aln is a short river falling from the Cheviot Hills, holding trout, and with a sea trout and salmon run. Fly fishing only is

Map shows the course of the main rivers of Northumberland and their fishing spots. (Below) the Tweed at Innerleithen.

allowed above the short tidal reach. Day tickets (trout only) can be bought from tackle dealers in Alnwick at 62½p day, £2 week, £2.50 month, £4 season. There is no Sunday fishing.

The Coquet

The River Coquet is the major Northumbrian salmon river. Bull trout feature here and arguments still run over whether these deep-chested fish are a unique strain of trout. Nearly 16 miles of this lovely river, from Tosson Ford to the Brinkburn Estate, are owned by the Duke of Northumberland and fished by the Northumbrian Federation of Anglers which issues 14-day tickets at £11 to genuine visitors to the area. The tickets cover salmon, sea and brown trout fishing.

At Weldon Bridge, about 1½ miles above the Federation water, the 'Angler's Arms', (Tel. Long Framlington 271) stands against a bridge carrying the Wooller-Morpeth road. No charge is made to residents of the hotel for three rods on a short section.

The River Wansbeck rises near the North

14

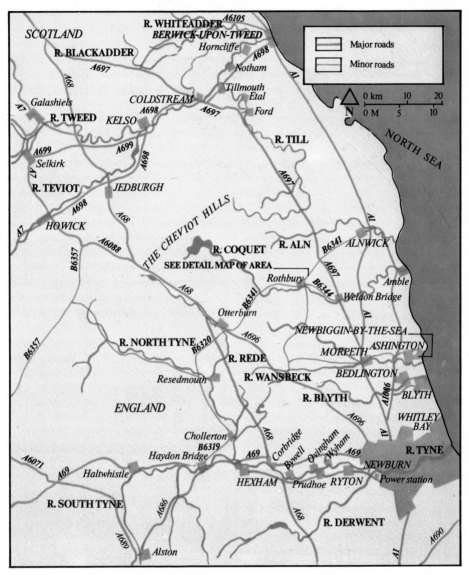

River Tyne, and supports a good population of brown trout. Fishing is mainly restricted to fly and upstream worm. The installation of a fish pass at Morpeth failed to induce migratory fish to run up this river. Though most fishing is in private hands or under club control with no permits issued, a short section running through Morpeth town is free on both banks. Mainly a shallow river, it still holds good fish. Another short section of free fishing is available at Sheepwash.

The River Blyth offers trout upstream and limited sport with roach, grayling and gudgeon in the lower and middle reaches. Blyth Council issue day tickets. Permit fishing is available in Plessey Woods, a National Park, where the river flows through a series of pools. Tickets (for fly fishing only) are obtainable from Bedlington and Blagdon Angling Club at 50p, but are restricted to

Tyne and Tweed

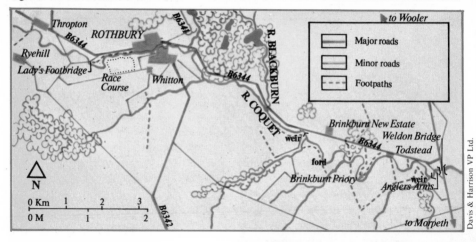

Detail map shows the day-ticket water available on the River Coquet. (Below) the River North Tyne at Barrasford.

genuine visitors from over 80 miles away.

The River Tyne, once a great salmon river, has salmon returning, and its brown trout to 5lb offer good sport. A prolific head of dace dominate the tidal reaches with roach returning after vanishing several years ago. Two major rivers, the North and South Tyne, join at Waters Meet above Hexham, and the parent river flows from this point down to Newcastle alongside the main A69 Carlisle-Newcastle road.

The upper Tyne

In its upper reaches, the Tyne is bubbling and fast-falling and in places scarcely wider than a stream. The Alston and District AA issues day tickets at 25p, obtainable from tackle dealers in Alston.

At Haltwhistle, the river widens and has some nice pools and mainly a gravel bed. Dace mingle with trout, and week tickets for this stretch, issued by the Haltwhistle and District Angling Assoc, cost £3, obtainable at Freggs Sports Shop.

Beyond Haltwhistle, the South Tyne Angling Assoc restrict the issue of day tickets to visitors staying in the village of Heydon Bridge, while at Reedmouth Junction, the North Tyne and Rede rivers join, and the Bellingham AC controls 4½ miles of river.

16

By Chollerford, the river has become quite wide, but is still quite shallow over a rock, gravel and sandy bottom. A dam holds back the flow just below the roadbridge where the A6079 road from Newcastle to Carlisle crosses the river. Trout are plentiful here, dace shy, but large fish to 1lb are found, and the odd roach The George Hotel issues day tickets at 75p for the right bank.

Downstream at Hexham, permits (fly only) to fish the steady deep swims fronting Tyne Green are available from Tynedale District Council, Council Offices, Hexham. Tel 0434 4011. Tickets cost £1 day, £12.50 season, with a reduced fee for residents.

At Corbridge the river runs fast over gravel. Fishing is free for a short section upstream and downstream of the Corbridge-Hexham roadbridge on both banks and the swims upstream on the right bank are favoured for trout and dace. The limits of free waters are indicated by signposts.

Northumbrian Federation

The Northumbrian Federation of Anglers controls both banks on most of the water from Bywell to Ovingham, and easy access is provided by a B road along the north bank. Fourteen-day permits are available to genuine visitors at £11, and should be booked well in advance.

Spectrum Colour Library

At Wylam, from the pumping station above the village to just below the road-bridge, Wylam Angling Club controls the fishing. The river holds good trout, perch and dace, and a fine salmon pool ends the water below the bridge. Day tickets (week-days only) are available at £1 for salmon, 50p for trout and coarse fishing (juniors and OAPs half-price) and can be bought from Dr Jones, 6 Stephenson Terrace, Wylam.

West Denton AC

Farther downstream, a traffic-light-controlled, single-lane, bridge spans the river between Newburn and Ryton. Upstream on the left bank West Denton Angling Club claim the fishing rights but allow individual anglers to fish at no charge. Visiting club bookings for matches are also accepted on

INFORMATION

WATER AUTHORITY
Northumbrian Water Authority, Northumbria House, Regent Centre, Gosforth, Newcastle-upon-Tyne NE3 3PX. Tel 843151.

LICENCES
Salmon, trout and freshwater fish: season £5, month £2.
Trout, migratory trout, freshwater fish and eels: season £3 (juniors £1.50), month £1.50.
Trout and freshwater fish excluding migratory trout: season £2 (juniors £1), month £1.
Freshwater fish and eels: season £1 (juniors 50p).
Close seasons: salmon 1 November to 31 January; sea trout 1 November to 2 April; brown trout 1 October to 21 March; coarse fish 15 March to 15 June.
Size limits: migratory trout 10 in (25 cm). There are similar limits for trout taken from specified waters in the Authority's area.

FISHERIES
Ford and Ethal Estates Office, Ford, Northumberland (Tel Crookham 224).
The George Hotel, Chollerford, Northumberland (Tel Humshaugh 219).
Percy Arms Hotel, Otterburn, Northumberland (Tel 261).

LOCAL CLUBS AND ASSOCIATIONS
Alston and District Angling Club, P Renwick, Ram's Head

Spectrum Colour Library

application to the Secretary. The water is very tidal and the banks muddy. Bottom fishing is recommended, the best results being in winter months with dace and roach.

The lowest reaches of the river considered worth fishing are on a short section below Newburn Bridge at Stella South Power Station—water controlled by the Middlesbrough Angling Club. Beyond that point, above the confluence with the River Derwent, pollution and deoxygenation combine to levels fatal to fish.

River Rede

For those who prefer stream fishing, the River Rede, tributary of the Tyne, is a fine trout fishery. Fly fishing only is allowed and tickets are available from the Percy Arms Hotel, Otterburn (Tel 0830 20261) at £1.25 for a day, 75p for a half day.

The River Aln is a short Northumberland river emptying into the North Sea at Alnmouth. It holds trout, with a run of sea trout and salmon, and is available on day ticket. A section of water by Alnwick Castle. South of the Aln, the River Coquet is the major Northumberland salmon river, and nearly 16 miles of good water are available here from Rothbury downstream.

Inn, Alston Cumbria.
Bellingham Angling Club, T H Armstrong, 24 Westlands, Bellingham, Hexham, Northumberland.
Bedlington and Blagdon Angling Club, S Symonds, 8 Moreland Drive, Bedlington, Northumberland.
Haltwhistle Angling Club, R J Smaile, 8 Wyden Terr, Haltwhistle, Northumberland.
Hawick Angling Club, A V Tokely, Lowood, Sunnyhill, Hawick, Borders, Scotland.
Kelso Angling Assoc, C Hutchinson, 55 Horsemarket, Kelso, Borders Scotland.
Middlesbrough Angling Club, B Watson, 53 Tollesby Lane, Marten, Middlesbrough, Cleveland.
Northumbrian Anglers' Federation, C Wade, 2 Ridge Villas, Bedlington, Northumberland.
Peebleshire Anglign Improvement Assoc, J Allan, 35 Edderston Rd, Peebles, Borders, Scotland.
South Tyne Angling Assoc, J Moore, 12A Radcliffe Rd, Haydon Bridge, Northumberland.
Wylham Angling Club, T R Bailey, Harby House, Wylham, Northumberland.
TACKLE DEALERS
McDermotts, 112 Station Rd, Ashington, Northumberland. Tel 812214.
Greys of Alnwick, 24 Hipsburn Cres. Lesbury, Alnwick.
Frasers Sports and Handicrafts, 27 West St. Berwick-on-Tweed. Tel 6844.

Cramsports Ltd, 13 Dudley Court, Cramlington.
Greeggs Sports Shop, Market Place, Haltwhistle. Tel 255.
Pyle, Hencoats, Hexham, Northumberland.
D O Stothert, 6 High St, Howick, Northumberland.
John Dickenson and Son, 35 The Square, Kelso. Tel 2687.
Redpath and Co, Tweedside Works, 55 Horse Market, Kelso. Tel 2578.
Rod and Line, 12 High St, Newbiggin-by-the-Sea. Tel 731.
R S Tackle Co, 36 Collingwood St, Newcastle-on-Tyne.
North East Sports, 60 Shields Rd, Newcastle-on-Tyne. Tel 651518.
Hall and Carr, 100 West Rd, Newcastle-on-Tyne.
Bagnall and Kirkwood, 52 Grey St, Newcastle-on-Tyne. Tel 25873.
John Robertson, 101 Percy St, Newcastle-on-Tyne.
Affleck Sports, 282 Shields Rd, Byker, Newcastle-on-Tyne. Tel 659300.
I Frazer (Sports), Northgate, Peebles. Tel 20979.
The tackle Shop, 106A Westoe Rd, South Shields, Tyne and Wear. Tel 60565.
J W Welch. 206 Ocean Rd, South Shields. Tel 63953.
Whales Tackle Shop, 22 Winchester St, South Shields. Tel 7445.
W Temple. 43 Ocean View. Whitley Bay, Tyne and Wear. Tel 56017.
The Tackle Shop, 34A High St, Wallsend, Tyne and Wear. Tel 626004.

North West Scotland

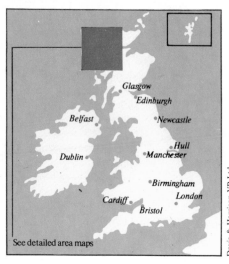

Davis & Harrison VP Ltd

See detailed area maps

The North West of Scotland is possibly the region least known and explored by itinerant anglers. It is not endowed with a vast network of roads and time and effort have to be taken to get there. Even then there might be little fishing of consequence unless earlier plans have been made. The area produces a high rainfall, but can also offer some wonderful fishing for migratory fish when the water is just right.

From the River Naver in the north down to Fort William there are myriad rivers, streams and lochs. Some, like the Naver and Laxford, have legendary reputations, but most do not offer fishing to the casual enquirer. At Bettyhill the Bettyhill Hotel provides for its residents two miles of sea trout fishing in the estuary of the Naver, and trout fishing on about 16 local trout lochs, while at Altnaharra the hotel provides fishing in Loch Naver, the river Mudale and Loch Hope. The season extends from 12 January to the end of September, with the best salmon fishing in March and April, trout from May to August, and sea trout from June to August. The best beats of the Naver, are reserved for long-standing

and permanent tenants or the riparian owners and their guests.

Fabulous salmon fishing

Salmon fishing, when it is just right, can be little short of the fabulous—with the possibility of double-figure catches per rod per day. All fishing is with fly, and at peak times frequently with single-handed rods, small flies and floating lines.

At Durness, the Cape Wrath Hotel has rights on the rivers Dionard, Grudie and Dall. Best times for migratory fish are from mid-June to mid-September, and there is also good brown trout fishing on several lochs—all at very modest cost. At Kinlochbervie the Garbet Hotel has rights on over 40 lochs and on a small spate river

The tiny fishing centre of Ullapool, in Ross and Cromarty, nestling amid the beautiful surrounding Highland mountains.

where sea and brown trout can be plentiful. For hotel guests the fishing is free.

Scourie is an excellent centre for the three game fish species. Out of 200 trout lochs, the Scourie Hotel has extensive fishing rights on over 100 of which four have salmon and sea trout. Boats and gillies are available and day fishing on Loch Stack and Loch More by special permit. Nearby, the Laxford river is strictly preserved.

Lochinver

At Lochinver, the rivers Inver and Kirkaig can give excellent fishing for migratory fish. The Inver, draining Loch Assynt, is private, but on the Kirkaig the Culag Hotel has residential facilities with instruction courses. If not required by guests, the hotel waters are opened to the public. Sea trout can be fished in Manse Loch, Kirkaig Seapool and Loch Culag, all of which offer boats, and there is bank fishing for brown trout on innumerable lochs nearby. Good sea fishing can be had.

Loch Assynt Angling Club has good trout fishing on 35 lochs and issues day and week tickets. These can be obtained from the secretary of the club, the Tourist Information Office in Lochinver (Tel 330), the Post Office at Stoer (Tel 201), the

A charter boat sets out from Ullapool in what anglers call a 'Force Nought'.

Spectrum Colour Library

North West Scotland

Len Cacutt

Drumbeg and Culag Hotels, or the Lochinver Fish Selling Co Ltd in Lochinver (Tel 228). Nearby Loch Roe and Manse Loch offer sea trout and salmon fishing from bank or boat, with day tickets available (except Sundays) during the season from 15 March to 6 October.

At Assynt, the Inchnadamph Hotel (Tel 202) has fishing facilities and boats available to residents. When the fishing is not used by guests, non-residents can apply.

June and July the best time

The best fishing begins with the first spates of June or July and much of the angler's success will depend entirely on the state of the water. In fact, this point cannot be too highly emphasized. Some of the West coast spate rivers do have legendary reputations, but they have been gained only at times when the river has been running off following a good flood. Sometimes the sport may be confined to hours rather than days, and there is no known way of predicting conditions. A well-planned holiday even at the peak of the season can be futile if the weather does not cooperate. If this happens, there is still a chance on the lochs for brown trout.

The Altnacealgach Hotel has famous brown trout fishing on Lochs Cama, Veyatie, Urigill and Borallan, with ten boats and gillies. Trout to 3lb are frequently encountered with even bigger fish a possibility in late spring and summer months.

(Above) South Uist, 40 miles away on the horizon, seen across the isle of Soay, and photographed from Elgol, on Skye.
(Right) Western Scotland and its waters.

Farther south at Achiltibuie, the Summer Isles Hotel has salmon and sea trout fishing on Loch Oscaig and the River Garvie from July to mid-October, and brown trout from mid-March—all at very modest cost. Loch Broom at Ullapool drains the rivers Ullapool, Dundonnell, Oscaig and Broom, and fishing is available from the Royal Hotel or the Warehouse Buildings at Ullapool. Try also J Macdonald of Inverpolly and D P Morrison of 30 Walker Street, Edinburgh.

Four famous salmon rivers

Farther east, four famous salmon rivers, the Oykel, Carron, Shin and Cassley, are not for the casual visitor. Occasionally, the Benmore Estate Office at Ardgay, Ross-shire offers fishing, or the Oykel Bridge Hotel. Most of the best fishing, however, is not only expensive, but let in advance. For the Cassley, rods can sometimes be negotiated through Bell-Ingram, 7 Walker Street, Edinburgh; but advance booking is essential.

No guide to angling in western Scotland could be complete without some mention of Loch Maree which, from July to October, is noted for its sea trout. The little River Ewe has good runs of salmon and sea trout from Poolewe up into the loch but most anglers

prefer to base themselves at the loch itself. There is the Kinlochewe Hotel or the Loch Maree Hotel which is owned by an angling syndicate and provides excellent facilities. Owing to a heavy demand for sea trout fishing, early reservations are advised.

Moving south there is yet another vast network of small rivers, streams and lochs. Many are hard to reach by road and only local knowledge would prove helpful. At

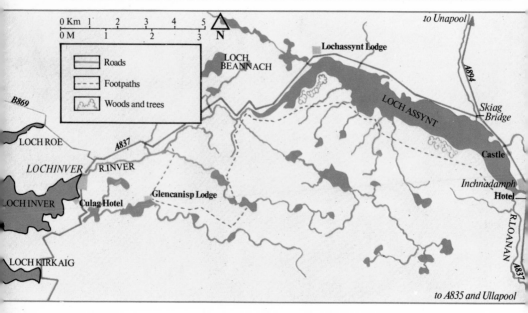

0 Km 1 2 3 4 5 N
0 M 1 2 3

Roads
Footpaths
Woods and trees

to Unapool
Lochassynt Lodge
LOCH BEANNACH
A894
B869
LOCH ASSYNT
Skiag Bridge
LOCH ROE
A837
RINVER
LOCHINVER
Castle
Inchnadamph Hotel
LOCH INVER
Culag Hotel
Glencanisp Lodge
LOCH KIRKAIG
R.LOANAN
A837
to A835 and Ullapool

Malaig, however, Loch Morar can provide good sport with the three main game fish species. Bank fishing is free and boats are available from the Morar Hotel. Between the loch and sea the short river Morar can be prolific for salmon, but it is all preserved.

The River Shiel which drains Loch Shiel and runs to the sea at Ardnamuchan is again preserved. On the loch, however, there is some salmon and trout fishing, and motor boats are available from Glenfinnan where guests may stay at the Stage House Inn.

The Hebrides

The best fishing is not necessarily found on the mainland. Some truly wonderful sport is available in the Inner and Outer Hebrides and in Orkney and Shetland—an area well worth exploration and development.

In the north, the islands of Lewis and Harris provide wonderful fishing for salmon and sea trout. The famous Grimersta river is a short distance from Stornoway, but it might prove very difficult to reach—not to mention the cost. The river belongs to Grimersta Estate and is let annually to a syndicate. Occasionally rods become available. Enquiries to the secretary.

Forty miles south-west of Stornoway, the

(Above) Detail map of the area round Loch Assynt and the myriad waters nearby. (Below) Amhuinnsuidhe Castle, North Harris, in the Outer Hebrides.

North Harris Estate controls a network of rivers and lochs over their 60,000 acres. Anglers can stay at the magnificent Amhuinnsuidhe Castle and have within easy reach the lochs Scourst, Voshimid and Ulladale. Most waters drain into Loch Resort, and the runs of migratory fish following the first July rains can be quite fantastic. Costs to stay at the castle include all fishing dues. The peak season price is £250 per rod per week.

Benbecula

North and South Uist offer many angling possibilities as does Benbecula. At Lochboisdale the hotel has brown trout fishing and some excellent sea trout fishing, but bookings must be made well in advance.

Orkney and Shetland has sea and brown trout together with big skate, halibut and ling. Intending visitors would be well advised to seek more comprehensive information before making a journey, however. Useful contacts include the secretaries of the Shetland Anglers' Association or the Orkney Trout Fishing Association.

Arthur Oglesby

INFORMATION

FISHERIES

Amhuinnsuidhe Castle, The Tulcan Estate Office, Grantown-on-Spey, Moray. Tel Advie 200.
Altnacealgach Hotel, by Lairg, Sutherland. Tel Elphin 231.
Altnaharra Hotel, Altnaharra by Lairg, Sutherland. Tel 222.
Benmore Estate Office, Ardgay, Ross-shire.
Bettyhill Hotel, Bettyhill, Sutherland.
Culag Hotel, Lochinver, Sutherland. Tel 209.
Drumbeg Hotel, Drumbeg, Sutherland. Tel 236.
Garbot Hotel, Kinlochbervie, by Lairg, Sutherland. Tel 275.
Grimersta Estate, 7 Melville Cres, Edinburgh.
North Harris Estate, The Tulcan Estate, Grantown-on-Spey, Moray. Tel Advie 200.
Inchnadamph Hotel, Inchnadamph, Sutherland. Tel Assynt 202.
Kinlochewe Hotel, by Achnasheen, Ross-shire. Tel Kinlochlewe 253.
Loch Maree Hotel, Achnasheen, Ross-shire. Tel Gairloch 2200.
Morar Hotel, Morar, Mallaig, Inverness-shire. Tel 2346.
Oykel Bridge Hotel, Ardgay, Ross-shire.
Royal Hotel, Ullapool, Ross and Cromarty. Tel 2181.
Scourie Hotel, Scourie, Sutherland.
Stage House Inn, Glenfinnan, Inverness-shire. Tel Kinlocheil 246.
Summer Isles Hotel, Achiltibuie, Ross-shire. Tel 282.

LOCAL CLUBS AND ASSOCIATIONS

Assynt Angling Club, A M McKenzie, Brackloch, Lochinver, Sutherland. Tel 253.
Orkney Trout Fishing Assoc, 36 Quaybanks Cres, Kirkwall.
Scottish National Federation of Angling Clubs, F McGuckin, 175 Dochart Terr, Dundee, Angus.
Sheltand Anglers' Assoc, Andrew Miller, 3 Gladstone Terr, Lerwick.
South Uist Angling Club, Major E W Jenno, 14 Truro Close, Isle of Benbecula.

TACKLE DEALERS

J H Murray, Dalrymple St, Girvan.
James Kirk Ltd, 25 Klye St, Ayr.
Sports Shop, High St, Irvine.
Aquatron Marine Ltd, 99 Temple Hill, Troon.
W G Morrison. 117 Main St, Prestwick, near Troon.
McCririck and Sons, 38 John Finnie St, Kilmarnock. Ayrshire.
Fullerton Bros, Dockhead St, Saltcoats.
Sports Shop, Glasgow St, Ardossan.
St Molios Shop, Lanlash, Isle of Arran.
R Savage, Main St, Largs.
MacLeod Marines, Pier Buildings, Rothesay. Tel 3950.
F V G Mapes and Son, 4 Guildford St, Millport.
Messrs Ourdie, Queen's Hall Shop, Dunoon.
Ian Tyrell, Sinclair St, Helensburgh.
Clyde Marine Charter Agency, Clynder.
Wild Cat, Achtercairn.
K Gunn, Strath and Sands Holiday Centre, Strath.
John MacLennen and Co, Marine Stores, Kyle of Lochalsh.
W J Wiseman, 45 Mellon Charles, Aultbea, Ross-shire.
Tackle Shop, Warehouse Bldgs., Shore St, Ullapool.
Lochinver Fish Selling Co, Lochinver. Tel 228.
The Tackle Shop, 7 Main St, Tobermory. Tel 2458.
The Harbour Shop, Portree, Isle of Skye.
Skeabost House Hotel, Skeabost, by Portree. Tel Skeabost Bridge 202.
Misty Isle Hotel, Skyeramics, Uiginish.
J S Morrison, Tarbert, Isle of Harris.
Electro Sports, Cromwell St, Stornoway, Isle of Lewis.
W Sinclair, Stromness, Orkney.
N Spence, Kirkwall, Orkney.
J A Manson, 88 Commercial St, Lerwick, Shetlands.
Macdonald's Tackle Shop, 23 Sinclair St, Thurso.

Solway Firth, Eden

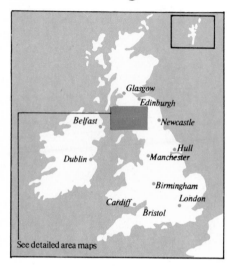

See detailed area maps

Over 2,000ft high up on the broad shoulders of Mallerstang Common, two rivers rise and flow eastwards—the beginning of the famous Yorkshire Swale, and the River Ure. A third river, rising nearby, might well have become a Yorkshire river but instead runs south-west before traversing Cumbria to empty into the Solway Firth. This is the aptly named River Eden.

The Eden is a famous trout water, but has an excellent run of sea trout. Smaller herling and salmon run the river up as far as Kirkby Stephen, below Ask Fell, and later in the season sometimes run a little farther. It is also a noted river for grayling, and in its lower reaches has a vast coarse fish population with quality chub predominating, and dace to a pound in weight.

Running out of the soaring Fell country of Cumbria the Eden cuts through high buffs, with clear water breaking over a shingly bed. It is little more than a beck in its early journey, but is continually charged by lesser streams splashing in from the Pennine wilderness on the one side and the high lake country on the other. Beyond Kirkby Stephen it changes to an easy, wide river

which is fishable throughout its length.

Traditionally, Eden sea trout anglers use fairly large pattern flies based on the big moths that flutter down from the banks at twilight. They are heavy flies with fat bodies often of chenille with a white tag added. In July and August they are deadly when used on a long line, often in tandem, across the tails of pools.

Early in the season it is stonefly time. These emerge in the shallows from the larval stage and are found in three forms; the great stonefly, yellow sally, and later a more restricted crop of the willow fly.

Wet fly is used more than dry, often upstream on a short line, but usually across and down on a long line. Eden trout are not big by Test standards—on average three to the pound—but the Eden can yield larger ones. The delicate and difficult art of upstream worming is also worth employing.

For salmon, the best time is probably from January until March, as the lighter spring run continues from then until May. Very few private owners issue permits for salmon or sea trout, but coarse and brown trout fishing is available along much of the bank for three months from mid-October.

Fishing at Carlisle

Carlisle Angling Association controls about seven miles of the Eden, and a considerable length of the nearby River Caldew. Permits are available from E Cave, 9 Brunton Crescent, Carlisle, or from Holmegate Farm, Holmegate, Carlisle. Groundbaiting is not allowed during the salmon season.

Upstream at Warwick-on-Eden permits are available on application to Warwick Hall. The Yorkshire Fly Fishers Club control water at Wetherall together with Great Corby, and some permits and further information are available from P Garnett, 2 Hallcroft Drive, Addingham, Ilkley, West Yorkshire.

At Armathwaite, the Dukes Head and Edendale Hotels have waters available for residents, and also issue a few day tickets to visitors. Tickets can also be obtained from E Eckroyd, Low House, Armathwaite, or from the Red Lion Hotel.

The Bracken Bank Hotel at Lazonby controls about 3½ miles of the Eden which regularly yield good sea trout and salmon. At Kirkoswald the Featherstone Arms Hotel has about two miles of bank and issues some day tickets. Downstream at Great Salkeld there is a fair amount of permit fishing available with Great Salkeld Parish Council issuing a number for a short stretch in the village, and day tickets are also available from the Highland Drove Hotel or from Major W Gubbins, Eden Lacy, Gt. Salkeld.

Penrith waters

Penrith Angling Association has water at Penrith with day tickets obtainable from the secretary. They also have day-ticket waters at Culgaith, Kirkby Thore, Temple Sowerby, and along a number of major Eden tributaries like the Eamont, Lowther and Petterell. On the River Petterell the Crown and Mitre Inn has about three miles of fishing for its guests.

The Yorkshire Federation of Fishing Clubs controls waters at Langwathby, Culgaith and Temple Sowerby where the Kings Arms Hotel has a 1½-mile stretch for residents. In Appleby, Appleby Angling Association controls excellent water—about seven miles upstream and roughly the same downstream. Permits are obtained from J Henderson, West View, Kirby Thore. There is some free fishing in Appleby for overnight visitors and the Tufton Arms Hotel issues some day tickets for guests for about 10 miles of bank. It is all very good wet fly water.

Solway Firth

A mile or so from the mouth of the Eden. the border Esk flows into the Solway Firth, and a few miles along the north coast the Annan enters. The Water of Fleet enters along Wigtown Bay, the Cree enters at

The Eden—famous salmon river—also has brown and sea trout, with a recent increase in coarse fishing around Carlisle.

England Scene

27

(Above) Portpatrick Harbour, eight miles from Stranraer. Boats are available from McIntyre in Main St, and there is shore fishing to the north. (Right) Area map.

Newton Stewart, and the Water of Luce lends its name to a famous bay which has fabulous shore fishing.

Many stretches of the lower Esk yield very good dace, chub and grayling, but its fame rests primarily on a large annual run of sea trout. For waters at Langholm, Canonbie and Longtown, permits are issued by the Esk and Liddle Fishing Association. For the Longtown area, permits and information can be obtained from the Netherby Estate Office in Longtown, from Major T Westoll, Ginger Bank, Longtown, or from A Tuddenham, 21 Netherby St, Longtown.

The Annan chub

The River Annan is well known for the former British record chub of 10lb-plus taken some years ago, and holds hosts of quality chub. Available coarse fishing is limited, however. The Red House Hotel in Wamphray issues permits, and in the Locherbie area local tackle dealers will supply information. Permit waters are at Copewood Farm, at Hallheaths Estate where tickets are available from the lodge, and at Shillahill Bridge where water is controlled by the Royal Four Towns Commission.

Nearby, there is excellent bream fishing on Castle Loch and Lochmaben, with catches to 80lb not infrequent. Worm is a favourite bait.

For sea trout, trout and salmon fishing, there are many first-rate permit waters along the Annan with Sunday fishing allowed. Fishing styles are similar to those on the Eden and Esk.

Noted waters near Annan are along the Newbie Estate and at Newbie Mill, while at Ecclefechan the Applegirth Water and the Kinnell Water near Lockerbie are also good. Day tickets are obtained at Clockhouse Cottage, Mill House Bridge, Lockerbie, or

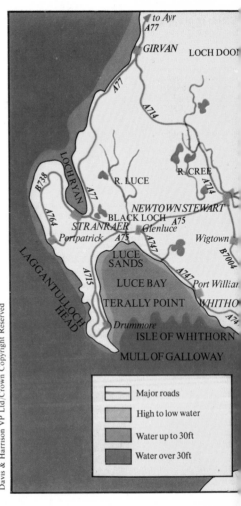

Map legend:
- Major roads
- High to low water
- Water up to 30ft
- Water over 30ft

from the Castle Milk Estate Office, Lockerbie, which also issues tickets for the Royal Four Towns water at Shillahill. For a four-mile stretch at Beattock, contact the Upper Annandale Angling Association.

The River Fleet trout fishing permits are obtainable from the Murray Arms Hotel, Gatehouse of Fleet, while permit fishing is also possible along the River Luce and on many locks and reservoirs in the Galloway and Dumfries area. Sunday fishing is allowed on Dalbeattie Reservoir and more good stillwater trout fishing is offered at Loch Dee, Auchen Loch near Beattock, for which permits are issued at Auchen Castle

Hotel, and on Black Loch near Newton Stewart. The New Galloway Angling Association issues permits for Clatteringshaws Reservoir and Stroan Loch, and the whole area is dotted with lakes with fishing available on most.

The Solway Firth

The Solway Firth has a vast sea fishing potential only now beginning to be realized. The Mull of Galloway has produced two shore-caught record fish—a 19lb thornback ray and a $15\frac{1}{2}$lb bull huss, while just across the Mull in Loch Ryan a superb shore-caught tope of $54\frac{1}{2}$lb was beached. The area is ripe for development, and increasingly

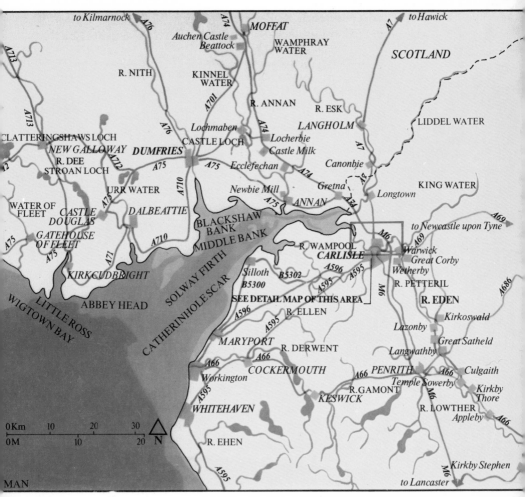

charter boats are becoming available at places like Port William.

The Solway Firth is a hot spot for tope with fish near the 50lb mark, and has potential for lunker halibut and skate. Lure and pirk fishing have also tempted many big cod. The south coast off the Isle of Man, and the coast slightly north of Mull are most productive areas.

The Firth's boat marks

Good boat marks along the north Solway Firth are the Mull of Galloway coast, a stretch along the 10 fathom line off Port William across Luce Bay to Drummore, Wigtown Bay, Little Ross and Abbey Head.

Along the south shore, Silloth is a good starting point for Catherinehole Scar, the Middle Bank and the Blackshaw Bank. Cod are usually thought of as a winter species but in these little-fished waters they can be caught through most of the year by shore anglers. Conger are also worth fishing and during October there is an inshore migration of pollack.

Anglers are only just realizing that the Mull and the Cumberland coast are particularly

(Above) The wide waters of the Solway Firth. Mackerel, pollack, coalfish and flatfish are shore-fished, and cod, conger, ray, flatfish and mackerel from boats.
(Below) Detail map shows the lower reaches of the Eden. Ticket water on the Eden can be found near Carlisle.

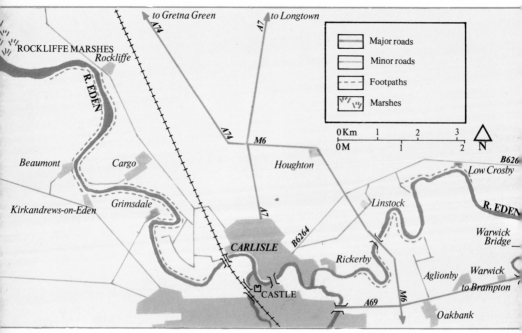

England Scene

good for bass. Whitehaven is good for shoal fish, and larger specimens are taken from shore marks in Luce Bay—renowned for its miles of sandy beaches and white breaker lines.

If you are interested in plaice, try spinning in the quieter 'up-Firth' estuaries. Or for haddock, a single-hook flowing trace will be successful.

The area described remains mainly unfished although most species can be found. Coalfish and pollack are plentiful and the porbeagle shark is a possible target. Record proportion ballan wrasse are taken off the many rocky outcrops of the Mull of Galloway from Laggantalluch Head to Terallt, and off Whitehorn from the Point of Lag to Palmallet Point.

INFORMATION

WATER AUTHORITY
North West Water Authority, Dawson House, Great Sankey, Warrington WA5 3LW. Tel Penketh 4321.
LICENCES
Salmon and migratory trout: season £15.60, part season to 31 May £7.80, part season from June £9, week £2.60 (juniors age 14–16 and OAPs season £6.50, part season to 31 May £3.25, part season from 1 June £4). A licence marked * entitles the holder to fish for eels, non-migratory trout (brown and rainbow) and char and freshwater fish for the whole of the respective seasons. Non-migratory trout: season £2.60, week 65p (juniors and OAPs season £1.25). Freshwater fish and eels: season £1.25, week 35p (juniors and OAPs season 65p).
Close seasons: Salmon, rivers Eden, Annas, Bleng, Esk, Mite, Irt, Calder and Ehen 1 November to 31 March; rivers Derwent, Ellen, Waver and Wampool 1 November to 14 February; all waters in the NW region 1 November to 31 January. Migratory trout, rivers Eden, Annas, Blang, Esk, Mite, Irt, Calder and Ehen 1 November to 30 April; all waters in the NW region 16 October to 30 April. Non-migratory trout (brown and char) 1 October to 14 March. Freshwater fish, all waters NW region whether or not connected to any river or stream, 15 March to 15 June. Rainbow trout and eels, no close season.
For fishing in Scotland: trout 7 October to 14 March, but many clubs extend this close season still further to allow the fish to reach better condition. Trout may not be sold between the end of August and the beginning of April, and not at any time if less than 8in long.
For salmon the close season depends on the area. River Annan, rod fishing 16 November to 9 February, net fishing 10 September to 24 February. River Cree, rod fishing 1 October to 28 February, net fishing 14 September to 28 February. Fleet (Kirkcudbright) rod fishing 1 November to 24 February, net fishing 10 September to 24 February. River Luce, rod fishing 1 November to 24 February, net fishing 10 September to 24 February.
Size limits: salmon 12in (30.5cm), migratory trout 10in (25cm), non-migratory brown trout and char 8in (20cm), carp 9in (23cm), roach, perch and rudd 8in (20cm), crucian carp 7in (18cm), dace 6in (15cm), gudgeon and ruffe 4in (10cm).

FISHERIES
W Graham, Clerk, Commissioners of Royal Four Towns Fishing, 'Glenelg', Hightae, Lockerbie, Dumfriesshire. Tel Lockerbie 220.
Bracken Bank Shooting and Fishing Lodge, Lazonby. Tel 241.
Warwick Hall, Estate Office, Warwick on Eden, Carlisle.
Hallheaths Water, Messrs McJerrow and Stevenson, Solicitors, Lockerbie. Tel 2123.
T Nelson, Newbie Mill, Annan, Dumfriesshire. Tel: Annan 2608.
Castle Milk Estate Office, Lockerbie, Dumfriesshire. Tel: Kettleholm 20314.
LOCAL CLUBS AND ASSOCIATIONS
Appleby Angling Assoc, J A Henderson, West View, Kirkby Thorpe, Penrith, Cumbria.
Carlisle Angling Assoc, E Cave, 9 Bruton Cres, Carlisle CA1 2AX.
Esk and Liddle Fisheries Assoc, R J B Hill, Solicitor, Langholm, Dumfriesshire. Tel 428.
New Galloway Angling Assoc, J Kentley, The Cafe, High St, New Galloway, Kirkcudbrightshire.
Penrith Angling Assoc, J Norris, 21 Victoria Rd, Penrith, Cumbria.
Upper Annandale Angling Assoc, 1 Rosehill, Grange Rd, Moffat, Dumfriesshire.
Yorkshire Fly Fishers Club, P Garnett, 2 Hallcroft Drive, Addingham, Ilkley, W Yorks.
TACKLE DEALERS AND LICENCE AGENTS
Appleby Sporting Supplies, Market Place, Appleby.
Beck and Leslie Ltd, 67 Denton St, Carlisle.
D Hodgson, Lane End Stores, Plumbland, Aspatria, Carlisle.
G Easton, 40 Lowther St, Carlisle.
McHardy's, 9 London Rd, Carlisle.
P Black, Post Office, Armathwaite, Carlisle.
Raine and Co, 21 Warwick St, Carlisle.
McCowan and Millar, High St, Dalbeatie. Tel 610270.
McKinnell and Watson, 15 St Cuthbert St, Kirkcudbright. Tel 30693.
E Metcalfe, 46/48 Market St, Kirkby Stephen.
The Tackle Box, 67 Main St, Kirkby Lonsdale.
Armstrong and Stockdale, 4 Gt Dockray, Penrith.
R N Burton, Bracken Bank Shooting and Fishing Co, Bracken Bank, Lazonby, Penrith.

Scottish Lowlands

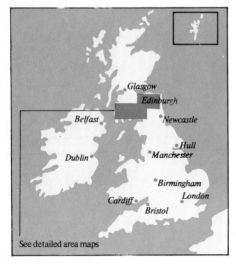

See detailed area maps

east and, 100 miles later, empties into the North Sea at Berwick. For many of its latter miles it forms the border between England and Scotland, but is under the jurisdiction of Scotland, where salmon may not be legally taken on a Sunday.

There are, as yet, no licence requirements for any form of fishing, but it is essential to have legal access to the water, and this may take the form of renting water from an owner or estate agent; membership of a club; acquiring weekly or daily tickets, or enjoying the facilities provided by some hotels.

The Tweed has noted runs of salmon during the early spring and the late autumn. The classic beats for early and late fishing tend to be from Kelso downstream. The

When a Scot talks of fish he always means salmon. Other things with fins are not 'fish' but are merely trout, pike, herring or whatever species they happen to be. Most freshwater species are regarded as vermin, but trout can be tolerated. Trout are, in fact, widespread throughout the country together with pike and other coarse fish but the Scots are not interested.

For the angler, the country is synonymous with salmon and trout fishing, and there can be little doubt that Scotland represents one of the last outposts of good game fishing. It follows, therefore, that most of the good salmon fishing is not only expensive but hard to come by. Trout fishing, however, can usually be had at very modest cost, and most coarse fishing is there for the taking.

The Tweed

Not many people cross the border on the eastern flank of Scotland without encountering the River Tweed. Although it now competes for praise with the River Tay, there is little doubt that it was once the most prolific salmon river in Scotland. It rises within almost a stone's throw of the westerly flowing Annan near Moffat, heads north and

famed junction pool at Kelso, for instance, where the Teviot and Tweed meet, may cost the visitor as much as £150 per week for one rod, but he is just as likely to find the river in roaring flood or like a skating rink as the angler paying a tenth of that sum and fishing upstream at Walkerburn or Peebles. There is, however, not much fishing of note up there until the last weeks of the season. Much fishing, controlled by the Peeblesshire Salmon Fishing Association, is made available through Blackwood and Smith of Peebles on a day or weekly ticket basis. The season is from 21 February to 30 November, and no Sunday fishing is allowed.

Tweed fishing centre

At Walkerburn, Peeblesshire, the Tweed Valley Hotel, established in 1960 as a Scottish Sports Council approved fishing centre, offers residential salmon and trout fishing facilities. Salmon fishing is from

£1.50 per day (£3 per week). The trout season is from 1 April to 30 September, and during this time the hotel run special weeks and weekends in April, May and June, when professionals are in attendance for the benefit of the residents, offering help with starting or advanced casting. The salmon season is from 21 February to 30 November, and special weeks are held in October and November. They also run an evening programme with talks, films and fly-tying.

For fishing guests not attending special fishing weeks, the usual hotel tariff applies, plus permits available from the hotel.

Angling facilities are also available at the Park Hotel in Peebles and The Traquair Arms in Innerleithen.

Downstream at Melrose there is occasional fishing available from Swallow Hotels, PO Box 35, Sunderland, and there is good trout fishing available from the Kelso Angling Association. Below Kelso, there is some first class roach and grayling fishing. Most owners will allow access on permit, but usually on condition that all coarse fish are removed from the water.

Tweed's reputation

The Tweed has, however, built its reputation entirely on its fantastic salmon resource, sadly now being over-exploited by an increase in illegal fishing at sea.

The Tweed has many worthwhile tributaries including the Whiteadder; the Blackadder, Till, Teviot, Leader, Gala, Ettrick, Leithen and Caddon. Some are noted for salmon while others offer free trout fishing.

On the western side of Scotland, the first river to cross the border is the Esk. Together with its tributary, the Liddle, it is more renowned for its summer and autumn runs of sea trout than for salmon, but there is much good fishing available at modest cost.

(Left) The River Annan at Lockerbie. One of the most noted of the south-west rivers, the Annan is a spate river where it is always advisable to plan one's visit after consulting the local ghillie.

Ray Forsberg

Scottish Lowlands

The Esk and Liddle Fisheries Association controls much of the fishing over a distance of 20 miles and tickets may be obtained from J I Wylie, River Watcher, Byreburnfoot, Canobie, or J G Elliot, River Watcher, Thistlesyke, Newcastleton. The River Esk shares dual nationality and it is important to comply with North West Water Authority requirements when fishing in England, while for the Scottish portion no licence is required.

Farther west are the rivers Annan, Nith, Urr, Water of Fleet, Cree, Dee, Stinchar and Girvan. They all offer salmon fishing of some description, but most would be classed as spate rivers where it is almost essential to plan a visit when the local ghillie or keeper phones to say it is right.

Perhaps the Annan and Nith are most noted of these south-west rivers. The Annan, for instance, rises near Moffat in the same watershed as the Tweed and then flows 30 miles south to the Solway Firth. There is frequently a modest run of spring fish in March, April and May, some sea trout and herring in June, July and August, and more salmon in late autumn.

On the Hoddom Castle water, 15 rods daily are allowed and tickets may be

Map of the area shows the principal rivers of the Lowlands; the Tweed, the border Esk and Liddle, and the western rivers Annan, Nith, Urr, Water of Fleet, Cree, Dee, Stinchar and Girvan. The Tweed is famous for salmon, the Esk and Liddle for sea trout.

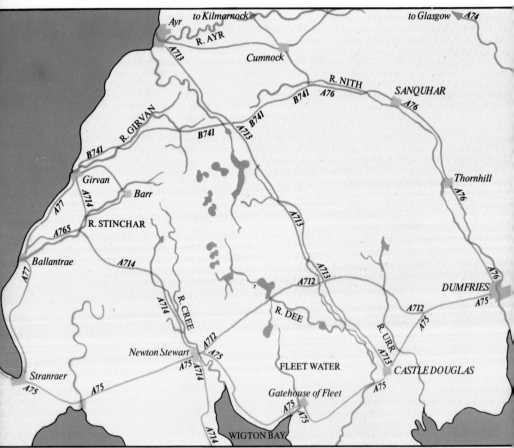

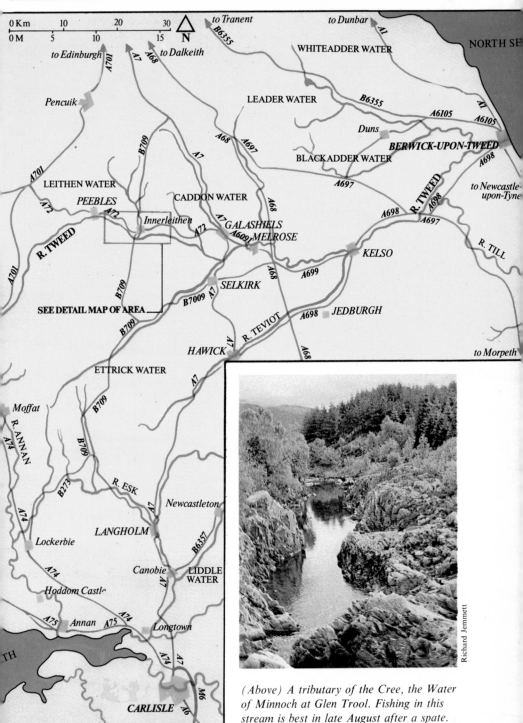

to Tranent

to Dunbar

WHITEADDER WATER

NORTH SE

to Edinburgh

to Dalkeith

Pencuik

LEADER WATER

B6355

A6105

A6105

A1

Duns

BERWICK-UPON-TWEED

A698

LEITHEN WATER

BLACKADDER WATER

PEEBLES

CADDON WATER

A697

to Newcastle-
upon-Tyne

Innerleithen

R. TWEED

A698

A698

A697

GALASHIELS

R. TWEED

MELROSE

R. TILL

KELSO

A699

SELKIRK

SEE DETAIL MAP OF AREA

B7009

A698

JEDBURGH

R. TEVIOT

HAWICK

to Morpeth

ETTRICK WATER

to Morpeth

A68

Moffat

R. ANNAN

B709

R. ESK

Newcastleton

LANGHOLM

Lockerbie

Canobie

LIDDLE
WATER

Hoddom Castle

Annan

Longtown

CARLISLE

M6

Richard Jemmett

*(Above) A tributary of the Cree, the Water
of Minnoch at Glen Trool. Fishing in this
stream is best in late August after a spate.*

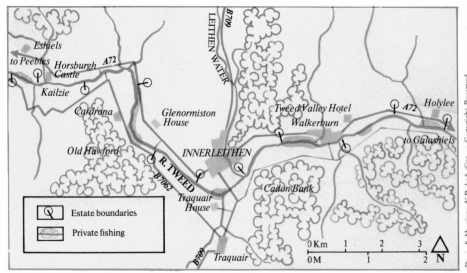

(Above) Detail map shows a section of the famous River Tweed in the Peebles–Innerleithen region. Day and week tickets are available from the Peeblesshire Salmon Fishing Association, and hotels offer residential angling facilities. (Below) The Tweed-Innerleithen junction at Innerleithen.

obtained from Peter Helm, River Watcher, 22 Fernlea Crescent, Annan, Tel 2922.

The Nith has its source just south of Ayr and it too flows south to Dumfries and the Solway Firth. The upper reaches offer modest trout fishing and there are good runs of both salmon and sea trout throughout the season. Some of the better known stretches are controlled by the Mid-Nithsdale Angling Association and the Upper Nithsdale Angling Club.

The Nith and Urr

Both Thornhill and Sanquhar make good centres, and enquiries for tickets should be directed to R W Coltart, 49 Drumlanrig Street, Thornhill. Like the Tweed, the Nith remains in open season until the end of November—a time of year when the legendary, big, grey-back salmon are supposed to enter the river. In fact, in 1812, a fish of 67lb is reputed to have been caught in the Nith by one Jock Wallace. Wallace, a well-known poacher, was said to have played the fish from 8am to 6pm. However, the claim was never authenticated!

At Castle.Douglas, where most of the Dee is private, the River Urr may be fished by members of the Castle Douglas AA. Permits are available from tackle shops in the area and there are good runs of sea trout and grilse from June onwards. However, fishing here depends on the state of the water and the casual visitor must have a local contact in order to take full advantage.

The Cree

Moving west, the Cree drains Loch Moan southerly to Wigtown Bay. It has recently improved as a salmon river and can be very good for both salmon and sea trout in summer. Recent runs have been reported to be getting earlier in the season which is unusual for these west coast rivers. The Secretary of the local angli association is D Frank, 9 Victoria Street, Newton Stewart.

The other most notable river is the Stinchar. This, however, is very much a spate river where local information is essential. Ballantrae and Barr make good centres, and fishing may be arranged at both the Kings Arms and the Jolly Shepherds hotels in Barr. It is, however, a river where the best salmon fishing undoubtedly comes late in the season.

The *Northern Angler's Handbook,* published by the Dalesman Publishing Co at 60p, and *An Angler's Guide to Scottish Waters,* published by the Scottish Tourist Board, both provide useful information of the facilities available in the area.

Arthur Oglesby

INFORMATION

FISHERIES
Dryburgh Abbey Hotel, St Boswells, Tel 2261.
Esk and Liddle Fisheries Assoc, R J B Mill, Solicitor, Langholm, Dumfriesshire. Tel 428.
Ettrick Shaws Lodge Hotel, Ettrick Bridge, Selkirk. Tel 229.
George and Abbotsford Hotel, Melrose, Roxburghshire. Tel 2308
Old Manse Guest House, Abbey St Bathans, Berwickshire. Tel 230.
Park Hotel, Peebles. Tel Peebles 20451.
Peeblesshire Salmon Fishing Assoc, Blackwood and Smith W S, 39 High St, Peebles. Tel 20131.
The Traquair Arms, Innerleithen. Tel Innerleithen 229.
Swallow Hotels, PO Box 35, Sunderland, Tyne and Wear.
Tillmouth Park Hotel, Cornhill-on-Tweed. Tel Coldstream 2255.
Tweed Valley Hotel, Walkerburn, Peeblesshire. Tel Walkerburn 220.
LOCAL CLUBS AND ASSOCIATIONS
Scottish National Federation of Angling Clubs, F McGukin, 175 Dochart Terr. Dundee. Angus.
Castle Douglas and District Angling Assoc, A Muir, 12 Cotton St, Castle Douglas, Kircudbrightshire. Tel 2849.
County of Peebles Angling Improvement Assoc, James Allan, 35 Edderstone Rd, Peebles, Peeblesshire. Tel 20507.
Greenlaw Angling Club, A Lamb, Waterford, Wester Row, Greenlaw, Berwickshire (water on the R Blackadder).
Melrose and District Angling Assoc, J Broomfield, Ravensbourne, Douglas Rd, Melrose, Roxburghshire. Tel 2219.
Upper Annandale Angling Assoc, J Black, 1 Rosehill Grange Rd, Moffat, Dumfriesshire. Tel 20104.
Whiteadder Angling Assoc, R Welsh, Abbey St Bathans, Duns, Berwickshire. Tel 210.
TACKLE DEALERS.
Frasers Sports 27 West St, Berwick-on-Tweed. Tel 6844.
John Dickson and Son, 21 Frederick St, Edinburgh.
F and D Simpson, 28 West Preston St, Edinburgh.
John Dickenson and Son, 35 The Square, Kelso. Tel 2687.
Redpath and Co, Tweedside Works, 55 Horse Market, Kelso. Tel 2578.
J Stewart and Son, Ironmongers, High St, Melrose.
Ian Fraser (Sports), 1 Bridegate, Peebles. Tel 20979.

Wear and Tees

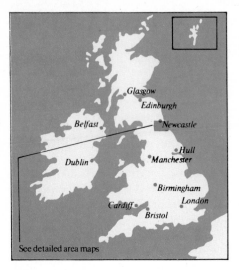

Glasgow

Edinburgh

Belfast

Newcastle

Dublin

Hull

Manchester

Birmingham

Cardiff

London

Bristol

See detailed area maps

The rivers Derwent, Wear and Tees run through some of the finest scenery in the North. The Wear and Tees are gravel-bottomed and have shallow streams with deep pools suitable for fly and coarse fishing, but the Derwent, a trout stream, narrow with a gravelled bottom is polluted in its lower reaches before it joins the Tyne. The Wear, one of the best sea trout rivers in the North of England, has a small run of salmon and contains a good head of coarse fish in the lower reaches. The Tees has good trout, especially above Croft, and is also an excellent coarse fish river, containing large dace, chub, roach, gudgeon, pike, and some barbel up to 7lb in weight below Darlington. Unfortunately, much of the fishing on these rivers is controlled by landowners who do not give permits, or by local clubs that have leased the water.

River Tees

The River Tees rises below Cross Fell in the Pennines and flows eastwards to join the North Sea near Middlesbrough. For most of its length it forms the boundary between Yorkshire and Durham. At the head of the river, between Cow Green and Middleton in Teesdale, there is a 7 mile stretch for trout and grayling on the north bank from Broken Way to Cow Green. Permits are issued by the Raby Estate office, Middleton in Teesdale, during office hours only, at a cost of £5.40 (season), £2.16 (week), and £1.62 (day) or from the office in Staindrop. They also issue permits for a stretch downstream at Piercebridge for winter coarse fishing. On the south bank, Strathmore Estates issue permits for 7 miles of fishing from Lune Foot to Cronkley Bridge, and these may be obtained from the Cleveland Hotel, Middleton at a cost of £5.40 (season) and £2.16 (week).

Farther downstream there is good trout fishing at Lartington Hall water on the south bank of the river from Cooper House, Cotherstone to the Aqueduct at Barnard Castle. Permits can be obtained from Mr W. Crocker, Gamekeeper, Deepdale Cottage, Barnard Cottage, Barnard Castle at a cost of £8 (season) or £1 (day). Nearby Lartington Lake holds brown trout and rainbow trout of up to 5lb and offers excellent fishing from bank and boat. The cost is £4.50 per day or £3 from 4.30pm to dusk, and permits are obtainable from Mr M. Innes, 66 High Riggs, Barnard Castle (Tel 2976).

Free fishing

In Barnard Castle there is free fishing on both banks between Stone Bridge and Thornton Bridge, while at Gainford there is a small stretch on the north bank good for trout and coarse fishing. Trout season permits cost £1.50 and coarse fishing permits £1, and may be obtained from Mrs Raine, Eddleston House, School Lane, Gainford.

Darlington Anglers' Club controls various waters between High Coniscliffe and Croft, and the Darlington Brown Trout Angling Association has good trout and coarse fishing water on the north bank at Low Coniscliffe and on the south bank from Croft Bridge to Clow Beck. Both clubs have

(Above) An improving salmon and trout river, the River Wear in its lower reaches at Lambton Castle near Chester-le-Street.

(Below) Codling, flatfish, coalfish, whiting, mackerel and gurnard are fished from the five miles of sand and rock at Redcar.

Spectrum Color Library

England Scene

day tickets at 50p and allow a member to obtain a permit for a visitor living beyond a 20 mile radius of Darlington.

At Croft there is about 300 yards of free fishing on the north bank from Croft Bridge to the River Skerne where trout, grayling, roach, chub, dace and pike may be fished. The Thornaby Angling Association controls 6 miles of fishing between Croft Bridge and Hurworth on both banks. They do not issue permits, but members may sometimes obtain permission for a visitor to fish for a fee of 60p a day. At Neasham, downstream of Croft, th .~ is about 200 yards of free fishing in the village. At Middleton-on-Row there is also 200 yards of free fishing on the north bank.

Tidal river at Yarm

Darlington Brown Trout Angling Association also has fishing on the north bank of the river between Dinsdale Spa and the end of the wood, and small clubs can fish their waters on Saturday on application to the Club Secretary who will take about 25 visitors at 25p each.

Below Yarm the river is tidal with good coarse fishing and occasional trout. Yarm Angling Club has 6 miles of water and issues day tickets at 20p. Farther upstream from the pleasure boat station to the skinyard there is free fishing.

River Wear

The River Wear rises in Co. Durham on Kilhope Moors and flows into the North Sea at Wearmouth. It was once noted for salmon but was spoilt by pollution, and is only now improving with restocking and with the closure of the collieries. Upstream of Chester-le-Street brown trout fishing, although difficult, is rewarding. Generally there are brown trout, sea trout and some salmon. At St John's Chapel the Upper Weardale Angling Association issues day tickets (except for Sundays) for a stretch from Long Lea Railway Bridge upstream, and downstream the Stanhope Angling Association issues day tickets for two miles of fishing on both banks for large sea trout and trout. At Willington there is fishing for salmon, brown trout and sea trout and the

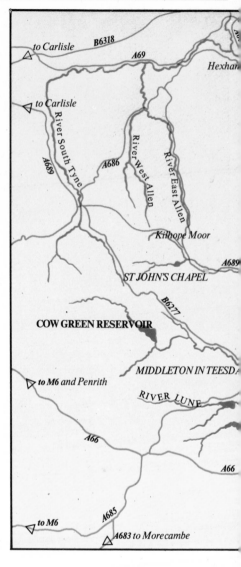

(Above) Our map shows famous trout-fishing rivers the Tees and Wear, and the Derwent, tributary of the River Tyne. The sea-fishing area extends along the coast from South Shields to Saltburn.

Willington and District Angling Club has waters that run from Sunnybrow Bridge to Page Bank.

Farther downstream, the Bishop Auckland & District Angling Club has 14

*(Above) The River
Derwent, a tributary of the
Tyne, is narrow with a
gravelled bottom and is
polluted towards Newcastle-
upon-Tyne. Trout here are
fairly small, about $\frac{1}{4}$lb in
weight, and hard to catch.
Our picture shows grayling
fishing on the stretch
Winlaton Mill to Lintz Ford.*

Arthur Oglesby

41

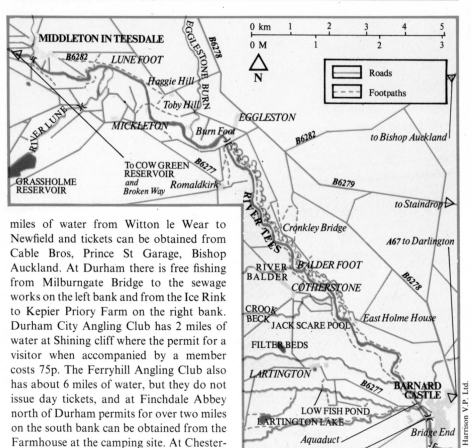

MIDDLETON IN TEESDALE
LUNE FOOT
B6282
EGGLESTONE BURN
B6278
Haggie Hill
Toby Hill
MICKLETON
Burn Foot
EGGLESTON
B6282
to Bishop Auckland
RIVER LUNE
To COW GREEN RESERVOIR and Broken Way
B6277
Romaldkirk
B6279
to Staindrop
GRASSHOLME RESERVOIR
Cronkley Bridge
RIVER TEES
A67 to Darlington
RIVER BALDER
BALDER FOOT
COTHERSTONE
B6278
CROOK BECK
JACK SCARE POOL
East Holme House
FILTER BEDS
LARTINGTON
B6277
BARNARD CASTLE
LOW FISH POND
LARTINGTON LAKE
Aquaduct
Stone Bridge
A67
Bridge End
B6277
to Bowes

0 km 1 2 3 4 5
0 M 1 2 3
N
Roads
Footpaths

Davis & Harrison V.P. Ltd.

miles of water from Witton le Wear to Newfield and tickets can be obtained from Cable Bros, Prince St Garage, Bishop Auckland. At Durham there is free fishing from Milburngate Bridge to the sewage works on the left bank and from the Ice Rink to Kepier Priory Farm on the right bank. Durham City Angling Club has 2 miles of water at Shining cliff where the permit for a visitor when accompanied by a member costs 75p. The Ferryhill Angling Club also has about 6 miles of water, but they do not issue day tickets, and at Finchdale Abbey north of Durham permits for over two miles on the south bank can be obtained from the Farmhouse at the camping site. At Chester-le-Street there is trout and sea trout and the angling club issues day tickets at 25p. Their waters are at Bishop Auckland, from Newton Gap Bridge to Birtley, and from Chester-le-Street to Finchdale Abbey.

The River Derwent is a less exciting prospect to the angler as there are few trout and these are hard to catch as they are not short of food. Those caught are rather small, on average $\frac{1}{4}$lb in weight. A 2 mile stretch from Winlaton Mill to Lintz Ford is controlled by the Axwell Park and Derwent Valley Angling Club. Then the Derwent flows into the Tyne and passes Newcastle to join the sea at Tynemouth.

Along the coast from South Shields to Saltburn there is good rock, beach and pier fishing. At Sunderland, cod, codling, mackerel, whiting, coalfish, gurnard, flounders,

dabs, plaice, pouting and skate can be caught either from Roker Pier and South Pier where fishing is free, or from the South Dock where permits, obtainable from the Council, cost £2 per year.

At Ryhope there is fishing from beach and rocks for plaice, sole, whiting and some skate, and Seaham with its sandy coast offers summer fishing for flatfish, whiting, coalfish, dogfish, codling and pouting, and good winter fishing for coalfish, plaice and whiting. Both the North and South piers are unfortunately only open to members of the Seaham Sea Angling Club, but there is good fishing along the Blast Beach from Dawdon Colliery to Hawthorn Point.

Eric Birch

(Above) The River Tees in its upper reaches near Barnard Castle is fast-flowing and boulder-strewn. There is good trout fishing at Lartington Hall water, and nearby Lartington Lake holds rainbow trout of up to 5lb.

The Blast Beach at Horden is one of the best local beaches for winter codling after dark and Blackhall is known for its rock fishing and good storm beaches. Hartlepool is good for all year round fishing and has five piers, the Heugh, Pilot Pier, Banjo Pier, Middleton Pier and Skeleton Pier, all accessible to the angler.

North and South Gare have good beach and rock fishing, best in winter but dangerous in rough weather. Cod, coalfish, dabs, plaice and gurnard can be fished, and a permit costing £1 (juniors and OAPs half price) from the Tees and Hartlepool Port Authority allows the angler to fish from the South Gare Breakwater.

Redcar and Saltburn

The piers at Redcar and Saltburn are now closed, but Saltburn has a sheltered harbour and bay, and Redcar has 5 miles of rock and sand where fishing is best 2hrs before and after low tide.

INFORMATION
WATER AUTHORITY
Northumbrian Water Authority, Northumbria House, Regent Centre, Gosforth, Newcastle-upon-Tyne NE3 3PX. Tel 843151.
LICENCES
Salmon, trout and freshwater fish: season £5, month £2.
Trout, migratory trout, freshwater fish and eels: season £3, month £1.50 (juniors £1.50). **Trout, freshwater fish and eels:** season £2, month £1 (juniors £1).
Freshwater fish and eels: £1, juniors 50p.
Close seasons: salmon November 1 to January 21; sea trout November 1 to April 2; brown trout October 1 to March 21; coarse fish March 15 to June 15.
Size limits: migratory trout 10in (25cm), and similar limits for trout taken from specified waters in the Authority's area.
LOCAL CLUBS AND ASSOCIATIONS
Darlington Anglers' Club, F C Birkbeck, 11 Charleville Rd, Darlington.
Darlington Brown Trout Angling Assoc, G Coulson, 5 Grange Ave, Hurworth Place, Darlington.
Thornaby Angling Assoc, A G Butler, 5 Melsonby Grove, Hartburn, Stockton-on-Tees.
Yarm Angling Club, F Flynn, Tackle Dealer, 12 Varo Terrace, Stockton-on-Tees.
Upper Weardale Angling Assoc, J K Hetherington, Hood St, St John's Chapel.

Stanhope Angling Assoc, J Green, Union Square.
Willington & District Angling Club, J Clarke, 7 High St, Howden le Wear.
Bishop Auckland & District Angling Club, Mr Mallam, 32 Low Willington, Crook.
Durham City Angling Club, C Johnston, 3 St Monica Grove, Durham.
Chester-le-Street Angling Club, J Colling, 1 Pennine Ave, Chester-le-Street.
Axwell Park & Derwent Valley Angling Assoc, F Olpin, 4 Thirlway Terrace, Sunniside, Bishop Auckland.
TACKLE DEALERS
J W Wright & Son, 107 Parkgate, Darlington.
W P Adams, 42 Duke St, Darlington.
Anglers' Corner, 121 Victoria Rd, Middlesbrough.
Anglers' Services, 45 Claypath, Durham.
Anglers' Services, 27 Park Rd, Hartlepool.
Harry Brough, 20 West Terrace, Redcar.
Frank Flynn, 12 Varo Terrace, Stockton-on-Tees.
Gents Stores, 85 Musgrave St, Hartlepool.
Richardson, 31 St John's Rd, Shildon.
D Smith, 23 Station Rd, Redcar.
A Ward Thompson, 6 Albert Rd, Stockton-on-Tees.
Ward Thompson Bros, 87 Borough Rd, Middlesbrough.
Dalesports, 35 Market Place, Barnard Castle.
P C Sports, 72A Galgate, Barnard Castle.
J Raine, Ironmonger, Market Place, Middleton in Teesdale.

West Cumbria

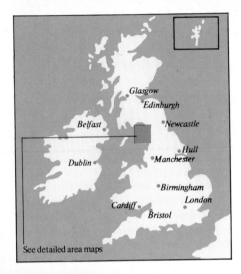

See detailed area maps

From the mountainous hub at the centre of the Lake District, lakes and rivers radiate out to the Eden Valley, the Solway Firth and the Irish Sea. Most of them are westerly inclined, arriving at the coast at points from Morecambe Bay on Solway in the north, to the Duddon-Lickle estuary bordering the old Furness district of Lancashire in the south-west.

Mainly spate rivers

These West Cumbrian rivers are mainly spate rivers, rain-fed owing to the impervious nature of their watershed and the naturally high rainfall of the area and, latterly, to the improved drainage system which affects many of the great northern rivers. They are precipitous streams, some rising well over 2,000ft above sea level and reaching the coast in a relatively short distance. For example, one tributary of the little River Annas falls 1,600ft in approximately $1\frac{1}{2}$ miles, taking a further two miles to fall 200ft to sea level.

These are, then, essentially game fish rivers – the domain of the sprightly brown trout, the dashing sea trout and the majestic salmon. The angler fishes for salmon and sea trout in the lower reaches of these rivers on the narrow coastal plain, in the peaceful, sheltered valleys, tree-lined and often bracken-clad; or high up in the fells, where the wild little brownies, three or four to the pound, will take his fly or upstream worm.

Summer salmon and grilse

The brown trout here are mainly small, with the better fish coming from the lower reaches. The salmon, too, tend to be on the small side, averaging 8lb, with the odd heavier specimens. Summer salmon and

(Left) An attractive corner of the River Duddon at Ulpha, north of Duddon Bridge and Broughton-in-Furness.
(Above right) Area map of the complex waters to be found in West Cumbria.

W F Davidson

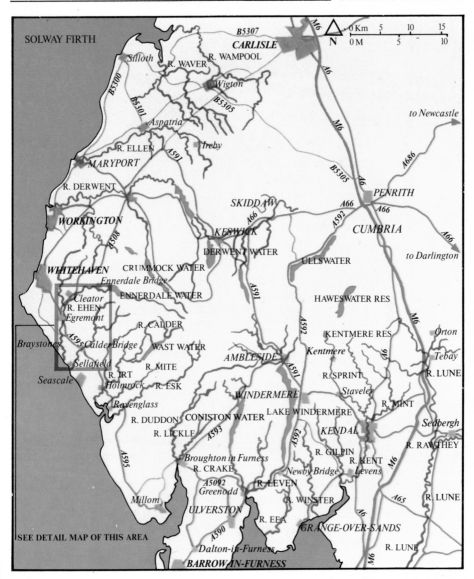

SEE DETAIL MAP OF THIS AREA

grilse constitute the main runs occurring from June onwards, augmented by sea trout and herling. The sea trout, in contrast to the salmon, are often found to be heavier than their counterparts in the Border rivers and the Eden. The little River Irt, for example, is renowned for its sea trout.

The exceptions to the rule are the Rivers Wampool and Waver, which are about 12 and eight miles long, respectively, and meander over the northern coastal plain to Morecambe Bay on Solway. They provide small but sporting brown trout, some limited sea trout fishing and, on the former, roach fishing. Permits are obtainable from Messrs Wilson, Blacksmith's Shop, Abbey Town, Carlisle.

A slightly longer river, the Ellen rises on the Uldale Fells and flows by Ireby, Aspatria and Bullgill villages before reaching

West Cumbria

Spectrum Colour Library

Maryport on the Solway Firth. It is crossed by the A595 and A596, Carlisle-to-Dalton-in-Furness and Carlisle-to-Workington roads, and is easily reached by minor roads along its course. Since the trout and salmon disease struck our rivers in 1966-67 the River Ellen has made a better recovery than most, and continues to make a slight but steady increase annually.

Permits to fish the lower river may be obtained from the River Ellen Anglers' Association, while the Aspatria Angling Club controls part of the middle reach. On the private waters upstream, permission to fish may be granted by local riparian owners.

June for salmon and sea trout

The River Ehen drains Ennerdale Water and runs through Ennerdale Bridge and Egremont villages on its short course to the sea at Sellafield. Salmon and sea trout abound from June to October and there are brown trout too. Wath Brow and Ennerdale Angling Association controls fishing on the lake and part of the upper Ehen. Lower down, the Egremont and District Angling Association waters may be fished, and tickets for part of the lowest reaches go to caravan residents by R Lockhart, Tarn Bank, Braystones, Beckermet.

Permits are available to fish the River Calder, a little river which also enters the sea near Sellafield. They are obtained from the Calder Angling Association, but the water controlled by the Sella Park Hotel, Calderbridge, Seascale, is reserved for guests and permanent residents.

The River Irt drains gloomy Wastwater, one of the remoter lakes, and lends its name to one of the engines on the famous Ravenglass and Eskdale Railway *La'al Ratty*, as does the little River Mite and the more impressive Esk. Permits to fish the Irt may be obtained from Gosforth Anglers' Club or from the Lutwidge Arms Hotel in Holmbrook, which has $5\frac{1}{2}$ miles of fishing.

The River Esk, the best known of the South-west Cumbria rivers, is renowned for its excellent sea trout and salmon fishing. This explains why it remains private. Rising high on the western slope of Scafell, England's highest mountain, the Esk reaches the sea at Ravenglass in approximately 13

miles, sharing part of its route with the miniature Eskdale railway. There is just one stretch available on permit, which may be obtained from the Pennington Arms Hotel in Ravenglass. The river is best reached via the A595, Whitehaven-to-Dalton-in-Furness coast road which, with minor roads, serves all rivers from the Ehen to the Lickle.

Wry Nose and Hard Knott passes

The River Duddon rises above, and flows through the valley linking the Wry Nose and Hard Knott passes (both are challenges to the motorist) and marks the old Cumberland, Furness and Lancashire borders. This river apparently suffered more than most when salmon disease struck, but it was once a very fine migratory game fish river, and will no doubt recover. Unfortunately, at the time of going to press, tickets are not available for this water, which is mainly private or under the control of angling syndicates.

The rivers Lickle and Duddon have a common estuary, the head of which is a little downstream of the A595 at Duddon Bridge. The River Lickle, a short river, draining the Dunnerdale and Seathwaite Fells, was until recently a ticket water on part of its lower reach. Permits were available in Broughton-in-Furness, and may possibly be made

(Top left) Great Gable and closer hills mirrored in the calm surface of Wast Water.
(Left) Draining Coniston, the Crake is a tributary of the River Leven.
(Below left) The Irt estuary.
(Below) Detail map of the River Calder, Kirk Beck and River Ehen.

Nick Yates

W F Davidson

Davis & Harrison V P Ltd/Crown Copyright Reserved

47

England Scene

available once more in the near future.

Those wishing to fish Duddon and Lickle rivers might apply for membership of the Millom and District Angling Association which also has fishing on parts of the rivers Esk, Irt and Annas.

Although only five miles long, the River Crake has a fair flow since it drains Coniston Water. The head of its estuary is at Greenodd, on the A590 Barrow-to-Levens road, making it one of the more accessible rivers. Unfortunately, it is all privately owned, apart from a little 'parish' water.

River Leven

A little farther along the A590 is the River Leven, which leaves Windermere, the largest lake in the area, near Newby Bridge on a short, picturesque run to the estuary which it shares with the Crake. The Leven is mainly privately owned, but permits to fish game and coarse species are available for the upper reaches. These are issued by the Swan Hotel in Newby Bridge, Ulverston.

Moving farther into old Lancashire, one reaches the little River Eea, a brown trout and sea trout water, with fishing controlled by Cark and District Angling Association. Permits are available from the club or from Mr Balmer, Commodore Hotel, Grange-over-Sands, Cumbria.

The next notable estuary easily reached from the A590 is that shared by the rivers Gilpin and Kent. The former provides fishing for brown trout and sea trout with

(Above) The limpid Leven at Newby Bridge. (Below) The Lune in its upper reaches is an attractive, rock-lined stream.

Spectrum Colour Library

some late salmon. Although privately owned, permission may be obtained from some riparian owners and farmers, and enquiries should be made locally.

The River Kent, which flows under Levens Bridge on the A6 road, rises high on Kentmere Common, with Kentmere Reservoir near its source. The river becomes accessible by minor road to Kentmere from Staveley, on the A591 road from Windermere to the A6 link. A little above Kendal it is swelled by the tributaries Mint and Sprint, which also provide sport with the game species. Permission to fish the higher reaches of these two streams may be granted by local farmers.

At Kendal there is a stretch of public water, but most of the main river is either privately owned or is under the control of the Kent Angling Association, the Burnside AA, or the Staveley Angling Association in the middle reaches. There is also good fishing on the lower river, for which permits may be obtained from Mr L Parsons, Low Levens Farm, nr Kendal. Apart from the A591 and A6 roads, the Kent, Mint, and Sprint valleys are fairly well served with minor roads.

The upper reaches of the River Lune and its tributaries are within view of the motorist travelling on the M6 motorway through the impressive Tebay Gorge. Tebay LMS Fishing Club controls most of the upper river, and issues permits to fish through three local hotels, the Cross Keys and the Junction at Tebay, and the George Hotel in Orton.

Late-season trout and salmon

There is good brown trout fishing, and late season sea trout and salmon fishing in the water controlled by the Sedburgh Angling Association. In its middle reaches the Lune is controlled by the Kirkby Lonsdale Club and beyond their waters the River Lune leaves Cumbria.

The Rivers Clough and Rawthey, tributaries of the Lune, also have a run of migratory fish. Parts of both streams are controlled by the Sedburgh Angling Association and permits may be purchased in Sedburgh, which lies on the A684 Kendal-to-Wensleydale road.

Lake District

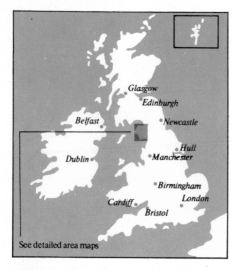

See detailed area maps

Comprising roughly 16 well-known lakes, many tarns and a wealth of small becks and larger rivers, the Lake District offers a variety of fishing controlled by the North West Water Authority.

Now served by the much-improved A66, the link between West Cumberland and the M6 Motorway, Keswick stands on Derwentwater near the heart of the Lake District. The lake is a link in the River Derwent chain, connected by the middle Derwent to Bassenthwaite, the district's most improved trout fishery.

(Right) The National Trust beauty-spots of the Lake District offer much good fishing.
(Below) Derwentwater seen from Prior Crag.

H. M. Frawley/Natural Science Photos

50

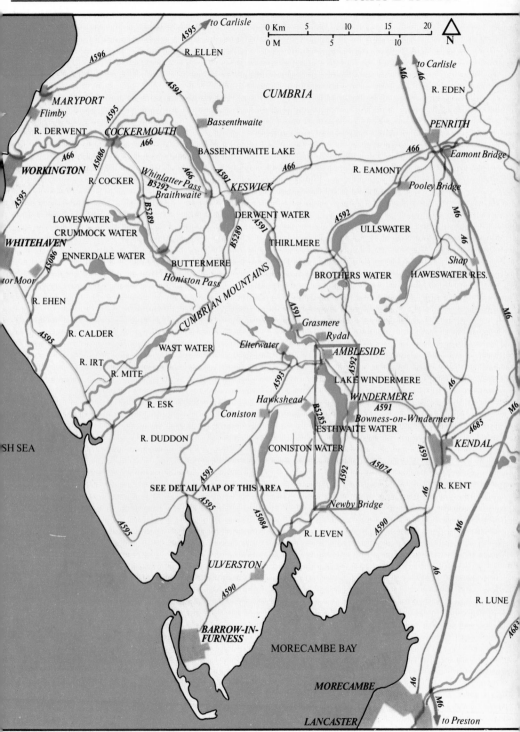

Lake District

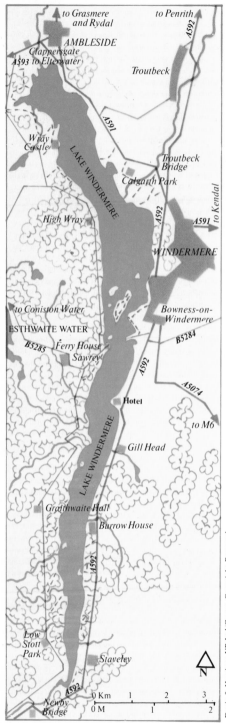

The upper reaches of the River Derwent contain brown trout, while the lakes hold trout, perch and pike. A late run of sea trout and salmon may also be expected, usually after July.

Bassenthwaite

For Bassenthwaite, permits are obtained at the Estate Office, Cockermouth Castle, Cockermouth, or at Piel Wyke boat landings off the Keswick–Cockermouth A66 road. For Derwentwater, permits may be obtained from the Keswick Anglers' Association. Below Bassenthwaite, the Derwent is mainly privately owned, but permits for salmon and sea trout fishing may be obtained by applying to the Estate Office, as above, or to the Broughton Angling Association.

The main tributary of the Derwent, the River Cocker, drains the neighbouring

(Left) Detail map of Lake Windermere.
(Below) A beautiful, quiet winter-evening study of weed-fringed Rydal Water.

Davis & Harrison, VP Ltd/Crown Copyright Reserved

52

valley containing the lakes Buttermere, Crummock and Loweswater. These are reached by taking the Whinlatter Pass, the B5292 spur off the A66 at Braithwaite village. An alternative route is the B5289 from Keswick, via Honister Pass.

Buttermere and Crummock contain brown trout, perch, pike and char, while Loweswater, a smaller, shallow lake, has no char. There is a salmon run through Crummock after July, and limited permits are issued for the River Cocker by the Estate Office, as above, or on application to Southwaite Farm, near Cockermouth. Permits for the three lakes are obtainable from the National Trust at the North Western Regional Office, or more locally at Buttermere and Loweswater villages.

The North West Water Authority controls several waters and limited numbers of permits to fish Thirlmere and Haweswater, both of which contain brown trout, perch and pike, may be obtained on application to the Eastern Division, North West Water Authority, Oaklands House, Talbot Road, Old Trafford, Manchester. Thirlmere lies south-east of Keswick on the A591 Keswick–Ambleside–Windermere road, which continues to Kendal, the A6 and M6. Haweswater, a remote reservoir, is best reached by a minor road from Penrith or Shap village on the A6.

Ullswater

Lying some five miles distant from Penrith, and easily reached via the A592 or B5320 roads to Pooley Bridge, Ullswater attracts thousands of anglers every year, as it is a free fishery. Ullswater itself, and Brotherswater, a neighbouring, much smaller lake, both contain brown trout, perch and pike (a recent introduction). However, the fish of Ullswater are much bigger on average. The rare schelly, a deep-water salmonid, is also found in Ullswater, but few are taken on rod and line. Both lakes may be fished without permits, but parts of their shores are privately owned and enquiries should be made locally before fishing either.

The River Eamont, which connects Ullswater to the River Eden, a Solway river, is mainly controlled by the Penrith Angling Association which issues brown trout permits for the upper reaches. Below Eamont Bridge, the water is mostly privately owned, but some fishing on the left bank is controlled by the Yorkshire Fly Fishers' Club, whose game water also holds fair numbers of very good chub.

Permits for the Penrith Angling Association water are available at tackle dealers in Penrith, while for the Yorkshire Fly Fishers' waters permits are available from the club secretary.

Windermere

Windermere is a good centre for the angler wishing to fish Grasmere, Rydal Water, Coniston, Esthwaite Water and Windermere itself. Grasmere, Rydal Water and Windermere all lie on the A591, Keswick–Windermere–Kendal route and are easily reached from the A6 and M6 to the south. There is no problem of access.

A. F. Kersting

Grasmere provides free fishing for brown trout, perch and pike, whereas Rydal Water is controlled by the Windermere Ambleside and District Angling Association. Permits are issued from several addresses in Grasmere, Ambleside, Hawkshead, Windermere and Bowness.

River Leven

Lake Windermere, more famous for good pike, trout and perch fishing, contains a great table fish, the char, which is fished for semi-commercially by deep trolling with lures. Several areas may be fished without permits, for most of the north-western shore north of Ferry House is National Trust property, but the rest is mainly privately owned and enquiries should be made locally in Windermere or Bowness. For the River Leven, for salmon, sea trout and coarse fishing, permits may be obtained from the Swan Hotel, Newby Bridge, near Ulverston.

Esthwaite Water is best approached from Ambleside, via the A593 then the B5286 road to Hawkshead village. The lake holds brown trout, perch and pike, and is owned by the Esthwaite Estates Company. Permits are available at Hawkshead Post Office.

Coniston, of water speed trials fame, is best reached via the A593, and offers good free fishing for brown trout, perch and pike. Char are also taken here on baits fished from the shore into the deeper water, which is mainly in the middle reaches. Most of the shore is National Trust property, but some parts are private and access should be obtained through local tackle dealers.

Ennerdale and Wast Water, though less accessible, are also worth fishing for their brown trout, char and late migratory fish. Permits for Wast Water are as for Bassenthwaite, and for Ennerdale are obtained from D F Whelan, Wath Brow and Ennerdale Angling Association, 11 Crossings Close, Cleator Moor, Cumbria.

Coarse angling

For coarse angling, the larger lakes are recommended, particularly Windermere, Coniston, Derwentwater, Bassenthwaite and Crummock. These lakes also tend to produce the bigger trout. Fortunately, the boats which are essential for this kind of fishing are available at these waters.

As mentioned in earlier pages, the west-coast late salmon and sea trout rivers, Calder, Ehen, Ellen, Esk and Irt offer fine sport, and may be fished, in part, on visitors' permits. The reader may also be given permission to fish in the many small un-mentioned becks and tarns, by applying to local riparian owners.

Lake Windermere contains pike, perch and trout. There is permit-free fishing on a number of areas round the lake. A two-month netting in 1969 collected over 7,500 perch for age and population-density studies.

England Scene

WATER AUTHORITY
North West Water Authority, Head Office, Dawson House, Great Sankey, Warrington WA5 3LW. Tel: Penketh 4321. Eastern Division, Oaklands House, Talbot Road, Old Trafford, Manchester.
LICENCES
Salmon and migratory trout: Season £15.60, part season to 31 May £7.80, part season from 1 June £9, junior and OAPs £6.50; part-season to 31 May £3.25; part season from June £4; seven days (salmon only) £2.60. 'Junior' applies to children of 14-16 years: up to 13 years no licence is needed. All except the seven-day licence also entitles the holder to fish for eels, non-migratory trout (brown, rainbow and char) and freshwater fish for the whole of the respective seasons. Non-migratory trout: Season £2.60; junior and OAPs £1.25; seven days 65p. Freshwater fish and eels: Season £1.25; junior and Oaps 65p; seven days 35p. Rod and line (old Mersey and Weaver Authority areas): Freshwater fish and eels: season 65p; junior and OAPs 35p.
LOCAL CLUBS AND ASSOCIATIONS
Broughton Angling Assoc, G B Clark, 'Deneldene', Ryehill Rd, Flimsby, Maryport, Cumbria.
Keswick Anglers' Assoc, W Ashcroft, 'Springhaven', How Lane, Portinscale, Keswick, Cumbria.
Penrith Angling Assoc, J S Norris, 21 Victoria Rd, Penrith.

Wath Brow and Ennerdale Angling Assoc, D F Whelan, 11 Crossings Close, Cleator Moor, Cumbria.
Windermere, Ambleside and District Angling Assoc, R T Parry, Yew Bank, Clappersgate, Ambleside, Cumbria.
Yorkshire Fly Fishers' Club, P R Garnett, 2 Hallcroft Drive, Addingham, Ilkley, W Yorks.
TACKLE DEALERS AND LICENCE DISTRIBUTORS
P Musgrave & Sons Ltd, Lake Road, Bowness-on-Windermere.
E R Barker, The Post Office, Broughton-in-Furness.
Dr G L Watson, Ulpha Post Office, Broughton-in-Furness.
W Bound, Wath Store, Wath Brow, Cleator Moor.
M Nicholson, Shop No. 3, Lakeland House, Tilberthwaite Ave, Coniston.
J Hazlehurst, Post Office, Hawkshead. Tel 201.
South Lakeland Fishing Tackle Specialists, 64 Kirkland, Kendal. Tel 24867.
Mrs M Barnard, Lake Leisure, Pooley Bridge.
Messrs Burnyeates, 26 Lowther St, Whitehaven.
M Taylor, 21 King St, Whitehaven.
A Simpson, 1 South William St, Workington.
M Taylor, 4 Murrey Rd, Workington.
FISHERIES
The National Trust, North Western Regional Office, Broadlands, Borrans Rd, Ambleside, Cumbria.
The Estate Office, Cockermouth Castle, Cockermouth.
Esthwaites Estates Company, Estate Office, Hawkshead.

Midlands Reservoirs

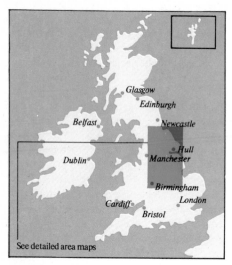

See detailed area maps

The Midlands and North are provided with many reservoirs, controlled by the Anglian, the Yorkshire, the Northumbrian and the North West Water Authorities, and offer excellent fishing. They are all frequently restocked and are available on day ticket.

The Anglian Water Authority controls several reservoirs ranging from the large Rutland Water, 3,100 acres, to the smaller Toft Newton Reservoir, 40 acres.

The latest venue for anglers, opened in 1977, is the Rutland Water at Empingham, Oakham, Leicestershire. Already the largest man-made water in Western Europe, it is hoped to make it Europe's premier trout fishery. Horn Mill trout hatchery, on a 5-acre site, is only two miles away, and makes possible annual restocking with 1,000,000 fish. This water has 16½ miles of bank fishing and is restocked each year with 75,000 rainbow and 25,000 browns.

Day tickets are issued at £3 (juniors, accompanied by an adult, half-price), motor boat tickets £9, rowing boat tickets £4.50, season £100, and are available from Whitwell fishing lodge open daily at 5.30am, or from the Reservoir Manager.

Sixty boats are available, fishing is by fly only, and there is a catch limit of eight fish.

In Huntingdonshire, Grafham Water is at West Perry, with easy access from the A1. It is a vast water of 1,670 acres well-stocked with brown and rainbow trout, with top catches in 1976 including a fishery record of 12lb 5oz and another giant of 11lb 2oz— and a record total catch for the season of 36,283 trout.

Grafham Season

The season is from 1 May to 13 October, and fishing from the banks, motor boats or rowing boats is fly only with a catch limit of eight fish. Day tickets (exclusive of boat hire) are available from the self-service unit at the lodge for £2.50, and season tickets (only 100) costing £75 (juniors accompanied by an adult £1.25) are available from the Water Authority.

Ravensthorpe Reservoir is a landscaped reservoir of 114 acres near Northampton, reached via the A60. Fishing is available from bank and boats throughout the season from 1 April to 30 September. Day

tickets cost £1.60, boats £1.90 extra and are obtainable from the lodge. Season tickets from the Water Authority cost £42.50.

Pitsford Reservoir, 739 acres, is near Brixworth, Northampton, and reached via the A508. It is an attractively landscaped water stocked with brown and rainbow trout—again fishing is by fly only with a catch limit of eight fish. Tickets are the same price as for Ravensthorpe.

Also near Northampton is Hollowell Reservoir, offering bank and boat coarse fishing, and with a variety of species including pike of nearly 30lb. A limited number of day tickets can be bought in advance from Reservoir House.

In Lincolnshire, Newton Toft Reservoir, near Market Rasen, is reached via the A631. It is a man-made concrete reservoir stocked frequently with brown and rainbow trout, and offers bank fishing. The season is from 9 April to 30 September, fishing is by fly only, and a catch limit of six fish applies. The water is controlled by the Lincolnshire Division of the Anglian Water Authority and day tickets at £3 are issued at the self-service unit at the water.

In Leicestershire, Eyebrook Reservoir, 400 acres, is at Caldecott, near Uppingham,

reached via the A43 or the A47. Stocked with brown and rainbow trout and with all the trout bred and reared in the reservoir's own hatcheries. Fishing is by fly only, there is no catch limit, and shooting-heads are not allowed. The season extends from 1 April to 30 September and there is fishing from bank and boats. Corby and District Water Company (Northants) controls this water and issues day tickets at £2, evening tickets £1.50 (boats £3 per day extra) available at the reservoir.

Cheshire reservoirs

In Cheshire, Lamaload Reservoir, 70 acres, is controlled by the Prince Albert Angling Society; Vale House Reservoir, 62 acres, and Bottoms Reservoir, 55 acres, by the North West Water Authority. Lamaload Reservoir is east of Macclesfield and reached via the A537 Buxton road. It is landscaped and well-stocked with brown and rainbow trout. A two-fish catch limit applies; fishing is fly only, and no wading is allowed. The season is from 1 April to 10 October, and day tickets at £2 (a limited number) are available from R Newton, tackle dealer.

Vale House Reservoir and Bottoms Reservoir are near Stalybridge and reached

(Left) The sun sets over anglers fishing the 3,100-acre Rutland Water.
(Below) A peaceful corner at Pitsford.

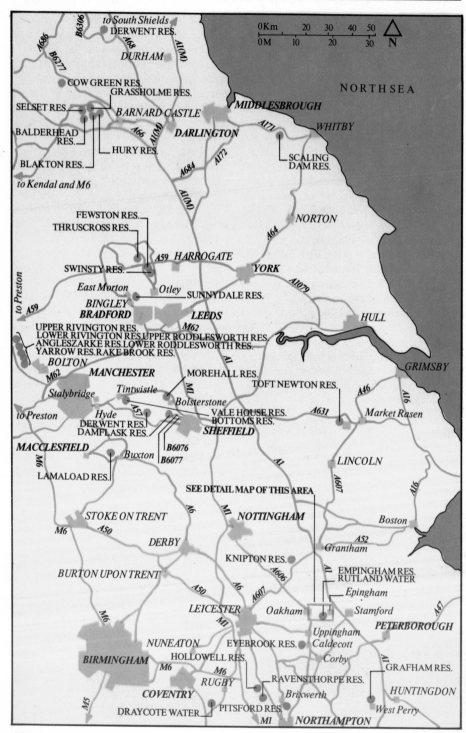

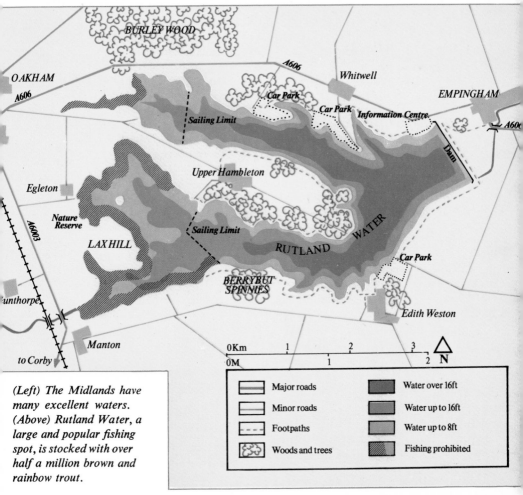

OAKHAM
A606
BURLEY WOOD
A606
Whitwell
EMPINGHAM
A606
Car Park
Car Park
Information Centre
Sailing Limit
Dam
Egleton
Upper Hambleton
Nature
Reserve
A6003
LAX HILL
Sailing Limit
RUTLAND WATER
Car Park
unthorpe
BERRYBUT
SPINNIES
Edith Weston
Manton
to Corby
0Km   1   2   3
0M   1   2   N

(Left) The Midlands have many excellent waters. (Above) Rutland Water, a large and popular fishing spot, is stocked with over half a million brown and rainbow trout.

Major roads		Water over 16ft
Minor roads		Water up to 16ft
Footpaths		Water up to 8ft
Woods and trees		Fishing prohibited

via the A628 Manchester-Sheffield road. They are stocked monthly with brown and rainbow trout, and fishing is by fly, spinning and bait. The season is from 31 March to 30 September and day tickets at 70p (reductions for OAPs) are issued on the site.

Durham reservoirs

The Northumbrian Water Authority controls several reservoirs around Durham. A group of five moorland reservoirs consisting of Blackton 66 acres, Balderhead 289 acres, Hury 127 acres, Grassholme 140 acres and Salset 275 acres, are reached via the B6277 from Barnard Castle. They hold native brown trout and are stocked with rainbow trout, offering fly and worm bank fishing during the season from 22 March to 30 September, with no catch limit.

Cow Green Reservoir, 770 acres, is at Upper Teesdale, also reached via the B6277 from Barnard Castle. Opened in 1971, the reservoir holds native brown trout and offers fishing by fly and worm from 24 March to 30 September. Day tickets at £2 (juniors and OAPs half price) are issued at the lodge, and season tickets can be obtained from the Water Authority.

Near Consett, Durham, Derwent Reservoir, 1,100 acres, at Edmundbyers, is stocked annually with several thousand

59

Midlands Reservoirs

brown and rainbow trout and offers fly fishing with a 10-fish catch limit. There is boat and bank fishing from 1 May to 14 October with day tickets at £1.80 (juniors and OAPs half price) issued at the reservoir. Motor boats cost an additional £7, rowing boats £3.50 per day. The reservoir is controlled by the Sunderland and South Shields Water Company.

Yorkshire is rich in reservoirs within easy reach of the main towns. Scaling Dam, 120 acres, is controlled by the Northumbrian Water Authority and reached via the A171 from Whitby. Day tickets at £2 (juniors and OAPs half price) are issued at the reservoir lodge for fly and worm fishing from 1 April to 30 September. The reservoir contains brown trout to 7lb 3oz.

Sheffield's reservoirs

Yorkshire Water Authority controls a number of reservoirs near Sheffield and Otley. Near Sheffield, Damflask Reservoir, reached via the B6077, 115 acres, and underbank Reservoir, 103 acres, hold trout and coarse fish, and all legal methods of fishing are allowed. They also hold big roach with a fine fish of 3½lb taken in 1965. The trout season is from 1 April to 30 September and the coarse season from 16 June to 15 March. Day tickets at 50p are available from the reservoir attendant's office.

Morehall Reservoir, a large landscaped water holding brown trout, lies between Underbank and Damflask reservoirs. Fishing is by fly only from the bank, with a catch limit of two fish. Day tickets at 50p are issued by the Yorkshire Water Authority for the season 1 April to 30 September.

Thrushcross, Fewston and Swinsty

Near Otley, there is a group of three reservoirs—Thrushcross, a long, narrow reservoir of 360 acres, Fewston and Swinsty. They are all reached via the A59 and hold brown trout. Fishing on Thrushcross is by fly only, while at Fewston and Swinsty it is by fly and minnow. There are no boats and the catch limit is six fish. Day tickets cost £1 from self-service units. The season is from 1 April to 29 September.

The Bingley Angling Club controls Sunnydale Reservoir, three acres, at East Morton near Bingley. The reservoir is annually restocked with brown and rainbow trout, and a brown trout of 6lb 4oz was caught there. Fly and bait fishing are allowed, but no spinning. The catch limit is two fish. Day tickets at 40p are available from tackle dealers in Bradford for the season from 25 March to 30 September.

Bolton reservoirs

The North West Water Authority controls a large group of reservoirs near Bolton in Lancashire, reached via the A6. The Rivington reservoirs, holding trout and coarse fish and totalling 600 acres, comprise Anglezarke, Yarrow, Rake Brook, Upper and Lower Roddlesworth, Upper and Lower Rivington. Fishing on all the reservoirs is by fly and bait (excluding maggots) and dry fly only on Upper Roddlesworth and Upper Rivington. Day tickets are available from the water authority or from local tackle dealers from the trout season from 16 March to 30 September and the coarse season from 16 June to 15 March.

In Leicestershire, Knipton Reservoir, said to be 160 years old, offers good fishing for bream, tench and roach, and became

INFORMATION

WATER AUTHORITIES
Anglian Water Authority, Diploma House, Grammar School Walk, Huntingdon PE18 6NZ. Tel. 56181.
Northants Division, Cliftonville, Northants.
Lincolnshire Division, 50 Wide Bargate, Boston, Lincs. Tel. 65661.
North West Water Authority, Dawson House, Great Sankey, Warrington WA5 3LW. Tel. Penketh 4321.
Northumbrian Water Authority, Northumbria House, Regent Centre, Gosforth, Newcastle-on-Tyne. Tel Gosforth 843151.
Yorkshire Water Authority, West Riding House, 67 Albion St, Leeds LS1 5AA. Tel. 448201.
CONTROLLING BODIES
Corby (Northants) and District Water Co, Geddington Rd, Corby, Northants. Tel. Corby 2121.
Duke of Rutland Estate, Estate Office, Belvoir Castle, Grantham, Lincs.
Sunderland and South Shields Water Co, 29 John St, Sunderland. Tel. 57123.
LOCAL CLUBS
Bingley Angling Club, B Howard, 26 Spring Park Rd, Willesden, Bradford, Yorks. Tel. Cullingworth 2115.
Prince Albert Angling Society, C Sparkes, High Lodge, Upton, Macclesfield, Cheshire.

famous for pike fishing in 1967 when a 39lb fish was caught. It is situated on the Duke of Rutland's estate eight miles from Melton Mowbray, reached via the A607. The season is from 16 June to 15 March, and day tickets at £1 can be obtained from the Estate Office or reservoir keeper.

Draycote Water

In Warwickshire, Draycote Water, 600 acres, near Rugby, is owned by the Severn-Trent Water Authority (Avon Division) and reached via the A426. It is a landscaped reservoir stocked on a put-and-take basis with several thousand brown and rainbow trout during each season and offering bank and boat fishing from 8 April to 9 October.

Fishing is by fly only with a catch limit of eight fish. Day tickets cost £2.50 (OAPs and the disabled £1), (juniors accompanied by an adult 70p), and rowing boats cost £2.50 per day, electric boats £6, and petrol boats £8. Bookings made at the lodge.

There are many other reservoirs in the Midlands and North, with the fishing rights of many controlled by water authorities or clubs. A useful fishing water can often be tracked down by enquiry at tackle dealers, or by writing to water authorities.

Draycote Water, near Rugby, holds both brown and rainbow trout. Bank and boat fishing is available.

Eric Birch

TACKLE DEALERS

Dalesports, 35 Market Place, Barnard Castle, Durham.
P C Sports, 72A Galegate, Barnard Castle, Durham
G F Wilkins, 79 Banktop, Blackburn, Lancs.
H Le Moine, 22 Accrington Rd, Blackburn, Lancs. Tel. 58719.
Richmond's Tackle, Morley St, Bradford, Yorks.
Carter's Sports, Bridge St, Bradford.
Steve's Fishing Tackle, 237 Bridgeman St, Bolton, Lancs.
Angler's Services, 45 Claypath, Durham.
J W Wright, 107 Parkgate, Darlington, Durham.
The Tackle Shop, 42 Tooley St, Gainsborough, Lincs. Tel. 3002.
Armley Angling Centre, 220 Armley Rd, Leeds 12.
D B Sports, 16 Queen's Parade, Leeds 14.
Gledhills of Leeds, 60 The Headrow, Leeds 1. Tel. 455336.
P T S Fishing Tackle, 250 Tong Rd, Leeds 12. Tel. 637019.
Kirkgate Anglers, W R Edge, 95 Kirkgate, Leeds 1.
Savage Sports Shop, 114 Cross Gates Rd, Leeds 16.
John Adams, 41 Humberstone Gate, Leicester. Tel. 22510.
Boundary Pet Stores, 16 Bunkers Hill, Lincoln LN2 4QP.
A Brough, 8 Waters Green, Macclesfield, Cheshire.

Ray Newton, Park St, Macclesfield.
J Gilder, 532 Oldham Rd, Fallsworth, Manchester, Lancs.
Arrowsmith, 1A Gordon Lane, W. Gorton, Manchester M12 5DF.
Buckley's of Manchester Ltd, 955 Old Ham Rd, Newton Heath, Manchester. Tel. 205-2829.
The Northern Angler, 29 Market Place, Middleton, Manchester. Tel. 643-3524.
Smith's of Salford, 167 Regent Rd, Salford 5, Manchester. Tel. 872-1367.
R S Tackle Co, 36 Collingwood St, Newcastle-on-Tyne. Tel. 25731.
Bagnall and Kirkwood, 52 Grey St, Newcastle-on-Tyne. Tel. 25873.
John Robertson, 101 Percy St, Newcastle-on-Tyne. Tel. 22018.
Afflech Sports, 282 Shields Rd, Byker, Newcastle-on-Tyne. Tel. 659300.
Gilders, 250 Wellingborough Rd, Northampton.
Banks and Burr, 27 Claremont Rd, Rugby, Warcs.
Steve's Fishing Tackle, 204 Yorkshire St, Rochdale, Lancs.
A Watts, 4 Herriots Lane, Wellingborough, Northants.
Whitby Angling Supplies, 56 Haggersgate, Whitby. Tel. 3855.
J C Dowson, The Board, Leaholm, Whitby, Yorks.

North East Yorkshire

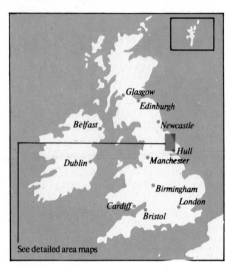

See detailed area maps

£19 per season or £7.50 per week. However the rates change each April, check with the Water Authority. Other worthwhile fishing is in the hands of the Egton Estates between Grosmont and Egton Bridge. Early application from the Estate Office at Egton Bridge is essential, but day tickets are occasionally available at £4.50.

The upper reaches of the Esk have excellent trout fishing. Danby and District Angling Club offers week tickets for stretches at Castleton, Danby and Leaholm. These can be obtained from Ward Tompson, Borough Road, Middlesbrough; the Duke of Wellington Inn, Danby; Castleton Post Office or Danby Post Office.

From Glaisdale to Ruswarp much of the fishing is either controlled by the Esk Fishery

No other county in the British Isles is as well endowed with good fishing venues as Yorkshire. It can offer the angler just about everything in the 'fishy' catalogue. In North Yorkshire especially, the rivers Esk, Rye and Derwent offer myriad possibilities.

The Esk rises 1,300ft above sea level and drains the moors of Baysdale, Farndale, and Westerdale before, approximately 29 miles later, flowing into the sea at Whitby. It is the only worthwhile salmon river in the county. However, its runs of fish, albeit prolific, can be as fickle as a politician's promise. The first worthwhile run of fish comes with the first floods of June or July, and with the salmon come a good proportion of sea trout. All legitimate fishing styles are permitted.

Yorkshire Water Authority
Unfortunately, much of the best fishing is in the hands of the Esk Fishery Association where the annual subscription is currently £110, but where the waiting list is too long to offer any hope to all but the very young. In addition, Yorkshire Water Authority requires the angler to take out a special licence for the Esk which, for salmon works out at £10 per season or £4 per week—rising shortly

(Below) Trout fishing on the River Esk. (Right) The picturesque River Derwent offers a variety of fishing. Our picture shows Jack Martin fishing for trout at Hackness.

Arthur Oglesby

Arthur Oglesby

Association or is in private hands. This stretch of the river offers the best of the fishing for migratory fish, but the casual visitor will have problems finding access. From Ruswarp downstream to Whitby, however, some day-ticket water is available, but it is mostly tidal and is subject to strict control. Tickets at £1 may be obtained from Mr Hall, Boatyard, Riverside, Ruswarp, and early application is advised.

River Rye
The River Rye has its small beginnings on the south side of the Cleveland Hills, at Rye Head. From there to Nunnington it offers the angler some sparkling streams where trout and grayling abound, but, from Nunnington downstream to its junction with the Derwent, it is a mixed coarse fishery with mostly sluggish and deeper water.

Some notable feeder streams join the Rye, but most fishing is in the hands of clubs or syndicates where the casual visitor cannot find easy access. At Hawnby on the Rye there is good brown trout fishing available from the Hawnby Hotel (Tel: Bilsdale 202) but early application is advised and the fishing is with fly only.

From Helmsley downstream to Nunnington Bridge. Ryedale Anglers' Club has ten miles of excellent water which is limited to members and their guests. At Nunnington, tickets are available from the keeper's cottage or from the Estate Office, Nunnington Hall, to fish varying sections of their preserves. The top beat of this water costs £2 per day and is for fly fishing only; the middle section costs 75p per day, and the lower, Holbeck Fishery, 25p per day.

Several notable tributaries, such as the Dove, Seven, Costa and Pickering Beck join the Rye. Members of both the York and Leeds Amalgamations of Anglers have access to good trout and grayling fishing, and the Pickering Fishery Association have first-class stretches on both the Costa and the Pickering Beck.

Wykeham High Moor
Rising a little to the south of the Esk, and at an altitude of 900ft, the picturesque Yorkshire Derwent has its source on Wykeham High Moor. It offers a wide variety of fishing and in its upper reaches is a highly rated trout and grayling fishery. From Langdale End to Hackness it resembles a

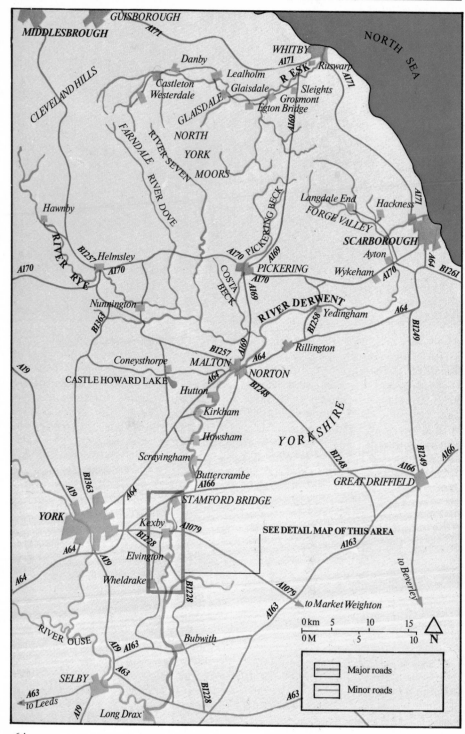

MIDDLESBROUGH
GUISBOROUGH
A171
WHITBY
A171
Ruswarp
NORTH SEA
Danby
Lealholm
R ESK
Castleton
Westerdale
Glaisdale
Sleights
Grosmont
Egton Bridge
GLAISDALE
CLEVELAND HILLS
NORTH
YORK
MOORS
FARNDALE
RIVER SEVEN
RIVER DOVE
Hawnby
Langdale End
Hackness
A171
FORGE VALLEY
SCARBOROUGH
RIVER RYE
B1257
Helmsley
A170
A170
PICKERING BECK
A170
A169
PICKERING
Ayton
Wykeham
A170
A64
B1261
A170
COSTA BECK
A169
A170
Nunnington
RIVER DERWENT
B1258
Yedingham
A64
B1363
B1249
A19
B1257
A169
Coneysthorpe
MALTON
A64
Rillington
CASTLE HOWARD LAKE
A64
NORTON
Hutton
B1248
YORKSHIRE
Kirkham
Howsham
B1249
A166
Scrayingham
B1248
A166
Buttercrambe
A166
GREAT DRIFFIELD
STAMFORD BRIDGE
YORK
B1363
A19
A64
Kexby
A1079
SEE DETAIL MAP OF THIS AREA
B1228
A163
Elvington
to Beverley
A64
A19
Wheldrake
B1228
A1079
A64
A163
to Market Weighton
RIVER OUSE
A19 A163
Bubwith
0 km 5 10 15
0 M 5 10
N
SELBY
A63
A63
A63
A63 to Leeds
A19
B1228
Long Drax

Major roads

Minor roads

(Left) Map showing the rivers Esk, Rye and Derwent in North Yorkshire.
(Above) the river Esk at Whitby.

Ray Forsberg

small highland stream. The scenery is magnificent and the river winds and topples to offer a kaleidoscope of changing views.

Ten miles of river in this vicinity are preserved by the ancient and much-respected Derwent Anglers' Club and the water is well stocked with both brown and rainbow trout from the club's own hatchery. Fly only is allowed; no trout under 10in must be taken and a three-brace day limit operates. After the end of June, it is possible to get day tickets on the club water at £5 per day, and these can be obtained from the Hackness Grange Hotel; The Everley Hotel or Pritchard's Tackle Shop, Eastborough, Scarborough.

West Ayton
Through Forge Valley the river slows its pace and offers trout fishing comparable with that in many chalk streams. Below West Ayton, the river assumes an even more tranquil pace. At Yedingham, Rillington, Malton and Huttons Ambo there is some excellent coarse fishing.

Malton and Norton Angling Club no longer issues day tickets, but some good bream, perch, tench and roach day-ticket

fishing is available at Castle Howard Lake (20 acres; fishing one side only), Coneysthorpe for 75p. The angler is advised to apply early in writing, to the bailiff, Mr H Cook, The Lodge, Coneysthorpe, York. Farther downstream, Huttons Ambro Angling Club issues day tickets at 30p for a 1½ mile stretch on both sides of the footbridge on one bank at Huttons Ambro. Tickets can also be obtained from Huttons Ambro Post Office (Tel: Malton 2803).

Stamford Bridge
Downstream of Malton there is some fine scenery at Kirkham Abbey, Howsham, Buttercramber and Kexby, but day tickets are not issued by the Bradford No. 1 Angling Club for their water at Howsham Wood, nor by the Leeds and District Amalgamated Society of Anglers for their water at Kexby and Scrayingham.

Stamford Bridge is a particularly noted venue producing specimen chub and most other varieities of popular coarse fish. It was quite a noteworthy salmon fishery, and even today, fish are occasionally seen trying to leap the weir. York and District Amalgamation of Anglers issue day tickets at 30p (rising shortly to 50p) for two stretches at Stamford Bridge; for a ½ mile left-bank stretch below the viaduct, and for 4 miles of the right bank from Stamford road bridge down to Kexby. Car parking is at Kexby where the A1079 Hull-York road is being diverted.

Sutton upon Derwent
Downstream of Elvington, the Leeds and District Amalgamation of Anglers has a 1½ mile day-ticket stretch on the right bank downstream from the road bridge, and at Sutton upon Derwent, the Leeds and York Amalgamations of Anglers have 4½ miles of joint day-ticket water at 30p. At nearby Wheldrake, there is more day-ticket water for 1½ miles on the right bank upstream of the swing bridge.

Yorkshire and District Amalgamation of Anglers issues these tickets at 30p (subject to price increase). They can be obtained directly from the York and District Club, or for the

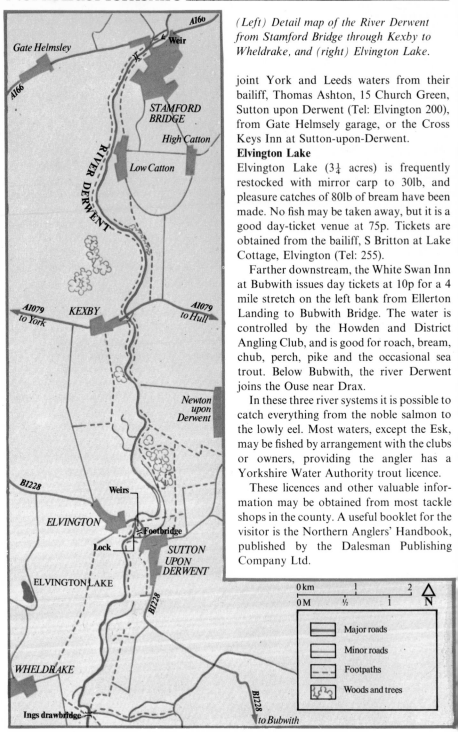

(Left) Detail map of the River Derwent from Stamford Bridge through Kexby to Wheldrake, and (right) Elvington Lake.

joint York and Leeds waters from their bailiff, Thomas Ashton, 15 Church Green, Sutton upon Derwent (Tel: Elvington 200), from Gate Helmsely garage, or the Cross Keys Inn at Sutton-upon-Derwent.

Elvington Lake

Elvington Lake ($3\frac{1}{4}$ acres) is frequently restocked with mirror carp to 30lb, and pleasure catches of 80lb of bream have been made. No fish may be taken away, but it is a good day-ticket venue at 75p. Tickets are obtained from the bailiff, S Britton at Lake Cottage, Elvington (Tel: 255).

Farther downstream, the White Swan Inn at Bubwith issues day tickets at 10p for a 4 mile stretch on the left bank from Ellerton Landing to Bubwith Bridge. The water is controlled by the Howden and District Angling Club, and is good for roach, bream, chub, perch, pike and the occasional sea trout. Below Bubwith, the river Derwent joins the Ouse near Drax.

In these three river systems it is possible to catch everything from the noble salmon to the lowly eel. Most waters, except the Esk, may be fished by arrangement with the clubs or owners, providing the angler has a Yorkshire Water Authority trout licence.

These licences and other valuable information may be obtained from most tackle shops in the county. A useful booklet for the visitor is the Northern Anglers' Handbook, published by the Dalesman Publishing Company Ltd.

0 km	1	2
0 M	½	1

Major roads	
Minor roads	
Footpaths	
Woods and trees	

S. Britton

INFORMATION

WATER AUTHORITY
Yorkshire Water Authority, West Riding House, 67 Albion St, Leeds LS1 5AA. Tel 448201.

LICENCES
Salmon, trout, freshwater fish and eels, excluding salmon and migratory trout in the Esk and its tributaries and in streams north of the Esk, season £1.90 (OAPs and the disabled 95p), 7-day 75p (OAPs and the disabled 40p). Children under 14 years do not require a licence. Salmon, migratory trout, freshwater fish, non-migratory trout and eels throughout the Authorities' area, season £19 (OAPs and the disabled £9.50), 7-day £7.50 (OAPs and the disabled £3.75), 1-day £3.75 (OAPs and the disabled £1.90).
Close seasons: salmon and migratory trout November 1 to April 5, non-migratory trout October 1 to March 31, freshwater fish February 28 to May 31.
Size limits: barbel 11.8in (30cm), carp 10in (25cm), trout, sea trout, bream, tench, chub and grayling 9in (23cm), dace, perch, roach and rudd 7in (18cm). Keepnets not allowed during the freshwater fish close season.

FISHERIES
Castle Howard Estate, H Cook, Bailiff, The Lodge, Coneysthorpe, York.
Nunnington Estate, P J B Clive, Estate Office, Nunnington Hall, Yorks.

LOCAL CLUBS AND ASSOCIATIONS.
Bradford No 1 Angling Association, C W Smith, 44 Fleet Lane, Queensbury, Bradford, W Yorks. Tel 815630.
Danby and District Angling Club, F Farrow, Green Bank, Danby, Whitby, Yorks.
Derwent Anglers' Club, I V Brett, Quarry Garth, Burniston, Scarborough, N Yorks.
Esk Fishery Association, H B Thomas, Angrove House, Great Ayton, Teesside, N Yorks.
Howden and District Angling Club, M Redman, 46 Mansfield Ave, Goole, Yorks.
Huttons Ambro Angling Club, Mr S King, 1 Danby Cottages, Thornton-le-Clay, York.
Leeds and District Amalgamated Society of Anglers, A G Copley, 6 Mount Pleasant, Middleton, Leeds 10. Tel 75059.
Malton and Norton Angling Club, M Foggin, 123 Welham Rd, Norton, Malton, N Yorks. Tel 3208.
Pickering Fishery Association, C Hardy, 3 Westbourne Grove, Pickering, Yorks. Tel 72212.
Ryedale Anglers' Club, H M V Wright, Rose Cottage, Lund, Driffield, E Yorks. Tel Middleton-on-Wolds 274.
Stokesley Angling Club, K W Foggin, 57 Harrow Rd, Linthorpe, Middlesbrough, Cleveland. Tel 84640.
York and District Amalgamation of Anglers, E Woodward, 204 Salisbury Terr, Leeman Rd, York. Tel 58298.

TACKLE DEALERS AND LICENCE AGENTS
Yorkshire Water Authority, Eastern Division, 37 North Bar Within, Beverley, E Yorks.
J and E Everett, 3 Flemingate, Beverley, Yorks.
Mallisons Stores, Middle Street South, Driffield, E Yorks.
F G Grale and Son, 26 Copley Rd, Doncaster, Yorks.
Sawyers Ltd, Sawyer House, Doncaster DN1 3AJ.
Barry's High Class Fishing Specialists, 23 Westfields Ave, Goole, Yorks.
Geo Cooper and Sons Ltd, Bridge St, Helmsley, Yorks.
The Angling Centre, 22 Chapel Hill, Huddersfield, Yorks.
The Tackle Shop, 423 Holderness Rd, Hull, Yorks.
The Fishing Basket, 470 Beverley Rd, Hull, Yorks.
Armley Angling Centre, 220 Armley Rd, Leeds 12.
D B Sports, 16 Queens Parade, Seacroft Town Centre, Leeds 14.
Gledhills of Leeds, 60 The Headrow, Leeds 1.
Kirkgate Anglers, W R Edge, 95 Kirkgate, Leeds 1.
P T S Fishing Tackle, 250 Tong Rd, Leeds 12.
Savage Sports Shop, 114 Cross Gates Rd, Leeds 16.
J Anderson and Son, 10 Saville St, Malton, Yorks.
D Y Etherington, 58 Castlegate, Malton, Yorks.
Anglers' Corner, 121 Victorial Rd, Middlesbrough.
Ward Thompson Bros, 87 Borough Rd, Middlesbrough.
Group 2 Sports Ltd, 7 Market Place, Pocklington, York.
Geo Cooper and Sons Ltd, 33 Market Place, Pickering.
Sports Toys and Model Shop, 14 Finkle St, Richmond.
Mrs B Wilkinson, 7 Queen St, Ripon, Yorks.
Buckley's Angling Supplies, 6 Leading Post St, Scarborough.
Mr J P Longbottom, 2 The Square, Stamford Bridge.
J C Dowson, The Board, Leaholm, Whitby.
R W and V Swaby, Mill Beck, The Carrs, Ruswarp, Whitby.
Shipley Sports Centre, 23 Westgate, Shipley.
The Salmon Leap Hotel, B Gibson, Sleights, Whitby.
Whitby Angling Supplies, 56 Haggersgate, Whitby. Tel 3855.
Hookes of York Ltd, 28-30 Coppergate, York. Tel 55073.
George Hill's, Clarence St, York.
Bulmer's Selling Service, Lord Mayor's Walk, York.
Anglers' Corner, Walmgate, York.
Morely Bros, Bishopthorpe Rd, York.

NorthWest Yorkshire

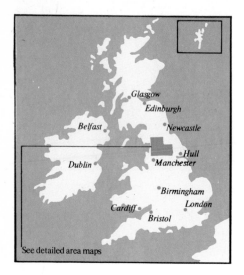

See detailed area maps

The rivers Nidd, Ouse, Swale, Ure and
Wharfe form the backbone of Yorkshire's
water structure, and all eventually become
the River Humber. Their individual qualities
are best seen in the upper reaches and most
are associated with the name of a dale—
Nidderdale, Swaledale, and Wharfedale.
Uredale is known as Wensleydale, but is no
less attractive for that reason.

Possibly the most attractive river, sceni-
cally, is the Wharfe. It rises 1,400ft up on
Cam Fell and flows 60 miles to join the Ouse
at Cawood. In its upper reaches it offers the
fly fisherman some very good trout fishing.
Much is in the hands of clubs and syndicates
but there is some day-ticket water. The
venues, however, are numerous and the
intending visitor is advised to acquire *The
Northern Angler's Handbook* published by
the Dalesman Publishing Company at 60p.

One very popular spot is at Grassington,
where a limited number of tickets are
available from Grassington Post Office or
the Devonshire Hotel. Trout tickets cost £4
per week or £1.50 per day, grayling only £1
per day. There is no Sunday fishing.

The best fly fishing on the River Wharfe is
available at Burnsall where the Burnsall
Angling Club has a 3-mile stretch from
Burnsall to Barden. Day tickets for trout
(weekdays only) cost £3.50 and week tickets
£15, and are available from 1 June to 30
September. Day tickets for grayling (1
November to 31 January) cost £2.

For 20p a day water is also available along
a 20-mile stretch from Leeds to Gargrave on
the Leeds and Liverpool Canal, and tickets
are obtainable from tackle dealers in the
area.

Bolton Abbey is very picturesque, and
there are five miles of Estate ticket water.
Day tickets for trout at £2.30, and for
grayling at £1.50, are available from the
Estate Office in Bolton Abbey. The trout
season is from 1 April to 30 September, but
grayling may be caught in October with fly,
and with worm in November and December.

Although good trout fishing is still
available in some downstream sections, by
the time it passes Otley, the Wharfe slowly
becomes a good mixed fishery. Much of the
water is again open to paying visitors and in
its lower reaches it can offer some excellent
coarse fishing.

River Ure

Next on the scenic list comes the river Ure.
Some claim it is the top Yorkshire sporting
river, for it is not many years since it had a
modest run of salmon. Even today the odd
fish can occasionally be seen following a
good flood. But those anglers who catch
salmon in the Ure keep very quiet about it.
The upper reaches offer trout fishing at
modest cost; but the best trout fishing is in
the middle reaches at Masham and Tanfield.
Here, however, it is very difficult for the
casual visitor to gain access.

There is some good day-ticket water
upstream at Bainbridge where the
Wensleydale Angling Association has six
miles of water on either side of the bridge at
Bainbridge and up to Carperby. They also

control Semer Water and the 2-mile-long River Bain. Day tickets for trout cost £1 (week £3) and the season is from 1 April to 30 September, while for grayling day tickets cost 50p and the season is from 1 April to 28 February. The Rose and Crown at Bainbridge (Tel 225) issues tickets.

From Ripon and on downstream there is much good mixed fishing. The Ripon Piscatorial Association has five miles of day-ticket water containing trout, grayling, dace, chub, perch, roach, barbel and pike. Day tickets at £1 and week tickets at £1.50 can be obtained from Mrs R C Hodgson, 7 Queen Street, Ripon, or from A Anderson, Brewers Arms, 2 Bondgate Green, Ripon.

Downstream of Ripon, until it becomes the Ouse, the Ure offers some first-class coarse fishing. Pike, chub, dace and roach are plentiful, and some noteworthy barbel are caught every year. Below Aldwark

Two seasonal views of Yorkshire's rivers: the Wharfe at Bolton Abbey (above) and the River Nidd at Knaresborough (below).

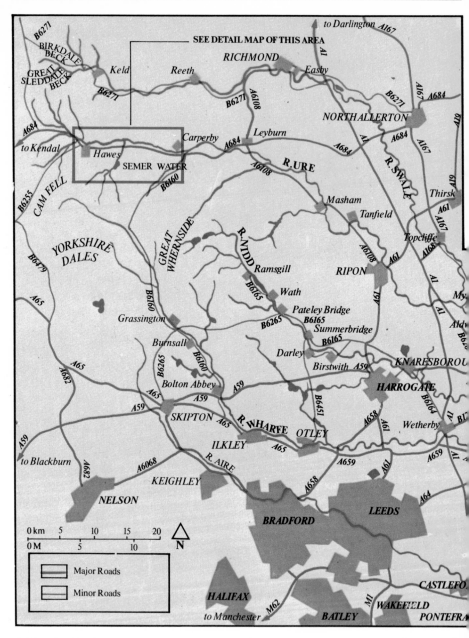

Bridge the Ure becomes the River Ouse.

At this point, the river is more sluggish and there is considerable boat traffic at weekends, but it provides good coarse fishing. Even in the centre of York roach and dace are plentiful. Below Naburn, although the river is tidal, there is much worthwhile coarse fishing down to Goole.

The Nidd at Nidd Head spring, 2,000ft up in Great Whernside, starts its simple life. At Goydon Pot the river goes underground, but on resurfacing offers good beck fishing for

Map shows NW Yorkshire's main rivers, the Ure, Nidd, Ouse, Swale and Wharfe; picture shows the Swale at Helperby.

Sportsman's Arms at Wath.

Below Gouthwaite the river takes on a more scenic aspect as it tumbles through Pateley Bridge and Summerbridge. Much of the fishing here is controlled by the Nidderdale Angling Club and day tickets at £1, week tickets at £3 or season tickets at £6 are available from most public houses and post offices in the area. The water contains a good head of both trout and grayling, but no day tickets are available until 1 June.

Rivers Nidd and Swale

At Darley and Birstwith, both the Harrogate Fly Fishers' Club and the Birstwith Private Angling Club have water on the Nidd offering first-class trout and grayling fishing. Unfortunately, the water is limited to members and their guests and waiting lists for both clubs are very long.

The river downstream of Birstwith tends to hold more grayling than trout, and by the time Knaresborough is reached, the Nidd has become a good mixed fishery. Continuing downstream the river writhes and loops and provides excellent coarse fishing down to its junction with the Ouse at Nun Monkton. Much of the fishing is in the hands of the Leeds Amalgamation of Anglers, with both day and season tickets.

The river Swale starts its life where the Great Sleddale and Birkdale Becks meet at Keld. Much of the upper reaches give good rain-fed river-type trout fishing and there are various centres where day tickets are available. At Reeth, for instance, the Black Bull Hotel offers weekly tickets for trout fishing at £10 and day tickets at £1.50. At Richmond there is good mixed fishing and day and weekly permits may be obtained from W Metcalfe, Market Place, Richmond or The Bungalow, Easby.

Below Richmond there is a mass of good coarse fishing water all the way down to its junction with the Ure at Myton. Noted venues include the well-known water at

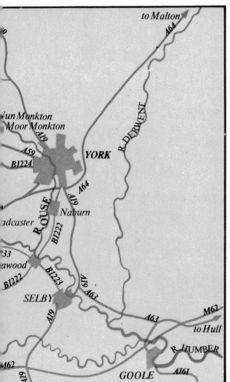

trout and grayling down to Ramsgill. Quite suddenly the river becomes Gouthwaite Reservoir which is well stocked with large trout and numerous grayling. Most of the lake is privately owned and fished, but there are tickets occasionally available from the

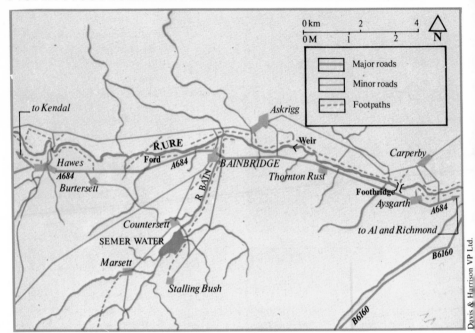

Detail map (above) shows the day-ticket water on the River Ure at Bainbridge.

(Right) Trout fishing at Aysgarth Falls, available on a £1 day ticket.

Topcliffe, reputed to hold some of Yorkshire's biggest barbel and chub. Even today, salmon are occasionally seen jumping at Topcliffe Mill, but the barbel in the mill race hold the greatest attraction. Residential angling facilities are available at Topcliffe Mill in conjunction with the Leeds Amalgamation and other owners of the water. Membership of the Amalgamation is not necessary, and for further details contact Mr A Smart at the Mill (Tel 395). Down to Myton, water is controlled by the Leeds Amalgamation and is available on ticket.

Scenic area

The rivers mentioned provide some of the best all-round fishing in Yorkshire, and within the same watershed there is a vast network of lesser-known rivers and still-water fisheries. The area is also particularly scenic. The dark, satanic mills in Yorkshire are still there, but a long way from Wharfedale, Wensleydale, Nidderdale and Swaledale.

INFORMATION

WATER AUTHORITY
Yorkshire Water Authority, West Riding House, 67 Albion St, Leeds LS1 5AA. Tel 448201.

LICENCES
Salmon, trout, freshwater fish and eels, excluding salmon and migratory trout in the Esk and its tributaries and in streams north of the Esk, season £1.90 (OAPs and the disabled 95p), 7-day 75p (OAPs and the disabled 40p). Children under 14 years do not require a licence. Salmon, migratory trout, freshwater fish, non-migratory trout and eels throughout the Authorities' area, season £19 (OAPs and the disabled £9.50), 7-day £7.50 (OAPs and the disabled £3.75), 1-day £3.75 (OAPs and the disabled £1.90). **Close seasons:** salmon and migratory trout November 1 to April 5, non-migratory trout October 1 to March 31, freshwater fish February 28 to May 31.
Size limits: barbel 11.8in (30cm), carp 10in (25cm), trout, sea trout, bream, tench, chub and grayling 9in (23cm), dace, perch, roach and rudd 7in (18cm). Keepnets not allowed during the freshwater fish close season.
FISHERIES
Chatsworth Settlement Trustees, E H Hey, Estate Office, Bolton Abbey, near Skipton.
Bolton Estate Office, Wensley, Leyburn.
Newby Hall Estate Office, 26 The Lodges, Skelton-on-Ure, Ripon.
Topcliffe Mill, A C Smart, Topcliffe, Thirsk.
LOCAL CLUBS AND ASSOCIATIONS
Appletreewick, Barden and Burnsall Angling Club, R C Whittington, Moorside Farm, East Keswick, Collingham Bridge, Tel 3135.

Arthur Oglesby

Bradford City Angling Assoc, T Stanly, 6 Newbourne Rd, Great Horton, Bradford 4. Tel 29729.
Bradford No 1 Angling Assoc, D B Arnett, 49 Templars Way, Bradford.
Boroughbridge and District Angling Club, J D Coates, Jasmine Cottage. New Row. Boroughbridge. York
Harrogate and Claro Conservative Angling Assoc, C Whittington, 107 Dragon Parade, Harrogate, HG1 5DG. Tel 62725.
Harrogate Fly Fishers' Club, J Darby Tredger, 18 St Catherine's Rd, Harrogate, Tel 884249.
Hawes and High Abbotside Angling Assoc, F Wilson, 2 Chapel St, Hawes.
Howden and District Angling Club, M Redman, 46 Marshfield Ave, Goole, N Humberside.
Hull and District Amalgamated Anglers' Assoc, K Bone, 151 Steynburg St, New Bridge Rd, Hull. Tel 71606.
Ilkley and District Angling Assoc, J A Cockerill, 31 Grange Estate, Valley Drive, Ilkley. Tel 3063.
Knaresborough Piscatorials, G Binks, 14 St Andrew's Place, Harrogate HG2 7RW.
Leeds and District Amalgamated Society of Anglers, A G Copley, 6 Mount Pleasant, Middleton, Leeds 10. Tel 75059.
Masham Angling Club, Mrs M Rennison, Moor Edge Farm, Darley, Harrogate. Tel 689.
Ripon Piscatorial Assoc, P Godden, 3 Oak Rd, Ripon. Tel 3021.
Richmond and District Angling Society, J O Hawitt, 73 Reeth Rd, Richmond. Tel 2182.
Skipton Angling Assoc, J W Preston, 18 Beech Hill Rd, Carleton, Skipton. Tel 5264.
Tadcaster Angling and Preservation Society, C Burton, 69 Leeds Rd, Tadcaster, N Yorks.
Wetherby and District Angling Club, P F Burnett, 10 Calder Close. Wetherby. LS22 4UW.

Wensleydale Angling Assoc, T Fawcett, 12 The Crescent, Bainbridge.
York and District Amalgamation of Anglers, E Woodward, 204 Salisbury Terr, York. Tel 58269.
TACKLE DEALERS AND LICENCE AGENTS
H Brady, Post Office, Arthington.
Rose and Crown Hotel, Bainbridge, Tel 225.
L Hodgson Ltd, Devonshire Arms, Bolton Abbey, Skipton.
Star Garage, Main St, Collingham.
W P Adams, 48 Duke St, Darlington.
J W Wright and Son, Fishing Tackle, 107 Parkgate, Darlington.
H Moisley Ltd, 18 Cambridge St, Harrogate.
The Tackle Shop, 423 Holderness Rd, Hull.
The Fishing Basket, 470 Beverley Rd, Hull.
P H Smith, 28 High St, Knaresborough HG5 0EQ.
Armley Angling Centre, 220 Armley Rd, Leeds 12.
D B Sports, 16 Queens Parade, Leeds 14.
Gledhills of Leeds,60 The Headrow, Leeds 1. Tel 455336.
P T S Fishing Tackle, 250 Tong Rd, Leeds 12. Tel 637019.
Malham Tarn Field Centre, R H L Disney, Malham, Settle.
J A Scott, Park Square, Masham.
Anglers' Corner, 121 Victoria Rd, Middlesbrough.
Ward Thompson Bros. 87 Borough Rd. Middlesbrough.
R M Wright, 5 Lascelles Lane. Northallerton.
J C Ellerton, Post Office, Reeth.
Sports, Toys and Model Shop, 14 Finkle St, Richmond.
J O Hewitt, 73 Reeth Rd, Richmond.
Mrs B Wilkinson, 7 Queen St, Ripon.
Norman Goodwin, 9 Water Lane, Skipton.
C R Burton, 69 Leeds Rd, Tadcaster.
A C Smart, Topcliffe Mill, Topcliffe.
Sports and Leisure, High St, Wetherby.
George and Dragon Inn, High St, Wetherby.

North, Central Lancs

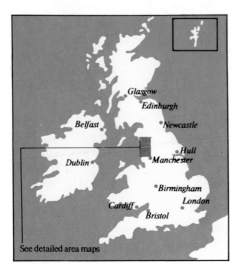

Glasgow
Edinburgh
Belfast
Newcastle
Dublin
Hull
Manchester
Birmingham
Cardiff
London
Bristol

See detailed area maps

Lancashire is a county of remarkable contrasts—of bare moorland and mountain, of rich farmland and extensive industrial areas. In the fishing domain it is also a county of contrasts, catering for excellent salmon, brown and sea trout fishing in rivers and lakes, and some first rate coarse angling in pools and canals.

Many people are surprised that Lancashire claims a large part of the Lake District. It includes one shore of Lake Windermere, all of Coniston Water, and the major part of the Duddon Valley.

The southern area encloses the rivers Lune, Ribble, Wyre, Hodder, Rawthey and the Greta, as well as excellent reservoirs such as the Rivington complex, and canals like the Lancaster, Haigh and the Leeds and Liverpool. These all form very important fisheries serving anglers from the great industrial conurbation.

The Lune

The Lune is the most northerly of the Lancashire rivers. Named after Lon, the mythological god of health, it rises on Wild Boar Fell near the source of the northwards flowing River Eden. It is a fairly fast flowing

river traversing some of our most glorious countryside and having a number of famous fishing tributaries. A first class salmon water, the best fish caught so far weighed over 38lb. It also has a good late sea trout run with fish to 9lb, and in its lower reaches is a superb coarse fishery which has yielded a 7lb chub, a 28¾lb pike, 8¾lb bream, 4lb plus perch and a superb roach of 3¼lb—the best ever from the North of England.

In its upper reaches approximately nine miles of Low Gill are controlled by the Tebay LMS Fishing Club and are available on a week permit. At Orton, the George Hotel can arrange fishing as can the Cross Keys and Junction Hotels in Tebay. At Sedbergh the Sedbergh and District Angling Association controls from below Broadraine Weir to Firbank and weekly permits are available from Lowis's Ltd, 43 Main Street, Sedbergh. The Association also has excellent brown trout fishing along the nearby rivers Rawthey, Dee and Clough.

Kirkby Lonsdale

Permits can be obtained from the Kings Arms, Kirkby Lonsdale, for a mile of good Lune fishing at Middleton and for another stretch along the River Rawthey. Sea trout to 8lb have been caught here, and the Kirkby and District Angling Association has a two mile stretch and issues weekly permits (no weekends) for visitors to the district. They can be obtained from The Tackle Box, Kirkby Lonsdale. The Royal Hotel has fishing for guests and a few miles downstream, day tickets are available for some very good fishing from Whittington Farm. Downstream at Caton, Lancaster and District Angling Association issues day tickets (no weekends) for a mile of fishing, and they can be obtained from Darwen & Gough, Moor Lane, Lancaster (Tel 64913).

North and Central Lancs, an area of very varied rivers, streams and lakes.

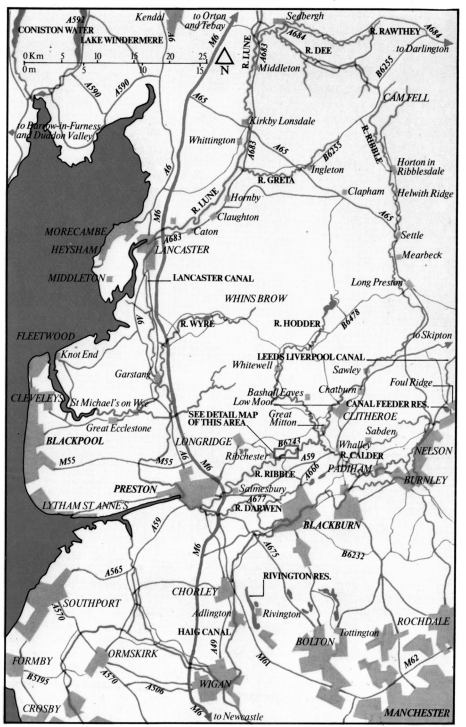

SEE DETAIL MAP
OF THIS AREA

The Castle Hotel at Hornby has fishing along the River Claughton for residents, while in the Lancaster area the North West Water Authority controls two highly rated mixed fisheries. For the stretch below Lower Halton weir they issue four daily salmon and four nightly sea trout permits, and for the fishing between there and Forge (Upper Halton) weir on the south bank, a similar number. For the Upper beat above Forge weir, they issue 12 salmon, 15 sea trout, six brown trout and six daily coarse fishing permits which can be obtained from Darwen & Gough, or after 6pm from A Corwen, Greenup Cottage, Hornby Road, Caton, Lancaster. They also issue permits for the North West Water Authority Skerton Fishery; six daily for salmon, six nightly for sea trout, and a dozen daily permits for some good coarse fishing with quality chub, roach and most other species.

The River Wyre is an elusive, twisting river. Rising near Whin Brow and the Forest of Bowland, it cuts the Fylde of Lancashire to enter the Irish Sea at Fleetwood. It has a hefty run of sea trout and salmon, good brown trout fishing higher up, and some of the area's best coarse fishing from Garstang downstream.

Wild Boar Farm

The Wyresdale Angling Association controls about seven miles of the shallow river for members only. The Garstang and District Angling Association has about four miles of good mixed fishing, and permits are available from the tackle dealer in Garstang. On the right bank downstream, the Ribble and Wyre Fishing Association has water, and other water at Wild Boar Farm, Great Ecclestone, and a stretch of nearly three miles from Fishery Field and below the bridge at St Michaels on Wyre. Permits are available from G Jones in Preston, or from Bridge Cottage, St Michaels, where permits can also be obtained for day-ticket fishing on a mile of good float water from St Michael's Bridge to Great Eccleston on both banks, and controlled by the St Michaels Angling Association. From the toll bridge for five miles to the sea at Knott End is free fishing.

The River Ribble is the area's longest river, running more than 50 miles from its Pennine source high on Cam Fell in Yorkshire. It has been called everybody's river, being claimed both by industrial towns and by some superb farming country. A historic river crossed by the Romans and by Cromwell's Model Army on its way to the Battle of Preston in 1648, it is also a very important North-West fishery famed these days for the superb quality roach in its middle reaches in particular. In 1976 it yielded a magnificent 8lb chub. A roach of 2¾lb has been caught with a number over 2lb recorded, and a 13lb trout.

A river of great looping horseshoe bends, the Ribble is the troutman's domain above Settle. The best sea trout fishing is in the middle sections where the North West Water

Arthur Oglesby

Authority has its famous Mitton Fishery.

Most fishing from the source to Helwith Bridge near Horton in Ribblesdale is preserved by the Manchester Angling Association for members only. Between Mere Beck and Stainworth the river is mostly controlled by the Settle Anglers' Association. Day tickets are available during licensing hours from the Royal Oak Hotel, or in advance from R Welsh, Midland Bank Ltd, Settle. Downstream, the Long Preston Angling Club have a mile of good fishing with permits from R Ellershaw, The Green, Long Preston and the Boars Head Hotel has fishing. Blackburn and District Angling Association controls waters with day tickets for members' friends, and another ¾ mile stretch from Low Bridge where day tickets are available along the bank.

Ribble day-tickets

At Sawley the Yorkshire Federation of Fishing Clubs has water, and at Chatburn the Clitheroe Angling Association has a lengthy fishery. The Ribble Valley Council have fishing at Edisford Bridge with day tickets from the Tackle Shop in Clitheroe, and nearby, the Roefield Hotel has day-ticket water, with permits also obtainable for the lengthy right-bank CWS Angling Club waters. They also control a stretch on the River Hodder.

The North West Water Authority Mitton Fishery allows ten daily permits from Mitton Bridge to Calder Foot along the south bank, four permits for the bridge to Hodder Foot, and 12 permits from Mitton Wood to Calder Foot (25 permits from 31 October to 31 January). These are obtained from Mitton Hall Farm, Mitton, nr Whalley.

Free fishing is available for about 300 yards of bank below Ribchester bridge and day tickets are available for a mile of right-bank fishing upstream to Marlswood. The

Northern Anglers' Association controls a considerable amount of fishing at the Preston Centre, having both banks upstream from Liverpool Road bridge. The Ribble and Wyre Fishing Association then has water from Ribblesdale Farm upstream to Salmesbury Church while the Northern Anglers' Association has water from Marsden Wood to Jackson's Bank Wood with permits from G Wilson, 11 Guildford Avenue, Chorley. In fact, this association controls most Ribble sections from here down through Preston, though there is a lengthy stretch of left-bank fishing available below Liverpool Road bridge. The Wigan and District AA issues day tickets for stretches on the Rivers Ribble and Wyre.

The Hodder—a joy to fish

Along the River Hodder, the well-known Whitewell Hotel water—about five miles of excellent trout and salmon fishing—is a joy to fish. The Hodder Bridge Hotel at Bashall Eaves has fishing, and at Withgill the CWS Angling Club controls a mixed fishery.

Lancashire is well blessed with quality stillwater fishing of most types. There are fighting brownies to be caught from hillside tarns, brown and rainbow trout at stocked fisheries such as the put-and-take Barnsfold

(Left) Arthur Oglesby playing a salmon on the famous River Lune.
(Below) Our detail map shows the Ribble in the Marles Wood area at Ribchester.

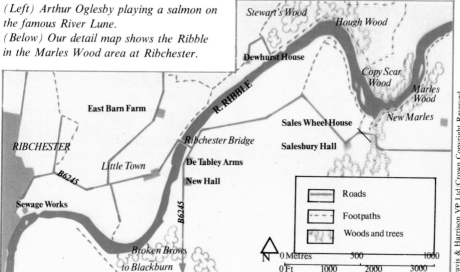

Part of the beautiful 50-mile-long Ribble, a river a huge looping horseshoe bends.

Waters or Longridge near Ribchester, or roach and carp fishing in many 'lodges'. Most local tackle dealers will give you information about these.

The wood-ringed Rivington Reservoirs complex can hardly be bettered as a scenic mixed fishery, and the North West Water Authority sets an example many other authorities would do well to follow. At Colne there is the Foulridge canal-feeder reservoir with more mixed fishing and day tickets available on the bank.

Blackpool has the well-known Stanley Park Lake with its roach and perch, and day tickets issued by the park ranger. Upper Roddlesworth Reservoir, controlled by the North West Water Authority, has coarse fish and trout, and Sabden Lodge water near Whalley has good carp and trout fishing. Tickets for the latter can be obtained from the Accrington and District Fishing Club, which controls the water, or from T Littler, 2 Pendle Street, West Sabden. The area also has many other stillwater fisheries with day tickets available; Heaping Lodges near Chorley, Carr Mill Dam at St Helens, Kirklees Lodge and Brenda Lodge at Tottington near Bolton, and Audley and Mitchell House Reservoirs controlled by the Accrington and District Fishing Club which also controls waters at Hag's and Sharm Hall reservoirs.

North-West canals

Canals also form a vital part of north-west fishing, and current matchmen had their grounding along the towpaths of these. The Lancaster Canal is fast improving now, particularly in the Garstang region where roach, perch, bream, pike and some tench are found, and the canal has easy access at many points along its 50-mile length. Day tickets, issued by the Northern Anglers' Association, are available along the bank.

The Leeds-Liverpool cut, at over 120 miles long, is England's longest. It is also important arm in north-west fishing, with quality roach now beginning to be caught. The section around Maghull is well-known, and access is good with much day-ticket fishing available, as it is along the 25 miles from Chorley to Ormskirk. Most of the fishing is controlled by the Northern Anglers' Association, the Liverpool and District Anglers' Association and the Wigan and District Angling Association.

Day-ticket fishing is also available along the arm of the Leeds-Liverpool known as the Haigh Canal which runs from New Springs, Wigan to Johnson's Hill Lock near Chorley. The best match catch recorded along the Leeds and Liverpool Canal was in excess of 20lb, with a roach of over $2\frac{3}{4}$lb on record and a trout of 11lb. Records are scarce for the Lancaster canal, although a 14lb match weight was recorded near Garstang in 1976 and in the same year a roach over 2lb.

Morcambe Bay

Sea fishing in this area is adequate if not outstanding. Morecambe Bay to the north has yielded catches of very big thornback ray, and there are a number of charter boats for hire in the area. Mackerel bait is a local recommendation.

It is an area of sand and mud shoreline. Marks are prolific, though most shore catches are made up with flounders, dabs, and in winter with whiting.

England Scene

Fleetwood is an important commercial fishing port with charter boats available. The main boat-caught species are cod, dogfish, skate, some conger, tope, and flatfish. Shore points offering fair possibilities are Easton beach, Marine beach, the Wyre Estuary, Jubilee Quay and Fleetwood town pier. There is also good shore fishing at Cleveleys and along the Anchorsholme Promenade.

During the high holiday period shore fishing at Blackpool is limited, for obvious reasons. In winter the local beaches are worth serious consideration. Lytham Promenade, the lengthy sea wall from there towards Blackpool, and Blackpool's North Pier often yield sizeable bass, cod and whiting to lugworm or mackerel baits.

INFORMATION

WATER AUTHORITY
North West Water Authority, Dawson House, Great Sankey, Warrington WA2 8JD. Tel: Penketh 4321.

LICENCES
Salmon and migratory trout: Season £15.60, part season tc 31 May £7.80 part season from 1 June £9, junior and OAPs £6.50; part-season junior to 31 May £3.25; part season from 1 June £4; seven days (salmon only) £2.60. 'Junior' applies to children of 14–16 years: up to 13 years no licence is needed. All except the seven-day licence also entitles holder to fish for eels, non-migratory trout (brown, rainbow and char), and freshwater fish for the whole of the respective seasons.

Non-migratory trout: Season £2.60; junior and OAPs £1.25; seven days 65p.

Freshwater fish and eels: Season £1.25; junior and OAPs 65p; seven days 35p.

Rod and line within the old Mersey and Weaver Authority area: **Freshwater fish and eels:** season 65p; junior and OAPs 35p.

Close seasons: salmon 1 November to 31 January; brown trout 1 October to 14 March; sea trout 16 October to 30 April; coarse fish 16 March to 15 June.

Size limits: salmon and migratory trout 10in (25cm); brown trout 8in (20cm); chub and barbel 10in (25cm); grayling, tench, bream and carp 9in (22cm); roach, perch and rudd 8in (20cm); crucian carp 7in (18cm); dace 6in (15cm); gudgeon and ruffe 4in (10cm).

LOCAL CLUBS AND ASSOCIATIONS
Accrington and District Fishing Club, Mr A Balderstone, 1 Grime Rd, Huncote, Accrington, Lancs.

Blackburn and District Angling Assoc, Mr A Smith, 25 Pickering Fold, Blackburn BB1 2LH.

Clitheroe Angling Assoc, Mr J Hodgson, 83 Starth Rd, Clayton-le-Moors, nr Accrington.

CWS Angling Club, D G Sandsford, CWS Ltd, Withgill Estate, Higher Hodder, Clitheroe, Lancs.

Garstang and District Angling Assoc, D E Irving, 33 High St, Garstang, Preston PR3 1EA.

Kirkby Lonsdale and District Angling Assoc, G Clough, Keeper's Cottage, Burrow, via Carnforth, Lancs.

Lancashire and District Angling Assoc, A L Marris, 12 Eden Park, Lancaster, LA 4ST.

Liverpool and District Anglers' Assoc, Jack Johnson, 97 Liverpool Rd North, Maghull, nr Liverpool, Merseyside.

Long Preston Angling Club, B Darnton, 7 Ledger Lane, Lofthouse, Wakefield, W Yorks WF5 3NG.

Manchester Federation of Anglers, D Lloyd, 37 Queenston Rd, W Didsbury, Manchester.

Northern Anglers' Assoc, G Wilson, 11 Guildford Ave, Chorley, Lancs.

Ribble and Wyre Fishing Assoc, G Jones, 1 Carnarvon Rd, Preston PR1 8PU.

St Michael's Angling Assoc, A J Moss, West Bungalow, St Michael's, Preston.

Sedbergh and District Angling Assoc, J P Lowis, Yarlside, Sedbergh, Cumbria.

Settle Anglers' Assoc, R P Robinson, Royal Oak Hotel, Settle, N Yorkshire.

Tebay LMS Fishing Club, J Ford, 14 Whinfell Terrace, Tebay.

Wigan and District Angling Assoc, G A Chamberlain, 15 Frog Lane, Wigan, Lancs.

Wyresdale Angling Assoc, J Croft, Orchard Farm, 115 Whittingham Lane, Barton, nr Preston.

TACKLE DEALERS AND LICENCE DISTRIBUTORS
Mr A Gibson, The Sports Shop, 98 Blackburn Rd, Accrington.

Brian Ogden, 254 Church St, Blackpool.

S Waterhouse & Son, 38 Cookston St, Blackpool.

Mr S Casey, 237 Bridgeman St, Bolton.

Mr F Chorlton, 137 Newport St, Bolton.

Mr H Windett, 84 Bradshawgate, Bolton.

Iretons, 50 Market St, Carnforth.

H Baker, 48 Bolton St, Chorley.

Mr K Varey, 32a King St, Clitheroe.

Messrs Langhornes, 80 Poulton Rd, Fleetwood.

J & M M Willacy, Market Place, Garstang, nr Preston.

Mr M A Roberts, Parkhill Rd, Garstang.

Darwen & Gough, 6 Moor Lane, Lancaster.

Riley Braithwaite (Sports) Ltd, 32 Market Sq, Lancaster.

Ted's Sports, 70 Linacre Rd, Liverpool 21.

Waterloo Angling Centre, 5 St George's Rd, Liverpool 22.

C P Phillips, 2 Railway Rd, Ormskirk.

T Carter, Church St, Preston.

Lowis's (Sedbergh) Ltd, 43 Main St, Sedbergh.

J R Lord, 14 Whinfell Terr, Tebay, nr Penrith.

Fred Alexander, 3 The Springs, Wakefield, Yorks.

T Blackledge, The Wiend, Wigan, Lancs.

H Glover, 217 Ormskirk Rd, Newton, Wigan.

South Yorkshire

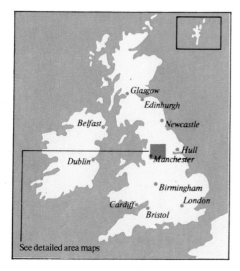

The Aire, Calder, Don and Went are the major rivers in heavily industrialized West Yorkshire. The upper reaches support a fair head of trout and coarse fish, but steel works, heavy engineering and woollen mills built on the river banks during the Industrial Revolution, have caused pollution in the middle and lower reaches.

The Yorkshire Water Authority instigated a vast clean-up campaign but only limited progress has been made, and it may be a few years before angling is possible again.

River Aire

The source of the Aire is in the heart of the Yorkshire Dales at Aire Head, ½ mile from Malham village. The river meanders its way through Airedale to Skipton and all fishing rights are in private hands. Angling clubs do not permit day tickets, even though the fishing is reported to be some of the best in the north.

At Skipton, Skipton Angling Club controls stretches of river with excellent fishing for trout and grayling, available on a 50p day ticket. Bradford Angling Club also has stretches of river between Skipton and Bingley, with day tickets at 25p available

This small trickle of water at Gordale Scar, Malham, is near the source of the River Aire.

from tackle shops. These reaches provide the best winter roach fishing with 2lb weights recorded every year. Operating on a similar basis, Bingley Angling Club controls stretches of water in and around the town.

Improved water

For years fishing ended at Bradford Beck, but new sewage plants at Bradford have improved the river as far as Leeds, and it is possible to catch fish in the centre of the town for the first time in decades. The rest of the Aire is polluted down to the sea. The Leeds and Liverpool canal runs parallel with the River Aire from Leeds to Skipton where it crosses the border into Lancashire. Most sections have been restocked, resulting in improved catches, and bream and quality perch have provided anglers with excellent sport. Local clubs have formed an association which has fishing rights on most of the canal and permits can be obtained from local tackle shops or the Leeds and Liverpool Canal Association Secretary.

Rising near Todmorden high in the

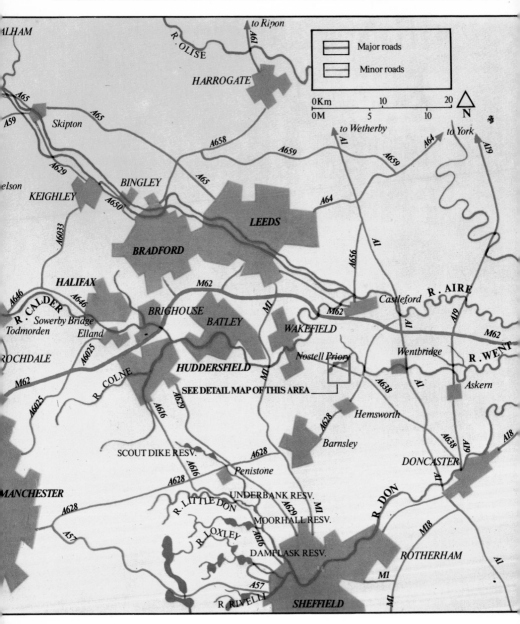

Map shows Aire, Went, Don, Calder.
(Above right) Peter Tombleson trout fishing
on the River Aire near Skipton. The upper
reaches of the river are in private hands,
but day tickets are available below Skipton.
(Below right) Quality trout and grayling are
found in the young river.

Pennines, the Calder flows only a few miles
before it is troubled by pollution from
woollen mills. From Todmorden to Sowerby
Bridge the fish have been able to re-establish
themselves despite effluent discharged into
the river. Trout are now caught in ever-
increasing numbers.

82

The best stretch of river in the West Riding is from Elland to Cooper Bridge in Huddersfield. Roach, bream, perch, dace and gudgeon are to be found, with catches up to 35lb recorded. There are no day tickets available at present but the situation is currently under review.

From Cooper Bridge the River Colne joins the Calder but, owing to the present level of pollution, fish are unable to survive. Slaithwaite and District Angling Club have numerous small dams, reservoirs and stretches of canal, some of which are open to day permits, available from Huddersfield tackle dealers.

Near Brighouse, Cromwell Lake is a 38-acre disused gravel pit stocked with trout on a put-and-take basis. Day permits are available at £3, fly only, with a bag limit of two brace. Access to the lake is off the A6025 Brighouse to Elland road.

River Don

Rising in the Pennines to the west of Sheffield, the River Don quickly increases in size, swollen by the waters of the Little Don, Loxley and Rivelin. Most of the fishing rights are controlled by Sheffield and District Angling Society who restock with trout annually. Below Sheffield the river is grossly polluted and was once rated the most polluted river in the country.

The head waters of the Don are tributaries to several reservoirs which are controlled by the Yorkshire Water Authority. Four of them are open to the angler on a day ticket basis.

Scout Dyke Reservoir

Scout Dyke, off the A629 Penistone road, has trout only and is restocked annually. Permits are available from the hut at the entrance to the dam, priced 60p.

Underbank and Dam Flask lie off the A616 and B6077 roads. Both are mixed fisheries restocked annually with trout, and contain a good head of roach, perch, bream, tench and pike. Day tickets at 60p (half-day at 30p) are available from the hut on the dam wall. Moorhall, a trout fishery (fly only), has limited day tickets available at 60p. Anglers are advised to apply in advance, from Yorkshire Water Authority. There are numerous small stillwater fisheries in Sheffield, but the majority are controlled by private works.

The River Went rises near Wakefield and flows westwards through open farmland to

83

SouthYorkshire

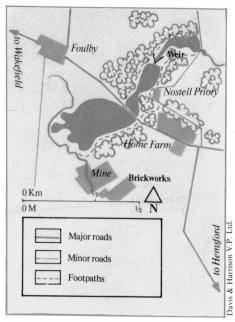

Davis & Harrison V.P. Ltd.

Map legend:
- Major roads
- Minor roads
- Footpaths

to Wakefield
Foulby
Weir
Nostell Priory
Home Farm
Mine
Brickworks
to Hemsford

0 Km   ½
0 M   ½   N

Spectrum Colour Library

(Left) The top lake of the Nostell Priory Estate which offers tench, bream and pike and is available on a season permit. The Estate is five miles east of Wakefield. (Below) The River Calder at Brierley, south-east of Wakefield. Once heavily polluted, it now offers some good coarse fishing.

Lord St. Oswald

its confluence with the River Don. Pollution has troubled this little river for years and only recently have fish re-established themselves. Today, trout, perch, roach and tench are found in most stretches. The only fishable reaches are between Wentbridge and Askern, but permission to fish must be obtained from the local land owners. Local angling clubs are now taking an interest in the waters, however.

Nostell Priory Lakes

At the headwaters of the Little Went, Nostell Priory Estate has recently opened its three ornamental lakes to the angling public. These are situated five miles east of Wakefield on the A638 Doncaster road.

The top lake, of 26 acres, offers some of the best fishing in the area with tench and bream catches over 100lb and pike to 28lb. Roach, perch and carp also abound in the lake. Season tickets only are available for this lake. Day tickets are available for the smaller, middle lake of 7 acres which contains tench, bream, roach, perch and pike. The bottom lake, 4½ acres, is a put-and-take trout fishery operating on a season permit only.

INFORMATION

WATER AUTHORITY
Yorkshire Water Authority, West Riding House, 67 Albion St. Leeds LS1 5AA. Tel 448201.

LICENCES
Salmon, trout, freshwater fish and eels, excluding salmon and migratory trout in the Esk and its tributaries and in streams north of the Esk, season £1.90 (OAPs and the disabled 95p), 7-day 75p (OAPs and the disabled 40p). Children under 14 years do not require a licence.
Salmon, migratory trout, freshwater fish, non-migratory trout and eels throughout the Authorities' area, season £19 (OAPs and the disabled £9.50), 7-day £7.50 (OAPs and the disabled £3.75), 1-day £3.75 (OAPs and the disabled £1.90).
Close seasons: salmon and migratory trout 1 November to 5 April, non-migratory trout 1 October to 31 March, freshwater fish 28 February to 31 May.
Size limits: barbel 11¾in (30cm), carp 10in (25cm), trout, sea trout, bream, tench, chub and grayling 9in (23cm), dace, perch, roach and rudd 7in (18cm). Keepnets not allowed during the freshwater fish close season.
FISHERIES
Cromwell Lake, near Brighouse, Halifax. Tel Mike Keighley, Halifax 73511.
Nostell Priory Fisheries, Head Bailiff, Foulby Lodge, Foulby, Wakefield. Tel Wakefield 863562.
LOCAL CLUBS AND ASSOCIATIONS
Bingley Angling Club, V H Spivey, 3 Moor View Court, Sand Beds, Keighley.
Bradford No 1 Angling Club, C W Smith, 44 Fleet Lane, Queensbury, Bradford.
Bradford City Angling Assoc, J D Illingworth, 2 Caryl Rd, East Bowling, Bradford.
Leeds and Liverpool Canal Angling Assoc, D Scott, 1 Tonngate, Horsforth, Leeds.
Sheffield and District Angling Soc, J W Taylor, c/o Station Hotel, Wicker, Sheffield.
Skipton Angling Assoc, J W Preston, Hill Crest, Beechill Rd, Carleton, Skipton.
Slaithwaite Angling Club, A Bamforth, 43 Binn Lane, Marsden, Huddersfield.
York and District Amalgamation of Anglers, E Woodward, 204 Salisbury Terr, Leeman Rd, York. Tel 58298.
TACKLE DEALERS
Carters Sports Shop, 15 Bridge St, Bradford 1.
Mathers and Craven Ltd, Market St, Dewsbury, W Yorks.
F G Grale and Son, 26 Copley Rd, Doncaster, Yorks.
Sawyers Ltd, Sawyer House, Doncaster DN1 3AJ.
The Angling Centre, 22 Chapel Hill, Huddersfield, Yorks.
Armley Angling Centre, 220 Armley Rd, Leeds 12.
D B Sports, 16 Queens Parade, Seacroft Town Centre, Leeds 14.
Gledhills of Leeds, 60 The Headrow, Leeds 1. Tel 455336.
P T S Fishing Tackle, 250 Tong Rd, Leeds 12. Tel 637019.
Savage Sports Shop, 114 Cross Gates Rd, Leeds 16.
Norman Goodwin, 9 Water Lane, Skipton.
Bennets of Sheffield, Stanley St, off Wicker, Sheffield.
Fred Alexander, 3 The Spring, Wakefield.
Normanton Anglers, High St, Normanton, Wakefield.

Leslie Bryce

Cheshire, Lancs

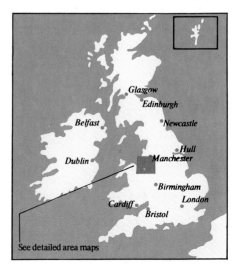

See detailed area maps

Between the grey-brown Pennine uplands and the hills of North Wales is a red sandstone country known by anglers for the big bream spawned in and caught from the Cheshire meres, and for the canals and small rivers which provide sport for fishermen from the industrial area of Greater Manchester. It is also a development ground for many future leading match anglers.

This area is a mixture of industry, farm-land, pasture, and woodland, with small rivers winding across the rich meadows of the Cheshire Plain. It is also a gently rolling region with an identity very different from that of the northern part of Lancashire.

The Bridgewater Canal

The canal network is a major fishing outlet. The Bridgewater Canal, one of the better known, has yielded perch to nearly 4lb, roach over 2lb and has a match record of 18¾lb set in 1970. It is one of the few privately owned canals in the country, and runs from Leigh, through Manchester, to Runcorn. From the top locks through Crawley Bridge

The picturesque Shropshire Union Canal at Wrenbury, in Cheshire.

to the bridge at Preston Brook the water is controlled by the Halton Joint Anglers, with season tickets obtainable from the secretary. The following six miles of towpath fishing from Preston Brook to Broadheath belongs to the Warrington Anglers' Association and is for members only. Then, from near Sale through Broadheath and Dover Lock, Leigh, Plank Lane, and as far as the Worsley motorway bridge, tickets can be obtained on the bank from the Leigh and District Association of Anglers. Fishing on this canal is improving, though still patchy and it would pay to enquire at local tackle shops where the current hot-spots are.

Bolton and Bury Canal

The short Bolton and Bury Canal offers permit fishing for a moderate head of coarse fish. Most are small roach, but larger specimens are to be found, and local tactics are to fish fine with small baits (pinkies or bloodworm), which encourages the capture of smaller fish. Bury and District Angling Society has some permit fishing from Bury to Withins, while in the Bolton district, the local association controls water and tackle dealers can give details about the open membership.

87

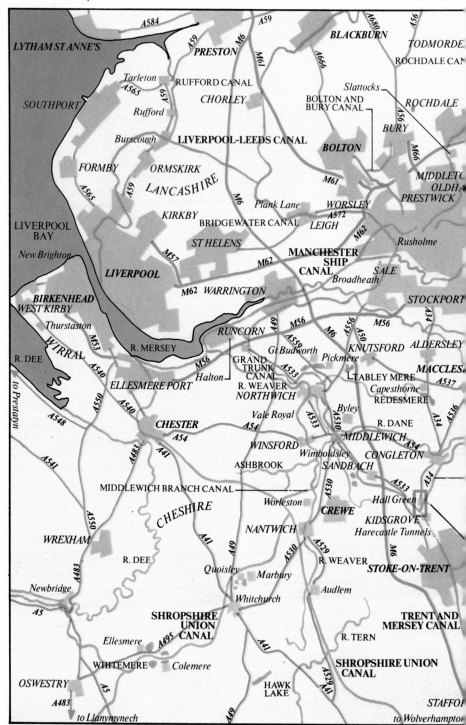

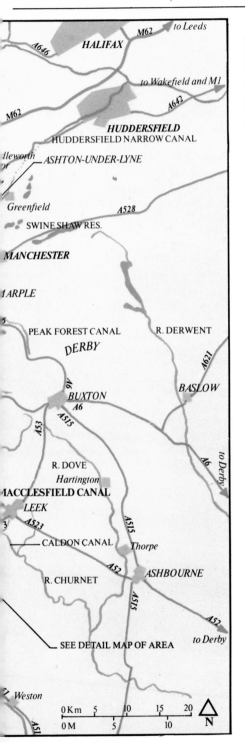

The privately owned Rochdale Canal falls into a similar category. It is a well match-fished water. From Slattocks Bridge to Manchester, the water is controlled by the Greenall Whitley Angling Association and day tickets are issued on the towpath. A lengthy stretch is then administered by the Todmorden Angling Society for members only. Bream to 7lb have been caught, and pike topping 20lb were taken near Slattocks Bridge about five years ago. There are also some hot-spots for tench.

The Macclesfield Canal is also a much-contested water. It holds large specimens of roach and bream, and one has the possibility of catching an 8–9lb carp. Most are caught with light tackle and small baits. The canal runs from Manchester through Macclesfield to join the Trent and Mersey Canal near the Cheshire/Staffs border near Kidsgrove.

'The Grand Trunk'

At Macclesfield, the Prince Albert Angling Association controls water and day tickets are available at tackle shops. Then from Bridge 61 to Bridge 65 near Congleton, a 9-mile section is controlled by the Stoke-on-Trent Angling Society with day tickets available on the bank. From the Hardings Wood Junction to Hall Green Lock, the North Staffordshire Angling Association has about three miles of very good fishing with day tickets available on the bank, and they also have a fair stretch of the Trent and Mersey Canal from Weston Lock to Hardcastle. Along most of the 16 miles of the Canal from Northwich, day tickets are issued on the bank. Once known by Midland bargees as 'The Grand Trunk', this canal was until recent years left alone by local anglers because of salt pollution. Now, it is fast recovering and yielding fair catches, mainly of roach.

Most of the 10-mile-long Middlewich Branch Canal, connecting the Trent and Mersey Canal with the Shropshire Union

Our area map of Cheshire and Lancs fisheries covers a wide range of waters varying from meres to rivers and canals.

Canal, is under the control of the Shropshire Union Canal Angling Association. Most of the sport is with small roach, although larger fish are sometimes caught. Day tickets are available along the bank.

The Shropshire Union Canal in this region often yields very good general sport, plus a few exceptional specimens like the 3lb roach caught in 1976 and a 7lb 1oz eel caught in 1957, both from the Montgomeryshire branch arm near Llanymynech. In the Cheshire area, most of the canal fishing is controlled by the Shropshire Union Canal Angling Association which has rights along many miles of towpath, most of which has day tickets obtainable along the bank.

Fishing this canal can create unusual problems, however, as it passes through areas controlled by the North West Water Authority, the Severn-Trent Water Authority and the Welsh National Water Development Authority. Check before fishing that you have the correct licence.

Many of England's best canal anglers originate from this region, where there are many other smaller canals. The Caldon Canal holds some fair tench and roach fishing and is under control of the North Staffs Angling Association. The Huddersfield Narrow Canal runs part of its path north of the area and has day tickets available along the bank from the Oldham and District Angling Association for sections from Lock 24 at Saddleworth to Bridge 85 at Greenfield, and for about three miles from Ward Lane to Hatshead.

Skimmers and belters
The Rufford Canal also has tickets available on the bank for a section from Burscough to Tarleton. It is an arm of the Leeds and Liverpool Canal and holds mainly small roach and skimmer bream with the odd 'belter' to liven things up. Also with tickets available along the bank, the Peak Forest Canal has great potential now that re-stocking has been completed in the section from Marple to Ashton.

Surprisingly, there is not much river fishing in terms of large waterways like the not-too-distant Severn or Trent. The River Weaver, with its tributary the Dane, is among the major local waters. Subjected to heavy boat traffic in the lower, navigable section, it has good fishing around Northwich and upstream. It is an easy-flowing water, averaging 5–7ft in depth, and has good roach and bream fishing which is improving each season. It is also an excellent trout water in the upper reaches around Audlem and for a considerable distance downstream from there, and is for the most part preserved. Near Middlewich the local angling association has fishing at Hulses Island, Vale Royal and Wimboldsley with tickets available. Upstream of Worleston is a good stretch of water belonging to the Nantwich Angling Society. From Newbridge to Saltersfield fishing is controlled by the Northwich Angling Association, and from Newbridge to Ashbrook by the Winsford and District Angling Association. They all issue tickets along the bank.

River Dane
Much of the River Dane is available on permit. At Byeley, good chub and dace fishing is found along the Middlewich Angling Society section, and the Northwich Angling Association also has a lengthy stretch in this area.

Richard Jemmett

Not too far away, there is excellent trout and grayling fishing in the Derbyshire Derwent and along the River Dove—known as 'Walton's Water'. Most of the upper Dove is preserved, but a number of hotels such as the famous 'Charles Cotton' at Hartington and the 'Izaak Walton' at Thorpe Cloud have excellent fishing for guests. On the River Derwent, the Cavendish Hotel at Baslow controls about six miles of grayling and trout water which has a high reputation among Continental and English anglers.

Cheshire's reputation is based on coarse fish, particularly on the big bream fished from its many meres. The meres are all that remains of a vast lake formed at the end of the last Ice Age, over 10,000 years ago. Greater Manchester Council controls many good pools which are fast becoming an important amenity. These include Lower Debdale, the Roman Lakes at Marple, Drinkwater Pool in Prestwich, Platt Fields at Rusholme, Swineshaw Mill Dam at Stalybridge and Myrtle Road Reservoir at Middleton. All are part of a Manchester plan for more fishing in the area, and all have day tickets available on the banks.

Cheshire's meres

For really big bream, however, one must fish in meres over the Cheshire border. Double-figure fish are caught here each season but are by no means easy to take. The best known mere is Redesmere with its gently curving contour. The best fish recently was the 12¾lb bream taken in 1976, while Whitemere just across the Salop border has produced fish over 12lb. Redesmere fishing is controlled by the Capesthorne Hall Estate and day tickets are available from the East Lodge there. The Lodge also issues tickets for the Capesthorne Pools on the estate near Aldersley Edge, and these hold excellent bream, tench, roach and sizeable pike.

(Left) The quiet and serene Derwent at Chatsworth, near Baslow.
(Right) Our detail map shows the old Macclesfield Canal at Kidsgrove and to the north. Day tickets are available.

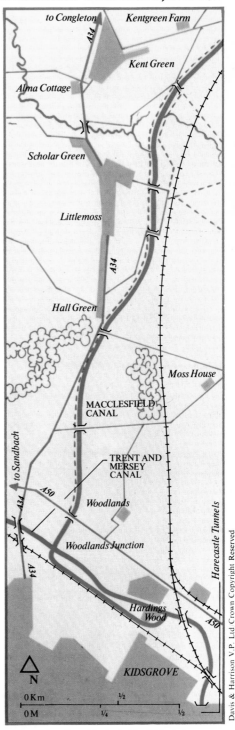

Near Kidsgrove, day tickets are available for fair fishing on the Leg O'Mutton Pool. There is good bream fishing at Taymere near Sandbach and permits can be bought at the tackle shop, G Fear, in Welles Street. Near to Knutsford limited day tickets are issued for boat fishing in Tabley Mere, and applications should be addressed to the Tabley Estate Office. For good mixed coarse fishing, day tickets are available from keepers on the bank at Great Budworth Mere and Pickmere Lakes, both controlled by the Northwich Anglers' Association.

Quoisley's meres

At Marbury near Nantwich, on the A49, are the two meres of Quoisley where day-tickets are available in advance for big bream fishing. The larger of the pools holds a fair head of rudd which during the late summer months give very good sport. Bream to nearly 10lb have been caught.

Another very well-known mere is near Ellesmere and known locally as 'The Mere'. Home of much wild life, it also holds big bream as well as roach, perch and pike. Not far away is Colemere, and permits for both can be obtained from Ellesmere tackle dealers or from the keeper on the bank at The Mere, where only boat fishing is allowed. Nearby Whitemere has tickets on the bank and good fishing on the ledges. Hawk Lake in Hawkestone Park is also not far away and is available on ticket. If you can find them in a feeding mood, good tench are to be caught here. The best spots are often those halfway along the bank opposite the

---

INFORMATION

WATER AUTHORITIES

North West Water Authority, Dawson House, Great Sankey, Warrington WA5 3LW. Tel: Penketh 4321.
Severn-Trent Water Authority, Abelson House, 2297 Coventry Rd, Sheldon, Birmingham B26 3PR.
Welsh National Water Development Authority, Shire Hall, Mold, Clwyd. Tel: Mold 2121.

LICENCES

North West Water Authority: *Salmon and migratory trout:* Season £15.60, part season from 1 June £9, junior and OAPs £6.50; part season to 31 May £3.25; part season from 1 June £4; seven days (salmon only) £2.60. 'Junior' applies to children of 14–16 years; up to 13 years no licence is needed. All except the seven-day licence also entitles holder to fish for eels, non-migratory trout (brown, rainbow and char) and freshwater fish for the whole of the respective seasons.
Non-migratory trout: Season £2.60; junior and OAPs £1.25; seven days 65p.
Freshwater fish and eels: Season £1.25; junior and OAPs 65p; seven days 35p.
Rod and line in old Mersey and Weaver Authority areas: Freshwater fish and eels; season 65p; juniors and OAPs 35p.
Severn-Trent Water Authority: *Trout and freshwater fish:* Severn catchment season £1, Severn and Trent catchments season £1.50. Severn and Trent catchments 28-day period 50p. Severn and Trent catchments season OAPs 20p.
Welsh National Water Development Authority: Rod licences are available in Categories A to G. Category A allows fishing for all species in all rivers in the Authority's area: season £21.60, juniors and OAPs £10.80, day £3.60. Categories B to E allow fishing for all species in progressively fewer selected rivers. Category F licence is for non-migratory trout: season £3, juniors and OAPs £1.50, week £1.80, day 60p. Category G is for coarse fish: season £1.80, juniors and OAPs 90p, day 60p. (see p.315).
Close seasons
North West Water Authority: salmon 1 November to 31 January; brown trout 1 October to 14 March; sea trout 16 October to 30 April; coarse fish 16 March to 15 June.
Severn-Trent Water Authority: (Severn area) brown trout and char (lakes and reservoirs) 16 October to 17 March, all other waters 1 October to 31 March. Salmon, 15 September to 1 February. Freshwater fish 15 March to 15 June. There is no close season for rainbow trout and eels. Spinning for trout during the close season for freshwater fish is prohibited. Trailing or trolling of natural or artificial spinning baits from boats in motion is prohibited. No float to be used with lure or bait when fishing for salmon, or during the close season for freshwater fish. No cereal or maggots to be used as bait during the freshwater fish close season. Keepnets (which must conform to the specifications set out in the byelaws) are not allowed during freshwater fish close season. (*Trent area*) Trout and sea trout 16 October to 17 March, rainbow trout in the catchment of the Derwent 15 November to 16 May, in the remainder of the River Authority area 16 October to 17 March. Coarse fish 15 March to 15 June. Welsh National Water Development Authority: salmon (Dee and tributaries) October 15 to March 1 except Grosvenor Bridge to Suspension Bridge Chester October 15 to June 15. (Clwyd and tributaries) October 15 to March 15. Sea trout (Dee and tributaries) September 30 to March 1 except Grosvenor Bridge to Suspension Bridge Chester October 15 to June 15. (Clwyd and tributaries) October 15 to March 18, elsewhere September 30 to March 1. Non-migratory trout and char September 30 to March 1 except Bala Lake August 14 to January 15. Freshwater fish and eels March 14 to June 16. No close season for eels.
Size limits
North West Water Authority: salmon and migratory trout 10in (25cm); brown trout 8in (20cm); chub and barbel 10in (25cm); grayling, tench, bream and carp 9in (22cm); roach, perch and rudd 8in (20cm); crucian carp 7in (18cm); dace 6in (15cm); gudgeon and ruffe 4in (10cm).
Severn-Trent Water Authority: Severn area: barbel all waters 15.7in (40cm), rainbow trout all waters 11.8in (30cm), brown trout and grayling below Shrewsbury Weir 9.8in (25cm), rest of river Severn 5.9in (15cm), all other waters within Authority area 7.8in (20cm). Trent area: pike 19.7in (50cm), barbel 15.7in (40cm), bream, carp, chub and tench 9.8in (25cm), trout 9.1in (23cm) dace, grayling, roach, rudd and perch 7.9in (20cm).
Welsh National Water Development Authority: Fishery byelaws are currently under review and may be substantially changed for 1978–79 season. At present they are: bream, tench and carp 12in, grayling, roach, perch and rudd 10in, dace 9in, trout 8in, gudgeon 4in.

monastery. In most other sections small roach are taken.

Sea fishing in the area is only modest. Bounded on the west by the Dee, and east by the Mersey is the wedge of land called 'The Wirral'—a coastline of mud or sand flats where currents can be dangerous. Local anglers tend to travel to the North Wales coast where more exciting fishing is found. Wirral shore marks are found at Thurlaston, West Kirby beach, New Brighton promenade and the nearby rocks. Farther north at Formby are shore marks at Southport, the Pinfold Channel in the Ribble estuary, and Southport pier, which has flatfish. In winter, whiting and cod move inshore and offshore marks yield tope, dogfish, mackerel, skate, cod and whiting.

Don Bridgewood

A Northern match catch of bream and hybrids from a water near Winsford.

LOCAL CLUBS AND ASSOCIATIONS

Altrincham and District Angling Club, J R Haslam, 77 Manley Rd, Sale.
Bury and District Angling Soc, F Booth, 142 Bury Rd, Tottington, Bury, Cheshire.
Davenham Angling Club, B Anderson, 2 Cranage Lane, Manchester Rd, Northwich.
Greenall Whitley Angling Assoc, J Robinson, 6 Birch Polygon, Rushmore, Manchester 14.
Halton Joint Anglers. W Durr, Footbridge Cottage, Canal St, Cheshire.
Kidsgrove and District Angling Assoc, C Woodcock, 29 Mitchell Ave, Butt Lane, Talke, Stoke-on-Trent.
Leigh and District Assoc of Anglers, J Scotson, 26 Glover St, Leigh, Greater Manchester.
Macclesfield Fly Fishers' Club, A Ashness, School House, Langley, Macclesfield, Cheshire.
Middlewich Angling Soc, D W Costello, 31 New King St, Middlewich.
Nantwich Angling Soc, J Haighton, The Bungalow, Worleston Rd, Reasen Heath, Nantwich.
North Staffs Angling Assoc, C Moore, 35 Debenham Crescent, Eaton Park, Bucknall, Stoke-on-Trent.
Northwich Joint Angling Assoc, F Egerton, 19 Bowden Drive, Northwich.
Oldham and District Amalgamated Anglers' Assoc, H Garside, 60 Queensway, Greenfield, nr Oldham, Greater Manchester.
Oldham and District United Anglers' Assoc, W Dawes, 171 Grange Ave, Oldham.
Prince Albert Angling Soc, C Sparkes, High Lodge, Upton, Macclesfield.
Shropshire Union Canal Assoc, F A Allwood, 73 Church St, Leigh, Greater Manchester.
Stockport Federation of Anglers, C Holland, 121 Northgate Rd, Edgeley, Stockport.
Stoke-on-Trent Angling Soc, S Broadgate, 5 Kingsfield Oval, Basford, Stoke-on-Trent.
Todmorden Angling Soc, D Howarth, 42 Hallroyd Cres, Todmorden.
Warrington Anglers' Assoc, J S Jackson, 23 Nora St, Warrington.
Winsford and District Angling Assoc, J Bailey, 24 Sandy Hill Rd, Winsford.

TACKLE DEALERS AND LICENCE DISTRIBUTORS

A Bredbury, 16 The Square, Hale Barnes, Altrincham, Cheshire.
R Vernon, 208 Stockport Rd, Timperley, Altrincham, Cheshire.
S J & L Powell, 142 Stamford St, Ashton-under-Lyne
W Hitchell & Son Ltd, 47 Oxton Rd, Birkenhead.
Cheadle Sports Ltd, 9 Gatley Rd, Cheadle.
D Gibson, 42 Upper Northgate St, Chester.
Terry's of Congleton, 10 Rood Hill, Congleton.
Joe's Fishing Tackle, 228 Broad St, Crewe.
R Jenks, 109 West St, Crewe.
E Dean, 27–9 Enfield Rd, Ellesmere Port.
Gilder's Fishing Tackle, 532 Oldham Rd, Failsworth.
B Hett, 2/4 Market St, Hyde.
J Kelly, 238 Market St, Hyde.
H Heath, 14a Market St, Kidsgrove, Stoke-on-Trent.
Whites, 61 King St, Knutsford.
Leigh Sports Centre, Lord St, Leigh.
S Sewart, Roman Lakes Cafe, Marple.
T Phelan, 32 Market St, Marple.
G & M Gibbins, 16 Leadsmithy St, Middlewich.
W Jones, 6 Beam St, Nantwich.
P Lovatt, 7 Brunswick St, Newcastle, Staffordshire.
Scotts, 84 Station St, Northwich, Cheshire.
C Humphrey, 25 London Rd, Northwich.
Aband Ltd, 10 Halton Rd, Runcorn.
Hobby Shop, Church St, Runcorn.
A Hugill, 136 Northenden Rd, Sale.
G & M Fear, 12 Welles St, Sandbach.
B Johnson, Wells St, Sandbach.
J E & J Robinson, 71 Sussex Rd, Southport.
F Fallows, 222 Shaw Heath, Stockport.
F Lonsdale, 45 Greek St, Edgeley, Stockport.
A Sherratt, 45 High St, Biddulph, Stoke-on-Trent.
Prince's 142 Eder Rd, Cobridge, Stoke-on-Trent.
F Steele, 65 Crewe Rd, Alsager, Stoke-on-Trent.
T Preston, 2b Forster St, Tunstall, Stoke-on-Trent.
H & L Hughes, 76 High St, Tarporley.
W McGann, 68 Water Lane, Wilmslow.
Ashley and Harrison, Delamere St, Winsford.
W Worral, 51 Green St, Warrington.
A Broadbent & Sons, 31 Walton Rd, Stockton Heath, Warrington.

Lincolnshire

The Lincolnshire Fenland offers well over 200 miles of bank fishing, most of which is easily accessible and available to all anglers upon the purchase of the appropriate fishing licence and permit.

The Fens have been reclaimed by land drainage over hundreds of years, and now drained and tamed, they represent some of the richest farming land in Britain, as well as providing some of the finest fishing. Often represented as flat uninteresting country, there are nevertheless areas where angling is the principal recreation. The Lincolnshire Fens are a patchwork of navigable drains and rivers, most of which offer an abundance of coarse fishing comparatively free of boat traffic.

The River Witham, the county's principal river, runs for a distance of 80 miles, rising at South Witham, some 10 miles from Grantham, in the iron mining district of Rutland. From its source to Grantham the river is a preserved trout fishery—and strictly private. The river runs through the town of Grantham and free fishing is available to licence holders in the area flowing through the park.

Immediately downstream of Grantham the local angling association control the fishing which begins on the Belton Trust Estate at Manthorpe village and continues downstream for approximately 9 miles to the village of Long Bennington. This section of river is narrow with a depth of between 1 and 3ft. It holds a good head of roach, dace, fine chub and also a few trout. Membership in the Grantham AA is open to all and costs £2.50 per annum.

From Long Bennington downstream the river forms a canal and has a much reduced flow. Much of the water down as far as Aubourn is leased to small angling clubs and fishing is restricted to club members. Lincoln and District AA control both banks between Beckingham and

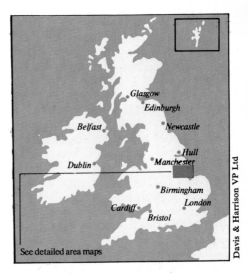

Glasgow
Edinburgh
Belfast
Newcastle
Dublin
Hull
Manchester
Birmingham
Cardiff
London
Bristol

See detailed area maps

Davis & Harrison VP Ltd

Stapleford for approximately 4 miles and the left bank from Stapleford to Bassingham Church footbridge for 1¾ miles.

The river along this stretch, renowned for its chub, varies from 2 to 4ft deep. No day tickets are issued on this length, but membership is open to all. Membership books are available at all Lincoln tackle shops and fishery bailiffs at a cost of £1.50.

The Witham to Lincoln

Fishing is private between Bassingham and the confluence with the River Brant. The River Brant runs into the Witham a couple of miles below the village of Auborn and from that point to the centre of Lincoln it is much more sluggish and almost wide enough to support double bank fishing. The depth of water is about 5ft, and the fish population includes pike, bream, roach, chub, dace, ruffe, and gudgeon. Lincoln and District AA control both banks to Lincoln and match fishing is permitted. (Enquiries to F Butler, 47 Nelsthorpe St, Lincoln. Tel. 134174.) Day tickets are available on this length at a cost of 35p from tackle shops and fishery bailiffs. On the Upper Witham access is

Lincolnshire

good at all villages and indicated by notice boards. Float fishing is the best method, close to the moderate weed growth.

The Witham and Fossdyke Canals flow into the Brayford Pool in the centre of Lincoln before flowing under the city's main shopping street and on to Stamp End Lock. From this point the next 31 miles to Boston are well known to many of the angling fraternity as one of the finest coarse fisheries in the country providing coarse fishing of all types, and are extremely popular with match anglers. The vast majority of the fishing from both banks is controlled by the Witham and District Joint Anglers Federation. Membership is open to all and temporary membership tickets indicated by notice boards are available all along the river at 40p.

The river is heavily booked for matches on all weekends throughout the summer and autumn until at least the end of October, but the Federation reserves areas solely for the non-competition angler.

Not match-pegged

The areas not match-pegged are currently found immediately downstream of Lincoln to ½ mile past Washingborough station (approximately 3½ miles); Bardney Deadwater and Branston Island on the inside bank from the local (3 miles), Stixwould on both banks (200 rods) Kirkstead on the left bank downstream of bridge (2 miles); Tattershall bridge upstream on both banks to the confluence with Billinghay Skirth (50 rods), and Anton Gowt to Boston (3 miles). In addition to these lengths of the main river, there is fishing on the Sincil Drain, which runs parallel for 9 miles from Lincoln before joining it at Bardney (a favourite spot during the late part of the season).

Martin Delph, a 2-mile length of straight water joining the Witham ½ mile downstream of Kirkstead Bridge on the right bank, provides good early season bream fishing and large pike. The area from Lincoln past Washingborough and Five Mile House to Bardney is a popular float

fishing stretch, with plenty of weed cover and a water depth of between 5 and 8f' Access is good and the fish population includes bream to 4lb and a few fine tench. There are also roach in quantity and bleak, ruffe, silver bream, gudgeon and pike.

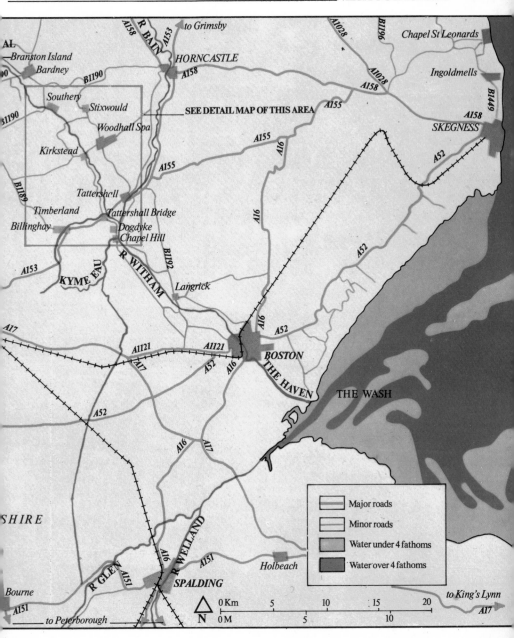

Major roads
Minor roads
Water under 4 fathoms
Water over 4 fathoms

From Bardney the river widens and deepens and is renowned for its large bream shoals along the whole of its length to Boston. Access is good at Bardney, Southrey, Stixwold and Kirkstead—and the river varies in depth between 7 and 14ft.

Map of the area shows the main river of Lincolnshire, the Witham, and the Witham and Fossdyke Canals and Sincil Drain. The Fens, now reclaimed by land drainage, offer an abundance of coarse fishing. Sea angling, however, is not particularly good.

Lincolnshire

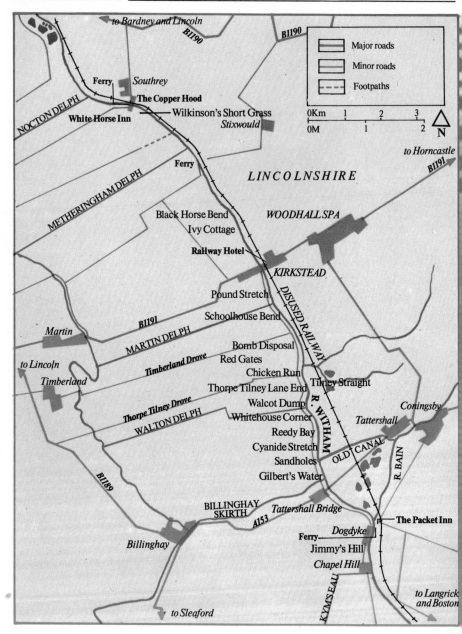

Ledgering tactics are favoured by the vast majority of match anglers. Worms, casters, maggots and breadflake make the best baits for the larger bream. The best pike fishing is at the Bardney Lock area of the Deadwater, Old River and Sincil Drain.

Kirkstead is the Mecca of the big open match angler and is the location of many competitions. This length of the Witham houses the famous bream spots such as 'Black Horse Bend' and 'Ivy Cottage', both upstream of the bridge. Downstream of the

England Scene

(Above) Boston on the River Witham. Upstream the river is at its widest and deepest and offers roach and bream. (Left) Detail map shows the River Witham from Southrey to Chapel Hill passing through Kirkstead. Famous bream swims include Black Horse Bend, Ivy Cottage, School House Bend, White House Corner and Sandholes. There is good access at Southrey, Stixwould and Kirkstead.

bridge is a 6-mile length of road running parallel and close to the river and ending midway between Dog Dyke and Chapel Hill. Notable bream swims include the Pound Stretch, Schoolhouse Bend, Timberland Lane End, White House Corner, Reedy Bay and also the famous Sandholes up to Tattershall. At Dog Dyke a tremendous shoal of bream congregate each winter on either side of the confluence with

Lincolnshire

the River Bain. At Chapel Hill the Kyme Eau joins the Witham—this area is popular with pleasure anglers. Downstream of Chapel Hill to Langrick Bridge there is no access other than along the bank, except with permission from the land owners. For the more energetic anglers, who are prepared to walk 1¾ miles downstream of Chapel or a similar distance upstream of Longrick, the rewards may be remarkable as this area is among the best on the river. Langrick is the wildest and deepest part of the Witham. Here there are plenty of weeds out from the bank and anglers can fish on either side without interfering with those on the opposite side. In this area huge catches of roach are taken on creed wheat, and bream catches often exceed 50lb. From Langrick to Boston the river runs a dog-leg course with good fishing all the way, although the only good access points are at Anton Gowt on the left bank and Boston West on the right bank and the Road End at Boston.

Trout fishing

There is very little trout fishing in Lincolnshire, and what little there is in the rivers and streams is strictly private. Until recently the county had only a sprinkling of small landlocked waters on which to practise fly fishing. However, a first-class fly-only water, administered by the Anglian

INFORMATION

WATER AUTHORITY
Anglian Water Authority, Lincolnshire Division, 50 Wide Bargate, Boston, Lincs. Tel. 65661.
LICENCES
Regional licence: adult £3.80, junior and OAPs £1. Weekly tickets 75p all categories.
Divisional licence: £2, no concessions for OAPs or juniors. The licences run from 1 January.

Close seasons: coarse fish 15 March to 15 June inclusive, but this does not apply to enclosed waters. Size limits: pike, common carp, barbel 18in (45cm), bream, tench and chub 14in (35cm), grayling, crucian carp and trout 11in (28cm), roach, dace, rudd and perch 9in (23cm). A keepnet must have a minimum depth of 5ft. Only 2 rods and lines allowed to be used at the same time by one person. Both rods must be licensed.
FISHERIES
Belton Trust Estate, Manthorpe, Stamford, Lincs.

LOCAL CLUBS AND ASSOCIATIONS
The Witham and District Joint Anglers Federation has 13 affiliated angling associations. Any of the affiliated organizations' membership booklets will entitle the member to fish practically the whole of the Witham between Lincoln and Boston, in addition to many other fisheries.
Witham and District Joint Anglers Federation, Ron Hobley, 30 Gunby Ave, Lincoln, Lincs LN6 0AW. Tel. 63688.
Boston and District Angling Assoc, J D McGuire, 6 Churchill Rd, Boston, Lincs. Tel. 64949.
British Rail Staff Assoc, North East Region, J L Oldfield, Toft Green Chambers, B.R. York.
Chesterfield and District Angling Assoc, B Thorley, 98 St Augustine's Ave, Chesterfield, Derby.
Doncaster and District Angling Assoc, E Cusworth, 55 Melbourne Grove, Balby, Doncaster, South Yorks DN4 0UN.
Grantham Angling Assoc, S C E Searle, 8 Arnold Ave, Grantham, Lincs.
Grimsby Angling Assoc, Paul Chamberlain,

Water Authority, opened in 1975 and has proved to be a tremendous attraction, not only to Lincolnshire anglers, but also to those from Midlands and South Yorkshire.

Sea Angling

Sea angling on the coast of Lincolnshire between the Humber and the Wash is probably the worst in Britain. The water is very shallow and 2 miles offshore at Skegness it is only 12ft deep, while at $\frac{1}{2}$ mile offshore one can stand up comfortably. It is therefore wise to fish off one of the points to get any sort of success. North to south these are at Chapel St Lennards, Ingoldmells, Skegness Pier (open summer season only, except when a competition is organized) and Gibraltar Point.

Cod are the predominant species caught, but there is also a sprinkling of bass, thornback skate, flounders and dabs. The baits to use are lugworm, ragworm, and mackerel strip. Tackle may be hired, bait obtained, and a mine of local information had from Pete Gibson, Tackle Shop, Roman Bank, Skegness.

The wide expanse of the lower Witham, where in 1966 a local team from Boston won the All-England NFA championship. The river here is noted for its huge bream shoals, and if a matchman holds such a shoal in his swim a big total is guaranteed.

Bill Howes

3 Trinity Rd, Cleethorpes, South Humberside.
Leeds and District Amalgamated Society of Anglers, A G Copley, 6 Mount Pleasant, Middleton, Leeds 10.
Lincoln and District Angling Assoc, A Gilbert, 35 Bristol Drive, Lincoln.
Rotherham and District United Anglers' Federation, T J Dickens, 18 Burns Rd, Herringthorpe, Rotherham, South Yorks.
Scunthorpe and District Angling Assoc, J D Mouncey, Sluice Rd, South Ferriby, Barton-on-Humber, South Humberside.
Sheffield Amalgamated Anglers' Society, W H Pursglove, 20 Manor Park Drive, Sheffield 2.
Sheffield and District Angling Assoc Ltd, Joe Taylor, c/o The Station Hotel, Wicker, Sheffield.
Worksop and District Amalgamated Angling Assoc, G D Rollinson, 31 Lincoln St, Worksop,
TACKLE DEALERS
H N Thornley, 23 Market Place, Alford, Lincs.
Claytons of Boston, Main Ridge, Boston, Lincs.
J Morley and Son, 5 Wide Bargate, Boston. Tel. 2544.
Pet's Pantry, 245 Grimsby Rd, Cleethorpes. 61766.

C F E Freeman, 9 West St, Horncastle.
Padgetts, 413 Weelsby St, Grimsby.
Lightwood's Fishing Tackle, Cleethorpes Rd, Grimsby. Tel. 43536.
Kirkstead Fishing Tackle, B A Gorman, Kirkstead.
Boundary Pet Stores, 16 Bunkers Hill, Lincoln, LN2 4QP.
Chambers Pet Shop, 14 Cornhill, Lincoln. Tel. 29359.
Nobbs Fishing Tackle, Norman St, Lincoln. 24365.
Beales of Lincoln, 108 Ripon St, Lincoln. Tel. 29267.
South End Pet Shop, High St, Lincoln.
Abbey Sports, John Burns, 263 Monks Rd, Lincoln.
Newport Tackle Shop, John King, 85 Newport, Lincs.
Wolsey's Fishing Tackle, 4 Market Hill, Scunthorpe. Tel. 2153.
Wolsey's Fishing Tackle, 17 Oswald Rd, Scunthorpe. Tel. 68948.
Bennetts, 70 Frodingham Rd, Scunthorpe. Tel. 2042.
Morgans, 125 Rowland Rd, Scunthorpe. Tel. 61786.
Hook Line 'n' Sinker, 85b Roman Bank, Skegness. Tel. 3623.
Palmer's Fishing Tackle, 11 High St, Skegness.
K W Storr, High St, Wainfleet, near Skegness.

Upper Trent

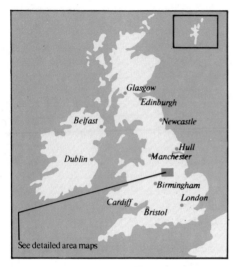

Glasgow
Edinburgh
Belfast
Newcastle
Dublin
Hull
Manchester
Birmingham
Cardiff
London
Bristol
See detailed area maps

The River Trent from Burton to Long Eaton was a superb fishery until sewage and industrial waste were discharged into it from Stoke-on-Trent killing fish and making the river uninhabitable for all life. Now, industrial pollution is being halted and the river seems to be regaining its cleanliness. In recent seasons the Trent here has developed into a fisherman's territory with most coarse species present. England international Tony Scott considers that on a good day he can take a good bag of fish from any of the hundreds of swims.

Trent species

Dace and chub predominate here early in the coarse fishing season, with plenty of roach later and gudgeon all the year round. A carp topping 20lb was recently caught on a single maggot fished on light match tackle near Swarkestone: barbel up to 3lb are caught regularly near Willington, and shoals of quite large bream are beginning to populate the stretch from there downstream to Thrumpton.

For most of the upper section, the Trent is broad, rarely deeper that 7ft, and fast

flowing. It is a pleasure to the angler. Even as far upstream as Rugeley, in Staffordshire, there are dace and roach by the power station. Just a short way downstream, at King's Bromley, the Birmingham Anglers' Association has waters along the left bank where fish, although not plentiful, give good sport to the angler not fishing at one spot.

Access points

The Birmingham AA, with an open membership and associate cards available from most tackle dealers in the area, has further stretches along a widening river through Yoxhall to Alrewas on the A38 trunk road. Access is at a number of well-signposted points along the A513.

From Walton northwards, fishing is controlled by clubs and is for members only. There is some free fishing in Burton on Trent, though it is residents-only fishing at the Pleasure Gardens and the tennis courts. Downstream from the town bridge is the well-known 'Bass's Island' where a number of open matches are held during the season for local club members only. This is the beginning of the part of the Trent where very good dace, chub and roach can be caught.

From Burton the B5008 follows the right bank through Newton Solney and Repton. Swadlincote Angling Club controls most of the fishing rights but it has a long waiting list for membership. This excellent fishing stretch upstream to Willington holds most species including barbel, carp, and some large bream. Near Newton Solney church there is a compact 200-yard stretch of free fishing.

The very lengthy Derby Angling Association waters start above Willington bridge. Day ticket fishing is available, with permits available from local tackle dealers and the Rising Sun Inn. Membership of the Derby AA is reasonable. The river can be reached at Willington bridge and above, all access

An angler fishing the fast-improving waters of the River Trent at Burton. Fish are returning to what was once England's premier river.

points being clearly marked by a large white disc on the gates.

Club waters

The association's waters run for many miles downstream, though the immediate section of the left bank at Willington is controlled by the Atherstone AA. Most coarse species can be caught here. Derby AA waters continue through Twyford on the A5132 and B5009 to Ingleby (where parking is available at the John Thomson Inn), through Barrow upon Trent where the Wheel Inn AC has waters, and on to Swarkestone bridge on the A514 and below to end near Stanton. Day tickets are available from the nearby Crew and Harper Inn.

From Weston on Trent the Derby Railway Institute Anglers' Association controls a lengthy stretch of prime river, holding roach, dace, chub and perch. Day tickets are available from dealers in the area, Grays (Newsagents) at Shardlow, or from the inn at Cavendish Bridge on the A6. There is access to the river at Kings Mills, approached from the A453 at Castle Donnington, and the Association's waters continue to just short of the confluence with the Derwent. Here the Pride of Derby AA waters start, strictly for members only, until Sawley where day tickets are available at the Harrington Arms.

Coventry's stretch

Farther downstream the Soldiers and Sailors Angling Club have waters at Trent Lock, which is approached by a lane from the A453, and where day tickets are obtainable from dealers in the area, as they are for the lengthy Long Eaton Victoria Angling Society waters in the same section. At Thrumpton, Coventry and District Angling Association has a very good stretch of water on the right bank with access near the church, approached from the A648. A single-bank 30-peg stretch is also available, and day-tickets can be obtained at Ferry Farm, Thrumpton.

Match waters

The Trent then passes on to Barton (right bank) and Attenborough (left bank) where day tickets are available. This stretch is recognised as the start of the big match-fishing area. The banks are fairly low, on average 2ft above the water. There is a fast flow, weed lanes, and good pegs for matches. The average depth is 8ft with 3-4ft near the bank.

Trent's potential

The Trent was once the equal of the Hants Avon, but it had the misfortune of passing through the heart of the industrial Midlands. This meant the march of pollution, foundries and factories happily making use of this nearby means of the disposal of toxic wastes. It nearly killed the river. But now it has a growing reputation as the fine fishery it once was. One day its huge potential will be fulfilled by the holding of a National Championship along its banks.

The approaches to the Upper Trent. Main roads and the M1 make locating the river simple. (Below) Our inset map of the King's Bromley-Alrewas stretch gives greater detail.

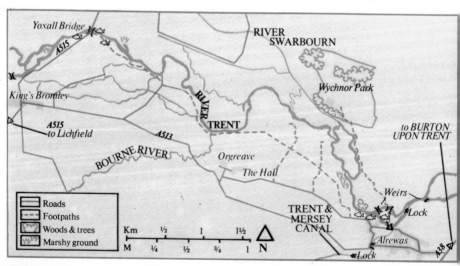

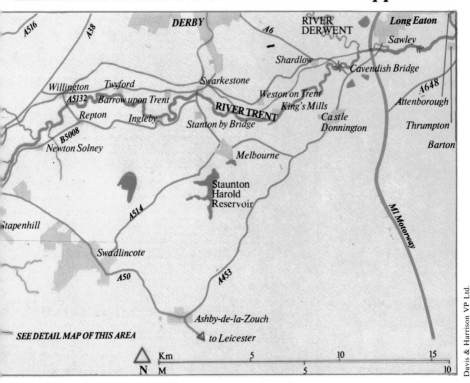

INFORMATION

WATER AUTHORITY.

Severn-Trent Water Authority, Trent Area, Meadow Lane, Nottingham NG2 3HN. Tel: 865007.

LICENCES

Trout, freshwater fish and eels: Trent area, annual from January 1 £1, combined Severn-Trent area annual £1.50, OAPs 20p, 28-day ticket 50p.
Salmon: season £15, day £2.25.

Size limits: pike 19.7 in (50 cm), barbel 15.7 in (40 cm), bream, carp, chub and tench 9.8 in (25 cm), trout 9.1 in (23 cm), dace, grayling, roach, rudd and perch 7.9 in (20 cm).
Close season: trout and sea trout October 16 to March 17; rainbow trout in the catchment of the River Derwent, November 15 to May 16, in the remainder of the River Authority area, October 16 to March 17. Coarse fish March 15 to June 16.

LOCAL CLUBS AND ASSOCIATIONS

Birmingham Anglers' Assoc, V S Hall, 40 Thorpe St, Birmingham B5 4AU. Tel: 6904.

Coventry and District Angling Assoc, E G Baxter, 15 Boswell Drive, Coventry. Tel: 615078.

Derby Anglers' Assoc, A E Descamps, Chapel Lane, Ticknall, Derbys. Tel: Melbourne 2362.

Derby Railway Institute Anglers' Assoc, 65 Leytonstone Drive, Derby DE3 4GS. Tel: 31855.

Long Eaton Victoria Angling Soc, J H Lewis, 138 Derby Rd, Draycott, Derbys. Tel: 2370.

Pride of Derby Angling Association, C. Titterton, 133 Matlock Rd, Chaddesden, Derby.

Soldiers and Sailors Angling Club (NFD&DS), W Walker, Tamworth Rd, Sawley, Long Eaton. Tel: (Mr Rees) Long Eaton 3639.

Swadlincote and Dist Anglers' Assoc, D Tye, 65 Main St. Linton, nr Burton on Trent, Staffs. Tel: 760669.

TACKLE DEALERS

J Rhone, The Matchman's Peg, 129 High St, Woodville, Burton on Trent. Tel: 216870.

Mullarkey & Sons, Waterloo St, Burton. Tel: 66777.

Blounts, Shaftesbury St, Derby. Tel: 40650.

J Burrowdale, London Rd, Alveston, Derby.

Derby & Burton Co-op, Exchange St, Derby. Tel: 44611.

Angler's Corner, Osmaston Rd, Derby. Tel: 43870.

Bridge Tackle, 30 Derby Rd, Long Eaton, Derbys. Tel: 68338.

The Horseshoe, 1 Station Rd, Long Eaton. Tel: 2972.

J & M Tackle, 59 West St, Arnold, Nottingham. Tel: 76990.

J Wright, 29 High St, Swadlincote. Tel: Burton on Trent 216608.

Rod and Tackle, Bridge St, Uttoxeter, Staffs.

Lower Trent

See detailed area maps

some wonderful sport is recorded in this area with match weights of 20lb not uncommon. Roach, dace, chub, bream and carp are taken on a variety of baits, with bigger fish found farther downstream.

Clifton Gorve on the right bank downstream from Beeston Weir has for two years produced the most astonishing sport. This 40p day-ticket water can boast a five hour match winning weight of 54lb and numerous pleasure totals to 60lb. The water here, fast and mainly shallow, makes for perfect barbel and chub swims. All baits are effective but the killing bait is wasp grub. The Clifton Grove water is packed with roach, chub, dace, bleak and gudgeon with a fair sprinkling of perch, bream and barbel and

The Severn-Trent Water Authority took several years to clean up the River Trent, Britain's third largest river. Now a considerable slice of the 170 miles gives the most exciting fishing in the country. Much progress must be made, however, before salmon can thrive in the river once again. From 1884 to 1887, on average 3,000 fish per year were killed, one fish caught on the Newark Dyke weighing 32lb, but then the river became polluted. In 1975, six fish made their way up the Trent, but only one fish has been reported since. Clearly the water quality is not yet good enough.

Barbel and carp

The Trent was once famous for its barbel stocks and these fish are beginning to show again, particularly near the weirs. With the possible exception of the power station swims where the water is artificially heated, hundreds and possibly thousands of carp to 30lb have been reported during the last two years. More remarkable is carp showing in quantity from Long Eaton to the tidal area downstream of Collingham.

The River Soar brings water of indifferent quality into the Trent near Long Eaton, but

Rodney S. Caldron

Rodney S. Caloron

(Above) Good roach fishing by Newark Castle, while Winthorpe Bridge (below) is one of the most popular stretches.

the occasional trout. The stretch is only a few minutes from Clifton Bridge, but ring bailiff Pete Mayne at Nottingham 215625 for more details. The left bank at Clifton also has good fishing. Several clubs control the water such as the Nottingham Anglers' Assoc and Raleigh Industries Ltd., but day tickets can be purchased on the bank.

Good roach fishing

Specialist tactics have taken many double-figure carp (several more than 20lb) from the swims near Wilford Power Station, while downstream there is plenty of free fishing available from the Nottingham Embankment. Roach fishing is good, particularly during the summer months on tares, chub, bream, perch and carp.

The Long Higgin and Little Higgin stretch is on the right bank and within sight of Nottingham Forest football ground. Access is from the A52 at Lady Bray, and the river at this point is deep. The first meadow is fast with an average depth of 12ft, but farther

Lower Trent

Rodney S. Caloron

downstream the water slackens. Average catches are around 7–8lb with the main species roach and gudgeon, and the occasional chub and bream. Day tickets are available on the bank.

Nottingham Federation control most of the right-bank fishing downstream to Radcliffe Railway Bridge, and this is members-only water. Day tickets at 30p for a lengthy stretch of the opposite bank at Colwick can be obtained, however, from the bailiff, Cliff Cox, on the bank. This is excellent roach fishing and gives some double-figure carp too.

Stoke Weir to Gunthorpe Bridge

Nottingham and District Federation of Angling Societies control the fishing on the left bank from 40-pegs upstream of Stoke Weir to Gunthorpe Bridge. This is mostly day-ticket water with tickets available on the bank. The stretch includes the famous Golden Mile bank at Burton Joyce where the access is easy. The 'Rack' at Burton Joyce has produced some astonishing nets of roach.

On the right bank, Nottingham Anglers' Association controls the fishing from Stoke

Weir to Gunthorpe Bridge. As far as Shelford day tickets are available, but from the Cherry Orchard to Gunthorpe Bridge it is members-only fishing. The right bank downstream from Gunthorpe Weir offers fine fishing, but is also members-only water and strictly bailiffed. From here downstream to Farndon is private fishing.

Hazelford Weir

Several different clubs control the fishing on the left bank downstream from Gunthorpe Weir to Hazelford Weir and day tickets are available on the bank. The fishing here is good, and a waggler/maggot combination often produces the best results.

The four fields immediately downstream of Hazelford Weir on the left bank produce some superb, varied sport with both float and ledger tactics. Several Trent Championship winners have come from this stretch, and it also produced Third Division National winner, 1977. Day tickets at 40p are available from Mrs Tavner, Bromley Arms, Fiskerton, Notts.

Nottingham Piscatorial Society controls the rest of the left bank downstream to

108

Staythorpe, but some of it is available to day-ticket anglers. The fishing at Rolleston is marvellous and well worth the long walk from the Rolleston to Bleasby Road. Day tickets are 40p and must be purchased in advance from tackle dealers in Nottingham, Mansfield, Warsop and Newark, or from the Post Office in Rolleston.

Day tickets are available on the bank to fish the picturesque river at Farndon. Float fishing is best on this stretch of water which varies in depth from 4ft to 12ft. Access is from the A46 Newark to Nottingham road into Farndon village.

Most of the Newark Dyke and its backwaters are controlled by Newark and District Piscatorial Federation and day tickets are available on the bank. Unlike much of the River Trent which now has its banks stoned, the Newark Dyke is natural and the flow tends to be slower than the main river, making it an ideal water for the float

Map shows the course of the Trent from Long Eaton to Gainsborough. (Left) Landing a carp near Collingham.

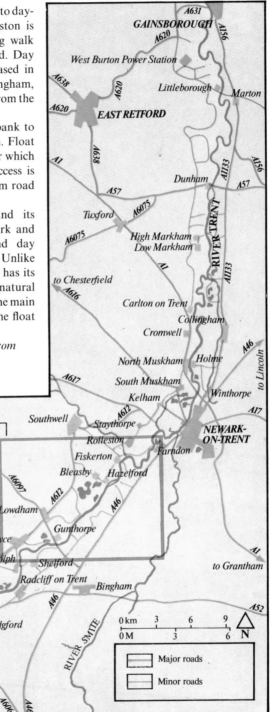

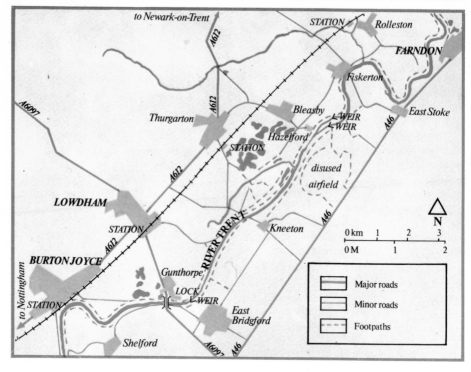

The excellent fishing from Burton Joyce to Farndon is shown in our detail map. Tickets are available on the bank. (Below) The Trent below Nottingahm.

angler. The dyke has a good head of fish including some barbel and carp, and the best baits are casters, maggots, and hempseed.

Fishing on the old river from Staythorpe Weir to Crankley Point is controlled by the Nottingham Piscatorial Society and is member-only water. A short stretch is available however in front of Kelham Hall, Newark, Notts, and day tickets at 40p are obtainable from Newark District Council, Kelham Hall, Newark.

Winthorpe stretch

The fabulous Winthorpe stretch from Crankley Shallows on the right bank to Winthorpe Lake can be fished on a day ticket available on the bank, but the stretch in front of the Lake is owned by the Severn-Trent Water Authority. Tickets for this stretch and for the Lake, must be purchased prior to fishing from the keeper at Winthorpe Crossing gates or from the Authority at Meadow Lane, Nottingham. They cost 40p.

The remainder of the right bank as far as Cromwell Weir, is controlled by Worksop and District Amalgamated Angling Association, with day tickets obtainable on the bank. The Holme Marsh stretch, particularly in the Weir Field, produces excellent sport with big chub and carp, while bream, which have shoaled here recently, make a fascinating day's fishing.

Day-ticket water

Some of the left bank from Crankley Point is private, but long stretches of day-ticket water are available near Winthorpe Bridge and Muskham. The Newcastle Arms' stretch and Walter Bower's bank at Muskham are marvellous roach and chub haunts. Worksop Angling Association issue day tickets for the remainder of the left bank to Cromwell Locks.

The tidal stretch starts at Cromwell Weir, and Collingham Angling Association con-trols six miles of first-class right bank fishing with day tickets obtainable on the bank. Roach and chub are the dominant species but there is also a very large head of bream. Several 20lb plus carp have been taken from the water recently, and some good class barbel have been showing. The best baits are casters, maggots, tares and hempseed. The river is easily reached by taking the lane behind Collingham church.

Most of the left bank opposite Collingham is private, but there is a good chub stretch at Carlton-on-Trent. Enquiries for day tickets should be made at the Great Northern Inn, Carlton-on-Trent. Other day-ticket water (particularly good in winter) is at Marnham, with tickets available from the Brownlow Arms in the village. The Water Authority has a good length of water upstream from Dunham Toll Bridge, and 40p tickets for this stretch are available from Mr Shucks, The Garage, Dunham-on-Trent, from Mr Beaumont, The Green, Dunham-on-Trent, or from the Severn-Trent Water Authority.

Mike Prichard

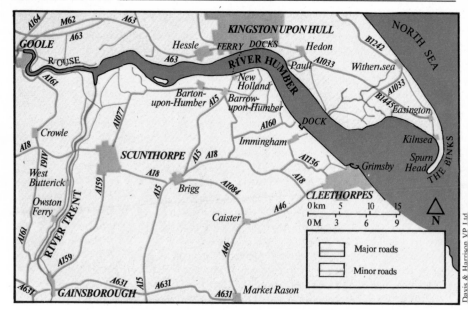

The tidal river at Dunham seems to produce its best sport in winter. Most of the stretches are controlled by Lincoln and District Angling Association, Rotherham and District United Anglers' Federation, Sheffield and District Angling Association and Doncaster and District Angling Association, and are for members only. Doncaster Angling Association has a productive stretch from Littleborough downstream to West Burton Power Station on the left bank, and this is probably the farthest point downstream at which serious match fishing is done.

Some good sport is recorded on the right bank at Gainsborough in the winter, and fishing here is mostly free. Fishing farther downstream is patchy, although some good catches have been made as far as Owston Ferry. The banks are difficult and the extreme tides make fishing unpleasant.

Humber Estuary

At this point, sea angling begins. The Humber Estuary is one of the few places in England where codling can be caught from the shore 52 weeks of the year. During the autumn months it is best to fish the estuary itself. Paull Foreshore and Stone Creek are

Map shows the Trent below Gainsborough and the Humber Estuary. (Right) The Humber by the docks of Hull.

particularly popular. Cod can be caught all the way up the estuary as far as Hull docks until December with the northern side of the estuary undoubtedly the best. Codling abound in the estuary but other species including whiting, pouting, school bass, dogfish, thornback ray, turbot, plaice, dab, flounder, eel are found, and occasional tope have made their way up the river.

Spurn Head

Spurn Head, the Yorkshire Naturalist Trust nature reserve, is a favourite spot for cod fishing from December onwards. From Hull to Kilnsea also cod can be caught, and for a small charge anglers can fish the Point.

The river side of the Head fishes best during northerly and north-easterly winds. There are two deep channels off the point of the Sprun known locally as the Binks, and in the right conditions these marks are the most productive. Lugworm can be dug along the mudflats of the estuary, but great care must be taken to watch the incoming tide. Other useful baits are mussel, crab and sprat.

A. F. Kersting

INFORMATION

WATER AUTHORITY

Severn-Trent Water Authority, Trent Area, Area Fisheries Office, Meadow Lane, Nottingham NG2 3HN. Tel 865007.

LICENCES

Freshwater fish: Trent area, season £1, Severn and Trent area season £1.50, (OAPs 20p), 28-day period 50p. Licences expire on December 31.

Close seasons: trout and sea trout October 16 to March 17. Coarse fish March 15 to June 15.

Size limits: pike 19.7in (50cm), barbel 15.7in (40cm), bream, chub, carp and tench 9.8in (25cm), trout 9.1in (23cm), dace, grayling, roach, rudd and perch 7.9in (20cm). A keepnet must not be used for retaining salmon or trout.

LOCAL CLUBS AND ASSOCIATIONS

Collingham Angling Association, Mrs June Wilson, 93 Braemar Rd, Collingham, near Newark, Notts.

Doncaster and District Angling Association, E Cusworth, 55 Melbourne Grove, Balby, Doncaster, S Yorks DN4 0UN.

Lincoln and District Angling Association, A Gilbert, 35 Bristol Drive, Lincoln.

Newark and District Piscatorial Federation, J N Garland, 58 Riverside Rd, Newark, Notts.

Nottingham and District Federation of Angling Societies, W Belshaw, 17 Springgreen, Clifton Estate, Notts.

Nottingham Anglers' Association, E Collin, 224 Radford Boulevard, Nottingham NG5 3EB.

Nottingham Piscatorial Society, H Waterfall, 8 Montfort Crescent, Sherwood, Notts.

Rotherham and District United Anglers' Federation, T J Dickens, 18 Burns Rd, Herringthorpe, Rotherham, S Yorks.

Sheffield Amalgamated Anglers' Society, W H Pursglove, 20 Manor Park Drive, Sheffield 2.

Worksop and District Amalgamated, G D Rollinson, 31 Lincoln St, Worksop, Notts.

TACKLE DEALERS

Foster's Sporting Services Ltd, 32 St John St, Ashbourne.

Anglers Corner, 344 Osmaston Rd, Derby. Tel. 43870.

Artisan Angling, 141 London Rd, Derby. Tel 53627.

J A Barradell, 976 London Rd, Derby. Tel 71472.

E Blount, 80 Shaftesbury Cres, Derby. Tel 40650.

Gibson's Aquatic Supplies, 248 Uttoxeter New Rd, Derby. Tel 48638.

J T Guy, 59 Annestey Rd, Hucknall. Tel 2868.

D A Wright, 136 Cotmanhay Rd, Ilkeston. Tel 301610.

Horseshoe Fishing Tackle, 1 Station Rd, Long Eaton. Tel. 2972.

A R Wainwright, 30 Derby Rd, Long Eaton. Tel 68338.

Brian Richmond, 2 Midworth St, Mansfield. Tel 77390.

J A Webster, 144 Outram St, Sutton-in-Ashfield, Mansfield. Tel 52943.

M & W Denby, 123A Newgate Lane, Mansfield. Tel 36554.

R and M C Dibble, 40 Belvedere St, Mansfield. Tel 23214.

C Smith and Sons, Clinton House, Lombard St, Newark. Tel 3839.

R Leach, 19 Boar Lane, Newark. Tel 74232.

P Kershaw, 7 Meering Ave, Newark.

W Lloyd, 43 Castlegate, Newark. Tel 2758.

Anglers Tackle, 572 Carlton Rd, Nottingham. Tel 53627.

Beeston Matchmen, 217 Queens Rd, Beeston, Nottingham. Tel 223034.

Terry Dorman, 272 Denman St, Nottingham. Tel 781695.

A Tizley, 100 Bunbury St, The Meadows, Nottingham. Tel 868960.

Tom Watson and Son, 1 Oak St, Carrington, Nottingham. Tel 609561.

Tom Watson and Sons, 198 Ilkeston Rd, Nottingham. Tel 76990.

J & M Fishing Tackle, 59 West St, Arnold, Nottingham. Tel 262644.

Matchmen, 5 Bannerman Rd, Bullwell, Nottingham. Tel 278859.

R E Smith, 472 Vernon Rd, Old Basford, Notts. Tel 782407.

Walkers of Trowell, Nottingham Rd, Trowell. Tel Ilkeston 301816.

R and M C Dibble, 6 Church St, Warsop. Tel 2448.

Bill Howes

Dee and Clwyd

See detailed area maps

Fishing in Welsh waters from lake, river or sea, does away with the fallacy that you cannot have the best of both worlds. The coast is within easy reach of the inland countries where the rivers, lakes and reservoirs are teeming with fish. Both inland and coastal areas are noted for their specimen fish.

The course of the Dee

The River Dee rises on the slopes of Aran Mawddwy in Gwynedd and flows through Bala, Llandderfel, Corwen, Llangollen, Overton, Holt and Chester and hence to the sea. Famous for its salmon and trout, the Dee also has grilse entering from June, and downstream from Bangor has mainly coarse fish—bream, roach, dace, perch and pike. Sea trout are found during July and August, but are small, and brown trout are found in Bala Lake (Llyn Tegid) and the River Alyn. Below Llangollen, dace and roach inhabit the waters in large numbers.

In its upper reaches the Dee is joined by mountain rivulets and has many waterfalls and small pools in which fingerling trout are found. Bala Lake holds coarse and game fish and also the gwyniad, found only in

this water. Bala and District Angling Association controls this lake (members only), but issues day tickets at 80p, week tickets at £3, for a stretch of approximately 600 yards near its outlet where trout, salmon and grayling are plentiful. From Rhiwlas Estate to Bala Junction Railway Station where the Dee is joined by the River Tryweryn, fishing is strictly preserved. The Bala and District AA also controls trout fishing (fly only) on Cwn Prysor Lake above Llyn Celyn on the River Tryweryn, and the River Llafar and River Craig-y-Tan.

Between Corwen and Llangollen, some water is controlled by Corwen and District Angling Club, but it is for members only. Glyndfrdwy Preserves controls nearly 2 miles of right bank fishing from Tyn Celyn to Glyndfrdwy Bridge with day tickets at 75p (trout and grayling) or £2 (salmon), available from W A Jones at the Berwyn Arms Hotel. The Midland Fly Fishers then have fishing rights beyond the bridge for 4 miles on the right bank as far as Groes Lwyd Gate, and on the left bank starting at Coedial just below Glyndfrdwy Bridge. Their day tickets cost £1, and are obtainable from the Berwyn Arms Hotel, the Royal Hotel in Llangollen, or Groes Lwyd Farm, Rhewl. This water, good for salmon, is strictly keepered.

Good salmon stretch

Llangollen Angling Association has 6 miles of water near Llangollen, all available on day ticket at 75p, week ticket £3, season ticket £7.50. These waters are on the left bank from Rhewl Mill to Horseshoe Falls and on the right bank from this point to 'Pendre' 1½ miles beyond. Then from the pool opposite the Canal Recording Station to Chain Bridge on the right bank below the Horseshoe Falls to the old weir. Beyond this there is a left-bank stretch as far as the field before Abbey Brook, and both banks on the meadows by the Jenny Jones Hotel. Also controlled are both banks by the Woodlands

Dee and Clwyd

(Above) Day tickets at 50p are available from the Bryn-y-Pys Angling Association for a trout stretch downstream of Overton.

Hotel, including Tip, Dee Mount, Skinyard Pools, and the Lingo Pool. Tickets for these waters are available from W N & H N Elbourn, 12 Chapel St, Llangollen and there is easy access from the A539 or the A5.

Near Chain Bridge, Liverpool and District Angling Association has a small left-bank stretch which is good for salmon at £5 a day.

Downstream of Llangollen the water is controlled by hotels which only let tickets to their residents. The Hand Hotel has the right bank and the Ponsonby Hotel the left bank downstream of Langollen Road Bridge, and the Golden Pheasant Hotel has a salmon beat near Pen-y-lan with day tickets costing up to £5.

South to Wrexham

In the Newbridge-Cefn Mawr area the Maelor Angling Association controls fishing on both banks between Pontcysyllte and the Cefn Viaduct Pool with day tickets costing 50p, week tickets £1.50, available from The Royal Oak at Newbridge. Access to these waters is via the A483 south of Wrexham.

The Dee then loops south through Chirk and passes through Overton and Erbistock to Bangor. At this point the river is fast flowing between steep, wooded banks with a very stony bed, and salmon, sea trout, trout and coarse fish are found. Chirk Angling Association has a small stretch on the right

Map of the area shows the game and coarse fishing of the rivers Dee and Clwyd, and the tributary rivers Alyn, Sarn, Ceiriog, Alwen, Tryweryn and Elwy. The Clwyd and Elwy river system is purely a game fishery, with

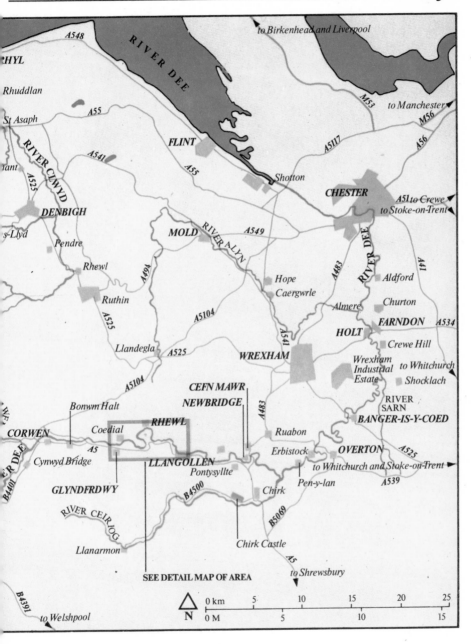

SEE DETAIL MAP OF AREA

large spring salmon from March to May and some fish of up to 12lb. Unfortunately, there is only one day-ticket stretch. The River Dee flows through Llangollen, Cefn Mawr and Chester to the sea, and at Bala

Lake (Llyn Tegid) one finds the gwyniad, a fish existing only in this lake. More accessible than the Elwy, the Dee is famous for its salmon and trout, but also offers many good coarse fishing spots.

117

bank downstream from Pen-y-Bont Pool to Sun Pool, and from Little Gleisha to Boundary fence. The Boat Inn at Erbistock issues day tickets at 75p for 500 yards on the left bank ¾ mile above the inn, and for the left bank by the inn.

Downstream of Overton, the Bryn-y-Pys Angling Association has a 50p day-ticket stretch from Clay's Ford to Bangor Bridge on both banks except for the small stretch on the river bank from Turn of Dee to Bangor Bridge. Access is via the A539.

Chester

From Bangor to Holt, the river loops and twists, passing the Wrexham Industrial Estate. The principal coarse fish species here are dace and roach with some perch, bream, gudgeon and chub. Bangor Angling Association controls both banks from Bangor Bridge downstream to Craig Lane, with day tickets at 15p (trout and coarse fish), £1 (salmon), and 62½p (salmon, after April 30th).

At Holt and Farndon, the river widens and flows to Chester where the Dee Anglers' Association has approximately 6 miles of

The very good salmon stretch controlled by the Midland Fly Fishers is shown in our detail map (below). Day tickets cost £1. (Left) On the Dee below Horseshoe Falls, Llangollen Angling Association offers day tickets at 75p.

bank starting at Farndon Bridge. Further details and season tickets (£1) are available from H. Wickham, 16 Lache Lane, Chester.

Chester Association of Anglers has water rented by the Dee Anglers' Association on 12 beats covering approximately 14 miles of the Dee at Farndon, Churton, Shocklach and Sutton Green. A map of the waters can be bought from the secretary for 25p. These stretches are—the Holt water, 1 mile of left banks upstream of Farndon Bridge, the right bank of the landing stages upstream and downstream of Chester Groves and Richmond Park Gardens, the left bank from the meadow's boundary upstream of the first intake to Bottom's Lane, both banks from Queensferry Old Road Bridge to the weir (except a stretch from the Old Dee Bridge to the weir), and both banks from Bottom's Lane downstream to the weir. They have only two day-ticket waters, both at 5p, on the lower Dee from the weir to opposite the White House, and below the weir from Sealand Road to Queensferry Bridge.

At Chester there is free fishing from the Suspension Bridge upstream to the Kissing Gates, on the south bank between Greenway Street and River Lane, and from one meadow below Grosvenor Road Bridge to the Railway Bridge. Below the town, the river flows past Shotton, and enters the sea at Flint. No rod licences are needed in the tidal waters, and close seasons and size limits are

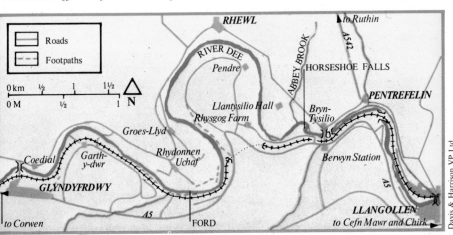

Dee and Clwyd

Our picture shows the estuary of the River Clwyd at Rhyl, upstream of the A548 road bridge. Fishing here is free, and good sea trout and salmon can be caught.

not applicable in these waters.

The Clwyd is purely a game fishery. There is some salmon from March to May, and some sea trout, but the major run is of grilse and small summer salmon in July and August. Migratory fish up to 12lb run into the estuary in June and are followed in August and September by smaller fish, generally whiting of $\frac{1}{2}$lb–$\frac{3}{4}$lb. Trout (average 9in) are numerous, but are better in the tributary rivers Elwy and Wheeler.

Very little water is available on the River Clwyd. The only day-ticket water, controlled by the St Asaph Angling Association, is between the two bridges at St Asaph, where day tickets cost £2.50 (juniors £1.50), week tickets £5 (juniors £3), and are available from the Post Office or Bevins Newsagents. In the Trefnant area, the Denbigh and District Angling Club controls 2½ miles of bank and waters on the River Ystrad and the River Elwy, as well as a reservoir at Pentre Saron. At Rhyl there is free fishing for approximately 3 miles from Rhuddlan to the sea. Salmon and sea trout are found but there are no holding pools.

The tributary rivers of the Dee and Clwyd

also offer good fishing. The tributaries of the Dee are the Alyn, Sarn, Ceiriog, Alwen and Tryweryn. The River Alyn, good for trout, has some waters controlled by the Llay Hall Angling Association on both banks from Abermoddue to Bradley with some exceptions; and from Hope to Abermoddue, for a mile, the Caergwrle Angling Club has water on both banks and issues season tickets.

River Ceiriog

The River Ceiriog is good for trout and has sea trout from August onwards. Chirk AA has several waters through the Chirk Castle Estate, the Trevor Estate, and both banks downstream from Ladies Bridge to the boundary fence above Pont-y-Blew Bridge and below Forge Farm to Mouses Bridge. Water is also controlled by the Golden Pheasant Hotel, which has water near Pontfaen Bridge and the West Arms Hotel, which has nearly 2 miles on both banks at Llanarmon.

The Golden Pheasant Hotel has nearly 2 miles of trout and salmon water near Druid on the River Alwen with a limited number of day tickets of £1. Upstream, the Crown Hotel owns reaches of the river near Llanfihangel.

The tributaries of the Clwyd are the Elwy, the Aled, and the Little Dee. St Asaph Angling Association has several waters on the Elwy near St Asaph Bridge and from

Pont-yr-allt Goch Bridge downstream. Maps are available from the Association, and day tickets at £2.50 (juniors £1.50), and week tickets at £5 (juniors £3) are available from the Post Office or from Bevins Newsagents.

Other waters are available on the rivers Aled and the Little Dee, and the Welsh National Water Development Authority, Dee and Clwyd Division, can give details.

Sea angling festivals

The Welsh coast from Colwyn Bay to Flint is noted for producing bass up to double figures during the summer months and the annual Welsh Bass Championships held in Colwyn Bay are regarded as one of Europe's top sea angling festivals. Shore fishing produces bass, flounder, plaice, dab, dogfish, small rays and gurnard, while boat fishing gives excellent sport with tope and thornback ray, with ling and conger in the deep channels. The area is plentiful in bait and is particularly noted for its black sewi lugworm, with soft and peeler crab found in abundance among the kelp at low water.

The Dee estuary holds mainly dab, flounder and eel, and Hilbre Island is a pleasant venue for family fishing and picnics. In the Clwyd estuary, flounder and eel are numerous at Rhyl, while flatfish, bass and eel are taken by the beach fisherman, with whiting taken during autumn and winter.

INFORMATION

WATER AUTHORITY
Welsh National Water Development Authority, Dee and Clwyd Division, Shire Hall, Mold, Clwyd. Tel: 2121.

LICENCES
Freshwater fish and eels: season £1.80 (juniors and OAPs 90p), day ticket 60p. Salmon and sea trout (also covers non-migratory trout, char, freshwater fish and eels) vary according to category A, B, C, D or E. Rivers Dee, Clwyd and tributaries fall under category C, D or E. Category C: season £10.80 (juniors and OAPs £5.40), week £5.40, day £1.80. Category D: season £7.20 (juniors and OAPs £3.60), week £3.60, day £1.20. Category E: season £4.80 (juniors and OAPs £2.40), week £2.40, day 90p. Non-migratory trout (also covers char, freshwater fish and eels): season £3 (juniors and OAPs £1.50), week £1.80, day 60p.

Close seasons: salmon: Dee and tributaries October 15 to March 1 except Grosvenor Bridge to Suspension Bridge Chester October 15 to June 15. Clwyd and tributaries October 15 to March 15. Sea trout: Dee and tributaries September 30 to March 1 except Grosvenor Bridge to Suspension Bridge Chester October 15 to June 15. Clwyd and trubutaries October 15 to March 18, elsewhere September 30 to March 1. Non-migratory trout and char September 30 to March 1 except Bala Lake August 14 to January 15. Freshwater fish and eels March 14 to June 16. No close season for eels.

Byelaws: fishery byelaws are currently under review and may be substantially modified for the 1978 season. Copies of byelaws currently in force may be obtained from the Authority's River Division offices.

FISHERIES
The Golden Pheasant Hotel, Llwynmawr, Dolywern, Wrexham. Tel Glyn-Ceiriog 281.
Boat Inn, Erbistock. Tel Overton-on-Dee 243.
Glyndyfrdwy Preserves, c/o W A Jones, Berwyn Arms Hotel, Glyndyfrdwy, Corwen. Tel Glyndwr 210.
Crown Hotel, Llanfihangel, near Cerrigydrudion.
West Arms Hotel, Llanarmon Dyffryn Ceiriog. Tel 665.
Hand Hotel, Llangollen.
Ponsonby Hotel, Llangollen.

LOCAL CLUBS AND ASSOCIATIONS
Bala and District Angling Association, E J Leary, Sarnau Mount St, Bala, Gwynedd.
Bangor Angling Association, R Johnson, 'High Trees', Dean Rd, Rhosnessney, Wrexham, Clwyd.
Bryn-y-Pys Angling Association, V Guest, Bryn Hovah, Bangor-on-Dee, Wrexham.

Caergwrle Angling Association, R Mathers, 29 Hawarden Rd, Hope, near Wrexham.
Chester Association of Anglers, J E Parry, 47 Marian Drive, Gt Boughton, Chester.
Chirk Angling Association, L Davis, 76 Longfields, Chirk, near Wrexham.
Dee Anglers' Association, H C Wickham, 16 Lache Lane, Chester.
Liverpool and District Angling Association, J Johnson, 97 Liverpool Rd, North, Maghull, near Liverpool.
Llangollen Angling Association, S I Evans, The Dingle, Abbey Rd, Llangollen, Clwyd.
Llay Angling Society, J Barlow, 54 Hatton Rd, Plas Newton, Chester.
Maelor Angling Association, N I Wright, 34 Heol Cefnydd, Cefn Mawr, Wrexham.
Midland Fly Fishers, A D Clark, 5 Deansway, Worcester.
Newbridge Angling Association, K Bathers, Sunnyside, Hill St, Cefn Mawr, Wrexham. Tel:Wynnstay 234.
St Asaph Angling Association, I D Jones, 18 Heol Afon, St Asaph, Clwyd.

TACKLE DEALERS AND LICENCE AGENTS
W E Pugh, 74 High St, Bala.
S Adams, The Stores, High St, Bangor-on-Dee, Wrexham.
W Hitchell & Son, 47 Oxton Rd, Birkenhead.
D R Ledgard, Post Office, Caergwrle, near Wrexham.
G D Jones, Parc Service Station, Carrog, near Corwen.
N Wright, Maelor Angling Club, 34 Heol Cefnydd, Cefn Mawr, Wrexham.
G F Boddy, 143 Westminster Rd, Hoole Chester.
D Gibson, 42 Upper Northgate St, Chester.
F J Proud & Sons, 27/29 Christleton Rd, Chester.
W F Nicholls, Church St, Chirk, near Wrexham.
R D Pickering & Son, 60 Abergele Rd, Colwyn Bay.
W R Tinniswood, Owain Glyndwr Hotel, Corwen.
J Longbottom, Cross Foxes Inn, Erbistock, Wrexham.
J D Jones, High St, Farndon, near Chester.
B Littlewood, Corner Stores, Church St, Holt.
E L Adamson, Happy Angling, 10–14 Sefton St, Liverpool.
Harrisons Tackle Shop, 51 Smithdown Rd, Liverpool 7.
Sullivans Sports, 15 Broadgreen Rd, Old Swan, Liverpool.
W N Elbourn, Newsagents, 12 Chapel St, Llangollen.
R A Jones, Post Office, Llanuwychllyn, near Bala.
Kirkham & Woolley, 6 High St, Rhuddlan, near Rhyl.
W Roberts Rhyl Ltd, 131 High St, Rhyl.
E R Bevins, Newsagents, High St, St Asaph.
Morrison & Co Retail Ltd, 40 Mount St, Wrexham.
L A Truby, 24 High St, Rhosymedre, Wrexham.

North West Wales

See detailed area maps

The sea fishing in the area—ranging from estuary-caught flounders to battling tope and shark—is excellent. The area caters for beach and rock fishing, inshore and deep sea boat angling.

Aberystwyth

Starting in the south, there is good fishing around Aberystwyth. Shore anglers can fish Ynyslas beach just along the coast towards Borth, and along the Constitution Hill and Castle rocks in the town. There is reasonable pier fishing (a 14lb bass was caught recently) too, and Aberystwyth has a number of charter boats to reach the superb tope, conger, black bream and skate offshore.

Aberystwyth Angling Association controls game fish waters along both the

Gwynedd, the most scenic corner of North-West Wales, is mainly the preserve of game fishermen, while for coarse fishing, Anglesey is practically the only area. Compensation for the loss of coarse fishing is in the superb countryside, however—in the stern grandeur of solid rock and tumbling, rushing streams gurgling through short lives on a fast journey to Cardigan Bay or the Irish Sea.

Two of the best-known rivers in the area are the Conwy and the Dovey. The former is famous for its spring run of salmon, the latter for a remarkable influx of sea trout. Gwynedd salmon are not generally big by Wye standards—around the 8lb mark in the average run—and they often seem puny in contrast to the sea trout caught. The brown trout are usually brook-sized, but they are endowed with excellent fighting qualities for the angler who tackles up appropriately.

This is also the part of Wales where char can be fished. These colourful relics of our Ice Age are found in Llyn Padarn and Llyn Cwellyn. Day tickets for the former are available from 17 Castle Street, Caernarfon, and for the latter from Castell Cidwm Hotel in Betws Garnmon.

(Right) The River Dovey has a run of sea trout including double-figure specimens. (Below right) The Mawddach Estuary at Barmouth has good fishing for large bass, mullet, eels and most flatfish.

Arthur Oglesby

Spectrum Colour Library

Rheidol and Ystwyth rivers, and issues day, weekly, and season tickets, with fly, worm and spinning tactics allowed. Along the Ystwyth, the Llanilar Angling Association has rights from Llanfarian Bridge upstream to Bontrhydygroes, and weekly tickets are obtainable from Llanilar Post Office.

New Dovey Fishery Association

The run of sea trout into the Dovey often includes specimens in double figures as well as salmon to 25lb. The New Dovey Fishery Association issues day tickets for sections of their upper waters which run for 15 miles on both banks from Afon Llynfnant to the Abergwybedyn brook. Sunday fishing is not allowed and all forms of bait fishing are prohibited. The Macclesfield-based Prince Albert Angling Association controls about five miles for members only, but guests of the Brigands Inn, Mallwyd, Machynlleth, are allowed eight rods for a good nearby stretch.

The A493 crosses Dysynni river which has good trout, sea trout and spring salmon fishing. Day tickets are available at Pen o

Wern Farm, Bryncrug, Tywyn and from Tywyn tackle dealer F Porter for two miles of double bank at Peniarth and for seven miles of the Eistimaner Angling Association water from Cedris Bridge to below Garth Bridge.

At Barmouth the Mawddach estuary is good for bass, mullet, eels and most flatfish. The harbour often yields quality mullet and fair rock fishing is available. Some fly fishing is allowed on weekend permits for salmon and sea trout, and above Dolgellau the Tyn-y-Groes Hotel controls three miles with free fishing for guests and day tickets for visitors.

Near Llanbedr, the estuary of the Artro holds good mullet and often a fair run of sizeable bass which, anglers have found, show a liking for red and yellow spoons. The Artro Angling Association has four miles of game fishing upstream to Llyn Cwm Bychan with day tickets available at the Wenallt Stores in Llanbedr. Nearby is Trawsfynydd Lake where perch to 3lb can be caught.

Glaslyn river gives excellent sport, with

Map shows Gwynedd, the most scenic part of North West Wales, and Anglesey. Good fishing is available along the coast from Aberystwyth to the Menai Straits, with Aberystwyth and Barmouth the main centres. The angler will find pier, rock and boat fishing. Inland, the Rivers Dovey and Conwy are primarily game fisheries, while Anglesey offers coarse fishing.
(Left) The River Glaslyn at Nantmor.

(Above) The fishing centre of Aberystwyth viewed from Constitution Hill.
(Right) The Aberystwyth area with good game fishing on the Rheidol and Ystwyth.

large sea trout and improving salmon fishing, and is best fished when falling from spate condition. The Glaslyn Angling Association controls long lengths covering most of the bank from Beddgelert to Porthmadog and day tickets are obtainable from the Prenteg or Nant Gwynant post offices or from Pugh's in Porthmadog. At Beddgelert on the A498, the Saracens Hotel controls about eight miles with free fishing for residents.

From Porthmadog and round the Lleyn Peninsula through Criccieth, Pwllheli, Llanbedrog and Abersoch, there is good estuary, beach and rock fishing for pollack, pouting, wrasse, cod and most other species. Bass fishing is excellent out of the high holiday season at spots like Porth Neigwyl west of Abersoch. This area tends to be shallowish with a two-fathom shelf extending well offshore.

Good boat marks are on the Gimblet off Aberdaron, Bardsey Sound and the Tripods. Tides tend to run fast, but are easily fishable.

Near Criccieth and Llanystumdwy are the Dwyfawr and Dwyfach rivers. Criccieth Angling Association controls most of the

126

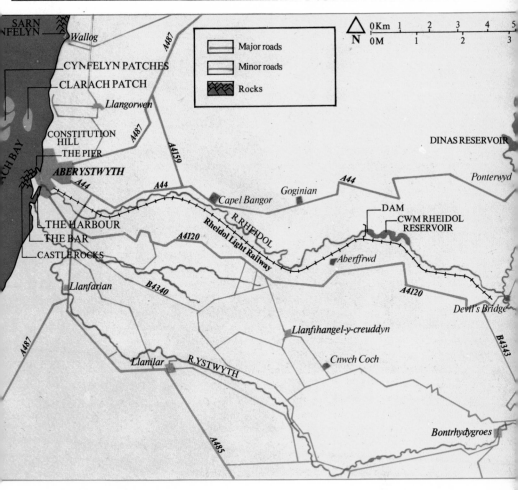

rivers and issues permits for some very good late-season fishing. They can be obtained from C Morgan, Criccieth. Spinning and bait fishing is usually allowed.

Caernarfon coastline

Caernarfon caters for most boat fishing south of the Menai Straits entrance. This coastline is again a mixture of broad beaches alternating with rock cliffs. Good beach fishing abounds at marks from Dinas Dinlle through Aberdesach to near Nefyn. Long casting ability is needed, and is rewarded with the possibility of double-figure bass, dogfish, most flatties and conger.

Caernarfon is also the headquarters of the Seiont, Gwyrfai and Llynfni Anglers Society

which issues permits for salmon and trout fishing. They are obtainable from most post offices in the area, and cover fishing in all three rivers. The waters include four miles of right bank Llyfni from Caerengan Bridge near Tal y Sarn, three miles of left bank Gwyrfai, and about five miles of the Seiont from Crawiau Bridge to Coed Helen and downstream from Pont Rhythallt.

A mile or so east is the river Ogwen which has reasonable runs of smallish salmon and sewin. The Penrhyn Fishing Club issues season tickets for stretches from Talybont Bridge to Halfway Bridge, and Pont Twr day tickets are issued by the Ogwen Valley Angling Club.

North West Wales

This is the coast of the famous Menai Straight, 12 miles long, about $\frac{1}{2}$ mile wide and with a 5 knot tide surge. The eastern end is renowned for bass, the western bar for tope, and the respected, though treacherous, mid-Strait 'Swellies' contain bass, tope, big conger, pollack and cod.

There are many good shore marks along both sides—Caernarfon golf course, Ysgubor Isaf, Port Dinorwic and Bangor on the South; the Mermaid Inn, Brynsiencyn, Moely Don and Beaumaris on Anglesey to the north.

Pier fishing

Pier anglers also have a fair choice at Bangor, Menai Bridge and Caernarfon Dock. Heavy tackle is necessary in this area and the best baits are often local peeler and soft-backed crab.

Anglesey abounds with beach, rock and shore marks. Local favourites are at Aberffraw Bay, Cymyrau Bay, north of Rhosneigr, North and South Stack, Church Bay, Cemlyn Bay, Dulas and Red Wharf. Good boat marks are at Carreg Goch off Rhosneigr, Bell Rock, The Skerries and Ethel Rock, Victoria Bank, Point Lynas, and near Puffin Island.

Anglesey also offers fine trout fishing. The Wygyr Fishing Association issue tickets for about two miles back from Cemaes Bay, while on the Cefni free fishing is available from the lake to the Malltraeth road bridge. There is also limited coarse fishing. Rudd can be caught from Llyn Bodafon, roach, rudd and perch at Llyn Twr, and at Llyn Dinam, while Llyn Cerig Back has the added attraction of tench fishing.

The River Conwy has sewin up to the 20lb mark, plus battling salmon and brown trout. The Dolgarrog Angling Association control five double-bank sections of the tidal river, and tickets are available from F Corrie in Dolgarrog. The Llanrwst Angling Club waters extend along both banks for $1\frac{1}{2}$ miles upstream of Gowers Bridge to Wall Pool, and their weekly permits, up to 19 September, can be obtained at The Library Shop, in Llanrwst.

Weekly permits are available from E W Jones in Betws-y-Coed for a stretch from, and along the Llugwy confluence to Waterloo Bridge where the Waterloo Hotel also issues permits. Permits are also issued for the lengthy Gwydr Hotel water along the left bank from the Lledr to Waterloo Bridge, the Llugwy to Wall Pool, both banks downstream of Gowers Bridge, and the famous Belmont Pool left bank.

National Trust waters

Above Betws, the National Trust controls rights along from Conwy Falls upstream, and the Ysbyty Ifan water. Day tickets at £1 are obtainable from the National Trust Office in Dinas, as are permits for fishing the nearby Machno and Glasgym rivers, which offer good small trout fishing in superb surroundings.

(Right) Sea fishing is good for bass, whiting and pollack in the Menai Straits near the suspension bridge and Bangor.

INFORMATION

WATER AUTHORITY
Welsh National Water Development Authority, Gwynedd River Division, Fisheries Officer, Highfield, Caernarfon. Tel 2247.
South-West Wales River Division, Penyfai House, 19 Penyfai Lane, Llanelli, Dyfed SA15 4EL. Tel 57031.
LICENCES
Trout, freshwater fish and eels: season £3 (juniors and OAPs £1.50), week £1.80, day 60p. **Freshwater fish and eels only:** season £1.80 (juniors and OAPs 90p). Licences to cover all the rivers in the WNWDA area: class A, all waters and all species, season £21.60 (juniors and OAPs £10.80), week £10.80, day £3.60. Class B, all rivers except the Wye and all species, season £18 (juniors and OAPs £9), week £9, day £3. For classes C, D, and E contact the area distributors for full details of the rivers and species covered. Class C, season £10.80 (juniors and OAPs £5.40), week £5.40, day £1.80. Class D season £7.20 (juniors and OAPs £3.60), week £3.60, day £1.20. Class E season £4.80 (juniors and OAPs £2.40), week £2.40, day 90p.
Close season: Gwynedd River Division, salmon and migratory trout 7 October to 10 March; brown trout 30 September to 3 March. South-West Wales River Division, salmon and migratory trout 7 October to 10 March; trout 30 September to 10 March; coarse fish 14 March to 16 June. Gaffs only to be used for salmon and sea trout from 1 May to 31 August.
Size limits: South-West Wales River Division, sea trout and trout 9in (23cm) in lakes and reservoirs, 6in (15cm) in other waters.
FISHERIES
Brigands Inn, Robin Tatum and John Meadows, Mallwyd, Machynlleth.
Gwydyr Hotel, Miss V C Smith, Betws-y-Coed, Gwynedd.
National Trust, Dinas, Betws-y-Coed, Gwynedd.

Pen-o-Wern Farm, Mrs Ellis, Bryncrug, Tywyn.
Saracens Hotel, Beddgelert, Gwynedd.
Tyn-y-Groes Hotel, Dolgellau.

LOCAL CLUBS AND ASSOCIATIONS

Aberystwyth Angling Assoc, Hon Sec, P O Box 15, Aberystwyth SY23 1AA, Dyfed.
Artro Angling Assoc, E Hoyle, Plas-y-Bryn, Llanbedr.
Betws-y-Coed Anglers Club, E W Jones, 25 Bro Gethin, Betws-y-Coed, Gwynedd.
Criccieth and Llanystumdwy Angling Assoc, G Hamilton, Morawel, Llanystumdwy, Criccieth.
New Dovey Fishery Assoc, D M Jones, Plas Machynlleth, Powys.
Dolgarrog Angling Assoc, F A Corrie, 3 Tayler Ave, Dolgarrog.
Eistaminer Angling Assoc, PC Edwards, Police Station, Abergynolwyn.
Glaslyn Angling Assoc, D G Pierce, 1 Bron Alltwen, Penmorfa, Porthmadog.
Llanilar Angling Assoc, c/o Llanilar Post Office.
Llanrwst Angling Club, D C Thomas, Erw Las Llwyn Brith, Llanrwst, Gwynedd.
Ogwen Valley Angling Club, E Parry, Llwyn-y-Gan, Rhos-y-Nant, Bethesda, Gwynedd.
Penrhyn Fishing Club, R H Jones, Minden, 3 Maes Coetmor, Bethesda, Gwynedd.
Prince Albert Angling Assoc, The Secretary, High Lodge, Upton, Macclesfield, Cheshire.
Seiont, Gwyrfai and Llyfni Anglers Soc, A Roberts, 17 Castle St, Caernarfon.
Wygyr Fishing Assoc, T Gillham, Crown Terr, Llanfechell, Anglesey.

TACKLE DEALERS AND LICENCE AGENTS

A H Lewthwaite, Trade Winds Yacht Services Ltd, The Harbour, Abersoch, Gwynedd.
Aberystwyth Sports Centre, North Parade, Aberystwyth.
E J Evans, Post Office, Crosswood, Aberystwyth.

R A Kendall, The Stores, Rhydyfelin, Aberystwyth.
W Morgan, Aberystwyth Angling Assoc, 6 Llanfihangel-y-Creddyn, Aberystwyth.
G M Hingley, All Sports and Hobbies, Beach Rd, Barmouth.
A Easton, Snowdonia Forest Park Camp, Beddgelert.
D H Griffiths, Gwynedd Enterprises, London House, Bethesda, Gwynedd.
E W Jones, 25 Bro Gethin, Betws-y-Coed, Gwynedd.
A· and C Hubbard, Compton, Borth, Dyfed.
E M Edwards, Siop y Bont, Bryncrug, Tywyn, Gwynedd.
R Gray Jones, RYZ Kiosk, Ferodo Ltd, Caernarfon, Gwynedd.
Mrs D Huxley Jones, 1-3 South Penrallt, Caernarfon.
Mrs M E Roberts, 79a Pool St, Caernarfon.
C Morgan, 1 High St, Criccieth, Gwynedd.
R T Pritchard and Son, Sheffield House, Criccieth.
Mrs N Corrie, 3 Tayler Ave, Dolgarrog, Gwynedd.
R G Jones, Waterloo House, Dolgellau, Gwynedd.
Mr McCaffrey, Celfi Diddan, Dolgellau.
Mrs O Ross, Post Office, Post Office, Llanbedr, Gwynedd.
Mrs M L Rees, Wern, Llanfihangel-y-Pannant, Tywyn.
E Fildes, Rhythallt Hotel, Llanrug, Caernarfon, Gwynedd.
B Roberts, Craiglwyd Hall (Caravans) Ltd, Brynteg Caravan Park, Llanrug.
T J Jones, The Library, Llanrwst, Clwyd.
T Evans, Service Garage, Cemmaes Rd, Machynlleth, Powys.
T A Hughes, 5 Penrallt St, Machynlleth, Powys.
Manager, Corris Caravan Park, Ceinws, Machynlleth.
J D Rees, Maelor Stores, Corris, Machynlleth.
Mrs Richards, Post Office, Derwen Las, Machynlleth.
K Johnson, Devon House, Menai Bridge, Gwynedd.
J M Pugh, 27 High St, Porthmadog, Gwynedd.
C T Noel, Studio Crafts, Station Rd, Rhosneigr, Gwynedd.
H K Lewis, Castle House, Trawsfynydd, Gwynedd.
F R Porter, 8 College Green, Tywyn, Gwynedd.
J J Roberts, Trefellyn Hairdressing Salon, Tywyn.

Welsh Reservoirs

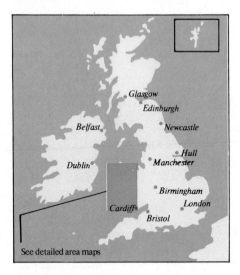

See detailed area maps

Wales abounds with reservoirs well-stocked with brown and rainbow trout. Managed on a put-and-take basis, they are frequently restocked and yield well. Pontisticill Reservoir in Glamorgan has produced trout to 14lb.

In Glamorgan, the reservoirs Ystradfellte, Beacons, Cantref, Llyn-on, Upper and Lower Neuadd, Dol-y-Gaer, Pontisticill and Talybont lie in an area north of Merthyr Tydfil and are easily approached by the A465, the A470 and the A4059. The Welsh National Water Development Authority (WNWDA) will give a map of the area when issuing licences and permits. The Glamorgan Division of the WNWDA also issue an annual rover ticket, the price being £25 for all reservoirs in the sector, £20 for a class 2 permit, £15 for a class 3, and £7.50 for a class 4 which permits fishing in the Pontisticill and Ystradfellte reservoirs only.

The angler can fish Pontisticill (253 acres) for a day ticket of 50p and Ystradfellte (59 acres) also for 50p; Beacons Reservoir (52 acres) for £1; Dol-y-gaer (96 acres) on Cantref reservoir for £1.50, Llyn-on (150 acres) for £2, and the Upper and Lower

Neuadd (57 and 12 acres) for £2. (Juniors and OAPs half-price). Fishing at these reservoirs is good. Each is stocked with trout of 12in average, except the Ystradfellte which has natural brown trout. Talybont Reservoir (318 acres) is controlled by the Gwent Water Division of the WNWDA, and may be fished with tickets costing £1.50 (day) or £20 (season). Spinning is allowed from one bank from June to the end of the season, and boats are available.

Vyrnwy Reservoir

In the Upper Severn area, there are two reservoirs owned by the Severn-Trent Water Authority. Llyn Clywedog (600 acres) is reached via the A483 from Welshpool and then the B4518 out of Llanidloes. Vyrnwy Reservoir (1,121 acres) is reached by the B4393 west of Shrewsbury, or from Welshpool via the A490 to meet the B4393. Both are restocked with brown and rainbow trout. At Vyrnwy fly fishing is allowed from boats only, which cost £1 per day. 24 tickets are available at £2.50 for the day, £1.25 the half-day, and £5 the weekend, obtainable from the Lake Vyrnwy Hotel, Oswestry, Salop SY10 0LY. At Llyn Clywedog Reservoir tickets cost £1.60 (day) £7.50 (week) and £16.50 (season).

In South West Wales, Dinas Reservoir and Nant-y-Moch Lake are both controlled by the Central Electricity Generating Board, (CEGB) North Western Region, and Llys-y-Fran controlled by the WNWDA. Dinas (60 acres) and Nant-y-Moch (860 acres) are both off the A44 Aberystwyth to Llangurig road, one and four miles out of Ponterwyd village respectively. At Dinas Reservoir fly and worm fishing and spinning are allowed from the banks but fly fishing only from boats; at Nant-y-Moch fly fishing only is allowed. Provision is made for disabled anglers at Dinas Reservoir, access being through a gate on the west side. For both these reservoirs tickets cost £2 (day), £10 (week), and for

A. F. Kersting

juniors, OAPs and the disabled, £1.20 (day) and £6 (week), obtainable from Evan's Garage in Ponterwyd, or from the CEGB. The Llys-y-Fran Reservoir (187 acres) is north east of Haverfordwest reached by the B4329. It is stocked with brown and rainbow trout, has four boats available and allows fly and worm fishing and spinning. Day tickets at £2, half-day tickets at £1.50 and season tickets at £20 (half-price for juniors and OAPs) are available from the Superintendent of the Pembroke Water Division or from the kiosk at the reservoir.

The Snowdonia area

Gwynedd, containing most of the Snowdonia National Park, has two reservoirs; Tan-y-Grisiau, owned by the CEGB is north of Blaenau Ffestiniog on the B4414, and Trawsfynydd Reservoir south of Ffestiniog on the A470. Tan-y-Grisiau is a 95-acre artificial lake stocked with rainbow trout. Spinning is allowed, but groundbaiting and swimfeeders are strictly prohibited. Wading is also forbidden because of the regular fluctuation of the water level caused by the power station. When buying tickets at the

(Above) The Dol-y-Gaer Reservoir in Powys, looking northwards.

Reception Centre it is advisable to ask which stretch is best to fish as rainbow trout tend to shoal. Tickets cost £2 (day) or £10 (week), and for juniors, OAPs or the disabled, £1.20 (day) and £6 (week). Trawsfynydd Lake (1200 acres) is owned by the CEGB and managed by the Trawsfynydd Lake Management Committee. It is south of Ffestiniog and reached via the A487. Tickets costing £1.60 (day), £7 (week), and £15 (season) are obtainable from H. Lewis, Newsagent at Trawsfynydd.

In Clwyd, the 368-acre Alwen Reservoir is owned by the WNWDA and controlled by the North West Water Authority. It is reached by the B4501 south west of Denbigh. In the top section, only fly fishing and four rods per side of the reselvoir are allowed, with floatbait and lure forbidden. In the middle and lower sections fly fishing and spinning are permitted. In all sections of the reservoir groundbait and maggot are prohibited, as is match and competition fishing. Day tickets at 50p and season tickets at £3.50 are available from the Superintendent's Office at the reservoir. Llyn Celyn (800 acres) owned by the WNWDA, is west of Bala on the A4212. Restocking with brown and rainbow trout is frequent. Other than a section reserved for fly fishing, spinning and worm are allowed. Tickets costing £1.50 (day), 75p (evening), £25 (season), with a reduction for juniors, OAPs and local residents, are available from the Post Office in Frongoch, or from W. E. Pugh, tackle shop in Bala.

In Gwent, Llandegfedd Reservoir (429 acres) owned by the WNWDA is reached via the A4042 south of Pontypool. In 1976 there were 10,500 brown trout and 10,000 rainbow trout, and restocking is on a monthly basis. 16 boats are avilable at a cost of £3 (day) and £1.50 (half-day), and motor boats £5 (day) and £2.50 (half-day). Day tickets at £2.50, week tickets at £12.50 and season tickets at £50 (half-price for juniors and OAPs) are obtainable from Sluvad Treatment Works, Panteg, Pontypool, or day tickets from the kiosk at the reservoir. Fly fishing only is allowed.

Ynysyfro, owned by the WNWDA, consists of two reservoirs, Upper and Lower, of 10 and 16 acres respectively and is approximately 1ml north of Newport. Details of fishing times may be obtained from the WNWDA Gwent Water Division, Station Buildings, Newport, Gwent, as may season tickets costing £40. Day tickets at £2 (half-price for junior and OAPs) can be bought from the Reservoir Superintendent.

Llyn Alaw in Anglesey

In Anglesey, the Llyn Alaw Reservoir (777 acres) is reached via the A5, then the B5111 to Llanerchymedd. It is controlled by the WNWDA which allows fly fishing on the north and east banks only, with spinning and worm fishing at the southern end. Stocked with brown and rainbow trout, ten boats are available at £1.50 per day (rowing) or £3 per day (outboard), with a fifty per cent reduction after 5pm. Day tickets are £2, evening tickets £1.50, week tickets £6 and season tickets £25, (half price for juniors and OAPs) and are obtainable from the Fishing Office, Llyn Alaw, Llanerchymedd, Anglesey, or in advance from the WNWDA, Gwynedd Water Division.

The Elan Valley Lakes, owned by the WNWDA and west of Rhayader on the

(Below) The Caban Coch Reservoir in Powys, is one of the famous Elan Valley Reservoirs.

LLYN ALAW

Holyhead

A5

A55

A5

A548

A548

Bangor

A4085

A543

DENBIGH

B4501

CONWY

CLWYD

A487

A498

LLYN CWELLYN

A5104

ALWEN RES

DE

A5

Blaenau Ffestiniog

A470

LLYN CELYN RES

A5

TRAWSFYNYDD RES

LAKE BALA

A470

A494

LAKE VYRNWY

B4393

A470

WELSHPOOL

A458

to Shrewsbury

SEVERN

A470

A489

CARDIGAN BAY

NANT-Y-MOCH RES

LLYN CLYWEDOG

NEWTOWN

A487

LLANDIDLOES

ABERYSTWYTH

A44

LLANGURIG

A4120

PONTERWYD

A44

RHAYADER

SEE DETAIL MAP OF AREA

A488

A487

ELAN VALLEY RESS

Newquay

B4343

A470

A44

LLYN BRIANNE

to Hereford

Builth Wells

A487

A483

WEY

Newport

TEIFI

FISHGUARD

A484

Llandovery

A440

BRECON

A478

A485

A440

St Davids Head

B4329

LLYS-Y-FRAN RES

USK RES

TALYBONT RE

ST

CARMARTHEN

to Newport

BRIDES

A40

LLYN FAN FAWR

BAY

HAVERFORDWEST

TYWI

MERTHYR

Milford
Haven

A40

A48

A4067

TYDFIL

A465

Llanelli

TAWE

NEATH

A470

A48

Tenby

SWANSEA

TAFF

BRISTOL CHANNEL

A48

CARDIFF

CRAY RES

YSTRADFELLTE RES

BEACONS RES

CANTREF RES

NAUADD RES

DOL-Y-GAER RES

LLYN-ON RES

| 0 km | 10 | 20 | 30 |
| 0 M | 15 | 30 | 45 |

N

Welsh Reservoirs

B4518, are probably the most popular and well-known reservoirs in Wales. The group consists of three lakes—Cerrig Llwydion, Llyn Carn and Llyn Gynin—and six reservoirs—Caban Coch (2170 acres), Dol-y-Mynach (40 acres), Garreg-Ddu (200 acres) and Pen-y-Garreg (124 acres). Claerwen (650 acres), Craig Goch (217 acres) and Dol-y-Mynach have brown trout which occur naturally, but the other reservoirs are restocked throughout the year. Groundbaiting and bubble floats are strictly prohibited and fly fishing only is allowed on all reservoirs except Craig Goch where spinning is also permitted. On Caban Coch and Claerwen rowing boats are available at £2.50 a day, and for £1 at Pen-y-Garreg. Tickets for all waters cost £20 (season), £6.60 (week), and £1.80 (day) (half-price for juniors and OAPs). For Claerwen, Craig Goch and Dol-y-Mynach, week tickets cost £4.40 and day tickets 90p and are available from the Elan Estate Officer, Elan Village, Rhayader, Powys, or from Mrs Hills, 'Kingsfield', Elan Valley.

For these reservoirs, as for all other Welsh reservoirs, it is advisable to check fishing dates, and local regulations with the controlling authority. Each reservoir has its particular bag and size limits, and also certain times of the year when fishing is best. Season tickets can be obtained from the addresses given, or from the WNWDA office

The Elan Valley Reservoirs, west of Rhayader on the B4518, are probably the most popular reservoirs in Wales. Pen-y-Garreg (above) is frequently restocked with brown trout and has boats for hire at £1 for the day.

for that area, or from local tackle dealers. As some reservoirs are small or are extremely popular, it is advisable to buy tickets in advance.

There are many more reservoirs in Wales than the ones covered in these pages. Those mentioned give a representation of the reservoirs throughout most regions, but the WNWDA can give more details of the others.

INFORMATION

WATER AUTHORITIES

Welsh National Water Development Authority, Cambrian Way, Brecon, Powys LD3 7HP. Tel 3181

Dee and Clwyd River Division, 2 Vicars Lane, Chester CHI 1QT. Tel 45004

Glamorgan River Division, Tremains House, Coychurch Rd, Bridgend, Mid-Glamorgan. Tel 2217

Gwynedd River Division, Highfield, Caernarvon. Tel 2247

South West Wales River Division, Penyfai House, 19 Penyfai Lane, Llanelli SA15 4EL. Tel 57031

Usk River Division, 4 St John St, Hereford. Tel 6313

Severn-Trent Water Authority, Severn Division, 64 Albert Rd, North Malvern, Worcs WR14 2BB. Tel 61511

North West Water Authority, Dawson House, Gt Sankey, Warrington WA5 3LW. Tel 724321

LICENCES

Welsh National Water Development Authority
Trout, freshwater fish and eels: season £3, juniors and OAPs £1.50, week £1.80, day 60p.

North West Water Authority
Non-migratory trout (brown, rainbow and char): season £2,

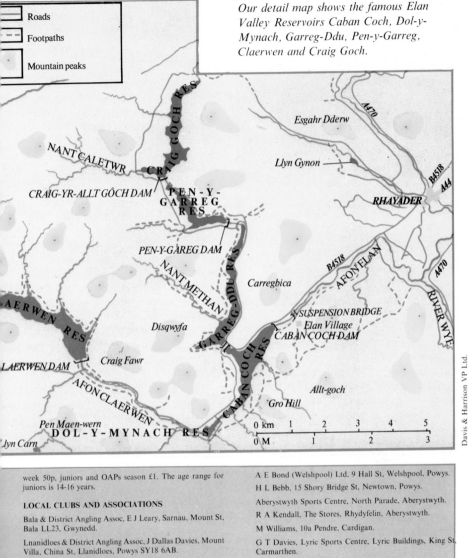

Our detail map shows the famous Elan Valley Reservoirs Caban Coch, Dol-y-Mynach, Garreg-Ddu, Pen-y-Garreg, Claerwen and Craig Goch.

Roads

Footpaths

Mountain peaks

CRAIG GOCH RES

NANT CALETWR

CRAIG-YR-ALLT GÔCH DAM

CRAIG

PEN-Y-GARREG RES

PEN-Y-GAREG DAM

NANT METHAN

GARREG-DDU RES

LAERWEN RES

Disqwyfa

Craig Fawr

LAERWEN DAM

AFON CLAERWEN

Pen Maen-wern

DOL-Y-MYNACH RES

llyn Carn

CABAN COCH RES

Esgahr Dderw

Llyn Gynon

RHAYADER

A470

B4518

444

Carregbica

B4518

AFON ELAN

A470

RIVER WYE

SUSPENSION BRIDGE

Elan Village

CABAN COCH DAM

Allt-goch

Gro Hill

0 km 1 2 3 4 5

0 M 1 2 3

Davis & Harrison VP Ltd.

week 50p, juniors and OAPs season £1. The age range for juniors is 14-16 years.

LOCAL CLUBS AND ASSOCIATIONS

Bala & District Angling Assoc, E J Leary, Sarnau, Mount St, Bala LL23, Gwynedd.

Lnanidloes & District Angling Assoc, J Dallas Davies, Mount Villa, China St, Llanidloes, Powys SY18 6AB.

Newport Angling Assoc, P Climo, 35 Claremont, Malpas, Newport, Gwent.

Rhayader Angling Assoc, G H Roberts, Belmullet, Rhayader, Powys.

TACKLE DEALERS & LICENCE AGENTS

H & G Supplies, 64 & 68 Countisbury Ave, Llanrumney, Cardiff.

Miles & Son, 172 Penarth Rd, Cardiff.

A Rees, 13 Alexandra Ave, Merthyr Tydfil.

F V Lewis, 29 Church Rd, Newport.

J D Davies, Mount Villa, China St, Llanidloes, Powys.

W J Vaughan, Penybank, Llanidloes, Powys.

A E Bond (Welshpool) Ltd, 9 Hall St, Welshpool, Powys.

H L Bebb, 15 Shory Bridge St, Newtown, Powys.

Aberystwyth Sports Centre, North Parade, Aberystwyth.

R A Kendall, The Stores, Rhydyfelin, Aberystwyth.

M Williams, 10a Pendre, Cardigan.

G T Davies, Lyric Sports Centre, Lyric Buildings, King St, Carmarthen.

D Evans, Post Office, St Clears, Carmarthen.

Country Sports, 3 Old Bridge, Haverfordwest.

B Llewellyn Stradey Sports, Llanelli Market, Llanelli.

E H Evans, Erwyd Garage, Ponterwyd, Aberystwyth.

Nash Sports, 41 St Helens Rd, Swansea.

W E Pugh, 82-84 High St, Bala.

D E Hawes, Oakley Arms, Blaenau Ffestiniog, Gwynedd.

J G & M Parry, Newsagent, Brynaber, Ffestiniog, Gwynedd.

J E Bradley, Joyces Jewellers, 13 Vale St, Denbigh.

J Ellis, Regal Sports Stores, Oswestry, Salop.

R G Forest, 12 Barker St, Shrewsbury.

South West Wales

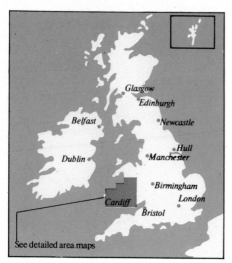

The South-West Wales River Division covers an area of approximately 1½ million acres, consisting of the old counties of Cardiganshire, Pembrokeshire and Carmarthenshire, now known as Dyfed. It is mostly a hilly area and the rivers are brisk, well-aerated spate streams. The most common species of fish caught in them are the Atlantic salmon, sewin (sea trout), brown trout, and some grayling.

From north to south the rivers of most note are the Clarach, Rheidol, Ystwyth, Wyre, Arth, Aeron, Teifi, Nevern, Gwaun, Western Cleddau, Eastern Cleddau, Taf, Tywi (including Gwili and Cothi), Gwendraeth Fach, Gwendraeth Fawr, Loughor and Tawe.

The River Clarach is two miles north of Aberystwyth and holds a few salmon, sewin and brown trout. Fishing rights are owned by local farmers who should be approached for permission to fish. It is reached along the B4512 road.

Aberystwyth is situated at the mouth of the rivers Rheidol and Yswyth. They contain salmon, sewin and brown trout, but of the two the Rheidol is the better. Most club

fishing is under the control of the Aberystwyth Angling Association or the Llanilar Angling Association. Fly, spinning and worm-ledger are the methods most used locally. Various lakes also lie within a 10-mile radius of Aberystwyth, and are stocked with trout. Day-tickets for these can be obtained from the above clubs.

Aberaeron is at the mouth of the River Aeron, which has a good run of sewin from June onwards and also holds plenty of small brown trout. As with all these small coastal streams, the fishing is best on falling water following a spate.

The Wyre and Arth

The Wyre and Arth are small spate streams north of the town. Fishing in the lower reaches of the Aeron is available with a daily or a weekly ticket from the Aberaeron Angling Association, but farmers control the middle reaches. There is good access to the Aeron valley via the A482 road.

The River Teifi, 70 miles long with a watershed of some 389 square miles, is one of the two principal rivers of South-West Wales. Cardigan is at the mouth and the A484 gives good access to the lower 10 miles. The main angling species are salmon, sewin, brown trout and a few grayling (between Lampeter and Llandyssul). Salmon run to beyond Tregaron, but the sewin do not penetrate in numbers much higher than Llandssul. The best brown trout fishing is from Lampeter up to the source. Regarding seasons, there is a small run of big sea trout in mid-May but the main run starts a month later. Some salmon are caught throughout the season, and brown trout fishing in the upper reaches is best in spring and early summer. Fly, spinning and worm-ledger are the most successful methods on the Teifi.

The Teifi Pools are six lakes situated on the Teifi headwaters about five miles east of Pontrhydfendigaid. These lakes are stocked with rainbows to supplement the native brown trout, and fly fishing only is allowed. Day tickets costing 75p are available in Pontrhydfendigaid.

Most of the Teifi is fishable on short-term permits issued through the clubs or the hotels. The Teifi Trout Association at Newcastle Emlyn controls parts of the lower reaches, the Llandyssul Angling Association Ltd and the Llanbyther Angling Club control extensive parts of the middle reaches, and the Tregaron Angling Association and the Strata Florida Angling Association have long stretches of the upper waters.

Teifi spins well on falling water following a small spate. Fly fishing after sundown is often deadly in July and August, while worm is nearly always effective during floods.

Newport is at the mouth of the River Nevern which contains salmon, sewin and brown trout. The best of the fishing is controlled by clubs or hotels, but access to the upper reaches is directly through farms. Visitors' permits can be obtained through the Newport and District Angling Association, at Dinas Cross. The A487 road reaches much of the Nevern valley, but access to the river is rugged.

The Gwaun at Fishguard

At Fishguard, the River Gwaun is a little sewin and trout river with some salmon late in the season. It is accessible from Lower Fishguard or anywhere along the Gwaun valley via the B4313 road. Fishing permission must be obtained from farmers.

The Western Cleddau lies north of Haverfordwest and contains sewin, brown trout and a small run of salmon. The Pembrokeshire Angling Association controls the best of the fishing, including the tributaries, and gives details of access points when issuing tickets. Night fishing with fly for sewin is often good from July onwards. Access to the Cleddau valley is via the B4330.

The Eastern Cleddau enters Milford Haven from the eastern shore and is the better of the two Cleddaus. Although the lower reaches around Canaston are in private hands, the visitor can obtain the right to fish from farms and pubs. The middle reaches are gained via the B4313 Fishguard to Narberth road. There is good sewin fishing after the summer spates, and the rare burbot may exist in the lower reaches.

Day tickets are available for Teifi Pools, wild moorland lakes stocked with trout.

Spectrum Colour Library

St Clears marks the lower parts of the River Taf, a quiet-paced little river carrying good runs of sewin, some salmon, and plenty of herring-sized brown trout. The upper reaches, between Llanfalteg and Llanglydwen, are pleasantly remote and reached on foot along the abandoned railway track. To reach it by car one should take the A478 then turn down the side roads. Tickets for the lower reaches are obtainable from the Whitland Angling Association in Whitland.

The Tywi is the second chief river of South-West Wales. It is about 60 miles long and drains a watershed of approximately 514 square miles. The water tends to be clearer than that of Teifi, and the river is slightly larger. It is a sewin river *par excellence* with specimens up to 17lb or more. One also finds salmon, sewin, brown trout and a few pike in the lower reaches, and a large sturgeon over 300lb was once caught on rod and line. Fly fishing, spinning and worm-ledgering are the main techniques used.

Visitors to the Tywi

Although much of the Tywi is private there is a club and hostel fishing in the lower, middle and upper reaches. Visitors' tickets for the lower reaches are issued by the Carmarthen and District Angling Association, for the middle reaches by the Llandeilo Angling Association, and by the Llandovery Angling Association for the upper reaches. Access to the Tywi valley is along the A40 which runs between Carmarthen and Llandeilo.

Kidwelly lies near the mouths of the small rivers Gwendraeth Fach and Gwendraeth Fawr. These streams are fished mostly for brown trout, although sewin and a few salmon also run upstream. Permission to fish is from the farmers. Access to the Fach valley is along the A484 road, and to the middle reaches of the Fawr along the B4309 road.

The River Loughor is a once-polluted stream that is recovering its runs of salmon and sewin, and is also stocked with brown

trout. The river enters its estuary at Pontardulais, and the river valley is reached from minor roads leading off the A483. Fortunately, nearly all the fishing is in the hands of clubs such as the Pontardulais and District Angling Association and the Llangyfelach and District Angling Association which issue tickets to visitors.

The Tawe recovers

Swansea is on the River Tawe, a river that was grossly polluted, but which since 1958 has started to run sewin and a few salmon. The brown trout fishing is also improving. Access to the river valley is along the A4607 road. Most of the water is controlled by such clubs as the Tawe and Tributaries Angling Association, or the Swansea and Pontardawe AA which issue permits.

Sea fishing

Sea fishing around South-West Wales is affected by the North Atlantic Drift—a

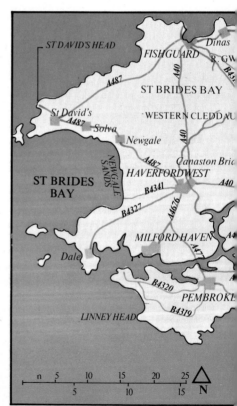

Our area map of the streams, rivers and mountain lakes of South-West Wales.

fairly warm current. Cod and haddock, which like cold water, are not found, therefore, and their place is taken by bass and pollack which prefer warmer water.

Aberystwyth is notable in having the only offshore reefs in Cardigan Bay to hold regular shoals of excellent black bream. These reefs, the Cynfelin Patches, lie one to five miles offshore, and are visited by bass, tope, thornback, stingray, and monkfish.

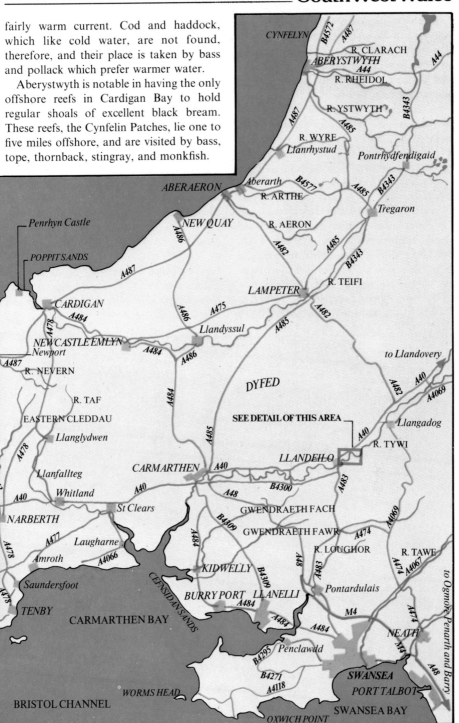

South West Wales

Beach fishing can be enjoyed from Aberystwyth down to Llanrhystyd and New Quay for bass, mackerel and flatfish. Farther southwards the coast becomes rocky and the rock-loving species such as pollack, conger and wrasse may also be added to the bag.

Farther south again, Cardigan is met on the estuary of the Teifi. This contains exceptionally good bass together with mullet and flounders. An $18\frac{1}{2}$lb bass was caught by a salmon fisher in 1956. Lug can be dug on the foreshore at Poppit or by the old lifeboat slip at Penrhyn.

South from Cardigan, the coast is mainly rock-bound and most anglers fish from the sandy beaches at Newport or from the breakwaters in Fishguard Harbour. Lug and razorfish can be obtained at low tide. Bass, flatfish and whiting are taken in autumn.

There are several good beaches around St David's as well as rock venues on St David's

Head. Lug can be obtained at Solva Harbour which is also a convenient point for launching towed dinghies. Newgale Sands is a well-known location for bass fishing at night using beachcasting techniques.

Razorfish and lug can be dug at Dale to fish beaches on the Dale peninsula, and boats may be hired at Dale and at Hobb's Point to fish the sheltered Milford Haven. Bass, flatfish, thornbacks, mullet, conger, mackerel and most other species are found in the Haven, including herring in season.

Surf-casting venues

The fishing from Linney Head to Worms Head embraces Carmarthen Bay and the resorts of Tenby and Saundersfoot. Access to most of this water is on long sandy beaches which are popular as surf-casting venues for bass, flats and other inshore species. Boats are obtainable at Tenby and Saundersfoot, or towed dinghies can be

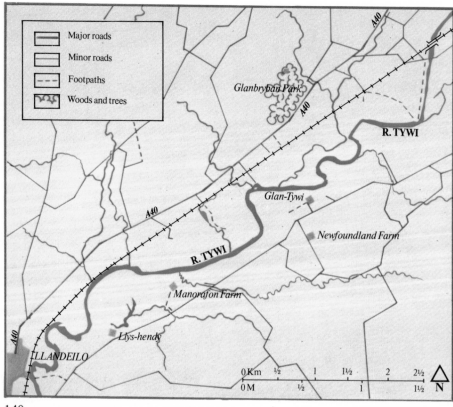

launched. The beaches between Amroth and Laugharne are often productive of good flounders and have yielded ray to 14lb.

Cefn Sidan Sands, accessible from Burry Port, is an extensive stretch of shallow water beach fishing producing bass, dabs and flounder. On the Gower Peninsula the venues are an interesting mixture of rock and beach locations with good bass reported from Worms Head.

Lug can be dug on Swansea beach and in the Burry estuary at Penschawdd. Good fishing is reported from Swansea and Port Talbot breakwaters; also from the rocks at Ogmore, Barry and Penarth. Codling tend to frequent the Bristol Channel and figure in the catches, while porbeagle sharks are frequently docked at the Swansea Sea Angling Centre. Anglers fishing off Oxwich Point have had considerable success with the black bream shoals.

Spectrum Colour Library

(Above) The tidal Teifi at Cardigan, where salmon and sea trout run each season.
(Below left) Detail map shows a stretch of the Tywi at Llandeilo. Open on day-ticket.

INFORMATION
WATER AUTHORITY
Welsh National Water Development Authority, South-West Wales River Division, Penyfai House, Penyfai Lane, Dyfed. Tel: Llanelli 57031
LICENCES
Each river has been placed in one of five different classes on the basis of potential and general quality of the fishing. The best waters are in Class A and the poorest in Class I. Class A licence permits an angler to fish for all species in all waters in the area and costs £21.60 (season), juniors and OAPs £10.80, week £10.80, day £3.60. Categories B to E allow fishing for all species but in progressively fewer selected rivers, e.g. a salmon/sewin Class C licence (covering also trout, char, coarse fish and eels) entitles the holder to fish the Teifi and Tywi plus lesser rivers. Category F licence is for non-migratory trout and costs £3 (season), juniors and OAPs £1.50, week £1.80, day 60p. Category G is for coarse fish: season £1.80, juniors and OAPs 90p, day 60p.
Close seasons: rod and line fishing, salmon and sewin 7 October to 10 March; coarse fish and eels 14 March to 16 June.
Size limits: Fishery byelaws are currently under review but stipulate at present a universal 6in for every kind of fish.
LOCAL CLUBS AND ASSOCIATIONS
'Aberarth Angling Assoc, E Griffiths, Fron Villa, Aberarth.
Aberaeron Angling Assoc, J H Evans, 1 Alban Square, Aberaeron, Dyfed.
Aberystwyth Angling Assoc, D A Williams, Rhandir, Penrhyncoch, Aberystwyth.
Carmarthen and District Angling Club, D T Lewis, 25 Park Hall, Carmarthen.
Llanilar Angling Assoc, W M Jones, Bryn Ystwyth, Llanilar, Aberystwyth.
Llandyssul Angling Assoc Ltd, A. Jones, Siop-y-Jones, Llandyssul, Dyfed.
Llanybyther Angling Club, R. Hogan, c/o Lloyds Bank Ltd, Llanybyther.
Llandeilo Angling Assoc Ltd, D Richards, Llys Newydd, Bethlehem Rd, Ffairfach, Llandeilo.

Llandovery Angling Assoc, D B Howells, Pentre House, Myddfai, near Llandovery.
Llangyfelach and District Angling Assoc, W L Griffiths, Glanmorfa, Penycae Lane, Loughor.
Newport and District Angling Assoc, C. C. Gaddum, Byfield, Dinas Cross.
Pembrokeshire Angling Assoc, A R Munt, 72 City Rd, Haverfordwest.
Pontardawe and District Angling Assoc, R H Lockyer, 8 Bwilfa Rd, Ynystawe, Swansea.
Pontardulais and District Angling Assoc, B J Davies, 23 James St, Pontardulais.
Strata Florida Angling Assoc, D Llovd Jones, Rhyd Teifai, Pontrhydfendigaid, Dyfed.
Swansea Amateur Anglers' Assoc, E R Coombs, Bryn Cothi Lodge, Abergorlech, Carmarthen, Dyfed.
Swansea Sea Angling Club, R Griffiths, 131 Rhondda St, Mount Pleasant, Swansea, West Glamorgan.
Tawe and Tributaries Angling Assoc, K Jones, 21 St David's Rd, Ystalyfera, Swansea.
Teifi Trout Assoc, Emlyn House, Newcastle Emlyn.
Tregaron Angling Assoc, Barclays Bank, Tregaron.
LICENCE DISTRIBUTORS
J Evans & Son, 1 Alban Square, Aberaeron.
E J Evans, Post Office, Crosswood, Aberystwyth.
M Williams, 10a Pendre, Cardigan.
D Meynard, 11 Lammas St, Carmarthen.
Tom's Sports Shop, 10 Market St, Haverfordwest.
Megicks & Herbert, Corner Shop, Lampeter.
R Thomas, Sports Outfitter, Stepney St, Llanelli.
W A Thomas, 6 Kings Rd, Llandovery.
Joseph Philpin & Sons, 66 Rhosmaen St, Llandeilo.
J Jones, Alma Stores, Llandyssul.
C Jones, Emlyn Boot Stores, Newcastle Emlyn.
J Llewellyn Havard & Sons, Newport, Dyfed.
J Morgan, Post Office, Pontrhydfendigaid.
D I Williams, Ironmonger, Dulais Square, Pontardulais.
D Evans, Post Office, St Clears, Dyfed.
Central Sports House, 113 St Helens Rd, Swansea.
Linnard Sports, High St, Swansea.
A Morgan, Caron Stores, Tregaron.

Lough Erne System

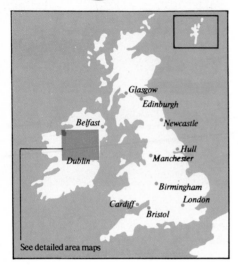

See detailed area maps

Ireland's prime angling is located in the 2,500 square miles of the Erne system—an extensive system of lakes, rivers and streams. It extends south to Dublin, west to the River Shannon, north to Loch Erne, and east to Carlingford. The myriad lakes and rivers are linked to the Boyne system—many of them are still largely unexploited.

Rules and facilities

Coarse angling in Eire is free. There are no rod licences or close seasons, although statutory fishery boards work to protect salmon and trout. Live-baiting is now prohibited, and no more than two rods may be used at a time. A recent bye-law was passed after the discovery that some anglers had not been returning species in danger of

Irish Tourist Board

(Left) A typical stretch of water in Co Cavan. (Right) Lough Owel (2,547 acres) in Co Westmeath, has trout and pike.

running into short supply, such as pike.

Most lakes have signposted approach roads, or are located alongside main or secondary roads. Car parking is easy, and when an angler wishes to cross fields, a polite request to the owner is rarely refused. The only enemy to the angler is the angler who litters, or carelessly lights fires and leaves gates open, allowing cattle to stray. The Irish Tourist Board (Bord Failte) maintains an advice service for visitors, and maps and advice on bait and techniques are provided by the Inland Fisheries Trust, a semi-state promotion organization offering membership for £3 a year. Guesthouses catering for visiting anglers can also help with directions.

Belturbet

Belturbet is a very good centre for coarse fishing and commands a maze of Lough (L) Erne lakes, linking streams, and the main River Erne. Boats are available on adjacent lakes, while the slow-flowing River Erne has ample bank facilities, and deep pools containing bream, roach and some pike. Putiaghan Lake, 2½ miles south, on the Belturbet-Butlers Bridge road, is a first-class tench fishery with fish of up to 6lb, and is fished from both stands and boats. North of Belturbet, Lough Shanncory and L Round, near Putiaghan, have pike to 10lb, with roach, rudd and perch. Farther south, by Milltown, L Arden and L Drumany have good fishing for bream, roach, perch and some pike. Richard Harris, Naughton, Belturbet, can give more details.

The numerous lakes of the Erne system are all within 3 miles of Butlers Bridge which is 4 miles from Cavan town, and on the River Annalee. Derryheen, 2 miles away, has excellent bream and roach fishing and bank fishing along the River Annalee offers an abundance of small roach. The up-river stretch near Ballyhaise also has good swims.

Cavan town lies 5 miles east of the maze of lakes of the Erne system which, all together,

are known as Lough Oughter. Favourite fishing places are found in Killykeen Forest Park which has good bank fishing for bream, and other waters with large stocks of bream and roach are L Rann, L Killagowan, L Carratraw and L Inchin. L Killymooney in Cavan town has fine tench to 4lb and bream to 3lb. Mrs B O'Hanlon, St Martin's, Creghan, Cavan, can give further details.

Killashandra, 2 miles from L Oughter, offers the same fishing as the other towns mentioned. In addition, there is L Green in the town providing good tench, L Tullyguide which is a good bream water, and L Derreskit and L Dunaweel, both good for bream and roach. Contact Matty Gaffney in Killashandra, for information.

Source of the Erne

L Gowna is a big dispersed lake of 1,000 acres on the Cavan-Longford border. Primarily a coarse fish water, it also holds brown trout and pike, and fishing is excellent, although algae growth is sometimes troublesome. Arvagh, within 3 miles, is where the Erne flow starts. L Garty has limited bank facilities on 500 acres, and there is good roach fishing in L Lisney and the

Lough Erne System _____

*Map of the Lough Erne system
from the N. Ireland border to Dublin.*

River Erne at Sallachan Bridge and Iron
Bridge. L Blue Gate is good for roach and
bream. Additional information can be
obtained from Jimmy Sloan at Lough
Gowna Post Office, Co Cavan.

In Co Monaghan, Clones has unlimited
bank space on the River Finn, chiefly near
Anlore, 4 miles east at Annie's Bridge. Here
the river is fast-flowing and weedy in places
and holds many roach and rudd. Five small
lakes in the area might be worth exploring,
but no boats are available. For further
details, contact Mrs A Woods, Clones.

River Dromore

Cootehill, Bailieborough, Shercock and
Ballybay form a triangle covering 60 square
miles. In Cootehill, there is good fishing on
the River Dromore flowing from Ballybay,
and excellent bream and roach fishing in L
White, at Baird's Shore, near Ballybay.
Other lakes are L Black and L Dromore,
both of 200 acres, L Inner and L Tacker, L
Mullanarry and L Corkeeran, which have
good roach fishing, and L Lisnalong which
has just one boat. Nearer Cootehill, L
Killyudran is good for bream and roach, and
L Drumlona is good for bream and pike.

Bailieborough has L Church of 150 acres
with adequate bank facilities and 4 boats, as
well as L Castle, L Skeagh, L Drumkerry,
and L Galbolie. L Sillan, 800 acres, is
alongside Shercock with fair pike and
bream, seven boats available, and bank
space for 60 rods. For further information
contact B Grennan, The Beeches, Cootehill,
or M Brady, Bailieborough, Co Cavan.

Monaghan town is a good centre for
fishing the Ballybay area which has the
Dromore River and 6 lakes. They are all
good for bream, rudd and perch, but no
boats are available. L Major, 800 acres, is
largely reserved for trout, although restricted coarse fishing is permitted, while L
Mullarney and L White provide good
bream, McCaughery, 1 Highfield Close,
Killygoan Co Monagham or G Maguire

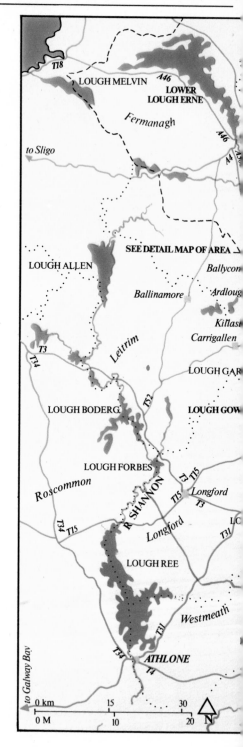

Lough Erne System

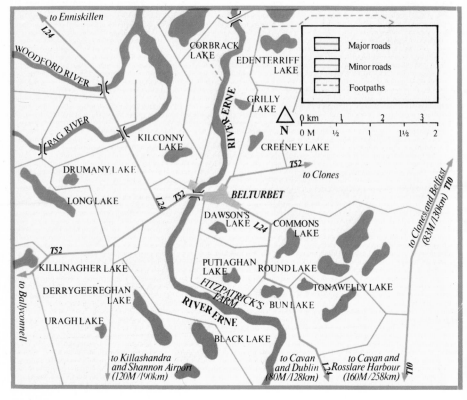

in Ballybay can give information.

Carrickmacross has many lakes, L Monalty, a shallow, weedy lake, has first-class bream, rudd, and rudd-bream hybrids, and nearby L Corcrin has bream. In the town, L Lisaniske is also good for bream, while Rahan's Lake, with fishing stands, provides good bream and pike. Contact Tom Ward, Coolfore, Carrickmacross, Co Monaghan, for further details.

Ballinamore, Carrigallen and Ballyconnel form another triangle west of the Erne system proper. The River Woodford, slow-moving near Ballyconnel, has high quality fishing for pike, bream, roach, perch and some rudd. L Cranaghan (50 acres), and L Clonty, near Ardlougher, have good fishing but limited bank facilities.

At Carrigallen, the little-fished L Glasshouse, 100, acres, is worth exploring by boat, and L Rockfield and L Gulladoo have good promise for bream and roach. Contact

J J Dolan, Carrigallen, Co Leitrim. Ballinamore has 10 lakes with some boats and attractive bank facilities, and L Carn at Ballyconnel has tench of up to $4\frac{1}{2}$lb. Ivan Price, Ballinamore, can give directions.

First-class boat fishing

L Muckno, near Castleblayney, offers roughly 1,000 acres of first-class boat fishing with many bays for pike and bream. Trolling for pike is popular and 3 boats are available. Contact the Secretary of the Bawn and District Gun and Angling Club at Gortubber Post Office, Castleblayney.

Drumconrath in Co Meath, has many lakes, known as the Ballyhoe lakes, holding good stocks of bream and rudd, and tench to 6lb. L Mentrim is good for tench and L Corstown for bream, while L Bracken has fine rudd-bream hybrids. Contact Jim Meade, Drumconrath, for further details.

Virginia in Co Cavan has fishing on L Ramor (800 acres), for fine perch and pike,

Bill Howes

(Above) Roach fishing on the slow-flowing River Erne in Belturbet, shown in our detail map of the Belturbet area (left).

with 6 boats available. Ramor feeds the River Blackwater, a River Boyne tributary. It is mainly a trout river but has pike in deep slow holes along a 15-mile stretch from Kells to Navan. Bank fishing is endless although angling leases are held mainly by trout clubs in Navan, Kells and Dublin. Further information from the motel at Ramor.

Mullingar, in Co Westmeath, is beside 3 big lakes, Derrevaragh (2,768 acres), Owel (2,547 acres) and Ennell (3,450 acres). They hold pike and perch and are good for trolling, but are mainly trout lakes. Ennell is heavily polluted. L Patrick, beside Multyfarnham, 6 miles from Mullingar, has small tench and is heavily fished. L Annalla, near Delvin, 10 miles north east of Mullingar, has good tench and rudd.

Enfield in Co Meath has a canal with shallow clear water and plenty of bank space. It is difficult to fish, but the angler will be rewarded with rudd and tench to 6lb.

INFORMATION

WATER AUTHORITY
There is no controlling water authority, but the Irish Tourist Board (Bord Failte) maintains an advisory service. Irish Tourist Board, Ireland House, New Bond St, London W1. Tel 493 3201.
Bord Failte, Baggot St Bridge. Dublin 2. Tel 76587.
Bord Failte, Stephen St, Sligo, Co Sligo. Tel 2436.
Inland Fisheries Trust Incorporated, Mobhi Boreen, Glasnevin, Dublin 9, Eire.
LOCAL CLUBS AND ASSOCIATIONS
Belturbet Coarse Angling Club, Mr O'Harris, Belturbet, Co Cavan.
LICENCES
No licence is required in Eire for brown or rainbow trout fishing, or for coarse or sea fishing. There is no close season for coarse fishing. The cost of licences for salmon and sea trout fishing is as follows:
Annual licence (all districts) £10, annual (valid in district of issue only) £5, 21-day licence (all districts) £5, seven-day licence (all districts) £3, late season licence valid July 1 onwards (all districts) £7, in district of issue only £3.
Licences may be obtained from the Department of Agriculture and Fisheries, Fisheries Division, Agriculture House, Kildare St, Dublin 2. Tel 789011.
TACKLE DEALERS
Fagan's, Main St, Belturbet, Co Cavan.
Allen's The Diamond, Belturbet, Co Cavan.
Magee's, Main St, Belturbet, Co Cavan.
Phil's Fishing Tackle, Main St, Ballinamore, Co Leitrim.
J J O'Reilly's, Main St, Canan Town, Co Cavan.
Garnett and Keegan's, Parliament St, Dublin 2.
Rory's Fishing Tackle, 17a Temple Bar, Fleet St, Dublin 2.
O'Malley's Fishing Tackle, 33 Domnick St, Mullingar, Co Westmeath.
Most tackle dealers do not stock maggots, but the main distributor of maggots is only 5 miles from Belturbet. Irish Angling Services Ltd, Ardlougher, Co Cavan.

Lough Erne System

Shannon System

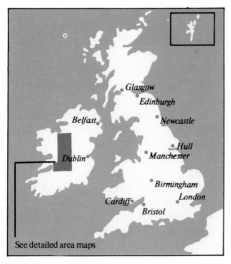

See detailed area maps

The River Shannon is approximately 160 miles long, running south from a pothole at Derrylahan, Co. Cavan, to a long estuary at Limerick, and then on to the Atlantic Ocean. The catchment area is 6,060 square miles, with tributaries of 1,130 miles.

The river bulges at places into great lakes (called loughs) and the incoming rivers and streams are fed by springs that rise in the rich limestone plains of central Ireland. It is a slow-flowing river: over almost 100 miles the drop in level is only 55ft from Lough Allen to Lough Derg.

The Shannon is now known as a coarse angling playground, but oddly enough, fishing only started, perhaps, with the increasing popularity of cruising holidays. The Guinness firm invested £1m in craft and encouraged French and German holidaymakers. They came equipped with bait and spinning rods and were delighted to find very large pike, perch, bream, rudd and, in some special places, big tench.

Unfortunately their enthusiasm led them to unfortunate practices—those of handling five or six rods at a time, and of removing large quantities of pike from the river. Eventually, to preserve the pike fishing, a bye-law was passed in October 1977 limiting each angler to two rods.

In the upper reaches of the Shannon, Drumshanbo, in Co Leitrim, just south of Lough Allen, is the major fishing base. Lough Allen (18 square miles) has both boat and bank fishing, while Drumshanbo has 12 listed lakes for coarse fish within three miles of the town, with car and foot access points signposted. Two miles west of Drumshanbo, the fast water below the sluices at Ballintra Bridge is good for pike. Catches of pike to 30lb are common, and James Earley of Mount Allen caught a 36lb pike there. At Lough Allen, local angler P. J. Reynolds caught 12 pike weighing 117lb in half a day.

Most of the lakes around Drumshanbo have only bank fishing, but Acres Lake will be available to boat anglers when a disused canal going south from Battlebridge is reopened. For further details of fishing in this area, contact Joe Mooney, Drumshanbo, or B. McGourty, Carrick Road, Drumshanbo, who will always help.

Carrick-on-Shannon

Carrick-on-Shannon is an important crossing point and angling centre on the River Shannon. A valuable angling tributary, the River Boyle, leads eight miles north-west to Lough Key, taking in Lough Drumharlow and Lough Oakport, both offering good boat fishing for bream, rudd, pike and perch. There are two stretches of bank fishing here with very good bream; one mile of bank from Knockvicar Bridge to Lough Key, and the Upper Boyle which feeds into Lough Key. Lough Key (six square miles) has pike, perch and rudd for boat anglers, with bank fishing in abundance around the lake, and 1½ miles on the Upper Boyle towards Boyle town. For further information contact Maria Finlay at the Tourist Office in Boyle, or one of the

Shannon System

local boat hirers who will always help.

Carrick-on-Shannon has a wealth of fishing from banks as well as from platforms located in reed-fringed pools in the town area. Cruiser traffic is busy here, but does not interfere with angling lines, except at narrow bridges. For more details contact the Tourist Office.

The Shannon then winds through Lough Curry for five miles to Jamestown, a good angling spot, with faster water and sluices. From here there is 3¾ miles of good bank fishing to Drumsna, but downstream the wildness of the Shannon becomes apparent and is perhaps best left alone by the angler.

Good angling starts again nine miles downstream. Just upriver of Rooskey, the branching Carrandoe lakes offer good boat fishing and are large enough to accommodate many anglers. Rooskey offers abundant bank fishing for bream, rudd and

(*Below*) *Lough Ree, 21 miles long, holds rudd × bream hybrids of 5lb.*

pike, and has numerous boats for hire on adjoining lakes. Downstream of Rooskey to L. Forbes there is good boat angling with bank sites on the northern shore where Rinn River flows in. For details of this area contact Mrs Duffy, Killianiker House, Rooskey.

Strokestown is not situated on the Shannon proper, but is a fine centre for boat or bank fishing at least 10 lakes. Notable among them are L. Cloonfree and L. Kilglass, especially good for boat fishing, and L. Lea. George Gearty, Conner House, Strokestown, can give details.

Fishing by the lock

Termonbarsy and Clondra, three miles below the Shannon outflow from L. Forbes, are familiar angling locations with bank places on both sides of the lock system. Clondra, however, has recently become polluted.

From this point, the seven-mile stretch leading to L. Ree has mainly unnamed and unknown angling points where the banks are often unstable and the locality wild.

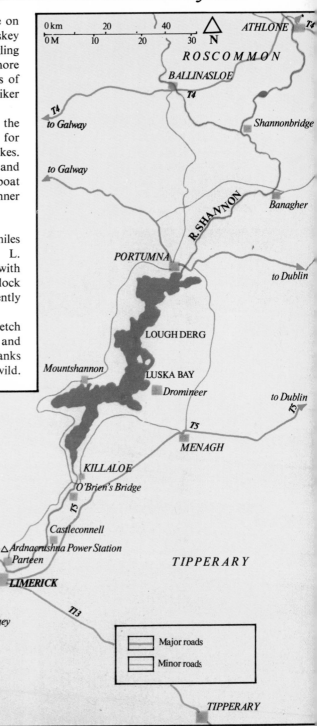

P. H. Ward/Natural Science Photos

Shannon System

Lough Ree is too big and uncharted to interest the bank angler, except perhaps at Anchor Bay and Cureen Point.

Lanesboro, where the Shannon enters L. Ree, has everything to recommend it as an angling centre. It is heavily fished, with anglers on some days queueing up.

In the town, fishing is on the left bank from the lake to the power station. At this point there is a hot water effluent from the power station and in the early season, the warm water attracts specimen bream, rudd, bream-rudd hybrids and perch. The Irish record bream-rudd hybrid, 5lb 13½oz, was

caught here and no fewer than 38 specimen bream up to 8lb 12oz. Since 1970 Lanesboro has become widely known for big tench. Up to 1974 it had recorded 138 specimens to 7lb 13¼oz with at least that number since then. The fishing bank extends from the power station on the left bank into the lake. Contact Tony D'Alton, 24 The Green, Lanesboro.

Lough Ree, from Lanesboro to Athlone, is 20 miles long, with expansions on both sides that are large enough to be called lakes. Most popular coarse fish species are found everywhere. The lough is fished from boats and cruisers strong enough to withstand sudden squalls. It can be a fearsome place in a storm and is not recommended to anyone with a small boat.

Most of L. Ree boat angling, mainly for pike, starts immediately upstream from Athlone. There is also a lot of trolling in the mile-long river stretch. The banks

Bill Howes

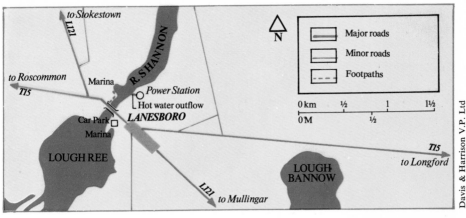

Davis & Harrison V.P. Ltd

(*Above*) *Detail map of the Lanesboro area between Lough Ree and the Shannon.*
(*Below, far left*) *Salmon spinning on the River Shannon. UDN has hit salmon of late but the Irish record stands at 57lb.*
(*Below*) *A match in progress on the fine coarse fishing venue at Ballinasloe.*

Irish Tourist Board

around the lake are firm, especially in the west, with a notable rudd spot on Charlie's Island, near the Jolly Mariner marina. Passing cruisers can be troublesome and boat anglers are advised to go three miles upstream to L. Coosan and L. Killinure, into a system of inner lakes holding plenty of bream, rudd, tench and hybrids.

Downstream from Athlone's lock and weir, still within the town, there is bank space on both sides. The west side is particularly good as is a disused canal nearby. Boat owners pass idle hours fishing from decks for perch at the lock. Three miles south of Athlone, Wren's Island has fine fishing from the main bank, but boat fishing is better. Big rudd live here. One of 2lb 12½oz was taken in 1976, as well as a 4lb 11½oz rudd-bream hybrid and a 6lb 2oz tench. Barry Brill, 31 Battery Heights, Athlone, or Aidan Gallagher, the secretary of the Athlone Anglers Association, can give further information.

Shannonbridge

At Shannonbridge, 12 miles below Athlone, the River Suck flows in from the west. It is an important sport river, and Ballinasloe is very popular with anglers. There is abundant bank fishing for tench, perch and bream, while The Suck at Culliagh, Coreen, and upriver at Derrycahill are favourite places for bream and rudd. The hot water at Shannonbridge produces good bream, rudd and tench.

153

Shannon System

Patrick Lawless, 4 Hillcrest, Ballinasloe, Shannonbridge or Dermot Killeen, Shannonbridge, can give more details.

Banagher is 10 miles south of the River Suck inflow to the Shannón and 20 miles south of Athlone. It is a good centre with lots of bank, footbridges and platforms.

Portumna

Portumna, at the north end of the vast L. Derg, has a mixed reputation for coarse angling. Silt from the peat bogs is continually being washed down, and then stirred up by cruiser traffic, so that angling is stopped at certain times. This does not mean, however, that angling is always poor. The main disadvantage is perhaps that local knowledge, while being essential, is in short supply. There is no local club contact to give information.

Lough Derg (50 square miles) is so big that most of the Norfolk Broads could be fitted into it, and angling space left over. A lake for boat and cruising anglers, it is dangerous in sudden storms, and has shoals. Dromineer on the east shore and Mountshannon on the west are locations for modest bank and safe boat fishing. Cruising anglers should try fishing at anchor at Luska Bay, six miles north of Dromineer, for truly big pike.

Killaloe, mostly a marina area with heavy boat traffic, is not recommended,

though an enquiring angler with time to spare could find surprises in many quiet, unfished spots.

The head race from Parteen, leading to the Ardnacrusha Power Station, has substantial stocks of perch, bream and rudd, with pike, while at O'Brien's Bridge, eight miles north of Limerick city, and at Plassey, there is an abundance of bream, rudd, hybrids and pike. Joe Maloney at O'Brien's Bridge can give more details of the area.

A large-capacity keepnet ready for the day's catch on the River Shannon at Shannonbridge, Co Offaly.

Irish Tourist Board

INFORMATION

WATER AUTHORITY
There is no controlling water authority, but the Irish Tourist Board (Bord Failte) maintains an advisory service.
Irish Tourist Board, Ireland House, New Bond Street, London W1. Tel. 493 3201.
Bord Failte, Baggot Street Bridge, Dublin 2. Tel. 765871.
Bord Failte, Stephen Street, Sligo, Co. Sligo. Tel. 2436.
Inland Fisheries Trust Incorporated, Balnagowan House, Mobhi Boreen, Glasnevin, Dublin 9.
Tourist Information Office, 17 Church Street, Athlone, Co. Westmeath.
Shannonside Tourist Information Office, 92 O'Connell Street, Limerick.
Tourist Information Office, Kickham St, Menagh. Tel. 610.
Information Office, Shannon Airport, Limerick, Tel. 61664.
Other offices are found in the following towns: Ballinasloe (May-Sept) Tel 2332, Balybunion (June-Sept) Tel 75, Boyle (May-Sept) Tel 145, Killaloe (July-Aug) Tel 76155, Longford (May-Sept) Tel 6566, Portumna (July-Aug) Tel 54, Roscommon (June-Sept) Tel 6356, Tipperary (July-Aug) Tel 51457.

LOCAL CLUBS AND ASSOCIATIONS
Midland Angling Club, B. Brill, 31 Battery Heights, Athlone, Co. Westmeath.
Banagher Tourist Association, D Corcoran, Banagher, Co. Offaly.
Carrick-on-Shannon Angling Association, S O'Rourke, Mullaghmore, Carrick-on-Shannon, Co Leitrim.
Drumshanbo Angling Club, J N Mooney, Drumshanbo, Co. Leitrim.
Kilgarvan Anglers' Club, Mrs B Fox, Brocka, Ballinderry, Nenagh, Co Tipperary.
Lanesboro Tourist Development Association, T. D'Alton, 24 The Green, Lanesboro, Co Longford
O'Brien's Bridge Angling Club, J Moloney, O'Brien's Bridge, Co Clare.
Portumna Angling Club, G Kinny, Palmerston Stores, Portumna, Co Galway.
Shannonbridge Anglers' Association, D Killeen, Shannonbridge, Co Offaly.
Scariff, Mountshannon and Whitegate Angling Club, J Murphy, Mountshannon Road, Scariff, Co Clare.
Ballinasloe Angling Committee, P Lawless, Bracknagh, Ballinasloe, Co Galway.

TACKLE DEALERS
J Dolan, The Creel, Carrick-on-Shannon, Co Leitrim.
Holts, Carrick-on-Shannon, Co Leitrim.
Conroys, Rooskey, Co Roscommon.
W T Wynne, Anglers House, Boyle, Co Roscommon.
McNally's, Lanesboro, Co Longford
D Connell, Mardyke Street, Athlone, Co Westmeath.
E Foy and Sons, Church St, Athlone, Co Westmeath.
O'Malleys, Dominick St, Athlone, Co Westmeath.
T Salmon, Ballinasloe, Co Galway.
G Kenny, Portumna, Co Galway.
A J Doherty, The Bridge, Ballina, Co Mayo.
P J Walkin, Tone Street, Ballina, Co Mayo.
P Maughan, Enniscrone, Co Sligo.
Barton Smith, Hyde Bridge, Sligo.
F. Nelson and Son, Castle Street, Sligo.
J J Killeen, Shannonbridge, Co Offaly.
M O'Sullivan, Moore Street, Kilrush, Co Clare.
Nestor Bros, 28 O'Connell Street, Limerick.
Limerick Sports Stores, 10 William Street, Limerick.

Eire-Sea Fishing

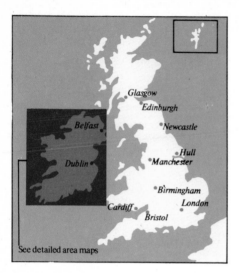

Glasgow
Edinburgh
Belfast
Newcastle
Dublin
Hull
Manchester
Birmingham
Cardiff
London
Bristol

See detailed area maps

Irish sea angling is very successful – both in terms of statistics and of variety. The Irish coastline covers 3,000 miles, not all of which is fishable, but which offers a mixture of vast beaches, offshore waters and bays, and rugged stretches leading to wrecks such as the *Lusitania* 10-12 miles off the Cork coast, and others off Donegal and Mayo.

Statistics show indisputably Ireland's sea angling wealth. In Leinster, for example, there are 53 clubs. Along the 150 miles of coast from Dundalk on the east coast to Kilmore Quay in the south, there were 1,266 boat anglers in competitions in 1977, who caught between them 4,740 fish. These included a tope of 39lb 4oz, specimen spurdog of 13lb caught at Bray, Co Wicklow and 12lb 9oz at Kilmore, a 13lb pollack at Kilmore, and cod to 20lb 5oz at Greystones, Co Wicklow.

The Leinster shore competitions proved equally successful – 2,953 anglers caught 1,869 fish weighing 2,381lb. Specimen fish included a 26lb 8oz conger eel taken at Arthurstown in the Hook Peninsula, a flounder of 3lb 7oz taken at Greystones South and 2lb 8oz at Ardcavan and a river

eel of 3lb 5oz taken in tidal water at New Rodd Bridge. Boat fishing competitions also yielded well, although the total of fish per angler was less than in other years – probably owing to the recent close inshore trawling.

In Connaught, 22 clubs entered the boat competitions in 1977. There was a drop in numbers and weight of fish caught, but there were only 39 fishing days as against 62 in 1976. In this time, 1,327 anglers caught fish weighing 21,102lb.

Greystones

Moving in a clockwise direction around the coast, Greystones, 20 miles south of Dublin, is the prime eastern venue, with three or four clubs and a membership of 500 or more. There is an abundance of fishing on steep shelving beaches north and south of the town – approximately eight miles in all, and codling, bass, pouting, dogfish and some gurnard are to be found. An unexpected addition in 1977 was a lobster. All along this section the tide-rip near the shore is strong at peak tides. Ballygannon Strand, two miles south of Greystones along the railway line, is the chief location.

There are many boats available at Greystones, and the boat fishing is located half a mile to a mile out, parallel to the coast, towards the Moulditch Buoy and the Ridge. The area is full of local marks. In winter, big cod are caught in north-flowing water, and all year round the area is noted for codling (especially in autumn), and for pouting, plaice, thornback, conger, pollack, and some skate, tope and wrasse.

Greystones, although a prime fishing venue, rarely figures in the specimen fish list. It gave a tope of 43lb 12oz in 1977, however, while Killiney Bay, eight miles north, gave one of 40lb 8oz.

Visitors to the area can obtain help and information from a number of contacts and clubs. In the Dundalk to Kilmore area, one should contact the Greystones Ridge Club in

Mount Merrion, Co Dublin, the Knights of the Silver Hook in Tallaght, Co Dublin, the Bray Sea Angling Club in Sallynoggin, Co Dublin, or the East Coast Ladies in Dublin.

The inquisitive shore angler who has a car will find numerous locations between Greystones and Wexford, notably at Kilcoole 'Breaches', Kilmichael and Courtown, where mullet in the tiny harbour are very catchable. The tidal stretches of the River Slaney at Wexford also offer good chances. Bass fishing at night can be good on both of the town bridges at Wexford, while numerous quay stands are excellent and there is a variety of beach fishing within three miles of the town. Two deep-sea clubs are active there and at adjacent Rosslare, leading to Tuskar Rock five miles out. Splaugh Rock, a vast undersea platform, was once fine for bass, but was overfished and now has fine cod, pollack, and conger.

Saltee Islands

Off Kilmore Quay there is plentiful angling all around the Saltee Islands, four miles out. The warmer water becomes evident here, and fishing for tope and pollack is excellent, especially when drifting along the Burrow beach near Kilmore Harbour. There is beach fishing everywhere here.

For more information about this area one should contact the sea angling clubs in Kilmore Quay, Co Wexford.

The mobile angler will find unlimited shore fishing at Dunmore East, a considerable fishing port, and along Bannow Bay, west of Kilmore, while all shore anglers would do well to explore the swift deep channel on the western side of Bannow Island for bass and flounder. Further information can be obtained from the Dunmore East Sea Angling Club in Waterford City.

Dungarvan

Dungarvan has had ups and down in deep sea angling mostly because of boat troubles, but has no shortage of good water. There is the four-mile estuary, fished from Connigar on shore, with a four-mile strand at Clones and then a vast crescent-shaped bay leading beyond to Helvick Head. Reports tell of estuary pollution or disturbance, but at sea it is a fine venue for tope and blue shark in summer.

Again, for more information about the area, one should contact Miss Patricia Horsom, Anchor Bar, The Quay, Dungarvan, Co Waterford.

Youghal has ideal general angling in reputable blue shark waters. In fact, the shark have been so heavily sought that future stocks are at a risk. Ballycotton, nearby, was once a popular Irish angling haven. Fifty

Angling is always possible in the huge, sheltered expanse of Westport Bay.

Bill Howes

Dunfanaghy
Moville
Rathmullan
LOCH FOYLE
DONEGAL
LONDONDERRY
LOCH SWILLY
N15
Killybegs
Donegal
NORTHERN IRELAND
Erris Head
Porturlin
N15
SLIGO
Belmullet
SLIGO
Killala
N59
N59
Inishcrone
DUNDALK
Achill Island
BALLINA
Louth
MAYO
N57
LOUTH
Achill Sound
Newport
DROGHEDA
CLEW BAY
WESTPORT
SEE DETAIL MAP OF AREA
T39
MEATH
T40
Clifden
GALWAY
DUBLIN
GALWAY
Tallaght
Killiney
REPUBLIC OF IRELAND
GALWAY BAY
GREYSTONES
Killco
T69
WICKLOW
Liscannor
N18
WICKLOW
ENNIS
ARKLO
CLARE
Kilmicha
Courtown
L51
LIMERICK
ENNISCORTHY
WEXFORD
N7
LIMERICK
R. SLANEY
N21
NewRoss
WATERFORD
WEXFORD
BRANDON BAY
L105
Fenit
WATERFORD
Rosslare
TRALEE
WATERFORD
Castlegregory
DUNGARVAN
T63
KILLARNEY
N25
Dunmore
Tuskar
Valencia
T68
Helvick Head
Island
Cahersiveen
CORK
Midleton
YOUGHAL
Saltee Islands
Kenmare
CORK
R. BARROW
T66
Courtmacsherry
Ballycotton
Kilmore Quay
N25
Banry
BANNOW BAY
CLONAKILTY
KINSALE
Rosscarbery
Baltimore
Glandore

0 km	25	50	75	100
0 M	15	30	45	60

N

(Left) Sea angling centres of Eire.
(Right) Fine mullet from Dungarvan, where large flounder are also numerous.

Irish Tourist Board

years ago, pioneers of sea angling in England went there, trained their boatmen, and set up a sort of angling dynasty. Later, when there were troubles in Ireland, the pioneers left and Ballycotton went off the angling map.

There are several contacts in this area – John Cronin, 73 North Main Street, Youghal, Co Cork; Myles Clancy, 13 Strand Street, Youghal; Mrs R Coughlan, Curragh, Ardmore, Youghal; and, for Ballycotton, P Murphy, 8 Bailick Road, Midleton.

Kinsale

After Ballycotton, enterprising promoters found Kinsale, west of Cork Harbour, with greater shelter and amenities. It is a highly organized angling boat station today, sophisticated and expensive. For those who like modest outgoings on holiday, however, some of the finest garfish and bass angling from small boats is to be found in the estuary of the River Bandon, going through Kinsale. Then, for the adventurous, the Irish Shark Club, with a 100lb qualifying weight for membership, is located in Kinsale. The Kinsale Sea Angling Club in Kinsale, Co Cork, will help with information about the area.

Sea loughs of Cork and Kerry

Centres such as Courtmacsherry, Clonakilty, Rosscarbery, Glandore, and Baltimore in West Cork are noted for shore fishing, but are rather expensive. Great sea loughs cut into the Cork and Kerry coasts, with angling spots such as Bantry, Kenmare, and Valentia. Boat fishing is not readily available, though the angler has never far to look for action on shore. Cahersiveen has boats suitable for truly big skate, but these, unfortunately, are becoming scarce in Ireland.

Local contacts for further information are G Jayes, Ahidelake, Clonakilty, Co Cork; D O'Dwyer, Silver Hill, Courtmacsherry; D McCarthy, Newtown, Bantry, Co Cork, and Comdt M J O'Connor, Ardree, Killowen, Kenmare, Co Kerry.

Next, working up the west coast, the Dingle Peninsula, jutting into the warm Atlantic, has wonderful shore fishing, with long strands noted for bass. Brandon Bay has a 14-mile strand perfect for bass fishing and it is only one beach out of dozens in the peninsula. Castlegregory also has good shore fishing.

At Fenit, in Tralee Bay, there is exciting fishing from the long pier with skate and ray coming regularly, while out in the bay specimen undulate ray are found in great numbers in June and July. Further information about the area can be obtained at the Old Bridge House in Fenit.

It was Jack Shine, of Co Clare, who caught the first porbeagle shark from the rocky shore at Liscannor, weighing 145lb – but it is certainly not a game for timid anglers. There are, however, 60 miles of rocky eminences from which to practice, all the way up to Galway Bay, which is well served by angling boats. They go along the Clare shore, into the path of north-going porbeagles and blues, and out to the Aran Islands. There is much bottom fishing. For more information about this area, contact Brian Higgins in Clybaunn Road, Galway, or Elmer Kavanagh at the *Elaine Jane* in Galway Harbour.

Clifden has been discovered by Dutch anglers who make it their holiday home. Blue sharks are numerous. There is little shore fishing, but general fishing is done

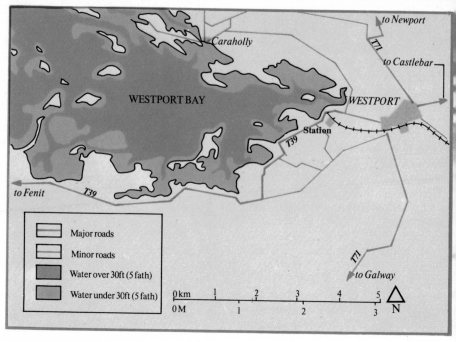

```
to Newport
Caraholly                                    T71
                                       to Castlebar
WESTPORT BAY                    WESTPORT
                        Station
                    T39
to Fenit    T39

Major roads
Minor roads
Water over 30ft (5 fath)                      T71
Water under 30ft (5 fath)                to Galway
                    0 km    1    2    3    4    5
                    0 M        1        2        3   N
```

from serviceable catamarans. Contact Jack O'Grady in Market Street, Clifden for further details.

Westport, in Co Mayo, was a pioneer in sea angling, and is still strong. It has the advantage of lying in a vast, sheltered, islanded bay that has few interruptions from storms outside, and is well established as a resort, with clubhouse and boats on call, frequent competitions, and a comradely spirit. Monkfish for years kept Westport famous, being caught even from the end of the pier. They are fewer now, however, and sustained fishing of other species is leading club members to return all fish alive.

Further information can be obtained from Michael Brooker, 17a Pinewoods, Westport, Co Mayo; Padraic Conlan, Rossmalley, Rosbeg, Westport; Michael Kennedy, c/o L Golden, The Mall, Westport, or from the Westport Angling Centre.

Achill Island has yet to be explored in shore fishing. Bullsmouth, however, has shown promise with ground fish in the fierce tidal sweep, and Purteen has boats for pollack fishing under the giant cliffs. Both

Westport Bay, venue for fine sea angling.

INFORMATION

No licence is needed to fish in Ireland, but help and information can be obtained from various regional centres: Irish Tourist Board, Ireland House, New Bond Street, London W1. Tel 493 3201.
Bord Failte, Baggot St Bridge, Dublin 2. Tel 765871.
Bord Failte, Stephen St, Sligo, Co Sligo. Tel 2436.
Dublin Regional Tourism Organization, 51 Dawson St, Dublin 2. Tel 747733.
Eastern Regional Tourism Organization, 1 Clarinda Park North, Dun Laoghaire, Co Dublin. Tel 808571.
South East Regional Tourism Organization, 41 The Quay, Waterford, Co Waterford. Tel 75823.
Cork-Kerry Regional Tourism Organization, Tourist House, Grand Parade, Cork. Tel 23251.
There are also smaller private contacts which will give information and make arrangements for boat hire etc: Inishcrone (Tel 22); Achill (Tel 70); Westport (Tel 269); Clifden (Tel: Cleggan 26); Killarney (Tel 31633); Quilty (Tel: Limerick 77107); Kinsale (Tel 021 72611); Youghal (June-Sept) Tel 2390; Dungarvan (Tel 058 41738).

SEA ANGLING CLUBS
Bray Sea Angling Club, B Reyniolds, 13 O'Rourke Park, Salynoggin, Co Dublin.
Dunmore East Sea Angling CLub, John Stewart, Tivoli, Marian Park, Waterford City.
East Coast Ladies, Mrs M Haydem, 22 Moatfield Ave, Dublin.
Greystones Ridge Club, J Cogan, 18 Clonmore Rd, Mount Merrion, Co Dublin.
Kilmore Quay Sea Angling Club, J Monaghan, Ballyteigue, Kilmore Quay, Co Wexford.
Irish Shark Club, Kinsale, Co Cork.
Kinsale Sea Angling Club, E Hurley, 2 Mandeville Terr, Kinsale, Co Cork.

Michael McHugh, Beach House, Bullsmouth, and Mrs Alice McNamara, Dugort P.O. Achill, Co Mayo, can give further details.

Belmullet, on the North Mayo coast has splendid venues – Porturin, Portacloy and Ballyglass. It is a wild area, however, and it takes organized parties to procure boats in advance. There is spectacular fishing for cod, bream, conger and skate off Erris Head, and the finest turbot are found in the water off Ballyglass. Belmullet gave a specimen turbot of 22lb, and a 31lb 2½oz whiting in 1977. Sean Gannon in American Street, Belmullet, can supply further local information.

Abundance of fish

Killala Bay, served by Killala and Inishcrone, has plenty of boats and an abundance of fish. In 1977, of all coastal areas, Killala gave the third highest average weight per fish: 3lb 12oz compared with 7lb 5oz at Clifden and 5lb 9oz fished by the Granuaile Ladies at Achill. Specimens caught at Killala included a red gurnard of 2lb 9¾oz, a tub gurnard 8lb 5oz, a blonde ray 26lb, and a pollack of 12lb 8oz.

More details of the area can be obtained from John Walkin in Ballina, Co Mayo, Jim Byrne, Alpine Hotel, Inishcrone, Co Sligo, or Mrs Grace Munnelly, The Close, Killala, Co Mayo.

Killybegs, in Donegal, has apparently fallen back in organized boat angling, principally because of commercial sea fishing. Along the high Donegal coast, however, places such as Dunfanaghy, Downings and Rathmullan, all with boats, have much mixed bottom fishing, and Lough Swilly was always famous for hordes of tope, although they are now much thinned. Moville, in neighbouring Lough Foyle, is noted for large amounts of gurnard, and holds a week-long fishing festival, usually in August.

For further information, contact Mrs Lena O'Callaghan, St Catherine's Road, Killybegs, Co Donegal; Mrs Madeleine McBride, Downings, Co Donegal, or Niall Docherty, 2 Market Street, Rathmullan.

Knights of the Silver Hook, J Carrigan, 109 St Melruin's Park, Tallaght, Co Dublin.
Rosslare Harbour Sea Angling Club, J F O'Brien, Villa Nova, Rosslare Harbour.
Saltee Sea Angling Club, L Devereux, 26 Pinewood Estate, Wexford.
Wexford District Sea Angling Club, M Guerin, Burren Lodge, Curracloe, Enniscorthy, Co Wexford.
Wexford Sea Angling Club, L D Meyler, Carryowen, Rosslare Strand, Wexford.
CONTACTS
Miss Patricia Horsom, Anchor Bar, The Quay, Dungarvan, Co Waterford.
John Cronin, 73 North Main St, Youghal, Co Cork.
Myles Clancy, 13 Strand St, Youghal.
Mrs R Coughlan, Curragh, Ardmore, Youghal.
P Murphy, 8 Bailick Rd, Midleton (for Ballycotton).
G Jayes, Ahidelake, Clonakilty, Co Cork.
D O'Dwyer, Silver Hill, Courtmacsherry, Co Cork.
D McCarthy, Newtown, Bantry, Co Cork.
Comdt M J O'Connor, Ardree, Killowen, Kenmare, Co Kerry.
Brian Higgins, Clybaunn Rd, Galway.
Elmer Kavanagh, *Elaine Jane*, Galway Harbour.
Jack O'Grady, Market Square, Clifden, Co Galway.
Michael Brooker, 17a Pinewoods, Westport, Co Mayo.
Padraic Conlan, Rossmalley, Rosbeg, Westport.
Michael Kennedy, c/o L Golden, The Mall, Co Mayo.
Westport Angling Centre, Westport, Co Mayo.
Michael McHugh, Beach House, Bullsmouth, Achill, Co Mayo.
Mrs Alice McNamara, Dugport P O, Achill.
Sean Gannon, American St, Belmullet, Co Mayo.
John Walkin, Ballina, Co Mayo.
Jim Byrne, Alpine Hotel, Enniscrone, Co Sligo.
Mrs Grace Munnelly, The Close, Killala, Co Mayo.
Mrs Lena O'Callaghan, St Catherine's Rd, Killybegs, Co Donegal.
Mrs Madeleine McBridge, Downings, Co Donegal.
Niall Docherty, 2 Market St, Rathmullan, Co Donegal.
TACKLE DEALERS
Sweeney & Son, Achill Sound, Achill, Co Mayo.
Walkins, Tone St, Ballina, Co Mayo.
J A O'Connolly, Corner Shop, Ballycotton, Co Cork.
Fuller & Co, Baltimore, Co Cork.
Field Sports, 6 Village Gate Arcade, Bray, Co Wicklow
Gerald Stanley & Son, Market St, Clifden, Co Galway.
H Sullivan, Main St, Clifden.
J E Spiller, 40-41 Pearse St, Clonakilty, Co Cork.
Day & Son, Cork.
S. Smyth Sports, 30 Shop St, Drogheda, Co Louth. Tel 7100.
Moorkens Ltd, 11 Abbey St Upper, Dublin 1. Tel 745704.
Nolans, 80 North Strand, Dublin 3. Tel 744520
Rory's Fishing Tackle, 17a Temple Bar, Dublin 2.
Irish Angling Services Ltd, Fishing Bait Farm, Monang, Dungarvan, Co Waterford.
O Bowman & Sons Ltd, 6 St Mary's St, Dungarvan, Co Waterford. Tel 41395.
Naughton's, Shop St, Kilcolgan River, Galway.
The Handy Stores, Killarney, Co Kerry.
R P Hilliard, Main St, Killarney.
McGuinness Fishing Gear, Main St, Killybegs, Co. Donegal.
Malahide Marine Ltd, The Green, Malahide. Tel 867450
Co-operative Stores, Moville, Co Donegal.
O'Connor's Tackle, Newport, Co Mayo.
Quinn's Tackle, Newport.
Hanley's Tackle, Newport.
F. Nelson & Son, Sligo, Co Sligo.
Barton Smith, Sligo.
Sports Shop, Quay, Waterford, Co Waterford.
Hewetson's, Dyar's Bridge St, Westport, Co Mayo.
Clarke's, The Octagon, Westport.

Warwickshire Avon

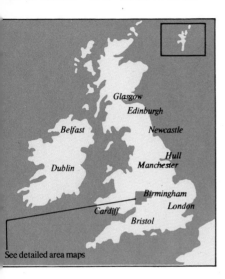

See detailed area maps

chub weighed 6lb; the best bream, 8lb 3oz, was from Pershore; the best roach, 2lb 14oz, from Strensham; the best carp, 15½lb, from Birlingham. Perch to 3lb, and double-figure pike are caught in middle and lower sections.

Birmingham Anglers' Association

Fortunately, there is a lot of water available and much of it is day ticket fishing. However, the Birmingham Anglers' Association has large holdings and it would probably be advantageous to the holiday angler to purchase an annual Associate Membership card at £5.50. They are available from most West Midland tackle dealers.

At Warwick and down through Barford to Hampton Lucy, local clubs control most fishing. The Warwick District Angling Society is open to membership at a reasonable cost and good catches of chub, dace and roach are to be made from their extensive fishery from Fulbrook to Charlecote. From Hampton Lucy to Stratford local clubs again control most of the water.

The Birmingham AA has a long right-

No other river of its size in England has so many places of distinction as the Warwickshire Avon. Rising near Naseby it skirts Rugby and passes Warwick and its castle, and Shakespeare's Stratford-upon-Avon before reaching Bidford. From here downstream to its confluence with the Severn there are the remains of three historical abbeys — Evesham, Pershore and Tewkesbury.

Specimen fish

Few Midland rivers have suffered more from industrial pollution than the Avon in its top reaches. This still shows to some extent, but downstream from Warwick it has become one of the most popular, and in places prolific, coarse-fishing waters in the country, yielding big catches and specimen fish. It also has one other virtue; differing tactics and techniques can be used with success at most venues.

The best Warwickshire Avon match weight tops the 75lb mark and was caught at Eckington. At Evesham, the best recorded

Good chub, dace and roach are to be caught in the young river at Warwick. (Right) The Mill Weir viewed from the castle.

Richard Jemmet

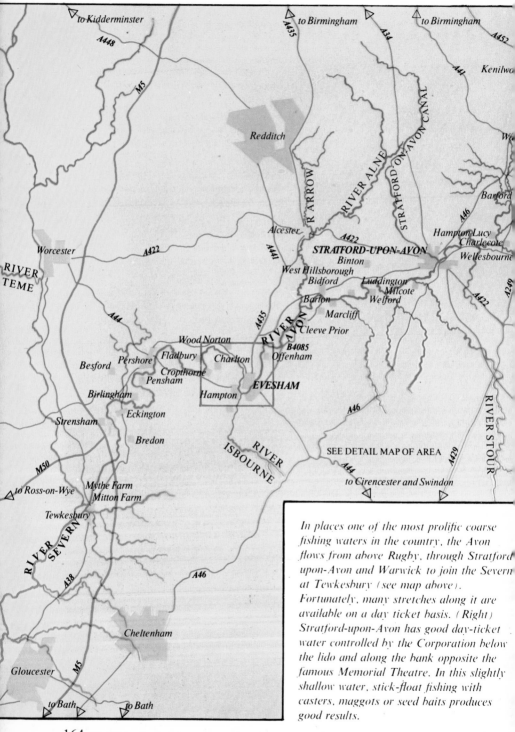

to Kidderminster

to Birmingham

to Birmingham

A448

A435

A34

A452

A441

Kenilwo

M5

Redditch

STRATFORD-ON-AVON CANAL

RIVER ALNE

R ARROW

Barford

A46

Wi

Alcester

Hampton Lucy
Charlecote

Worcester

A422

A441

A422

STRATFORD-UPON-AVON
Binton
West Hillsborough
Bidford
Barton
Marcliff
Cleeve Prior

Wellesbourne

RIVER
TEME

A249

A422

Luddington
Milcote
Welford

A46

RIVER STOUR

A444

Wood Norton

RIVER AVON

A435

B4085
Offenham

Pershore
Fladbury
Charlton
Crophtorne
Pensham
Hampton

Besford

EVESHAM

Birlingham

Eckington

A46

A429

Strensham

Bredon

RIVER ISBOURNE

SEE DETAIL MAP OF AREA

M50

to Ross-on-Wye

Mythe Farm
Mitton Farm

A444

to Cirencester and Swindon

Tewkesbury

A46

RIVER SEVERN

A438

Cheltenham

M5

Gloucester

to Bath

to Bath

In places one of the most prolific coarse fishing waters in the country, the Avon flows from above Rugby, through Stratford-upon-Avon and Warwick to join the Severn at Tewkesbury (see map above). Fortunately, many stretches along it are available on a day ticket basis. (Right) Stratford-upon-Avon has good day-ticket water controlled by the Corporation below the lido and along the bank opposite the famous Memorial Theatre. In this slightly shallow water, stick-float fishing with casters, maggots or seed baits produces good results.

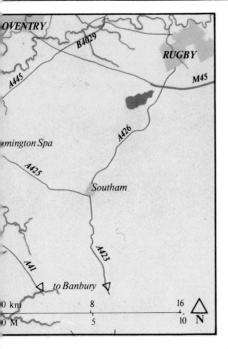

bank stretch at Hampton Lucy approached via the village from the A46. At Stratford, its 65-peg Avon Meadows venue is on the right bank running parallel to the A46 and with access points clearly marked. Below the lido and into Stratford the water is controlled by the Corporation, and day tickets are available from local tackle dealers.

The river in this area is generally shallow, down to 5ft, with a fair stream running. It is float-fishing water, the stick-float method with maggots, casters and seedbaits being the most successful. Excellent sport can be had from the park bank opposite the famous Memorial Theatre, especially for those who fish slightly overdepth with the terminal tackle held back against the current.

Below Stratford town the Birmingham AA control a 50-peg right-bank stretch called Seven Meadows, approached from the footbridge near the weir below St Mary's church. Opposite is a fine section controlled

Richard Jemmet

Warwickshire Avon

by the Hazeldine Angling Association which issues honorary cards. Farther down on the left bank the Birmingham AA have another 50-peg section with fishing also on a small stretch of the Stour which enters at Milcote. The match record here in 1975 was 34lb.

Club-controlled waters

On the right bank at Luddington, Stratford-upon-Avon Angling Society control a very good two-mile stretch which is for members only, although annual membership is available. From there down to Welford the waters are club-controlled except for the small but good day-ticket stretch from the Four Alls Inn near the bridge leading from the A439. More club-controlled sections follow from here to Bidford. The Birmingham AA have a good section of left-bank fishing at Barton where the upstream 'gully' pegs are best, and on the opposite bank the Worcester and District United Anglers' Association, which issues honorary cards, has a good length of productive water at West Hillsborough, reached via the A439.

The stretch immediately below Bidford Bridge is strictly members only along the park bank. Below this, though, runs a series of Birmingham AA venues through Marcliff and Cleeve Prior. Access points are from the B4085 and clearly marked. Downstream at Cleeve is free fishing for Severn-Trent Water Authority licence holders.

The water here provides excellent chub, dace and roach fishing. Casters and maggots are the standard baits, but very often seedbaits, particularly tares, yield good sport.

The next stretch of day-ticket water is at Court Farm in Offenham, on the left bank by the B4510. Below, on the right bank the Bridge Inn waters are approached by the Ferry at the inn, which issues day tickets.

The first class fishing of Evesham is now reached. In the town 50 pegs are available for the cost of a 25p day ticket. Downstream are the famous Hampton Ferry waters on both banks. The match catch record stands at $41\frac{1}{4}$lb and most species can be found here,

(Above) Welford-on-Avon, below Stratford, is good water for perch, roach and dace. From Luddington to Welford most of the water is club-controlled, but there is a good day ticket stretch at the Four Alls Inn near the bridge leading from the A439.

even carp. Depths vary from 5ft to 15ft with excellent swims above Abbey Bridge, through the Isbourne confluence, at Hampton Ferry and on to the railway bridge. Day tickets are available at the ferry from Mr Huxley, and for the town waters from bailiffs on the bank, if a contest is not in progress.

More right-bank and club-contest water is found at Haselor Farm, and from there down to Fladbury the Birmingham AA controls much of the water at Wood Norton, Chadbury Meadows and on the opposite bank Charlton and Cropthorne, and also on both sides of Jubilee Bridge in Fladbury. Here club catches of over 50lb have been made from the fence peg on the right bank below the bridge.

Downstream, the water is controlled by Redditch-based clubs, and farther down to Pershore it is also mostly club-controlled. The river noticeably changes character at this stage, changing from a younger, faster-flowing river to a wider, calmer, and distinctly breamy water. The lower part of the Avon is known particularly for its bream.

Generally, the river has many species including carp, chub, roach and dace, and if one is not successful at first with one tactic it pays to switch to another.

Big shoals of bream

The Birmingham AA has a lengthy stretch above the bridge at Pershore on the left bank, while there is free fishing on the right bank for licence holders. At Pensham and Nafford on the left bank, and on the right bank at Birlingham, the Association has long sections where there are big bream shoals. Downstream Cheltenham Angling Society controls a lot of water all the way through Strensham Lock and on to Bredon. Day tickets are available from the local inn, or from tackle dealer Jones in Selly Oak.

This is the best Avon bream water where club catches in excess of 100lb are not uncommon. Such large bags of bream are usually made with ledgered bread flake baits or with worm. For quality roach, float tactics are often very successful. Big eels are also found here, and large chub and carp are often caught by the early morning angler.

Day tickets in Tewkesbury

Along the flat banks at Twyning Fleet and Mythe Farm and at left bank Mitton Farm to Tewkesbury, the Birmingham AA controls more waters. In Tewkesbury itself good sections of the Avon and Severn are controlled by the Tewkesbury Popular Angling Club and day tickets are available on the bank.

The attraction of the Avon is the varied fishing it presents for anglers from all parts of the country. Here, Trentmen can use their method successfully just as the bream anglers of the Witham and Welland can fish their style. This is what makes the Avon the fabulous fishing river it is.

Warwickshire Avon

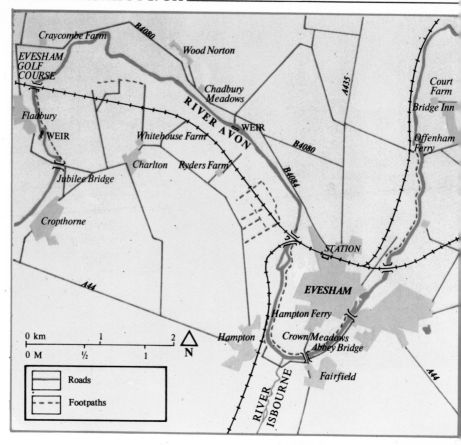

(Above) Our map shows the excellent day ticket waters of Evesham where most species can be caught. The Court Farm and Bridge Inn waters in Offenham are reached via the A435 from Redditch. In the town, the famous Hampton Ferry waters are from above Abbey Bridge, past the ferry, and on both banks down to the railway bridge. Downstream much of the water is controlled by the Birmingham AA.
(Right) The waters at Hampton Ferry yield good pike, perch and bream.

168

INFORMATION

WATER AUTHORITY
Severn-Trent Water Authority, Severn Area, 64 Albert Rd,
North Malvern, Worcs. Tel: Malvern 61511.

LICENCES
Trout and freshwater fish: £1. **Salmon**, season £15, day
£2.25.
Close seasons: brown trout and char (lakes and reservoirs)
October 16 to March 17; all other waters October 1 to
March 31. Salmon September 15 to February 1. Freshwater
fish March 15 to June 15. No close season for rainbow
trout and eels. Spinning for trout during the close season
for freshwater fish is prohibited. Trailing or trolling natural
or artificial spinning baits from boats in motion is
prohibited. No float to be used with lure or bait when
fishing for salmon, or during the close season for
freshwater fish. No cereal or maggots to be used as bait
during the freshwater fish close season. Keepnets (which
must conform to the specifications set out in the byelaws)
are not allowed during freshwater fish close season. No fish
to be taken from the River Severn within a distance of
approximately 50ft above and 148ft below the crest of
Shrewsbury Weir.
Size limits: barbel all waters 15.7in (40cm); rainbow trout
all waters 11.8in (30cm); brown trout and grayling River
Avon 9.8in (25cm). Bona fide matches may be fished "all
in", provided undersized barbel are returned to the water
with as little injury as possible after weighing, which must
take place on the river bank.

FISHERIES
Evesham
The Corporation holds rights for bank fishing. Tel:
Stratford-upon-Avon 67575. Day tickets costing 25p may
be obtained from Mr E Huxley at Hampton Ferry. Crown
Corporation meadows are free to individuals except when
contests are on. At Wood Norton 80 match pegs are
available. Apply to Mr S Lewis, 2 Severnside, South
Bewdley.

Stratford-upon-Avon
Day tickets for the Corporation water cost 20p. Sunday
fishing from the Fishery Bailiff, Capt A Heath, 3 Garrick
Way, Evesham Rd. Tel 3941, or from the bailiff on the
bank.

Leamington Spa
Day ticket for Association and Corporation water from the
Parks Director, 10 Newbold Terrace. Tel 27072. Day ticket
35p, juniors and OAPs 20p. Season ticket £3, juniors £1.50,
OAPs £1.

Offenham
Day tickets from Mr J A Coldicott, Court Farm,
Offenham. Tel Evesham 6113.

Pershore
The Severn River Division controls a stretch here, 2m on
one bank, 1m on the other; angling permitted to licence
holders, right bank. Some free water in recreation ground.

LOCAL CLUBS AND ASSOCIATIONS
Birmingham Anglers' Association, V S Hall, 40 Thorpe St,
Birmingham 5B5 4AU

Cheltenham Angling Club, F T Selley, 2 Hollis Gardens,
Hatherley, Cheltenham, Glos.

Gloucester United Anglers' Association, R H Ellis, 15
Armscroft Way, Barnwood, Gloucester.

Hazeldine Angling Association, J W Hazeldine, 8 Dudley
Rd, Sedgley, West Midlands, DY3 1SX.

Redditch Angling CLub, G W Blundell, 99 The Meadway,
Redditch, Worcestershire B97 5AE.

Redditch and District Anglers' Federation, C Wright, 16
Cyprus Avenue, Ashwood Bank, Redditch, Worcestershire.

Rugby Federation of Anglers, T Hilditch, 89 Balcombe Rd,
Rugby.

Stratford-upon-Avon Angling Society, Tony Mason,
Kewstoke, Luddington, Stratford-upon-Avon. Tel 750626.

Tewkesbury Popular Angling Association, R A Smith, 10
Tretawn gardens, Newtown, Tewkesbury, Glos.

Warwick and District Angling Society, R Phillips, 2
Lydstet Rd, Leamington Spa. Tel 34524.

Worcester and District United Anglers Association, W
Meadows, 101 Bransford Rd, St Johns, Worcester.

TACKLE DEALERS
A E Brookes, 958 Bristol Road South, Birmingham B31
28E.

Austin Clisset, 1801 Pershore Rd, Cotteridge, Birmingham
30.

Harold Greenway & Sons, (10 branches) main branch 1010
Chester Rd, Pype Hayes, Birmingham 24. Tel 373 0057.

Roy Jarvis, 364 Shirley Rd, Acocks Green, Birmingham 27.

Stan Jones, 17 Raddlebarn Rd, Selly Oak, Birmingham 29.

Simmonds & Priddey, Stratford Rd, Shirley, Birmingham.

J Keeling, 45 Market Hall, Bull Ring Centre, Birmingham.

M Robinson, 4 York Rd, Kings Heath, Birmingham.

W H Lane & Son, 31-33 London Rd, Coventry.

F Marshall, 360 Alderman's Green Rd, Coventry.

P Ruyssevelt, 467 Holyhead Rd, Coventry.

Joan Heritage, Merstow Green, Evesham, Stratford-upon-
Avon. Tel 3278

Evesham Sports Centre, 60a Bridge St, Evesham.

R J Russell, 93 Coventry Rd, Kidderminster, Herefs &
Worcs. Tel 64040.

M Storey, Sutton Rd, Kidderminster, Herefs & Worcs.

W H Norris, 24 Russell Terrace, Leamington Spa. Tel
26067.

Coopers, 17 Willes Rd, Leamington Spa. Tel 22539

W L Brown, 3 High St, Pershore, Worcester.

R W & D Powell, 28 Mount Pleasant, Redditch,
Worcester.

Banks & Burr, 26 Claremont Rd, Rugby, Worcs.

Donalds, 155a Bilton Rd, Rugby, Worcs.

West Mid Fishing Tackle, Stourbridge, W Midlands

A C Claridge's, Greenhill St, Stratford-upon-Avon. Tel
2778.

Ben's Pitch, 3 Shires Rd, Warley, W Midlands. Tel
Birmingham 429 4530.

Roger's Fishing Tackle, 166 Causeway Green Rd, Langley,
Oldbury, Warley. Tel Birmingham 552 6701

Bailey's, 55 The Saltisford, Warwick. Tel 41984

Allan's, St Johns, Worcester.

F Durrant & Son, Gun & Fishing Tackle, 3 Mealcheapen
St, Worcester.

Georges, 12 Bridge St, Worcester.

Richardsons, 28 St Johns, Worcester.

West Midlands Canals

See detailed area maps

A map of the West Midlands shows a myriad of waterways built around Birmingham in the canal boom era of the 19th century. Although some are now polluted and many exist only as pleasure craft waters, several remain in as clean a state as when they were built. The major canals are the Stratford-upon-Avon Canal, the Staffordshire and Worcestershire Canal, the Worcester and Birmingham Canal and the Grand Union Canal. Each gives handy fishing and some excellent sport can be enjoyed.

Birmingham Anglers' Association

The Birmingham Anglers' Association controls most of these waters, and the angler would be well advised to obtain annual membership. This is available at most local tackle dealers or at the Birmingham AA Headquarters.

The Stratford-upon-Avon Canal flows from Stratford to Birmingham, passing through Wilmcote, Wootton Wawen, Preston Bagot, Hockley Heath and Earlswood to join the Worcester Canal at King's Norton. It is a narrow waterway, opened in 1815. During summer fishing is somewhat hampered by heavy pleasure boat

traffic, but there is good sport from early autumn.

The Birmingham AA controls fishing rights along the Stratford Canal for 25 miles from King's Norton to a point near the junction with the River Avon. King's Norton, due south of Birmingham, is reached via the A441 through Edgbaston. Fish can be caught nearer the city, by Yardley Wood, Shirley, and Ilshaw Heath, but the better fishing starts at Hockley Heath at the junction of the A4023 and the A34.

The B4439 edges the canal from Hockley Heath to Lapworth and then crosses this canal and follows the Grand Union Canal down to Warwick. There is some fair roach fishing at Lapworth with the odd bream and crucian carp, while a little farther, from Lapworth to Lowsonford, Preston Bagot and Wootton Wawen, sport improves. These places are south of Hockley Heath. Lapworth is reached via A34, then the B4439; Preston Bagot via the A34 then the

West Midlands Canals

B4095, and Wootton Wawen is reached directly via the A34. Lowsonford is due south of Lapworth, reached via a minor road which follows the canal. From swims above Bridge 51 near Wootton Wawen double figure catches can be made during an evening's fishing.

Sport then deteriorates due to recent canal improvement work which necessitated draining. This continues as far as Wilmcote, but at Bishopton, tench and roach begin to show again. The best recorded pleasure catch from this canal was 77lb of tench caught near Wootton Wawen a decade ago.

The Worcester Canal

The most popular canal venues for local anglers are perhaps those found along the Worcester Canal. The Birmingham AA again controls most of this, from King's Norton as far as Blackpole Bridge near Worcester. The A38 Birmingham-Worcester road and the A441 Birmingham-Redditch road follow most of its length, and there is easy access to the canal from several major or minor roads which cross between them. In the area of Alvechurch, on the A441, fishing is improving and roach are on the

increase. At Stole Pound and Tardebigge, reached from Redditch via the A448, there are also bream and the odd fair-sized carp. The reservoir near Tardebigge is privately controlled. From Tardebigge to Stoke Prior, at the junction of the A38 and the B4091, anglers fishing the flight of locks with floated bread baits may be rewarded with a double figure catch of carp.

Favourite contest venues

Some of the best bream and roach swims are found above Hanbury where the B4090 road crosses the canal. For pleasure anglers, the 'boat turn' often yields catches of 30lb plus, and favourite contest venues are found at Oddingley, Tibberton, Pershore Lane and Tolladine. These stretches are reached via the A422 east of Worcester then turning left through Crowle to join the canal, or alternatively via the A38 north of Worcester then turning right to join the canal. The last section from Tolladine to Blackpole is currently the best for sport, with roach and skimmer bream predominating. From here and through Bilton to Worcester, fishing is controlled by the Worcester and District United Angler's Association. It has no day tickets, but issues honorary cards, and has other excellent waters on the rivers Severn, Teme and Avon.

The Staffordshire and Worcestershire Canal stretches from Wombourne Lock, through Swindon, Cookley and Kidderminster to Stourport. It holds roach, bream, carp, tench, gudgeon and even chub. Wombourne is reached via the A449 due south of Wolverhampton, which then continues south skirting the canal as far as Kidderminster. Stourport is South of Kidderminster reached via the A4025.

Whitmore Reans Angling Club

From Wightwick, just west of Wolverhampton on the A454, through Wombourne to Bolterham, near Bridge 42, the

The Worcester Canal has excellent roach and bream swims above Hanbury (left), while favourite contest venues are found upstream at Oddingley and Tibberton.

171

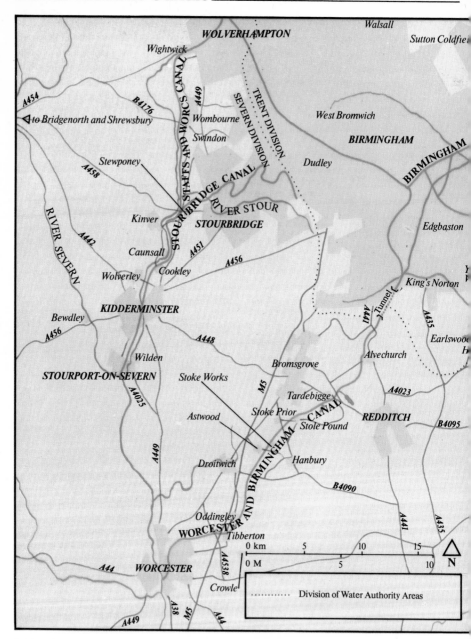

Wolverhampton-based Whitmore Reans Angling Club controls fishing rights. From there to Stewponey Bridge, where the A458 crosses the canal, the Birmingham AA controls the water. Good catches are often made at Greensforge using bloodworm or maggot fished with a roach pole close in, or casters fished near the opposite bank.

The Kinver Freeliner Club issues day tickets for the stretch from Stewponey to Hyde Lock at Kinver and the Kidderminster Angling Association controls the fishing rights along the Stourbridge Canal which joins at this point. Recently some good roach catches have been made in this canal, and on the Kinver waters bream to 4lb, roach to $1\frac{3}{4}$lb and carp of 6lb have been caught. The Birmingham AA then controls the water starting at Bridge 29 continuing through Caunsall, Cookley, off the A449, and Wolverley, where the B4189 road crosses the canal, and on through Kidderminster and Wilden to Stourport.

The Grand Union Canal, for its whole length from London to Birmingham, is let to various angling clubs. The Birmingham AA controls a 3 mile stretch from Shrewley near Warwick, reached via the A41 then the B4439, to Hatton on the A41. Currently, excellent roach catches are being made here, and quality perch, bream and the odd carp are also taken. A crucian carp of 3lb was caught near Bridge 58 in 1967.

(Right) The Grand Union Canal at Hatton. Map shows the main canals in the Birmingham area, while detail map (over) shows sections of the Stratford-upon-Avon and Grand Union canals, reached from Birmingham or Stratford via the A34.

Norman Worth

173

West Midlands Canals

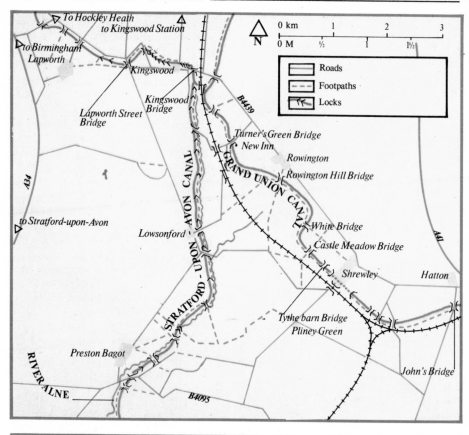

	0 km		1		2		3
	0 M	½		1		1½	

- Roads
- Footpaths
- Locks

To Hockley Heath
to Kingswood Station
to Birmingham
Lapworth
Kingswood
Kingswood Bridge
Lapworth Street Bridge
B4439
Turner's Green Bridge
New Inn
Rowington
Rowington Hill Bridge
GRAND UNION CANAL
STRATFORD - UPON - AVON CANAL
to Stratford-upon-Avon
Lowsonford
White Bridge
Castle Meadow Bridge
Shrewley
Hatton
A34
A41
Tythe barn Bridge
Pliney Green
Preston Bagot
RIVER ALNE
B4095
John's Bridge

INFORMATION

WATER AUTHORITY
Severn-Trent Water Authority, Abelson House, 2297.
Coventry Rd. Sheldon. Birmingham Tel 743 4222.
Severn Area, 64 Albert Rd, N. Malvern Tel 61511.
Trent Area, Area Fisheries Office, Meadow Lane,
Nottingham NG2 3HN. Tel 865007.

LICENCES
Trout and freshwater fish: Severn Area, season £1. Trent
Area season £1. Combined Severn and Trent area, season
£1.50, 28 day period 50p, OAPs 20p.
Close seasons: freshwater fish March 15 to June 15.
In the Severn area no float to be used and no cereal or
maggots to be used as bait during the freshwater fish close
season. Keepnets are not allowed during close season.
Size limits: (both areas) barbel 15.7in (40cm), pike 19.7in
(50cm), bream, carp, chub and tench 9.8in (25cm), dace,
grayling, roach, rudd and perch 7.9in (20cm).

CANAL AUTHORITIES
Stratford-on-Avon Canal, (Northern section) British Waterways
Board, Area Amenity Assistant, Reservoir House, Icknield Port
Rd, Birmingham 16. Tel 4547091.
(Southern section) National Trust, 34-36 Church St,
Tewkesbury, Glos.
Staffordshire and Worcestershire Canal, Grand Union Canal: British
Waterways Board.

LOCAL CLUBS AND ASSOCIATIONS
Birmingham Anglers' Association, V S Hall, 40 Thorpe St,
Birmingham B5 4AU
Kidderminster & District Angling Association, C G Wilcox, 35
Dunnington Ave, Sion Park, Kidderminster DY 10 2YS.
Kinver Freeliners Club, Roger Oliver, 38 High St, Kinver,
W Midlands.
Whitmore Reans Angling Association, R H Hughes,
Star Chambers, Prince's Square, Wolverhampton.
Worcester and District United Anglers' Association, W
Meadows, 101 Bransford Rd, St Johns, Worcester.

TACKLE DEALERS
S Lewis, 2 Severnside South, Bewdley, Worcs.
Sport'n Tackle, 31 High St, Bilston, W Midlands Tel 56200.
A E Brookes, 958 Bristol Rd South, Birmingham B31 28E.
Harold Greenway & Sons, (10 branches) 1010 Chester Rd.
Pype Hayes, Birmingham 24. Tel 373 0057.
Roy Jarvis, 364 Shirley Rd, Acocks Green Birmingham 27.
Simmonds & Priddey, Stratford Rd, Shirley, Birmingham.
M Robinson, 4 York Rd, Kings Heath, Birmingham.
Jack Stevens, 5 St Anne's Rd, Cradley Heath. Tel 67778.
Peter Gordon, 83 High St, Dudley, W Midlands. Tel 52413.
R J Russell, 93 Coventry Rd, Kidderminster. Tel 64040.
Powell's, 28 Mount Pleasant, Redditch, Worcs.
A C Claridge, Greenhaill St, Stratford-upon-Avon. Warks.
West Mid Fishing Tackle, Stourbridge. W Midlands.
M A Grinnall, 10 York St, Stourport-on-Severn.
Ben's Pitch, 3 Shires Rd, Bearwood, Warley, W Midlands.
Tel Birmingham 429 4530.
Roger's Fishing Tackle, 166 Causeway Green Rd, Langley,
Oldbury, Warley, W Midlands. Tel Birmingham 552 6701.
Bailey's, 55 The Saltisford, Warwick. Tel 41984.
Ron Haynes, 176 Stafford St, Wolverhampton. Tel 23777
F Durrant & Sons, Mealcheapen St, Worcester. Tel 25247.
George's, Bridge St, Worcester.

British Tourist Authority

West Midlands Canals II

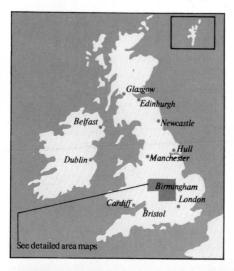

See detailed area maps

West Midlanders are fortunate in having a vast variety of waters to choose from—lucid trout streams in the Shropshire border country, the mighty, fish-filled River Severn, and the placid Warwickshire Avon. They also have the choice of myriad canals built a century and half ago and holding fair and, for the most part, fast-improving fishing. Several were discussed in the previous chapter but there are lesser known waters.

The Grand Union Canal holds most species of coarse fish, including carp, tench and record-sized eels. The Royal Leamington Spa AA, which has annual membership at £1.50, controls the fishing from Junction Bridge at Warwick on the A425 through Radford Semele, Bascote and

Long Itchington to Calcutt Lock and the junction with the Oxford Canal at Napton on the Hill, also on the A425.

Coventry club waters

Northwards, the Rugby Federation controls a long length from Elkington to the north end of Crick Tunnel on the A428, and day tickets are sold along the bank. From Crick to Norton, off the A5, the Coventry and District AA controls the waters, and honorary cards are available. They also control lengths of the Grand Union—from Braunston Tunnel on the A361 to the junction with the Oxford Canal; from South Kilworth on the A427, past and including the Welford Arm, where trout have been introduced, to Husbands Bosworth Tunnel; from Fenny Stratford on the A5 to Stoke Hammond Locks, Bridge 102, on the B4488 in Bucks; and from Buckby Wharf to Muscott Mill bridge near Daventry.

The Oxford Canal is known for its fine roach fishing. Here the Rugby Federation controls about 10 miles of towpath space from Cathiron on the B4112 west of the town to Willoughby on the A45, then the Coventry and District controls rights from Willoughby Wharf at Bridge 83 to Fenny Compton on the A423, a distance of 16 miles or so. They also control other long stretches from Banbury, Bridge 160 on the A422 to Nell Bridge 187; from Heyford Wharf, Bridge 206 on the A4030 to Shipton Weir Rock on the A4055 and on through Thrupp and Kidlington to Green Lock at Bridge 228 on the A423.

The Coventry Canal is a fast-improving water because the pollution is now being controlled. It has produced a large 5lb tench at Alvecote. The Coventry and District AA controls 21 miles of this canal from Coventry City through Nuneaton and Atherstone to the Bulls Head bridge in Polesworth on the B5000. From there, the Polesworth AC control a lengthy stretch followed by more day ticket waters to the junction with the Fazeley canal. Tamworth Working Men's Club control the nine miles between Polesworth and Fazeley.

Fishing near Spaghetti Junction

The Fazeley Canal is an often-ignored but fair water, the rights of which are controlled by the Birmingham AA. Regular East Birmingham anglers often find good sport at many points from along the 16-mile stretch from the A38 near Spaghetti Junction at Salford through Minworth on the A4097, Curdworth, Dunton, Bodymoor Heath, Kingsbury on the A51, Drayton Bassett on the A4091, Fazeley on the A5, Hopwas on the A51 and Whittington to Bridge 82 near the junction of the (part-disused) Wyrley and Essington Canal. Along this latter canal, fishing has deteriorated recently, but many stretches back through Brownhills on the A452, where roach are showing again,

A beautiful spot of unspoiled England. Reeling in to allow a horse-drawn barge to pass along the Shropshire Union Canal.

England Scene

West Midlands Canals II

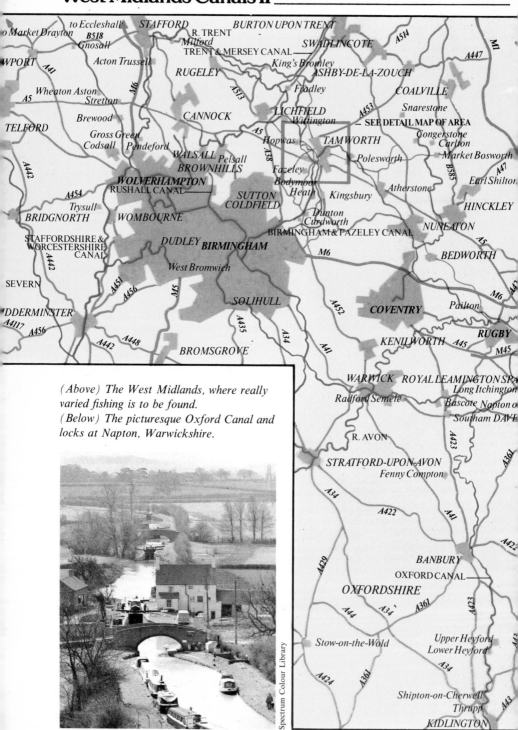

(Above) The West Midlands, where really varied fishing is to be found.
(Below) The picturesque Oxford Canal and locks at Napton, Warwickshire.

Spectrum Colour Library

Pelsall (B5154) and Bloxwich (A34) are available on day tickets which can be obtained on the bank.

Another canal in the area is the Ashby Canal, controlled mainly by the Coventry and District AA which has the rights from Bridge 22 at Dadlington, off the A447, to Bridge 45 at Market Bosworth on the B585. The Shackerstone and District AA then controls about eight miles of the canal from Snarestone on the B4116 to Congerstone and Carlton. Then, in the Hinckley area, most of the fishing rights are controlled by the Hinkley AA which has headquarters at the Wharf Inn on the A47.

Shropshire Union Canal

The Shropshire Union Canal, from its junction with the Staffs and Worcs Canal at Autherley near Wolverhampton Airport is controlled by the Provincial AA. This is a very long stretch passing through Brewood and Stretton on the A5 to Wheaton Aston, and the club issues honorary membership cards permitting one to fish. From the locks at Wheaton Aston, a stretch of two and a half miles to Bridge 23 near Little Onn is controlled by the Hazeldine AA of Bilston which issues honorary cards for this stretch, as they do for the stretch from Bridge 33 at Gnosall on the A518 to Bridge 35. Day-ticket waters can then be found at Norbury and the South Arm junction and from Norbury to Market Drayton where the canal winds its path across the Salop Plain through some superb countryside.

The Trent and Mersey Canal is controlled mainly by the Walsall and District AS which has the fishing rights from Kings Bromley and on towards Fradley Junction, where day tickets are available, and also all the way through Burton, Willington, which has excellent fishing, and Chellaston on the A514 near Derby.

The upper Staffs and Worcs Canal is controlled by several clubs. Around Stafford the local Izaak Walton (Stafford) AA controls and issue day tickets for long stretches from Milford on the A513 to Bridge 94 below Acton Hill. From there

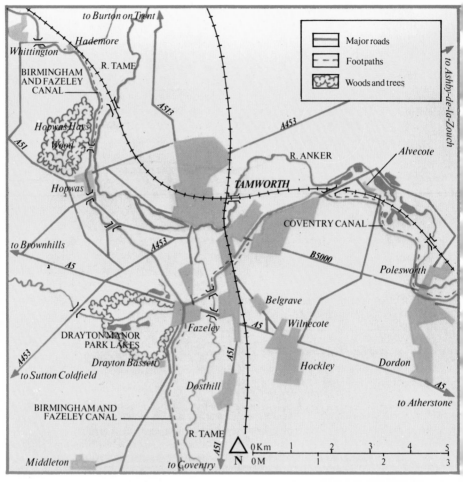

through Acton for four and a half miles to Penkridge the water is controlled by the Wolverhampton Whitmore Reans Constitutional AA. Then, from Cross Green on the A449 through Coven to Autherley and the junction with the Shropshire Union Canal three miles of water are controlled by the Provincial AA. Whitmore Reans then control from Pendeford, Wolverhampton (Bridge 4) to Bridge 16 at Broomhall, and from Wightwick lock by the A454 through Trysull, and Wombourne to Botherham where the Birmingham AA waters start.

Many more canals, with fishing of various quality, are also available in this area criss-crossed with waterways. Surprises are to be had from some canals passing through a very industrial landscape—for example, the Whitmore Reans have a stretch of the Birmingham Canal Navigation running from Alma Street in Wolverhampton.

Another canal, the Bentley Canal, holds fish, although it looks very unlikely, while in the Delph Canal near Brierley Hill, roach to 2lb have been caught with caster baits. The Rushall Canal by the A34 in Walsall holds roach, tench and perch, and the Birmingham arm of the Trent and Mersey Canal at Salford, Brookvale and Perry Barr in Birmingham often yields good specimen roach. Much of it is good free fishing but locals may think you mad for trying.

(Left) Our detail map shows the canals in the area of Tamworth, Staffordshire.

(Below) Food scraps thrown from barges will encourage fish into the area.

G. L. Carlisle

INFORMATION

WATER AUTHORITY
North West Water Authority, Dawson House, Great Sankey, Warrington, WA5 3LW. Tel Penketh 4321.

LICENCES
Rod and line licences, whole area: salmon and migratory trout, season £12, part-season to 31 May £6, part-season from 1 June £7, week £2, juniors (14–16 years) and OAPs season £5, part-season to 31 May £2.50, part-season from 1 June £3. A licence marked * entitles the holder to fish for eels, non-migratory trout (brown, rainbow and char) and freshwater fish for the whole of the respective seasons. Non-migratory trout, season £2, week 50p, juniors and OAPs season £1. Freshwater fish and eels, season £1.25, week 25p, juniors and OAPs season 65p. For the area within the boundary of the former Mersey and Weaver River Authority rod and line licences are issued for a period not exceeding three years from January 1976 for freshwater fish and eels: season 65p, juniors and OAPs season 35p. Juniors aged 13 years and under are exempt from rod and line licences for all the foregoing categories.

Close seasons:
Salmon 1 November to 31 January; brown trout 1 October to 14 March; sea trout 16 October to 30 April; coarse fish 16 March to 15 June.

Size limits:
Salmon and migratory trout 10in (25cm); brown trout 8in (20cm); chub and barbel 10in (25cm); grayling, tench, bream and carp 9in (22cm); roach, perch and rudd 8in (20cm); crucian carp 7in (18cm); dace 6in (15cm); gudgeon and ruffe 4in (10cm).

LOCAL CLUBS AND ASSOCIATIONS
Birmingham AA, V S Hall, 40 Thorpe St, Birmingham 5B5 4AU.
Coventry and District AA, E G Baxter, 15 Boswell Drive, Coventry, W Midlands.
Hazeldine AA, J W Hazeldine, 8 Dudley Rd, Sedgley, W Midlands DY3 1SX.
Hinkley AC, L J Aston, 75 Forest Rd, Hinkley. 611586

Izaak Walton (Stafford) AA, Dick Wilton, Brook House, Brook Lane, Brocton, Stafford. Tel 61429.
Royal Leamington Spa AA, E G Archer, 9 Southway, Leamington Spa. Tel 34185.
Provincial AA, W Hunt, 11 Central Ave, Bilston, Staffs.
Polesworth AA, Mr Hanbury, 8 Tanworth Rd, Polesworth.
Rugby Federation of Anglers, A G Brown, 4 Farm Grove, Rugby.
Shackerstone and District AS, Mrs B M Andrews, 6 Church Rd, Shackerstone, Nuneaton.
Walsall and Distric AS, Alan Clark, 18 Roche Rd, Mossley Estate, Bloxwich, Walsall. Tel Bloxwich 404670.
Whitmore Reans Constitutional AA, R Harold Hughes, FCA, Star Chambers, Princes Sq, Wolverhampton.

TACKLE DEALERS
G Bate Ltd, Colmore Circus, Birmingham 4.
A E Brookes, 958 Bristol Rd South, Birmingham B31 28E.
Austin Clisset, 1801 Pershore Rd, Cotteridge, Birmingham.
Harold Greenway & Sons (main branch), 1010 Chester Rd, Pype Hayes, Birmingham 24. Tel 373 0057.
Stan Jones, 17 Raddlebarn Rd, Selly Oak, Birmingham 29.
Simmonds & Priddey, Stratford Rd, Shirley, Birmingham.
J Keeling, 45 Market Hall, Bull Ring Centre, Birmingham.
Sports & Tackle, 31 High St, Bilston. Tel 46200.
W H Lane & Son, 31–33 London Rd, Coventry.
F Marshall, 360 Alderman's Green Rd, Coventry.
P Ruyssevelt, 467 Holyhead Rd, Coventry.
Peter Gordon, 84 High St, Dudley. Tel 52413.
Mr Hanbury, 6 Tanworth Rd, Polesworth.
A C Claridge's, Greenhill St, Stratford-upon-Avon.
Rod & Tackle, Bridge St, Uttoxeter, Staffs.
G Heath, 97 Rugeley Rd, Chase Terr, Walsall.
Bailey's, 55 The Saltisford, Warwick. Tel 41984.
Stan Molvey, Tackle Shop, Wilmcote.
Allan's, St Johns, Worcester.
F Durrant & Son, Gun & Fishing Tackle, 3 Mealcheapen St, Worcester.
Georges, 12 Bridge St, Worcester.
Richardson's, 28 St Johns, Worcester.
Ron Haynes, 176 Stafford St, Wolverhampton. Tel 23777.

Great Ouse

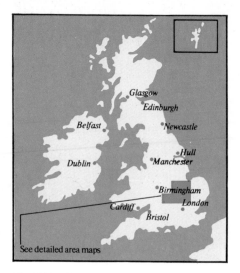

Glasgow
Edinburgh
Belfast
Newcastle
Dublin
Hull
Manchester
Birmingham
Cardiff
London
Bristol
See detailed area maps

The River Great Ouse which discharges into the Wash at King's Lynn, 160 miles from its source near Brackley in Northamptonshire, is one of England's major rivers. It has many tributaries and runs through a massive network of Fenland drains in its lower reaches, the whole of the catchment area containing over 1,000 miles of superb fishing. It is essentially a coarse fishing river system, although some tributaries rising in the chalk of Cambridgeshire and Norfolk support trout. Two man-made lakes in the area are particularly good for brown and rainbow trout; Rutland Water, and Grafham Water near Huntingdon. The high quality of the fishing is reflected in the British Record (rod-caught) Fish list, where six of the eligible freshwater species were caught within the Great Ouse catchment area.

Headwaters

The headwaters of the Great Ouse are narrow and fast, but below Buckingham, the river widens and takes on more character. It provides good chub, dace, perch, and occasionally barbel as it winds down to Bedford taking in the rivers Tove and Ousel. Below Bedford it becomes navigable,

widening and deepening as it is joined by the rivers Ivel and Kym. Bream and roach dominate this stretch which also offers fine chub. Big barbel are sometimes caught from the weir pools, and recently there has been a spate of large carp between Eaton Socon and Offord as the river curves gently down to St Ives. Here it becomes a fen river and is open to the tide below Brownshill Staunch, most of its flow being diverted down the Hundred Foot Drain, through the fens to the sea. The river proper follows its old pre-drainage course, known as The Old West River, takes in the rivers Cam, Granta, and Rhee, and becomes the Great Ouse again at Stretham. It is not tidal here and runs straight, wide and deep, through Ely until its rejoins its brother The Hundred Foot at Denver, taking in the rivers Lark, Little Ouse, and Wissey. Here it is joined by many famous fen drains, The Relief Channel, Cut-Off-Channel, Middle Level, Sixteen Foot, Forty Foot, Pophams Eau, and many others. In all, over 12,000 match pegs are available holding fish.

Fishing the Great Ouse

Anglers fishing the Great Ouse require either a Great Ouse River Division or an Anglian Water Authority Regional licence, and the appropriate season or day tickets. At Newport Pagnell, the Newport Pagnell Fishing Association has both banks above the town upstream to Kickles top meadow. Access to the right bank is from a car park at Kickles Farm, reached by Lakes Lane off the A422, and to the left bank from a car park at Quarry Hall Farm off the B526. Below the town the Newport Pagnell FA has the left bank to Gayhurst, and the right bank from Sherington Bridge to Filgrave, and access to both is from a car park at Park Farm reached by taking the Filgrave road off the B526. Day tickets are not issued but season tickets and a detailed map of these waters are available from the secretary. Downstream, the Leighton Buzzard Angling Club has the left bank from Gayhurst Spinney to Stoke Goldington Brook, the right bank from the Tyringham Estate boundary board to the Emberton Park boundary, and a stretch from the downstream park boundary to Olney Bridge. Below Olney they have Faireys Meadow and the adjoining Osier Cobs as far as the fence, and the remaining osier beds then form a bird sanctuary where there is no fishing. They also have three-quarters of a mile of the right bank at Manor Farm, Clifton Reynes, and access is from Midland Road, Olney or from the old railway track from Clifton Reynes. Other stretches are available at Sharnbrook and Renhold, and although no day tickets are issued, season tickets and further details can be obtained from the secretary.

Farther downstream Bedford Angling Club have both banks from Oakley Bridge to Oakley Viaduct, and the left bank as far

upstream as the spinney. In Bedford they have the right bank from the railway bridge near the boating lake to a point opposite Fenlake Anchor, and access is by the railway bridge or from the A603 by Fenlake Anchor. Day tickets are available as are season tickets for other waters at Bromham, Willington, and Biddenham. The stretch of river through the town from Queens Park to the railway bridge is free fishing.

Great Barford

The London Anglers' Association issues day tickets (weekdays only) and season tickets for both banks downstream of Great Barford north of Bedford on the A428, and for the left bank below Roxton to Tempsford

The River Great Ouse is wide and slow-flowing at Emberton where the Leighton Buzzard Angling Club has good fishing for chub, dace and perch.

Bill Howes

Bridge, except for half a mile owned by the Anchor Hotel. The hotel, situated right next to the A1, has a mile on the right bank, and issues day tickets. Below Little Barford Power Station, St Neots Angling Society has both banks, and above St Neots Paper Mill they have long stretches of both banks as well as substantial lengths below the mill, including the island. The club will issue day tickets on application to their secretary.

Superb backwaters

Below Offord Cluny, The Offord and Bickden Angling Society issues day tickets for both banks, for the right bank above and below the lock, and for a 3 mile left-bank stretch. Between Brampton and Huntingdon the London AA has Portholme meadow— the largest in England—on the left bank, and the West meadow downstream of the railway bridge on the right bank. Godmanchester Angling Society issues day tickets for the right bank opposite Brampton, the Godmanchester recreation ground, the right bank for one mile below Huntington Bridge,

(Above) Bedford Angling Club controls several stretches of quiet pasture along the River Ouse at Oakley.

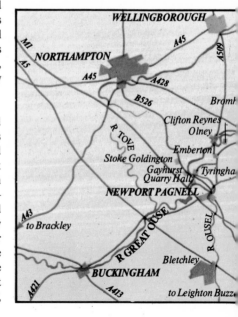

184

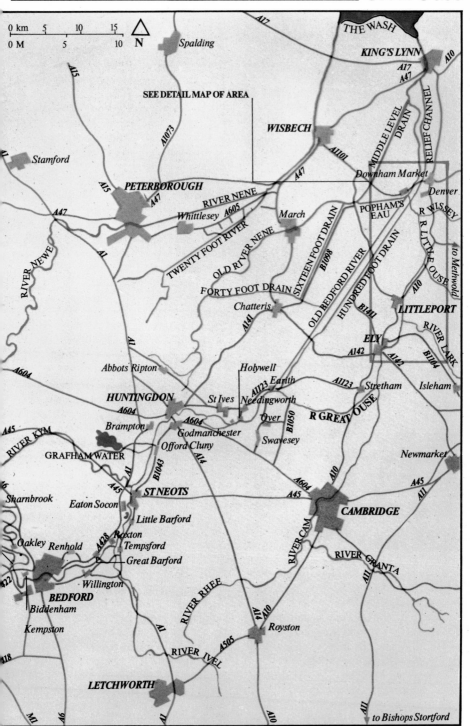

THE WASH

KING'S LYNN

Spalding

SEE DETAIL MAP OF AREA

WISBECH

MIDDLE LEVEL DRAIN

RELIEF CHANNEL

Downham Market

Denver

Stamford

PETERBOROUGH

RIVER NENE

POPHAM'S EAU

R WISSEY

Whittlesey

March

R LITTLE OUSE

to Methwold

RIVER NENE

TWENTY FOOT RIVER

OLD RIVER NENE

FORTY FOOT DRAIN

SIXTEEN FOOT DRAIN

OLD BEDFORD RIVER

HUNDRED FOOT DRAIN

B1098

RIVER NEWE

Chatteris

LITTLEPORT

RIVER LARK

Abbots Ripton

Holywell

ELY

Earith

Stretham

Isleham

HUNTINGDON

St Ives

Needingworth

Brampton

Godmanchester

Over

Swavesey

R GREAT OUSE

GRAFHAM WATER

Offord Cluny

Newmarket

RIVER KYM

Sharnbrook

Eaton Socon

ST NEOTS

CAMBRIDGE

Little Barford

Oakley

Renhold

Roxton

Tempsford

Great Barford

RIVER GRANTA

Willington

RIVER CAM

BEDFORD

Biddenham

Kempston

RIVER RHEE

Royston

LETCHWORTH

RIVER IVEL

to Bishops Stortford

Great Ouse

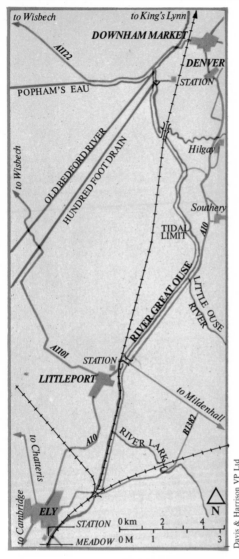

to Wisbech   to King's Lynn

DOWNHAM MARKET

A1122

DENVER

STATION

POPHAM'S EAU

to Wisbech

OLD BEDFORD RIVER

HUNDRED FOOT DRAIN

Hilgay

Southery

TIDAL LIMIT

A10

RIVER GREAT OUSE

LITTLE OUSE RIVER

A1101

STATION

LITTLEPORT

A10

to Mildenhall

B1382

to Chatteris

RIVER LARK

to Cambridge

ELY

STATION   0 km   2   4

MEADOW   0 M   1   3

N

Davis & Harrison VP Ltd

(Left) Detail map of the River Great Ouse from Ely to Downham Market. (Right) Typical view of the Relief Channel at Denver—bleak water with extensive reed beds and miles of artificial bank.

stretch below the lock on the right bank. At Holywell, well-known Fenman Tom Metcalfe-Arnold Arnold issues day tickets for stretches on both banks, and hires out angling punts as well. To reach Holywell, turn off the A1123 at Needingworth. At Brownshill Staunch the Over and Swavesy and District Angling Society has water on both banks above and below the Staunch. Over village is just off the B1050, and anglers should call at the Post Office for information and season tickets.

Most popular stretch

Downstream is the biggest and most popular stretch of the river from Ely to Denver. Above Ely there is a large meadow on the right bank which is excellent free fishing, and below the town the British Sugar Corporation issues day tickets for a $4\frac{1}{2}$-mile stretch that provides good winter roach fishing. The LAA then has a season ticket length, followed by the King's Lynn Angling Association which has the last few miles of the non-tidal Great Ouse. This is probably the very best fishing on the whole river and day tickets are available from the secretary, or from bailiffs. Access to all these fisheries is easy; a minor road hugs the right bank between Ely and Littleport and another road follows the left bank to Denver.

Mentioning briefly some of the major clubs which issue day tickets and accept club match bookings for the fenland drain network; The Anglian Water Authority has the Relief and Cut-Off Channels; Sheffield and District Angling Association has the Middle Level, Pophams Eau, Sixteen Foot, and Old Bedford River; The Chatteris Working Men's Angling the Club and Ramsey Angling Society share the Forty Foot; and the March Working Men's Angling Club shares the Twenty Foot with Whittlesey Angling Association.

and some superb backwaters. At this point the B1043 road skirts the river between St Neots and Godmanchester. Below Huntingdon Bridge, Huntingdon Angling Society has the left bank from the boathouse to Hartford Church, and two miles of the right bank opposite the church.

Farther downstream day tickets are issued by St Ives Angling Society for the right bank above the town, the big meadow below the town on the left bank, and for a

Barrie Rickards

INFORMATION

WATER AUTHORITY

Anglian Water Authority, Great Ouse River Division, Great Ouse House, Clarendon Rd, Cambridge. Tel. 61561.

LICENCES

Regional licence: adult £3.80, junior and OAPs £1. Weekly tickets 75p all categories.

Divisional licence: £2, no concessions for OAPs or juniors. The licences run from 1 January.

WATER AUTHORITY BAILIFFS

Above Bedford: Roger John, 31 Dagnall Rd, Olney, Bucks. Tel Bedford 711859.

Bedford to Earith: Don Prior, 6 Station Rd, Abbots Rippon, Cambs. Tel 375.

Earith to Littleport: Doug Cottrell, Isleham Lock, Isleham, Cambs. Tel 275.

Littleport to Denver and Cut Off Channel: Doug Yates, Brookville, Methwold, Norfolk. Tel 327.

Relief Channel: Cliff Cawkwell, Rudds Cottage, Wiggenhall, St Peter, King's Lynn, Tel St Germans 336.

Fens: John McAngus, 141 Green Park, Chatteris, Cambs. Tel 2597.

LOCAL CLUBS AND ASSOCIATIONS

Bedford Angling Club, R Meads, 155 Marlborough Rd, Bedford. Tel 54708.

Chatteris Working Men's Angling Club, B Knightly, 18 West St, Chatteris, Cambs. Tel 2015.

Godmanchester Angling and Fish Preservation Society (FPS), B P Docherty, 5 Kisby Ave, Godmanchester, Huntingdon. Tel 54365.

Huntingdon Angling Society and FPS, W Wallis, 8 Clayton Way, Huntingdon.

King's Lynn Angling Assoc, G T Bear, 63 Lynn Rd, Downham Market, Norfolk. Tel 2347.

Leighton Buzzard Angling Club, F Groom, 'Nancegollan', 29 Albany Rd, Leighton Buzzard. Tel. 3321.

London Anglers' Assoc, H J Wilson, 183 Hoe St, Walthamstow, London E 17.

March Working Men's Club, H Davies, 1 Percheron Drive, March, Cambs. Tel 3956.

Newport Pagnell Fishing Assoc, F J Read, 19 Chicheley St, Newport Pagnell. Tel 610342.

Offord and Buckden Angling Soc, A Plumb, 8 Latin Close, Offord Cluny, Huntingdon.

Over and Swavesey and District Angling Soc, D A Warren, Post Office, Over, Cambs. Tel Swavesey 217.

Ramsey Angling Soc, P Aldred, 143 Great Whyte, Ramsey, Huntingdon.

St Ives Angling and FPS, J Ives, 25 Greengarth, St Ives. Tel 62630.

St Neots Angling and FPS, S Smith, 10 River Terr, St Neots.

Sheffield and District Anglers' Assoc, J Taylor, Station Hotel, Wicker, Sheffield 3.

Whittlesey Angling Assoc, J Walton, 7 Mayfield Rd, Eastrea, Peterborough.

British Sugar Corporation, R M Lane, Sugar Beet Factory, Ely, Cambs.

TACKLE DEALERS AND LICENCE AGENTS

Ampthill Angling Centre, 14a Woburn St, Ampthill.

The Tackle Box, 109 Cambridge St, Aylesbury. Tel 21574.

Dixon Bros, 95 Tavistock St, Bedford.

Beecroft's, 207 Cherry Hinton Rd, Cambridge. Tel 49010.

Thornton's 46–47 Burleigh St, Cambridge.

Sports and Fashions Ltd, High St, Huntingdon. Tel. 54541.

Kempston Sports, 1 High St, Kempston. Tel 854744.

C Stevens, 55 London Rd, King's Lynn.

A S G Coleby, 15 Granby St, Littleport, Ely.

Anglers' Corner, 73 Austin Rd, Luton, Beds. Tel 51115.

Deryk Hawkes, 1 Scargill Lane, March, Cambs.

Gilder's, 250–252 Wellingborough Rd, Northampton, Tel 36723.

Arthur Smith, 91 Islip Rd, Oxford. Tel 56955.

Nene Sports, Town Bridge, Peterborough.

Paradene Ltd, 44a High St, St Neots.

Lake Bros, 28 Stratford Rd, Wolverton, Bucks.

Nene and Welland

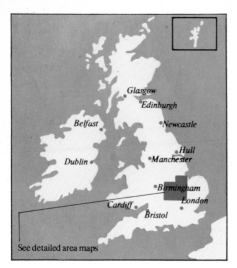

See detailed area maps

Two great slow-moving rivers amble down from Leicestershire and Northamptonshire to the Wash—the Welland and the Nene. The novice will find fishing easy here, while the massive bream, chub and huge roach shoals will tempt the expert.

The Welland and Nene offer a huge expanse of water, it being impossible to cast from one side to the other in many sections. They are also two of Europe's slowest rivers, their slowness a result of widening when the Fens were being drained. The former course of the Welland is just discernible and it is generally no more than 7ft deep.

Source of the Nene

The River Nene rises near Northampton and reaches the tidal section below Peterborough at the Dog-in-a-Doublet. The best fishing is in the lower reaches, especially from Oundle downstream. Near the town, bream of 4lb are common, and fish of 8lb not unknown. During summer, wheat accounts for many good bags of roach, while casters sort out some class fish in autumn.

Oundle Angling Association has the five miles of river looping round the town, and anglers can drive to within a field of the river.

Day tickets at 40p and weekly permits at £1.50 are available from the secretary.

Below Oundle there is another mile of left-bank day-ticket water from Cotterstock church to Perio Lock. Tickets must be obtained in advance from the bailiff, and there are certain restrictions operating. There is then a half mile of water at Fotheringhay with day tickets obtainable on the bank.

Then, near Elton Mill, Leicester and District Amalgamated Society of Anglers has the rights along a pleasant tree-lined stretch, with day tickets costing 40p, available at the Black Horse in Elton.

Downstream there is a four-mile day-ticket stretch at Nassington on alternating banks extending as far as Yarwell, with tickets obtained on the bank. At Yarwell itself, there is nearly a mile of left-bank fishing below the mill, with day tickets available on the site.

Backwaters give the best fishing

From just past Wansford, most of the available water as far the Dog-in-a-Doublet is controlled by the Peterborough and District Angling Association. Membership for those living outside a radius of 20 miles is £2.20, and tackle shops sell day tickets at 30p. Backwaters here offer the best-known fishing venues, including the one at Castor where chub and the occasional barbel are taken. Access is from the A47 near Ailsworth.

Milton Ferry is noted for the large head of chub, only yards from the main road, and there is a small car park near the ancient three-arched bridge. Lower down, Orton Staunch is another favourite venue, with its large weir pool that holds chub, pike, roach and bream.

This section runs down to the town, passing the 'Electricity Cut', once famed for its specimen carp. Now, after the closure of the Peterborough Power Station in 1976, the Cut is to be filled in.

Below the Town Bridge in Peterborough there is a short free stretch on the Embankment—a winter haunt of big bream shoals. Next come the four miles of the North Bank. This is controlled by the Anglian Water Authority and booked at most weekends by match anglers, but short sections are set aside for pleasure fishing.

On the south side, fishing is again held by the Peterborough club and there is a car park near the bank at Fitzwilliam Bridge, where most anglers will be looking for bream and roach. Maggots, casters and bread are favoured, although hemp and tares sometimes account for heavy roach bags in summer. There is a tackle shop, Nene Sports, just over the Town Bridge, close to the football ground.

Birth of the Welland

The River Welland starts its life near Market Harborough, and in its upper reaches is stocked with trout. Its middle reaches, starting around Stamford, are renowned for coarse fishing.

Three dace-populated streams tumble from the red lands of Rutland and slow down near the old stone-built town of Stamford, where chub and roach can be caught in the Meadows. The river slows and broadens here until, at Crowland Bridge, it is less than 3ft deep all the year. Shallowness and flow produce much weed growth. At times it reaches about 30ft from the bank, and there are often huge midstream islands.

The deepest parts of the river are the Crowland bank—the old course of the River Welland—and the Coronation Channel, a horseshoe-shaped relief channel at Spalding.

Pleasure craft moored on the River Nene at Wansford, south of Stamford. The stage is a likely place from which to fish.

Nene and Welland

The Stamford-Welland Angling Association has water at Barrowden and Collyweston, available on day ticket, and the Deeping St James Angling Club has day-ticket water at 50p from Tallington, above Market Deeping, to Willow Drove, a short way upstream of Crowland. Tickets for the latter can be obtained from the tackle dealer in Deeping St James.

Fat Fenland bream

Beyond Willow Drove, as far as Little London, upstream of Spalding, almost all the bank is owned by the Anglian Water Authority. Anglers seeking fat Fenland bream will do best at the small section above Crowland. Every summer weekend, 4lb-plus specimens are taken there. Day tickets can be obtained at Parnell's Pet Shop in Crowland.

Expect to find bream and roach all the way. The best roach show below Locks Mill at the Spalding end, where there are also some sizeable chub. Tickets for this stretch can be obtained from the Golden Ball, Hawthorn Rd, Spalding.

Fishing the River Welland requires special techniques. It is a highly popular match river, and match anglers developed the zoomer float specially to cast across its wide water. This is an 8in float of cane with a bulbous balsa base. The smallest models generally take two and a half swan shot; the biggest, five and a half swan.

Shot is bulked 4ft-5ft below the float, with a small indicator shot near the hook. This rig, fished overdepth, takes bream. Roach men, however, will bulk their shot immediately under the float, adding more

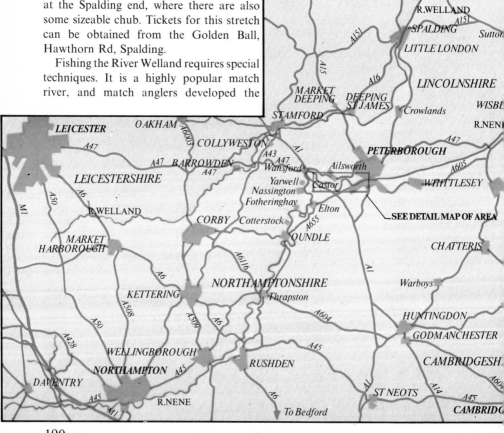

weight halfway down to get through the bleak, plus another indicator shot.

Swingtipping is the most successful method, with a long tail between bomb and hook. Welland bream often bite on the drop. Use worm, maggot, and casters to catch them, either on their own or in a cocktail. Regular changing often pays off. Roach like casters too, but will sometimes go crazy for tares in warm weather.

Chub abound at the Spalding end, and there is one very good area above Four Mile Bar—a footbridge near a pumphouse—marked by a concrete bay.

The hottest swim for large numbers of bream is above Crowland, at a spot opposite a clump of willow trees. This swim, known as 'The Willows', regularly produces 40lb bags, and in 1977 the winner of the National Championship was pegged there.

British Waterways Board

Nene and Welland

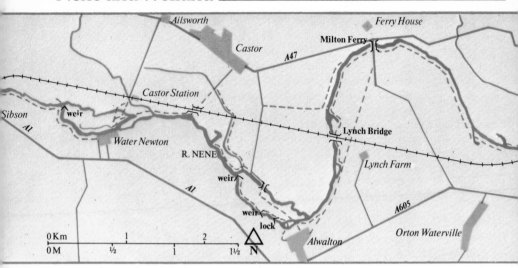

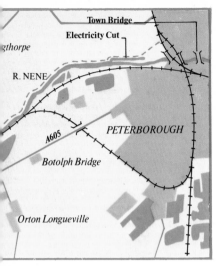

Davis & Harrison VP Ltd/Crown Copyright Reserved

(Left) Detail map shows the Nene between Water Newton and Peterborough, where a number of backwaters offer entertaining fishing for chub, bream, roach and pike. (Below left) There is good access to the Nene at Milton Ferry, Peterborough.

INFORMATION

WATER AUTHORITY
Anglian Water Authority, Diploma House, Grammar School Walk, Huntingdon PE18 6NZ. Tel 56181.
Lincolnshire River Division, 50 Wide Bargate, Boston, Lincs. Tel 65661.
Welland & Nene River Division, North St, Oundle, Peterborough PE8 4AS. Tel 3701.

LICENCES
Regional licence: adult £3.80, junior and OAPs £1. Weekly tickets 75p all categories.
Divisional licence: £2, no concessions for OAPS or juniors. The licences run from 1 January.
No charge for children under 12.
Close seasons: Lincolnshire River Division, coarse fish 15 March to 15 June inclusive, but this does not apply to enclosed waters. Welland & Nene River Division: trout in enclosed waters 30 October to 31 March, non-enclosed waters 29 September to end of February; pike 15 March to 30 September; other freshwater fish 14 March to 16 June.
Size limits: Lincolnshire River Division; pike, common carp, barbel 18in (45cm), bream, tench and chub 14in (35cm), grayling, crucian carp and trout 11in (28cm), roach, dace, rudd and perch 9in (23cm). A keepnet must have a minimum depth of 5ft. Only two rods and lines allowed to be used at the same time by one person. Both rods must be licensed. Welland & Nene River Division: no size limits but livebait must not exceed 7.8in (20cm).

LOCAL CLUBS AND ASSOCIATIONS
Deeping St James AA, J Cran, 53 Castle Drive, Northborough, Cambs.
East Midlands Federation of Anglers, W Hutchins, 63 Huntingtower Rd, Grantham, Lincs.
Leicester and District AS, R Green, 52 Skampton Rd, Thurnby, Leics. Tel Leicester 416605.
Nene and Welland Anglers' Consultative Assoc, J Beal, 150 Roland Ave, Holbrooks, Coventry, W Midlands.
Oundle AA, D Laxton, 31 St Peters Rd, Oundle, Northants. Tel Oundle 2289.
Peterborough and District, W Yates, 75 Lawn Ave, Peterborough, Cambs. Tel 67952.
Stamford Welland AA, K N Fowler, 13 Chatsworth Rd, Stamford, Lincs.

TACKLE DEALERS
Parnell's Pet Shop (children's tackle), 4 North St, Crowland, Cambs. Tel Peterborough 210380.
J K O'Brien, 44 Church St, Deeping St James, Peterborough, Cambs. Tel Market Deeping 342637.
Sports & Fashions Ltd, High St, Huntingdon, Cambs. Tel 54541.
Frank's Fishing Tackle, 38 Wellington St, Kettering, Northants.
Deryk Hawkes, 1 Scargill Lane, March, Cambs.
Gilders, 250 Wellingborough Rd, Northampton, Northants.
F Wade & Son, High St, Old Fletton, Peterborough, Cambs. Tel 65159.
Webbs, 196 Newark Ave, Peterborough, Cambs. Tel 66466.
Nene Sports, Town Bridge, Peterborough, Cambs.
Kirks Tackle Shop, 6 Bond St Court, Spalding, Lincs.
Tackle & Trains, Railway Station Yard, Spalding, Lincs.
Stamford Gun Shop, 8 St Mary's Hill, Stamford, Lincs. Tel 2796.
A Watts, 4 Herriotts Lane, Wellingborough, Northants.

Spectrum Colour Library

Norfolk

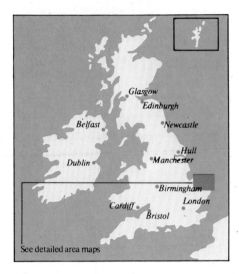

See detailed area maps

Most famous for its Broads, Norfolk probably has more accessible fishing than any other county.

Three major river systems feed the Broads—the Bure, Wensum and Yare, each with tidal stretches, and two tidal rivers, the Ant and Thurne. There are also numerous gravel pit complexes plus natural and man-made lakes, meres, ponds and minor rivers.

The River Wensum runs crystal-clear from its source above Fakenham along a 30-mile course to Norwich. It has 2lb roach, large dace, and chub to over 6lb, with perch, a few bream, a good head of native brown trout, and pike in plenty.

Fishing starts at Fakenham, where the local club controls a four-mile length. Trout day tickets at £1.50 and coarse day tickets at 50p are obtained from the local tackle shop.

Wensum trout and roach

The next available stretch, for trout only, is at Guist, and is controlled by the Anglian Water Authority. Day tickets, bookable in advance, cost £1.50. From Guist downstream, the LAA controls some good roach fishing at North Elmham with tickets from E Bond, 81 Lakenfields, Norwich.

There is more day-ticket fishing four miles downstream at Swanton Morley with 50p day tickets obtained from the bailiff of Morley Fisheries. These give access to excellent coarse fishing in the river and in three gravel pits.

At Lyng, the Dereham and District AA sells day tickets for a short length of the river, while on the opposite bank a little farther upstream, the LAA has a length, and another at Lenwade Common—both with good roach fishing.

Below Lenwade much of the fishing is private, except for a free stretch at Ringland Bridge, and around the sluice pool at Costessey, where the AWA introduced some barbel a few years back. All the fishing from here downstream to Hellesden is private except for a short length opposite Drayton Green Lanes where AWA day tickets at 50p are issued. Downstream from Hellesden to Norwich, much of the Wensum comes into the city boundaries and is free fishing. At New Mills the river becomes tidal and offers excellent free sport for roach, bream and pike. Eventually, after flowing close to Thorpe Station and beneath Carrow Road

194

Bridge, the Wensum joins up with the Yare.

The Yare is in two parts—the upper reaches, clear, weedy and shallow, hold specimen dace, roach, perch and chub, and the deep, wide, tidal reaches below Norwich hold good stocks of roach and bream. Many of the upper reaches offer fishing, particularly from Bawburgh to Norwich.

In this region, over 10 miles of excellent roach, dace and chub fishing is controlled by the AWA at 50p per day, with a fair amount of free fishing on common land in the Earlham-to-Keswick reach.

At Trowse, the Yare becomes tidal and the fishing is free wherever there is access. The AWA controls access at Postwick, reached via Ferry Lane, Strumpshaw Marshes, Buckenham Ferry, reached by the Beauchamp Arms roadway, Cantley, reached via the Red House Hotel grounds, and at Langley.

Between Strumpshaw and Buckenham on the southern bank, two dykes lead to Rockland Broad, an excellent fishery of about 50 acres. It is mostly shallow, 2ft–6ft, but is 12ft deep at the junction of the short

(Below left) Reed-fringed Filby Broad, so typical of the area's popular waters.
(Below right) Fine fishing water on the Wensum at Hellesden Mill, near Norwich.

dyke. Roach and bream fishing is good, and pike are plentiful in winter. Downstream from Langley, after Reedham Ferry, the new cut joins the Yare and the Waveney, which flow two miles apart at this point but gradually run together to Breydon Water and on to Great Yarmouth.

Superb tidal Thurne

Just five miles long, the tidal Thurne is a superb fishery, containing large quantities of roach and bream, particularly in the Potter Heigham to Martham reaches. The river links (via Candle Dyke) the Bure to Hickling Broad, Heigham Sounds and Horsey Mere. Before 1969, the fishing here was probably the finest in Britain, but then stocks were wiped out by toxins released in the water by decomposing algae. Now, sport is improving, and Hickling Broad and Heigham Sounds, joined by a deep dyke, are again producing good bags of bream and roach. The bream average close on 3lb, with roach over 1lb.

Boats can be hired at Hickling or Great Yarmouth and, from these points, taken anywhere along the Thurne and onto the Broads. There is also extensive free fishing along the Thurne from Martham, through Potter Heigham and to where the Thurne enters the Bure.

Although the Ant has a short non-tidal

Bill Howes

John Wilson

195

pike in winter. The Ant then flows out of the Broad's southern end, through Irstead Shoals, where the flow can be strong at times, and downstream through How Hill, Johnson Street, and to Ludham Bridge. The AWA controls sections of free bank fishing on these reaches, which are extremely good winter and autumn venues. Half a mile below Ludham, the Ant joins the Bure.

For most of its length, the Bure is tidal, deep and fast, and holds good roach, dace, and bream in its upper reaches. It connects with several Broads, and with the Thurne and Ant as it flows to Great Yarmouth.

Fishing in much of the upper Bure has deteriorated, but the AWA controls good lengths at Burgh, Oxnead, Buxton and Bayton Bridge. Roach and bream are few, but large, with roach over 2lb and bream over 6lb taken each season, and the occasional fair trout and pike.

The Bure becomes tidal at Horstead Mill Pool, and from this point the fishing is free. Good locations are at Coltishall, Belaugh and Wroxham, where quality bream and roach are to be found, with perch, rudd and numerous pike, some very large. The flow is not strong, but the Bure gathers pace and depth as it flows through Woodbastwick

Marshes and onto Horning, a good winter fishing location.

The AWA controls access to free fishing at Woodbastwick, South Walsham and Upton—and again, much farther downstream, at Acle and Burgh Marshes, where the flow is incredibly strong and ledgering is the only method of fishing. Access to these lower reaches is from the main Stokesby road.

Several miles downstream, the Bure reaches Great Yarmouth. Few anglers fish these last few miles because of the salt tides, particularly likely during the winter months.

Access to the Broads

Between Wroxham and Acle, the Bure feeds many publicly accessible Broads: Wroxham Broad, Salhouse Broad, Decoy Broad, Ranworth Broad, and South Walsham Broad.

Wroxham Broad, with over 100 acres of water of 2ft–10ft deep, has good roach fishing, and numerous bream and good pike in winter. Salhouse Broad offers similar fishing, but it not so deep. Boats are hired at Wroxham, or one can bank-fish by taking the road from Salhouse village.

Decoy Broad is an enclosed water reserved for Norwich and District AA members.

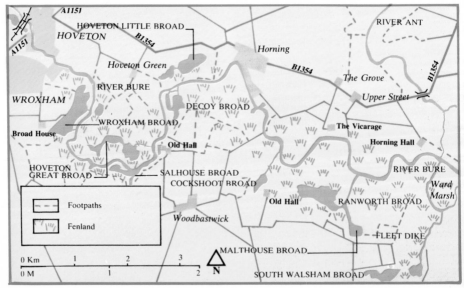

A. F. Kersting

(Above) There are plenty of bream to be taken from the Thurne at Potter Heigham. (Below left) Detail map shows a group of Broads to the north-east of Norwich.

Membership is £1.50 per day. This large Broad, with depths from 3ft–12ft, offers superlative summer fishing for sizeable bream, some roach and tench, and good pike in winter.

Ranworth Broad consists of an outer part which offers free fishing, and a large, shallow, inner Broad, also controlled by Norwich and District AA, which offers fishing from 16 June to 31 September and from 1–14 March. Summer fishing produces good bags of roach and bream, with big pike during the last fortnight of the season.

South Walsham Broad also has two parts: the inner Broad strictly private, the outer Broad offering free fishing. Roach and bream sport is good during summer and autumn, but winter fishing is variable.

The Great·Ouse Relief Channel and the Cut Off Channel—deep man-made drains cut between high flood banks—relieve the Great Ouse of much of its flood water and provide high quality coarse fishing. They abound with roach and bream, and also offer pike and zander. The Relief Channel is the larger stretch, being over 100 yards wide in many places and 11 miles long, stretching from Denver Sluice to King's Lynn. Access

to both banks is possible via the bridges spanning the channel at regular intervals.

The Cut-Off Channel stretches from Denver to Mildenhall, but accessible fishing is limited to the Denver to West Dereham stretch on both banks. Day tickets at 65p cover fishing on both channels and are available from local tackle shops.

The Little Ouse is a wonderful river, but many of its higher reaches are strictly private. After running through the pine forest of Thetford Warren, the Ouse reaches Thetford, where fishing is free within the town boundaries as far as the first staunch. Good roach and specimen dace exist in this clear-flowing, shallow and weedy river, which usually fishes best during the winter.

Fishing downstream is controlled by the Thetford and Breckland AC, for members only. Then at Brandon, the LAA and Bury St Edmunds AC control a good stretch, with day tickets for non-members in places.

The Ouse then flows to Lakenheath Halt and Wilton Bridge, where fishing rights are shared by the Thetford and Breckland AC and the Bury St Edmunds AC, which both issue day tickets. Bream start to show in this part of the river, along with sizeable roach and good chub and pike. The last four miles of the river, before the Little Ouse joins forces with the Great Ouse at Brandon Creek, is nearly all private fishing.

Enchanting Wissey

Although the Wissey is a long and enchanting little river, with hugh chub and trout in its higher reaches, it only becomes accessible to anglers at Stoke Ferry, close to its end. The King's Lynn AA controls some good stretches here and on both banks two miles upstream at Denver Sluice where the river joins the Great Ouse. Day tickets are available from the club. A section of the river at Five Mile House Farm is reserved for LAA members and one below Stoke Ferry Bridge is reserved for the Swaffham AC.

Several lakes near Lenwade, off the A1067 north of Norwich, are controlled by the LAA and available on a 40p day ticket. The four Bridge Lakes (up to 5 acres) hold

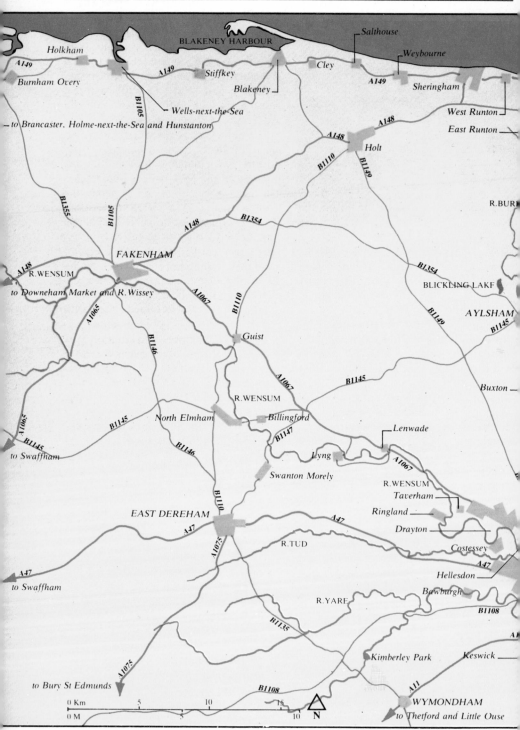

BLAKENEY HARBOUR

Salthouse

Holkham

Weybourne

A149

Burnham Overy

A149

Stiffkey

Cley

A149

Blakeney

Sheringham

B1105

Wells-next-the-Sea

West Runton

to Brancaster, Holme-next-the-Sea and Hunstanton

A148

A148

East Runton

B1110

Holt

R.BUR

B1355

B1105

B1149

B1354

FAKENHAM

A148

BLICKLING LAKE

A148

R.WENSUM

B1354

to Downeham Market and R.Wissey

A1067

B1149

AYLSHAM

B1110

B1145

B1065

Guist

Buxton

B1146

A1067

B1145

B1065

R.WENSUM

B1145

North Elmham

Billingford

Lenwade

to Swaffham

B1146

B1147

A1067

Lyng

R.WENSUM

Taverham

Swanton Morely

Ringland

EAST DEREHAM

B1110

Drayton

A47

A47

Costessey

A1075

R.TUD

A47

A47

to Swaffham

Hellesdon

Bawburgh

R.YARE

B1108

B1135

AI

A1075

Kimberley Park

Keswick

to Bury St Edmunds

B1108

A11

WYMONDHAM

0 Km   5   10   15

0 M   5   10

N

to Thetford and Little Ouse

stretch, the river is not of importance to anglers until it reaches Wayford Bridge over which runs the A149 Stalham road. The flow here is of medium pace, and the river is inhabited by roach, bream and pike, as in most of its length. Fishing is free wherever the banks are accessible.

Downstream from Wayford, the Ant enters Barton Broad—a huge area of shallow water offering good bream fishing, with

Norfolk's fisherman's paradise: great rivers and prolific, man-made Broads.

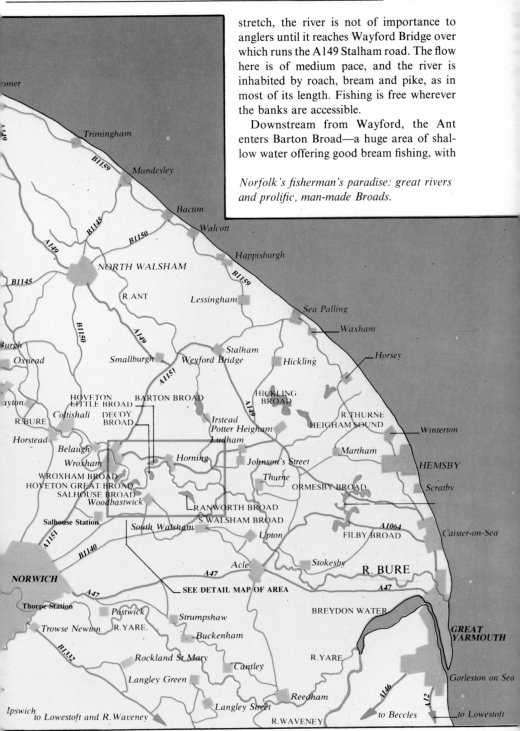

(Above) Ormesby Broad, an ideal place for a quiet and peaceful afternoon's fishing. (Left) The Great Ouse Relief Channel, where the angler can fish for bream, roach, pike and the exciting zander.

John Wilson

rudd, perch and pike; the two Common Lakes hold roach, rudd, tench and some good pike; and the six Station Lakes (up to 8 acres) hold specimen tench, rudd, carp to 32½lb, pike, roach, perch and big eels.

Day-ticket gravel pits

In the same area, there are also several gravel pits, controlled by the Dereham and District AC and offering fishing on a 50p day ticket. The two Worthing Gravel Pits, near Swanton Morley, hold good perch, roach and pike, while the Lyng Pit (4 acres), off the A1067, offers a good head of tench and bream, and large carp.

The Lyng Easthaugh Pit (20 acres) is reached via the A1067 at Lenwade, and holds an enormous roach stock, with tench and pike. Billingford Pit (3 acres), reached via the A1067 Bawdeswell road and the Swanton Morley road, holds perch, roach and big tench.

Other pits and lakes are controlled by the AWA and available on a season permit at £3 or day ticket permits at 50p. Taverham Pits,

reached from the A1067 via Taverham village, are three large waters containing roach, bream, good tench, carp to over 20lb and pike. Haveringland Lake (12 acres), off the B1149 Haveringland road, is a shallow lake holding good roach and bream stocks plus some large pike; while Blickling Lake (20 acres), off the A140 via Aylsham, is set in National Trust grounds and is a shallow, weedy lake with good roach, big pike, bream and carp, and plentiful tench.

Seven other well-matured pits are set in the beautiful Ringland Hills near Norwich, adjacent to the Wensum. Their depth is 2ft–20ft and they contain roach, perch, good tench, carp to over 20lb, big eels, and some small pike, and can be reached via the A1067 at Taverham.

Norfolk sea fishing

The entire Norfolk coast offers excellent beach and offshore fishing. Thornbacks, tope and bass are most sought after in summer, and whiting and cod from late September. Other species found all year

England Scene

East of Blakeney, one passes through Cley, which has good bass fishing near the wreck, Salthouse, Weybourne, with wreck fishing for bass, Sheringham, West and East Runton, and Cromer. The latter is the largest North Norfolk resort, and in addition to beach fishing offers anglers a comfortable pier.

Down the coast from Cromer, good spots are at Trimingham Cliffs, Mundesley, Bacton, which has good offshore boat fishing, Walcott, Happisburgh, Lessingham, Eccles, Seapalling, Waxham, Horsey, Winterton, Hemsby, Scratby and Caistor-on-Sea, all with excellent beaches.

Great Yarmouth

Great Yarmouth is Britain's second largest holiday resort, and offers good summer and winter offshore boat fishing, and fine beach and pier fishing for whiting and cod. The Wellington Pier caters especially for anglers. Across the river, Gorleston-on-Sea is another good location, particularly for whiting and cod.

round are dabs, flounders, soles and eels, with mullet and the occasional sea trout also taken, particularly between Hunstanton and Blakeney. Beach access points between these two are Holme-next-the-Sea, Branchester, Burnham Overy, Holkham, Wells-next-the-Sea and Stiffkey.

Several boats may be chartered at Blakeney Harbour to fish for offshore skate and tope, or for conger, pollack and ling off the wrecks.

Fresh Norfolk lugworms make an excellent bait for the whole region and can be obtained from tackle shops or from houses displaying 'lug for sale' notices.

Suffolk

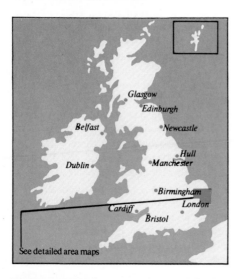

See detailed area maps

The River Waveney starts as a very small stream but quickly matures into a beautiful river. Good fishing starts in the Diss area where the Diss Angling Club controls many stretches. This area holds the same species as much of the River Waveney—good roach, dace, chub, perch and pike.

At Hoxne, the River Dove joins the main stream which flows down to Needham, and tench and a few bream start to appear, despite the clear water. The Anglian Water Authority has some day ticket fishing in this area and again at Weybread where the Harleston, Wortwell and District Angling Club controls some attractive sections of the bank, particularly productive for big roach and chub. Day tickets are available from

Denny and Sons, tackle dealers in Harleston.

The river then winds through picturesque farmland via Mendham, Homersfield and on to Earsham where one can fish free on the common. Downstream at Bungay, the Waveney stretches around Bungay Common providing good roach and chub fishing for 50p a day. After the town, the river reaches Wainford Maltings where the Anglian Water Authority controls day-ticket fishing, but much of the best fishing here, especially for bream averaging over 4lb, is controlled by the Bungay Cherry Tree Angling Club. The club has a fine stretch of water reaching half way downstream to Ellingham, a long piece farther upstream at Flixton, and a newly acquired piece on the tidal reaches. New members are always welcome.

The tidal Waveney

At Ellingham, the Waveney becomes tidal with little access other than by boat, until Geldeston where the Anglian Water Authority controls a short stretch on the left-hand bank which is free fishing.

Downstream from the old lock at Geldeston, the river widens and harbours some good stocks of roach and bream. It flows through Barsham Marshes towards Beccles where the Anglian Water Authority controls more free fishing with access via Pudding Lane and Farm Road.

Downstream from Beccles on the Gillingham side, two miles of water are controlled by the Anglian Water Authority. Their next piece of free fishing is at Worlingham on a 170-yard stretch of the Suffolk bank. The Waveney in this area is a deep, wide and strongly flowing river with good shoals of bream and quality roach. It passes Burgh St Peter and then reaches the junction of Oulton Dyke which provides access to Oulton Broad.

In the Broad proper, flow is not really noticeable, so light float tackle can be used to take roach and bream. There are also some pike and just a few perch. The large perch of yesteryear which made Oulton Broad famous have been absent for some time. There is little bank fishing, but boat fishing is better, and boats can be hired from J Mallet of Camping Boats near Carlton.

Downstream from Oulton Broad, the Waveney passes through wide bends down to St Olaves, and then to Haddiscoe where the New Cut flows off from the Norfolk bank linking the River Waveney to the River Yare at Reedham. This cut offers free fishing for 2½ miles, but the flow is very fast.

The River Gipping is not considered a worthwhile coarse fishery until it reaches Stowmarket. From here it flows to Baylham and offers good sport for roach, dace, bream, perch and pike. Depth fluctuates from 3ft to 6ft with the occasional deep hole.

(Left) John Wilson, noted angler, netting a good bream from a stretch of the Upper Waveney at Bungay. This part of the Waveney is well known for its large bream and roach.
(Right) Sunlight dapples the waters of the Mere at Diss, Norfolk. Among the coarse species found in this water are carp, bream, tench and rudd. Day tickets are available from a tackle dealer in Mere Street.

Richard Jemmett

Suffolk

The river remains quite shallow as it flows to Great Blakenham, Claydon and then to Bramford Bridge. Along much of the river, day tickets are available at 50p from the Gipping Angling Preservation Society which has done much over the last two decades to improve the state of the river following mild pollution. Numerous restocking programmes have been completed which have included the restocking of tench and bream. The Society welcomes new members, and also has other waters including a number of pits and a lake.

To the Orwell Estuary

From Bramford Bridge the River Gipping flows down to Sproughton where there is more day-ticket fishing with tickets available from local tackle dealers or from Sproughton Post Office. From the railway

(Right) Suffolk's picture-book scenery includes some of the most rewarding and entertaining fishing in the country.
(Below) The Deben at Wickam Market.

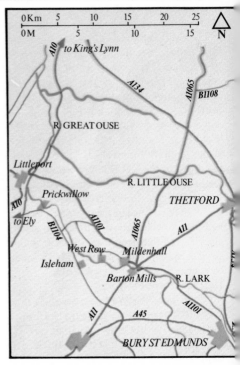

bridge, downstream fishing is entirely free from the towpath, and the water is quite deep. Then, after splitting between West End sluice and Horseshoe Weir in Ipswich, the Gipping becomes tidal and is known as the Orwell Estuary.

Similar to all Suffolk rivers, the Deben starts as a small, clear-flowing stream and matures into a full-blooded estuary in its tidal reaches. Much of the upper river is private fishing with clubs controlling large pieces of the bank at Cretingham, Kettleburgh, Easton and Wickham Market.

Near Wickham Market at Clevering Bridge, over three miles of the River Deben is controlled by the Woodbridge and District

205

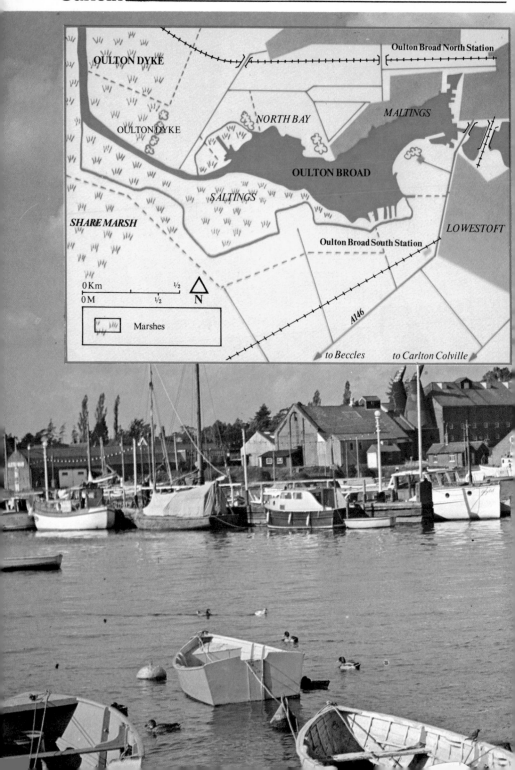

Suffolk

OULTON DYKE

Oulton Broad North Station

OULTON DYKE

NORTH BAY

MALTINGS

OULTON BROAD

SALTINGS

SHARE MARSH

LOWESTOFT

Oulton Broad South Station

0 Km   ½
0 M   ½

N

Marshes

A146

to Beccles   to Carlton Colville

Angling Club. They do not issue day tickets, but anyone interested in joining should contact the Secretary at the Rod and Gun Shop in Woodbridge (Tel 2377). Good catches of quality roach are regularly taken from the club's waters, along with some bream, dace, perch and pike which run on the small side.

Sea species

Below Wickham Market, the river flows to Ufford, and at Melton Mill Pool becomes tidal. The tidal reaches are free fishing and offer good sport with mullet, flounder, eels and the odd bass.

The River Lark rises above Bury St Edmunds and flows to Barton Mills where it flows beneath the A11 Norwich to London road. These upper reaches are fast, clear and shallow, harbouring trout, dace and some good chub. However, much of the fishing is strictly private. It is not until the river changes its pace to a more sluggish river at Mildenhall and towards West Roe and Isleham that bream and numbers of roach are found. Much of the fishing in this area is controlled by the Lark Angling Preservation Society which issues tickets.

Downstream from Isleham Lock, the Lark travels towards Prickwillow, with typical Fenland bream fishing all the way until it merges with the Great Ouse at Littleport.

There are also several lakes in the area. Redgrave Lake lies off the A143 road close

Photo: Spectrum Colour Library

Oulton Broad, facing the Maltings. This water yielded a record perch. (Left) Our detail map of the brackish Oulton Broad.

to the village of Botesdale, and can be fished with day tickets at £1. This long, wide, clear-watered and weedy lake offers superb tench fishing during the summer months in truly peaceful surroundings. Good bags, with fish averaging 4lb, are regularly taken, together with perch, rudd and bream. In the winter, fishing is very good for pike which have been caught to over 30lb.

Fritton Lake lies off the A143 close to the village of St Olaves, and is available on a day ticket costing 50p for bank fishing and £2 for boat fishing. This huge lake, the largest in East Anglia, is for most of its two-mile length over 10ft deep. Huge shoals of bream averaging 4–6lb are there for the finding—and for this one must groundbait heavily. Other species include roach, perch and some large eels and pike. There is a little bank fishing, but boat fishing is much better. The lake closes for fishing on 30 September.

There are also several stillwater gravel pits controlled by the Harleston, Wortwell and District Angling Club and available from Denny & Sons, Harleston, on a 50p day ticket. The Weybread gravel pits, reached from the A143 Harleston road via the Weybread road, consist of three large pits, one of which is over 50 acres, situated closely together and adjacent to the River Waveney. They vary in depth—from 2 to 3ft on the gravel bars to over 12ft.

Good pit fishing

All three pits hold good stocks of roach and bream, plus some good tench, and the smaller pits, called No 1 and No 2, hold really good stocks of mirror and leather carp. The average size of these is 3–8lb, with larger fish over 20lb taken each season. High-protein and cat food bait work well here, either freelined or link-ledgered. Some good-sized pike are also to be found.

Although covering only 50 miles, the Suffolk coastline offers superlative sea fishing—both off and inshore. Bass have been very much in evidence during the past few years and are a welcome addition to the summer shore species of dabs, flounders, plaice, sole and eels. Offshore, and in

The beautiful old gravel -pit workings near Harleston, Suffolk.

addition to the species mentioned, good skate, tope, dogfish and the occasional conger are to be found. Whiting and cod are the predominant species from September.

Travelling southwards along the coastline from Great Yarmouth, Hopton and Corton offer easy access to the beaches, as does Lowestoft where in addition to the beach there is Claremont Pier, and the South Pier harbour entrance—a long concrete promontory with plenty of room. Good mullet are also taken here.

Offshore anglers are well catered for by skippers Ron Culley (Tel: Great Yarmouth 73045) and Bob Williams (Tel: Lowestoft 66183) who specialize in skate and tope during the summer, and cod during the winter months. Additional information can be obtained from Sam Hook's tackle shop (Tel: Lowestoft 65821).

Travelling south of Lowestoft, Pakefield is another good spot, followed by Kessingland, Benacre and Covehithe, with good beach access all the way to Southwold.

Suffolk

John Wilson

Southwold offers good all-round sport in the harbour particularly for bass and mullet, and also from the pleasure pier. Additional local information can be obtained from Southwold's Angling Centre (Tel 722085).

Beach fishing

South of Southwold are Walberswick, Dunwich, Minsmere, and Sizewell. The latter, where the power station sends warm water into the sea, is a good bass spot.

South of Sizewell, there is good beach access at Aldeburgh, and at Orfordness where Orford Island can be reached from the quay with regular boat trips for anglers. For boats, contact R Brinkley (Tel: Orford 481). South of Orfordness is Shingle Street, a popular location which reaches down to East Lane and the mouth of the river Deben. Local information is available from the Rod and Gun Shop in Woodbridge.

At Bawdsey, fishing in the estuary of the River Deben is good for mullet and bass during the summer months, with the occasional sea trout.

Felixstowe, with the Deben flowing into the sea from the north, and Harwich Harbour draining the rivers Stour and

Orwell on the southern point, has excellent and varied fishing from beaches and estuaries. The British record bass was caught here in 1943. The pier offers alternative sport particularly for the winter cod and whiting fishing, while for charter boats for hire one should contact D Goodall (Tel: Felixstowe 5979).

Cod in excess of 40lb have been taken offshore from Felixstowe in past years. For additional information contact tackle dealer L T Bobby, Undercliffe Road, Felixstowe (Tel 2709).

INFORMATION

WATER AUTHORITY
Anglian Water Authority, Diploma House, Grammar School Walk, Huntingdon, PE18 6NZ. Tel 56181.
Norfolk and Suffolk River Division, Yare House, 62-64 Thorpe Rd, Norwich NR1 1SA. Tel Norwich 615161.

LICENCES
Regional licence: adult £3.80, junior and OAPs £1. Weekly tickets 75p all categories.
Divisional licence: £2, no concessions for OAPs and juniors. Licences run from 1 Jan. Children under 12 free. Norfolk and Suffolk River Division; only two rods are allowed to be used at the same time, and only then if in possession of two licences.
Close seasons: coarse fish 16 June to 14 March, trout 1 April to 30 September.
Size limits: Bream, chub, trout and grayling 10in (25cm), carp, roach, rudd, dace, tench, and perch 8in (20cm), pike 24in (61cm), Catch limit of trout four fish. No bait or lure other than dry or wet fly allowed when fishing for salmon or trout during the coarse fish close season.

LOCAL CLUBS AND ASSOCIATIONS
Bungay Cherry Tree Angling Club, I Gosling, 37 St Mary's Terr, Bungay. Tel 2982.
Diss Angling Club, Mr M Nelson, Skelton Rd, Diss. Tel 3359.
Gipping Angling Preservation Soc, G Alderson, 19 Clover Close, Chantry Estate, Ipswich. Tel 211402.
Harleston, Wortwell and District Angling Club, John Adamson, 21 Thomas Manning Rd, Diss. Tel 3952.
Lark Angling Preservation Soc, G J Amis, 22 Cricks Rd, West Row, Bury St Edmunds, Suffolk. Tel Isleham 614.
Woodbridge and District Angling Club, Mr Abbot, Rod and Gun Shop, 62 The Thoroughfare, Woodbridge. Tel 2377.

CHARTER BOATS
D Goodall. Tel Felixstowe 5979.
Ron Culley. Tel Great Yarmouth 73045.
Bob Williams. Tel Lowestoft 66183.
R. Brinkley. Tel Orford 481.
J Mallet, Camping Boats, Carlton.

TACKLE DEALERS
A Crack, Blyburgate, Beccles. Tel 712045.
L Bobby, Undercliff Rd, Felixstowe. Tel 2709.
G Denny, Market Place, Harleston. Tel 852248.
Bowman's, Orwell St, Ipswich. Tel 51195.
Sam Hook, Bevan St, Lowestoft. Tel 65821.
E Taylor, High St, Saxmundham. Tel 2102.
Southwold Angling Centre, High St, Southwold. 722085.
The Swim, Gaol Lane, Sudbury. Tel 74066.
Rod and Gun Shop, The Thoroughfare, Woodbridge. Tel 2377.
E Nunn, Mere St, Diss.

209

Essex Stour

Glasgow
Edinburgh
Belfast
Newcastle
Hull
Dublin
Manchester
Birmingham
Cardiff
London
Bristol

See detailed area maps

Rising at Wrattling Common near Weston Green, just inside Cambridgeshire, the Stour soon trickles over the border into Suffolk. Then, along nearly all of its length, it forms the boundary between Essex and Suffolk. By Wixoe and Clare it is a young river flowing between high grassy banks that wind through the farmlands. Dace and roach inhabit the water where mallards and moorhens haunt the reeds. After Sudbury the Stour widens to flow through Bures and into Constable country: Nayland, Stratford St Mary, Dedham, and Flatford hence to the sea. It is just over 40 miles long.

Constable country

The Stour is fairly wide, clean flowing, with weeds and lily pads, and on average 40ft across with an average depth of 6-8ft. Predominantly dace water, it meanders through the Suffolk valley to the estuary. In many places, especially Flatford Mill, it has hardly changed since Constable painted it.

The fish species are those common to the rivers of East Anglia; bream, dace, chub, perch, pike and big eels. Flounders and grey mullet are found where saltwater moves into the lower tidal reaches to provide ideal

brackish water conditions for these species. Down to the beginning of the brackish area, the freshwater angler may fish with light tackle baited with maggots and drift for roach, or ledger a bunch of lobworms for millpool bream. The roving fisherman carries bait and spare tackle in a holdall and hunts solitary chub and roach shoals in the glides and deep holes under banks, wandering upriver where tall reeds choke the footpaths. The gregarious and less dedicated fisherman picnics with his family on the crowded banks at Dedham and Flatford Mill, where all species can be caught.

Because the course of the Stour is winding and the road system does not always follow its banks, the river is almost invisible to the motorist. It sparkles under road bridges and its position can be judged by the stands of willows and reeds. But the only way to really see this river is to walk its banks.

'Private Water—No Trespassers'

Fishing the Stour is a problem. You cannot fish where you want. The river is strictly preserved and there are few day tickets and public stretches. There are many pools and backwaters where huge fish roll, but always on the banks or the approach roads are the inevitable signs 'No Fishing' or 'Private Water—No Trespassers'. The angler intent on fishing this river should consider applying for club membership, for the cost of subscription will be repaid in the quality fishing he gets. In this way he can gain access to the quieter waters.

The London Anglers' Association owns most of the stretches along the Stour, but issues day tickets at 40p for one stretch of water only—Secretaries Farm at Bures. Tickets are obtainable from Mr F Staples, 25 Nayland Road, Bures. The annual individual subscription of the LAA is £5.50 which entitles you to a wide selection of swims from Clare and Cavendish through Glemsford and Sudbury to Middleton,

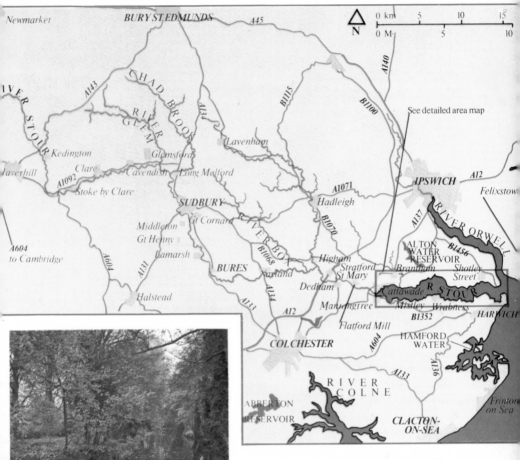

Newmarket · BURY ST. EDMUNDS · 445 · 0 km 5 10 15 · N · 0 M 5 10

RIVER STOUR · CHAD BROOK · RIVER GLEM · A143 · A134 · B1115 · B1100 · A140 · See detailed area map

Kedington · Clare · Glemsford · Lavenham · A1092 · Cavendish · Long Melford · IPSWICH · A12 · Felixstowe

Haverhill · Stoke by Clare · SUDBURY · A1071 · Hadleigh · B1070 · A137 · RIVER ORWELL

A604 to Cambridge · Middleton · Gt Cornard · Gt Henny · RIVER BOX · A131 · B1068 · Higham · Stratford St Mary · ALTON WATER RESERVOIR · Brantham · Shotley Street · B1456

Lamarsh · BURES · Nayland · Dedham · A134 · Cattawade · R STOUR · Mistley · Wrabness · HARWICH

Halstead · A133 · A12 · Manningtree · B1352

Flatford Mill · COLCHESTER · A604 · HAMFORD WATER · A136

RIVER COLNE · A133 · Frinton on Sea

ABBERTON RESERVOIR · CLACTON-ON-SEA

Richard Jemmet

Our map shows the course of the Stour from its source in Cambridgeshire, through Essex and Suffolk to the estuary at Mistley, Wrabness and Harwich. A section of the young river is seen in our photo taken at Clare. The banks are fairly high and wooded. Later the more mature river is wider, with lower banks as it flows through Sudbury, Bures and Flatford, meandering through valleys to reach the estuary.

Lamarsh, Bures and Nayland. Here you can fish bream, chub, dace, perch, pike, roach and tench, and these swims may be preferred to the more popular stretches which tend to get very crowded and noisy in summer.

Day tickets

Day tickets are also available from local angling clubs for a number of swims at Sudbury, Long Melford, Great Henny, Great Cornard and Brantham Lock by the A137 bridge at Cattawade. In many cases they can also be obtained directly from the bailiff on the site. Clovers Flour Mills at Dedham issue day tickets for their waters at Dedham and Higham Hall where there are fine bream and dace. Tickets are also available from Mr. W. Coote, at 'The Swan', Great Henny, for a stretch there.

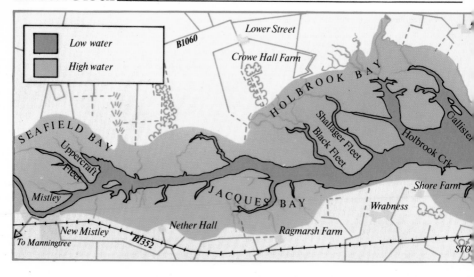

Low water

High water

B1060

Lower Street

Crowe Hall Farm

HOLBROOK BAY

Shallager Fleet

Black Fleet

Gallister

Holbrook Crk

SEAFIELD BAY

Uppercraft Fleet

Mistley

JACQUES BAY

Shore Farm

Wrabness

New Mistley

To Manningtree

B1352

Nether Hall

Ragmarsh Farm

STO

The River Stour at Dedham in its typical middle stage. The banks are grassy and even, the river peacefully flowing, and on average 40ft wide and 10ft deep. Dedham and Flatford (below) are two of the more picturesque spots on the river. Flatford Mill remains much as it was when Constable painted it in 1817. Today, both areas are popular day-ticket venues.

Richard Jemmet

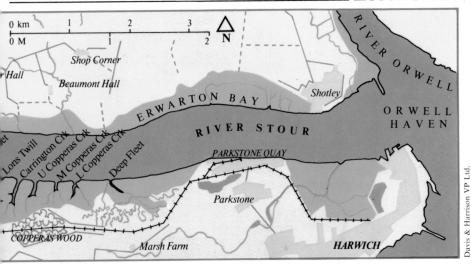

Davis & Harrison VP Ltd.

Woodmanstone Ltd

Our detail map of the estuary shows the lower reaches of the River Stour where the angler may fish unhindered by bailiffs, day tickets or permission. When the tide is in, a wide variety of stretches can be reached via the B1060 (north) or the B1352 (south).

Access to these stretches is by the A134 to Sudbury and Long Melford and by the A1090 to Clare and Cavendish. To reach the villages of Middleton, Great Henny and Lamarsh, take the A131 out of Sudbury and then turn left after two miles. Both the A134 to Nayland and Sudbury and the A133 to Bures are reached by the A12 from London, Chelmsford, Colchester and Ipswich, or by the A604 from Cambridge.

Fishing at Flatford Mill

By the picturesque Flatford Mill there are stretches of water between the club notice boards up to Judas Gap and at Brantham Lock by the A137 bridge at Cattawade, with day tickets again available from local clubs.

Downtide from the Mistley quays, the Stour opens out into the mudbanks and creeks of a large estuary. Here there are no licences, no bailiffs, no commercial restrictions. Subject to tide and season the fisherman can go where he pleases. Inshore creeks swarm with mullet and flounders. The mullet are notoriously difficult to catch, even

213

on bread paste, and are rarely caught on any other bait. The baited spoon method is well-known to account for flounders. Farther seawards, past Wrabness and Harwich, there are bass and whiting according to the time of year. Both species may be hooked by beachcasting, or caught from a dinghy in the channels.

Winter and summer fishing
Using paternoster tackle you can drift a ragworm over sandbanks to lure big summer bass, or ledger fresh herring for thornback rays. In winter, the Stour is a cold, inhospitable place, but out in the estuary dinghy anglers harvest whiting and floun-ders, and cod too in good years, although these are becoming rarer.

The estuary is laced with creeks which dry out as the tide recedes but provide good fishing when the tide is in. The angler has a choice of wide mud stretches and bays on both sides. On the north side, the B1080 leads from Manningtree to Brantham Hall, Stutton, Harkstead and Erwarton, while on the south side, the B1352 leaves Manningtree for Mistley, Bradfield, Wrabness, Parkstone Quay and Harwich. Beyond the estuary the sea fishing is excellent.

Felixstowe and Harwich
Felixstowe is considered the cream of East Anglia's fishing, having a great variety of fish. From the estuary and beaches the angler can fish lumpsuckers, plaice, dogfish, turbot, garfish and sea trout, and in warmer months plaice, sole, eel, bass and dab. Night fishing is especially good, and there is good fishing from the pier from September for a small charge.

At Harwich it is possible to get permission from the Trinity House Superintendent for parties of anglers to fish from the lightships in the estuary, provided one books in advance. There are fish of all species, with excellent whiting and cod from September onwards. Both rowing and power boats are available for fishing many miles of mudflats and deep creeks.

At Walton on Naze, bait can be dug locally, and boats are available for offshore

The estuary of the River Stour near the Maltings at Mistley Quays, Essex. This is typical estuarial water, the low tide exposing acres of food-rich mud-flats where mullet and flounder abound.

fishing when the local boatman have done their daily work of lobster potting or inshore trawling. Flatfish are caught in the back-waters, and conger, skate, dab, bass and codling from the beaches and pier. For sea fishing, advice is needed regarding local marks and obstructions.

Clacton-on-Sea
The pier at Clacton offers the best local fishing. A deep channel lies about half a mile offshore, and the boatdeck of the pier is reserved for anglers and boat passengers. Other than at a stretch near the pier by Holland-on-Sea, beachcasting is not advised as the water is less than 4ft deep. Lugworm is the best and most popular all-round bait at any time of the year and it can be dug from the local beaches.

Richard Jemmet

INFORMATION
WATER AUTHORITY
Anglian Water Authority, Essex Division, Rivers House, 129 Springfield Rd, Chelmsford, Essex CM2 7JN Tel 64721.
LICENCES
Regional licence: adult £3.80, junior and OAPs £1. Weekly tickets 75p all categories.
Divisional licence: £2, no concessions for OAPs or juniors. The licences run from 1 January.
Close seasons: salmon September 28 to March 1,

Size limits: barbel 15.7in (40cm), bream, carp, chub and grayling 11.8in (30cm), tench 9.8in (25cm), perch 9in (23cm), crucian carp, roach and rudd 7.8in (20cm), dace 7in (18cm), pike 23.6in (60cm) and trout 11.8in (30cm).
Waters at Wormingford, Wiston, Boxted, Langham, Stratford St Mary and Flatford are owned by the Colchester Angling Preservation Society. Colnes Angling Society owns a stretch at Little Horkesley. Hadleigh and District Angling Society has water on the River Brett which fishes better in winter.
Bures Lake, a little downstream from Bures Mill, is a large lake with very good tench (to over 8 lb) and Carp (to 37½ lb). It is owned by the London Anglers' Association and for members only. For more information conact the LAA bailiff, F Staples, 25 Nayland Rd, Bures. Tel: Bures 227 555.
LOCAL CLUBS AND ASSOCIATIONS
Clacton-on-Sea Angling Club, W. Marples, 352, Old Rd. Clacton-on-Sea, Essex.
Colchester Angling Preservation Society, N F J Binks, 7 Churnwood Rd, Colchester, Essex. No tickets.
Colnes' Angling Society, Mr K. W. Murrells, 1 Hillie Bunnies, Earls Court, Colchester, Essex.

Elm Park, Hornchurch and District Angling Society, Hotten, 4 Cairford Way, Harold Hill, Romford, Essex.
Great Cornard Angling Club, P. Franklin, 48 Queensway, Great Cornard, Sudbury, Suffolk. Tel: Sudbury 73766.
Hadleigh and District Angling Society, J S Hill, 18 Highlands Rd, Hadleigh, Ipswich, Suffolk. No tickets.
Kingcatchers Angling Club, King's Head, East Bergholt, near Colchester, Essex. Tel: East Bergholt 386.
Lawford Angling Club, R W Nunn, Mistley Hall Cottage, Clacton Rd, Mistley, Manningtree, Essex.
London Anglers' Association, H J Wilson, 183 Hoe St, Walthamstow, London E17 3AP.
Sudbury and District Angling Association, B Roberts, 45 Chelsworth Ave, Great Cornard, Sudbury, Suffolk.
NATIONAL ORGANISATIONS
National Federation of Sea Anglers, R W Page, 26 Downsview Crescent, Uckfield, Sussex, TN22 1UB.
National Shorecasting Association, G W Wilson, 71 McNamara Rd, Rose Hill, Wallsend, Tyne and Wear.
TACKLE DEALERS
Home and Sport, 31a St Botolphs St, Colchester, Essex. Tel 5382. (early closing Thursday)
K D Radcliffe, High Street, Colchester, Essex.
Sudbury Sports, Friar St, Sudbury, Suffolk. Tel 72687. (early closing Wednesday).
The Swim, Tower Lane, Sudbury.
Nunn's Norse St, Sudbury.
The Breakaway Tackle Co, 376 Bramford Rd, Ipswich. Tel 41393.
Godfrey's Tackle, 52 Moulsham St, Chelmsford, Essex. Tel: 84562.
Ronnie Crowe, Mouldon Rd, Great Baddow, Chelmsford.
Fishing tackle shop, Rosemary Rd, Clacton-on-Sea.
Tackle supplies at The Pier, Clacton-on-Sea.
M R Brien, 2a Bent Hill, Felixstowe. Tel 5318.
L T Bobby, 57 Undercliff Rd West, Felixstowe. Tel 2709.

Upper Severn

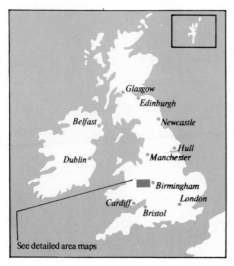

See detailed area maps

In its higher reaches the Severn is just a lusty little stream. This part gives little indication that it is to develop into England's longest river, 215 miles long. Rising on Plynlimon, it travels east before arcing through the Shropshire Plain where a switch in direction puts it in a southerly course past the Wrekin, through Ironbridge, and then through the rich pastures of Worcestershire and Gloucestershire to its wide estuary.

The Severn is a first-rate fishing river with improving salmon catches. The match catch record is 98lb 7oz caught at Bewdley, and many more catches topping the 80lb mark have been made at Bridgnorth, Shrewsbury, Arley, and from the deeper, breamy reaches around Tewkesbury. Individual specimens of near-record proportions are caught most seasons. The best chub, caught at Newtown, weighed 7lb 14oz. Bream over 8lb have been taken, roach of 3lb, barbel into double figures, pike over 30lb, brown trout to 8lb, a best salmon of 43lb, and comparatively large bleak and gudgeon.

Coarse fishing is available in all of the river's varied reaches—much of it on day ticket, but a lot controlled by the

Birmingham Anglers' Association which only issues associate membership on an annual basis. A regular visitor to the Severn would be well advised to obtain one of these. The cost is £5.50 for coarse fishing, £6.50 to include trout fishing, and for juniors just £1!

Down to Bewdley

From the mountains down to Bewdley the river is very popular. At Llanidloes the Birmingham AA has a mile-long stretch of shallow stream where a fair number of brook-sized trout are found, and below Caersws it controls both banks in two sections near the A492-A470 junction. Here, too, the Red Lion Hotel issues day tickets for a small stretch on the left bank, while not far away, the Dinas Estate has about 4 miles

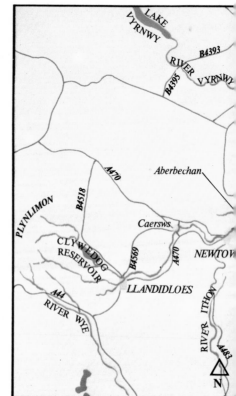

(Above) The River Severn in its upper reaches at Welshpool where there is good fishing for salmon, trout and coarse fish including grayling.
(Below) Map shows the course of the Severn from its source on Plynlimon, through Llanidloes, Caersws, Shrewsbury and Ironbridge to the Bewdley-Stourport area. It is a good river for salmon, and for chub in the upper reaches and barbel in the middle river. Bridgnorth to Hampton Loade is the most popular fishery on the Severn, and is also one of England's big match stretches.

Spectrum Colour Library

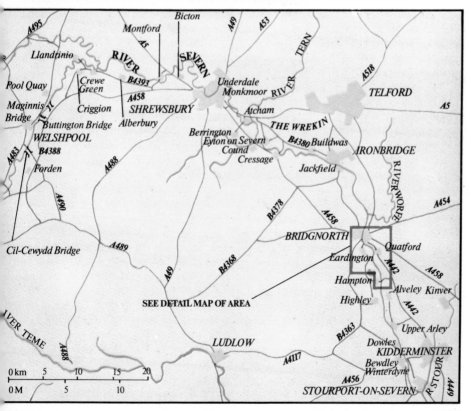

SEE DETAIL MAP OF AREA

0 km 5 10 15 20

0 M 5 10

Spectrum Colour Library

of both banks with day tickets available from Evan Jones in Llanidloes. Maesmawr Hotel below Caersws also has a stretch of day-ticket water.

In this area, with the exception of small trout, most fish are large—especially chub and dace. One is more likely to have large-sized fish than a big catch. The river here is affected by the influx of cold compensation water released regularly from the Clywedog Reservoir and this tends to make the fish spasmodic feeders.

The Birmingham AA controls water upstream of Newtown, and farther downstream a left-bank stretch above and below the bridge at Aberbechan. There are two other stretches near here, and tackle dealer L. Bebb in Newtown issues day tickets for these. Near Forden, by the B4388 road, the Birmingham AA controls about 2 miles of right-bank water where the dace fishing is excellent. Then downstream at Cil-Cewydd Bridge where the A490 crosses the river there is a long stretch of free fishing with access clearly marked.

At Welshpool, the Hazeldine Angling Association of Bilston controls a portion of the river, and the Birmingham AA has more double-bank fishing from here to Buttington Bridge where the river is crossed by the A483. It also has waters downstream near the Powis Arms and at many other venues; Maginnis Bridge, Maesydd, Pool Quay and on opposite bank at Criggion. Access is

directly from the A483, clearly marked, and with car parking available at most spots.

The Birmingham AA also controls a right-bank fishery above and below Llandrinio Bridge on the B4393, and the right bank downstream at Crewe Green and Alberbury. Again, most of this water is likely to yield the big fish rather than the big catch. Breadflake is a good bait and has tempted chub to 5lb.

In this area the River Vyrnwy joins the Severn and there is more free fishing for licence holders below the confluence. A lot of day ticket fishing is available along the good-fishing River Vyrnwy too.

Shrewsbury

Back on the Severn the Birmingham AA has water at Montford Bridge by the A5 and below at Bicton. Clubs then control most sections of the river down to Shrewsbury where local tackle dealers issue day tickets for considerable bank space in the town and below at Monkmoor.

The Quarry Park waters are noted for the dace fishing in the upper section on both sides of the Welsh Bridge, and roach and chub are to be caught in the deeper runs near the English Bridge. The record match catch here topped 84lb of chub for five hours' fishing. They were taken with wasp grub bait, though maggots, hemp, bread, tares and casters more usually account for good catches. There is also some excellent salmon fishing near Shrewsbury Weir, and local tackle dealers will give information.

218

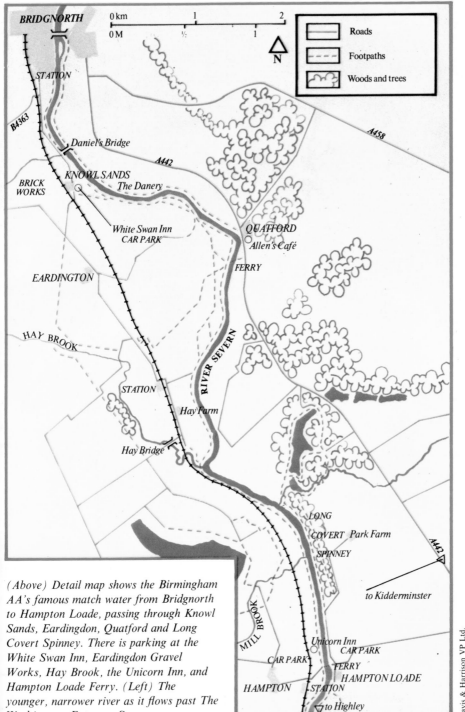

BRIDGNORTH

0 km   1   2

0 M   ½   1

N

	Roads
	Footpaths
	Woods and trees

STATION

B4363

Daniel's Bridge

A442

BRICK WORKS

KNOWL SANDS

The Danery

White Swan Inn
CAR PARK

QUATFORD

Allen's Café

FERRY

EARDINGTON

A458

HAY BROOK

RIVER SEVERN

STATION

Hay Farm

Hay Bridge

LONG
COVERT   Park Farm
SPINNEY

A442

to Kidderminster

MILL BROOK

Unicorn Inn
CAR PARK

CAR PARK

FERRY
HAMPTON LOADE

HAMPTON   STATION

to Highley

(Above) Detail map shows the Birmingham AA's famous match water from Bridgnorth to Hampton Loade, passing through Knowl Sands, Eardingdon, Quatford and Long Covert Spinney. There is parking at the White Swan Inn, Eardingdon Gravel Works, Hay Brook, the Unicorn Inn, and Hampton Loade Ferry. (Left) The younger, narrower river as it flows past The Wrekin near Eyton on Severn.

Davis & Harrison VP Ltd.

219

Upper Severn

Below Shrewsbury the Birmingham AA has an equally good salmon fishery at Underdale where large chub, dace and barbel are also found. The Monkmoor stretch lies downstream and is approached from the A5112 just past the hospital. This is available on a day ticket basis. Farther on, the Severn-Trent Water Authority has a lengthy fishery above the bridge on the left bank, and downstream on the right bank all the way to Berrington where the Birmingham AA rights start again. In this area the Provincial Angling Association and the Prince Albert Angling Society have fishing on the left bank.

More Birmingham AA waters follow at right-bank Cound Lodge and on both banks at Buildwas near the junction of the B4380 and the B4378. At Cressage there is a day-ticket fishery on the Braby Estate and the Estate Office is in nearby Eyton-on-Severn. Other day-ticket water is available at Ironbridge, with the tickets obtainable from

Hampton Loade is known for the excellence of its coarse fishing. At the limit of the Birmingham AA's Knowl Sands-Hampton Loade match stretch (see detail map), it also offers very good day-ticket fishing.

local tackle dealers. This is the section where double-figure barbel have been caught. Below the town the river bubbles and crashes through the gorge and there is superb free fishing along the left bank. Day tickets are also available from the Half Moon Inn at Jackfield for a stretch there where chub over 6lb have been caught.

The fishing from this point is club-controlled and strictly preserved as far as Bridgnorth, but immediately below the town is the start of the big match country famous all over England. Coventry and District Angling Association and the Whitmore Reans Angling Association control rights as far as left-bank Danery and right-bank Knowl Sands at which point the

220

Birmingham AA rights start again. They then control the fishing with few breaks through Quatford, Eardington, Hampton Loade, Highley, and Arley off the A442. This is the most popular fishery on the Severn and the Birmingham AA's proudest possession. Robin Harris won the 1971 National Championship on the famous Quatford stretch. At right-bank Hampton Loade day-ticket water is available, and at Alveley, the Kinver Freeliners Angling Society lets a 40-peg stretch for club bookings.

Alveley

This last stretch of water is really excellent for coarse fishing. Barbel to 9lb have been taken, catches of them in excess of 100lb (top match catch 83lb), plus quality chub, dace which are beginning to show again, and some superb roach in winter. River depths vary from 2ft to 12ft and swim characteristics are just as different, from fast-flowing fords to breamy-looking lies. Most fishing techniques will succeed, though the most popular at the moment is swimfeeder fishing.

Around Bewdley most of the water is controlled by the Kidderminster and District Angling Association which issues honorary cards at a reasonable cost. This is a section of the Severn with such famous bankside names Hawkbatch, Dowles and Winterdyne. It is the area which, in July 1977, yielded the Severn match catch record of 98lb. Barbel abound, as do big chub and large shoals of chub. Sometimes the water is black with barbel and chub feeding with abandon. The river here, as in the Arley section, varies in depth. In the deep downstream waters bream to 8lb have been caught while Lax Lane Ford, which runs only inches deep, has produced 40lb nets of dace. This then is the fabulous Severn. Already only half-way to its estuary, it is a river of a thousand moods and just as many different swims.

INFORMATION

WATER AUTHORITY

Severn-Trent Water Authority, Severn Division, 64 Albert Rd, North Malvern, Worcs WR14 2BB. Tel 61511.

LICENCES

Trout and freshwater fish: season £1, combined Severn and Trent season £1.50, 28 day period 50p. OAPs season 20p.
Salmon: season £15, day £2.25.
Spinning for trout during the close season for freshwater fish is prohibited. No float to be used with lure or bait when fishing for salmon or during the close season for freshwater fish. No cereal or maggots to be used as bait during the freshwater fish close season. Keepnets (which must conform to the specifications set out in the byelaws) are not allowed during freshwater fish close season. No fish to be taken from the River Severn within a distance of approximately 50ft above and 148ft below the crest of Shrewsbury Weir.
Size limits: barbel all waters 15.7in (40cm), rainbow trout all waters 11.8in (30cm), brown trout and grayling River Severn below Shrewsbury Weir 9.8in (25 cm), River Severn (including tributaries) upstream of Afon Clywedog confluence, River Vyrnwy (including tributaries) upstream of Dolanog Weir, River Banwy (including tributaries) upstream of Afon Gam confluence, River Tanet (including tributaries) upstream of River Rhaiadr confluence, 5.9in (15cm), all other waters within the Authority area 7.8in (20cm). Bona-fide matches may be fished 'all in', provided undersized barbel are returned to the water with as little injury as possible immediately after weighing, which must take place on the river bank.

LOCAL CLUBS AND ASSOCIATIONS

Birmingham Anglers' Association, V S Hall, 40 Thorpe St, Birmingham 5B5 4AU.
Coventry and District Angling Association, E G Baxter, 15 Boswell Drive, Coventry, W Midlands.
Hazeldine Angling Association, J W Hazeldine, 8 Dudley Rd, Sedgley, W Midlands DY3 1SX.
Kinver Freeliners Clun, Roger Oliver, 39 High St, Kinver, W Midlands.
Kidderminster & District Angling Association, C G Wilcox, 35 Dunnington Ave, Sion Park, Kidderminster DY10 2YS.
Prince Albert Angling Society, C Sparkes, High Lodge, Upton, Macclesfield, Cheshire.
Provincial Angling Association, W Hunt, 11 Central Ave, Bilston, W Midlands. Tel 42313.
Tewkesbury Popular Angling Association, R A Smith, 10 Tretawn Gdns, Newtown, Tewkesbury, Glos.
Whitmore Reans Angling Association, R H Hughes, Star Chambers, Prince's Square, Wolverhampton.

TACKLE DEALERS AND LICENCE AGENTS

Stan Lewis, 2 Severnside South, Bewdley, Worcs.
G Bate Ltd, 16 Colemore Circus, Birmingham. Tel 2367451
A E Brookes, 958 Bristol Road South, Birmingham B31 28E.
Austin Clisset, 1801 Pershore Rd, Cotteridge, Birmingham.
Harold Greenway & Sons, (10 branches) main branch 1010 Chester Rd, Pype Hayes, Birmingham 24. Tel 373 0057.
Roy Jarvis, 364 Shirley Rd, Acocks Green, Birmingham 27.
Stan Jones, 17 Reddlebarn Rd, Selly Oak, Birmingham 29.
Simmonds & Priddey, Stratford Rd, Shirley, Birmingham.
J Keeling, 45 Market Hall, Bull Ring Centre, Birmingham.
M Robinson, 4 York Rd, King's Heath, Birmingham.
Mrs E K Francis, The Stores, Caersws, Powys.
R J Russell, 93 Coventry Rd, Kidderminster, Herefordshire and Worcestershire. Tel 64040.
M Storey, Sutton Rd, Kidderminster.
Evan Jones, Llanidloes, Powys.
B Rowlands, R & E Garages, Dolwen, Llanidloes.
B J Hall, The Corner Shop, Llanymynech, Powys.
H L Bebb, 15 Short Bridge St, Newton, Powys.
Jayeff Sports, 48-49 Windsor Rd, Griffithstown, Pontypool.
A E Bond (Welshpool) Ltd, 9 Hall St, Welshpool, Powys.
Mrs L J McCrae, Roverband Caravan Park, Llangadfan, Welshpool, Powys.
Ron Haynes, 176 Stafford St, Wolverhampton. Tel 23777.

Lower Severn

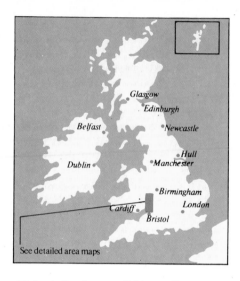

See detailed area maps

Gloucester is the lowest point along the River Severn for serious coarse fishing. From Stourport downstream to Gloucester the river deepens and looks leisurely—but the usually placid surface hides a fierce current which urges the Severn to the sea.

The fishing throughout most of this long section is excellent. Below Tewkesbury, the river is tidal, and many anglers have learned, from soaked feet and submerged tackle, to tread warily, for tides topping the 10ft mark have, in many places, left steep and dangerous banks.

At Stourport, the Birmingham AA controls a good fishery on the right bank at Ribblesford known as the Roadside Stretch because the B4194 Bewdley-Stourport road follows the river. This section holds a large head of big barbel, 5-6lb bream, good winter roach, perch, dace and the odd quality carp.

From this point down to and through

(Below) Good coarse fishing at Stourport. The Birmingham AA controls a fine stretch here, holding a large head of barbel.

Bill Howes

Stourport, the Lytellton AA controls an excellent fishery on the right bank with day tickets available on the bank—although most weekends it is match-booked. The section on the right bank from 'Stony Bottom' up past Gladder Brook and on to the well known 'sunken boat' swim below Little Gladder, is a famous contest water. The 'sunken boat' swim recently yielded a 67lb contest catch of barbel, and chub, dace and roach abound.

Below Stourport

Most of the left bank from Ribbesford to Stourport is inaccessible, being club-controlled for members only. Below Stourport, however, the BAA has a small right-bank water known as Newhall's Meadow. Then, below Lincombe Weir, where good roach are found, some free fishing is available for Severn-Trent Water Authority licence holders, and day tickets are issued at the Hamstall Inn on the right bank for a short section here.

Opposite, on the left bank, and extending downstream for about five meadows, are the well-known Kidderminster DAA Winnal and Lady Ham waters. The association sells annual honorary membership cards. For the fishing downstream at Boreley, Bewdley tackle dealer Stan Lewis issues day tickets. All of this water yields regular good catches of most species with the best contest haul of bream weighing 51lb, catches of chub exceeding that, and bags of roach to 30lb often being taken.

Above Holt Fleet on the A443, the BAA has a lengthy left-bank water, while downstream, day tickets for some good mixed fishing are available from the Wharf Inn and from Holt Castle on the right bank. Barbel to 9lb, and 2lb-plus roach have been caught.

The Severn now begins to widen and deepen, carrying much pleasure boat traffic in summer. The average depth is 8ft, with a deeper central channel, and good sport is to be had with float or ledger.

(Below) The Severn above Holt Fleet where the angler can find not only good barbel fishing but sport with game species.

Bill Howes

At Grimley, off the A443, the BAA has two miles of right-bank fishing, and after a short break, nearly two miles at Hallow. On the opposite bank, between Bever and Barbourne, is the well known, but members-only, Blackheath AS water, where monthly open matches are held.

Northwick

Downstream is a stretch of free fishing and a section at Northwick controlled by the Hazeldine AA. The river now reaches the cathedral city of Worcester, where there is more free fishing for licence holders below the main town bridge down to Diglis Weir.

The Worcester DUAS controls more than five miles of water on the rivers Avon, Tame and Severn. They do not issue day tickets, but sell annual honorary membership cards. The main Severn waters are at Pitchcroft, fronting Worcester race-course, on both banks below the city at Diglis, at Beauchamp Court near Callow End on the B4424, at Clevelode on the right bank, and opposite Oak Meadows bank and Lathams Farm, approached from the A38.

Near Kempsey and the Ketch Hotel on the A38, there are more Severn-Trent WA free fishing. The BAA then controls much of the left bank at Severn Stoke on the A38 and at Upton upon Severn. On the right bank at Upton, on the A4104, the local club has good water, with day tickets at 35p available from tackle dealer Geoff Shinn. Below the town, on the right bank, there is more free fishing for Severn-Trent WA licence holders.

Downstream the BAA controls the left bank at Uckinghall and Ripple, and ten meadows on the right bank at Bushley and on to Mythe Bridge on the A438. At Ripple, between the BAA waters at Uckinghall and Ripple, there is more free Severn-Trent WA fishing along the left bank, reached via the A38 and then the small lane down to the ferry from Ripple. There is a weekend bankside cafe and ferry at Uckinghall, where good bream catches are made from the

'Cables' swim upstream of the BAA car park, and on the downstream stony section.

This is now bream country, and maggots, casters, luncheon meat, bread flake and tares are the usual baits. The water also holds chub (best contest catch 55lb), barbel and roach. Ledger or float tactics pay off, and it was here that the technique of 'bobbing for bream' was born. This technique, particularly effective in deep water to 20ft, and in slow-flowing rivers like the lower Severn, uses an Arlesey bomb ledger and a slider float of bulky quill or balsa. The float is allowed to drift downstream until it forms a right-angle with the bait and the bank. The angle, essential for this method, heightens sensitivity, causing the float to bob during a bite.

Downstream from here, on the left bank above and below Tewkesbury Weir, water is controlled by the Tewkesbury Popular AA,

(Below) Good bream fishing at Tewkesbury.

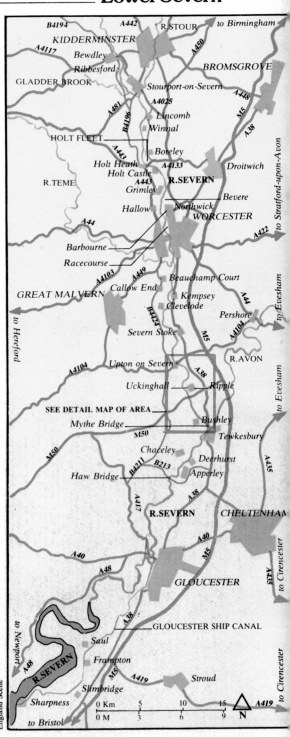

England Scene

225

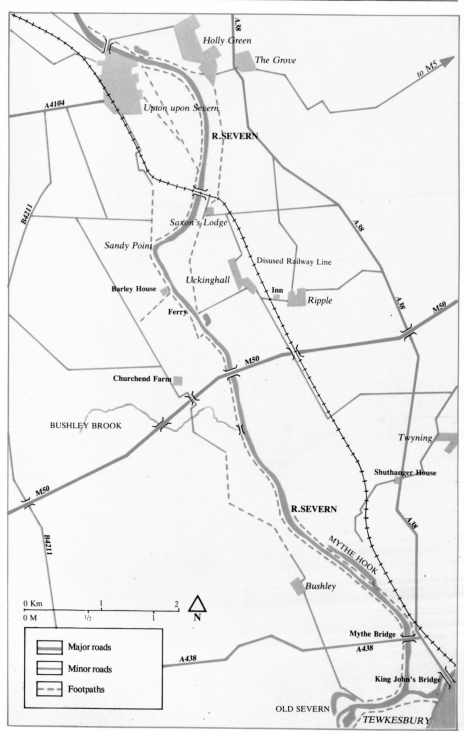

with day tickets available on the banks for some excellent fishing.

The river is now tidal. Some day-ticket fishing is available at the Lower Lode Hotel, and the BAA has more water here and downstream at Chaceley, where the Hazeldine AA also has a stretch.

Opposite Lower Lode, water is controlled by the Gloucester UAA, which issues honorary cards. All of these venues, particularly the Tewkesbury Popular AA water, have good bream and autumn roach fishing. Sport is particularly good on some of the downstream swims along 'The Big Ham'—created by a diversion of the River Avon which enters here.

Deerhurst and Apperley

The RAA has water downstream at Deerhurst, and controls the fishing on two riverside pools at Apperley. At Haw Bridge on the B4213 the Gloucester UAA then controls an extensive right-bank fishery which stretches all along the way to Ashleworth, and where some club bookings are permitted. The water holds big bream, very large eels, chub, roach, and large barbel which are rarely seen.

The A38 closely follows the Gloucester and Sharpness Canal, which averages 12ft in depth and offers good fishing in most parts. Day tickets are issued at most toll bridge houses and good areas are Pilot Bridge, Frampton, Saul, Slimbridge, and Rea and Hempstead Bridges near the centre of Gloucester. Species found are bream to 4lb, chub to 3lb, roach and perch.

Returning to the lower Severn, there are day tickets available for a good stretch of left-bank fishing at the Red Lion Inn at Wainlode Hill, approached from the A38, while at Maisemore in Gloucester, the BAA controls a five-meadow section.

Whatever your choice of fishing, the Severn most certainly has it. That is why it is probably the most popular fishing river in the country.

(Left) Detail map shows the area where 'bobbing for bream' was born.

INFORMATION

WATER AUTHORITY
Severn-Trent Water Authority, Abelson House, 2297 Coventry Rd, Sheldon, Birmingham B26 3PR.
Severn Area, 64 Albert Rd, North Malvern, Worcs WR14 2BB. Tel: Malvern 61511.

LICENCES
Trout and coarse (regional) £2.25, trout and coarse (divisional) £1.50, trout and coarse (seven day regional) 75p, concessionary for children from 12 to 15 years, OAPs and the registered disabled (divisional) 30p.

Close seasons: salmon 15 September to 1 February, freshwater fish 15 March to 15 June. There is no close season for rainbow trout and eels. Spinning for trout during the close season for freshwwater fish is prohibited. Trailing or trolling of natural or artificial baits from boats in motion is prohibited. No float to be used with lure or bait when fishing for salmon, or during the close season for freshwater fish. No cereal or maggots to be used during the freshwater fish close season. Keepnets are not allowed during freshwater fish close season.

Size limits: barbel all waters 15.7in (40cm), rainbow trout all waters 11.8in (30cm), brown trout and grayling River Severn below Shrewsbury Weir 9.8in (25cm). Bonafide matches may be fished 'all in' provided undersized barbel are returned to the water with as little injury as possible immediately after weighing, which must take place on the river bank.

RIVER REPORT SERVICE
The Severn-Trent Water Authority runs an up-to-date information service. Phone Gloucester 37180.

LOCAL CLUBS AND ASSOCIATIONS
Birmingham AA, V S Hall, 40 Thorpe St, Birmingham 5B5 4AU.
Blackheath AS, John Green, 73 Regis Heath Rd, Rowley Regis, Warley, W Midlands B65 0PB.
Gloucester UAA, R H Ellis, 15 Armscroft Way, Barnwood, Gloucester, Glos.
Hazeldine AA, J W Hazeldine, 8 Dudley Rd, Sedgley, W Midlands DY3 1SX.
Kidderminster DAA, C G Wilcox, 35 Dunnington Ave, Sion Park, Kidderminster DY10 2YS.
Lytellton AA, I Cooper, 64 Mostyn Rd, Stourport-on-Severn, Herefs & Worcs.
Tewkesbury Popular AA, R A Smith, 10 Tretawn Gdns, Newtown, Tewkesbury, Glos.
Upton upon Severn AA, R Webster, 8 Furlongs Rd, Upton upon Severn, Herefs & Worcs. Tel 2253
Worcester SUAS, W Meadows, 101 Bransford Rd, St Johns, Worcester, Herefs & Worcs.

TACKLE DEALERS
Stan Lewis, 2 Severn Side South, Bewdley, Herefs & Worcs. Tel 403358.
D Caldwell, 45 Bristol Rd, Gloucester, Glos..
Jeff Aston Fishing Tackle, 78 High St, Gloucester. Tel 23009.
Fred Harvey & Co Ltd, 18 Barton St, Gloucester. Tel 21609.
Allsports, 86 Barton St, Gloucester, Glos.
Fletcher (Sports) Ltd, 24 King Square, Gloucester, Glos.
Ron Russell, 93 Coventry St, Kidderminster, Herefs & Worcs.
Malcolm Storey, 106 Sutton Rd, Kidderminster. Tel 5221.
Mick Grinnall, 10 York St, Stourport-on-Severn. Tel 2212.
John White, Raven St, Stourport-on-Severn.
Ivor Griffiths, 2 Barton St, Tewkesbury, Glos. Tel 293234.
Geoff Shin, 23 Old St, Upton upon Severn, Herefs & Worcs.
George's, Bridge St, Worcester, Herefs & Worcs.
W Richardson, St Johns, Worcester, Herefs & Worcs.
F Durrant & Sons, Mealcheapen St, Worcester.

Wye

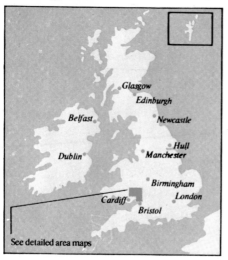

Rightly recognized as England's premier salmon river the Wye is also one of the best coarse fishing rivers in Europe. The river has produced pike to 37lb, dace to $1\frac{1}{4}$lb, roach of 2lb 14oz, eels to $6\frac{1}{2}$lb, a chub of 7lb 3oz at Symonds Yat, grayling of 3lb 10oz and even a bream nearing 8lb. It also yielded a record salmon of $59\frac{1}{2}$lb (with bigger seen on the spawning redds), a brown trout of 5lb and sea trout to near 9lb. It makes the Wye an exciting prospect for all anglers.

The course of the Wye

Rising on the heights of Plynlimmon, the Wye is a rushing, boulder-strewn and busy water in its upper reaches. Here is the game angler's preserve. Not until Builth Wells is the Wye recognized for its coarse fishing, and not until Hay-on-Wye is this fishing described as of 'quality'. It was near here at Whitney in the autumn of 1976 that Austin Clisset set a new five-hour match catch record for the Wye with a bag of chub totalling 87lb.

But Wye fishing is overshadowed by the salmon. This inhibits full-season coarse fishing in many places. In most cases coarse fishing is allowed only after the salmon season closes in October. Most fishing rights are privately owned or syndicated, and a ban on the use of maggots applies from March 14 to October 26 except along the major tributary, the River Lugg in Herefordshire.

Tackle and techniques for fishing the Wye are generally heavier than those used along the Trent or Thames, Welland or Witham. Bread flake or maggots, when permissible, are standard baits fished with four or five swan shot on balsa floats. Heavy terminal tackle such as this is needed to get to the midstream chub. Comparatively heavy tackle is also used to catch the fine dace whose huge shoals inhabit this fabulous water.

Much of the Wye is privately controlled. Fortunately it is a long river and a lot of bank space is still available with a reasonable amount of all-season coarse fishing. Some day ticket water is available near Builth Wells and enquiries should be addressed to Mrs Asbrey, 17 High Street, Builth. Llyswen lies a few miles downstream on the A470. Here the Bridgend Inn has about half a mile of single bank and issues day tickets. Nearby, too, is the famous Llandrindod Wells carp lake which can also be fished by the purchase of day tickets at 75p.

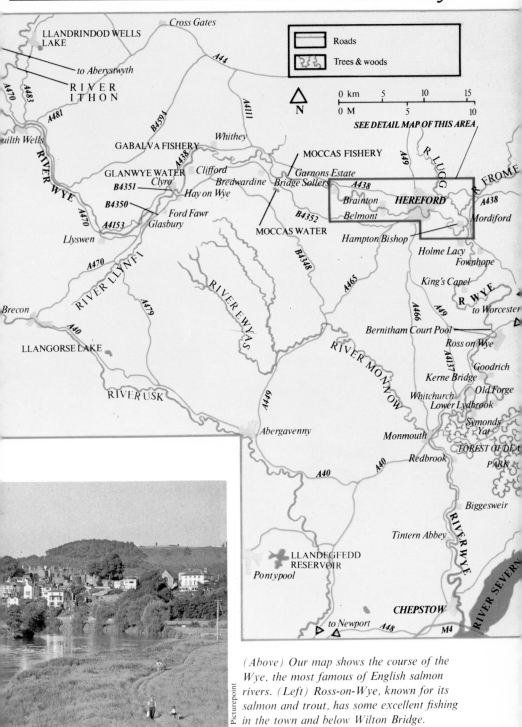

Roads
Trees & woods

0 km ⎯⎯ 5 ⎯⎯ 10 ⎯⎯ 15
0 M ⎯⎯ 5 ⎯⎯ 10

SEE DETAIL MAP OF THIS AREA

LLANDRINDOD WELLS
LAKE

Cross Gates

to Aberystwyth

RIVER
ITHON

uilth Wells

A470
A483
A481

A4594

A44

A4111

Whithey

GABALVA FISHERY

MOCCAS FISHERY

Garnons Estate

A449

R LUGG

R FROME

GLANWYE WATER
B4351

Clifford
Clyro

Bredwardine
Hay on Wye

Bridge Sollers

A438

HEREFORD

Brainton

A438

B4350

A438

Ford Fawr
Glasbury

B4352

Belmont

Mordiford

A4153

MOCCAS WATER

Hampton Bishop

Llyswen

RIVER WYE

A470

Holme Lacy
Fownhope

King's Capel

R WYE

RIVER LLYNFI

A479

RIVER EWYAS

A465

B4348

A466

A449

to Worcester

Brecon

A440

Bernitham Court Pool

LLANGORSE LAKE

Ross on Wye

A4137

Goodrich

Kerne Bridge

Old Forge

RIVER USK

A449

Whitchurch
Lower Lydbrook

RIVER MONNOW

Symonds Yat

Abergavenny

Monmouth

FOREST OF DEA
PARK

A40

A40

Redbrook

Biggesweir

LLANDEGFEDD
RESERVOIR

Pontypool

Tintern Abbey

RIVER WYE

RIVER SEVERN

CHEPSTOW

to Newport A48

M4

Picturepoint

*(Above) Our map shows the course of the
Wye, the most famous of English salmon
rivers. (Left) Ross-on-Wye, known for its
salmon and trout, has some excellent fishing
in the town and below Wilton Bridge.*

Wye

At Treble Hill Cottage, Glasbury, Mr R. Bufton issues day tickets for two miles of right-bank fishing at Ford Fawr and a mile of the right bank upstream of the B4351 bridge at Hay-on-Wye. This is a particularly good section for dace fishing (best catch so far is over 80lb), and, for the angler who likes river pike fishing, specimens to 25lb are regularly taken. Nearby is Llangorse Lake with free fishing for roach, perch and good pike, and where there are boats for hire.

Hay-on-Wye

Day tickets and club contest bookings can be had on application to H. Brodie-Smith of Poolpardon Cottage, Clifford, near Hay-on-Wye, who controls a mile of double bank at Hay Castle and Clyro, and a very productive length of the river downstream at Kerne Bridge below Ross.

Moving downstream one finds the Glanwye water. This stretch is a mile long, with 30 day tickets to be had from W. Potter, Glanwye, Hay. Farther down, the Gabalva Fishery is one of the best Wye stretches for chub and dace. It is two miles long on the left bank upstream of Whitney toll bridge on the A438-B4350. The season is October 1 to January 24 and 40 day tickets are available from the Rhydspence Inn at Whitney. It was near this stretch that Clisset's record was set, from a right-bank peg above the old railway bridge near the B4350.

The famous Moccas Water

The A438 trunk road now closely follows the path of the river as it winds down to Hereford. Most of the access points are from this road. The Whitney Court Estate controls about five miles of both banks and the Estate Office issues day tickets which are for club bookings only. As on much of the Wye, night fishing is not allowed on the estate water.

On the famous Moccas Water stretch 200 day tickets are available for 8½ miles of the right bank. The coarse fish season runs from October 1 to January 1 and permits are obtainable from the Red Lion Hotel, Bredwardine, near the B4352 Hay to Hereford road. Like much of the Wye this

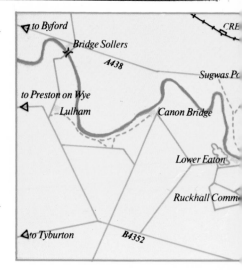

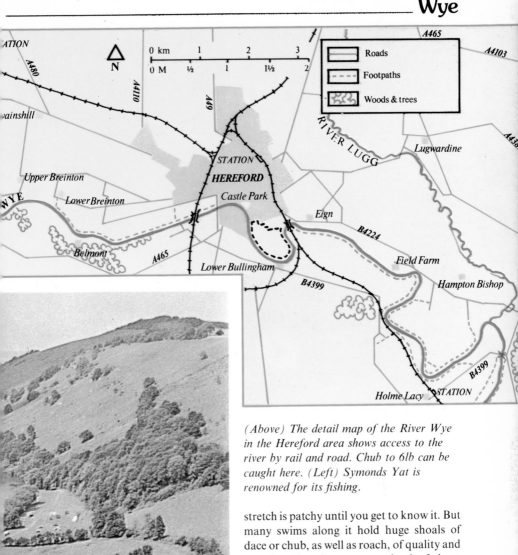

(Above) The detail map of the River Wye in the Hereford area shows access to the river by rail and road. Chub to 6lb can be caught here. (Left) Symonds Yat is renowned for its fishing.

stretch is patchy until you get to know it. But many swims along it hold huge shoals of dace or chub, as well as roach, of quality and big pike. There is an average depth of about 5ft. At Bridge Sollers the Garnons Estate water covers $2\frac{1}{2}$ miles from the bridge and 100 day tickets are available on application to the estate office. There is some great chub fishing to be had along this slightly deeper water where fish to 6lb have been caught. The Birmingham Anglers' Association controls about $1\frac{1}{4}$ miles of both banks at Brinton for members-only fishing. Associate membership cards are available from most tackle shops in the Midlands.

In and around Hereford the local

Len Cacutt

231

association controls the fishing along 6½ miles of the Wye. This is match and pleasure fishing country and day tickets are available for many stretches. The Hereford and District Angling Association controls several excellent fisheries; the left bank at Belmont above the city, at Castle Park, at Eign where there is superb dace fishing immediately below the railway bridge, at Bartonsham on both banks and at Field Farm on the right bank near Hampton Bishop where there are big roach, chub and dace. The Association also controls stretches near Holme Lacy and Fownhope. A map of local fishing is issued with day tickets.

Holme Lacy

Hereford tackle-dealer H. Hatton, 73 St. Owen Street, controls and issues day tickets for a stretch at Holme Lacy, and downstream at King's Caple, on the left bank, day tickets are available from Pennoxtone Court, King's Caple, Herefordshire.

Ross-on-Wye has some first-class fishing. Birmingham AA controls 800 yards in the town, on the left bank below Wilton Bridge (access from A40) and the Ross Angling Club issues day tickets for this stretch running from the town rowing club HQ to Wilton Bridge. Nearby, too, is the famous and strictly preserved Bernithan Court pool.

The Birmingham AA controls a mile or so of both banks above the Saracens Head Hotel at Symonds Yat. There is good fishing here for eels, also for other coarse species. At Old Forge, near the junction of the A40 and A4137, the Worcester and District United Anglers Association, has a stretch and issues honorary membership cards.

Kerne Bridge

A short way upstream is the famous Kerne Bridge where some day tickets are available on application to local hotels. At Lower Lydbrook, too, the Courtfield Arms has a short stretch available for visitors.

At Monmouth, the Birmingham AA controls a lengthy stretch of both banks upstream of the A466 bridge. Monmouth tackle dealer H. Keeling, 48 Monnow Street, issues day tickets for some excellent fishing

The River Wye at Chepstow is wide and tidal. It has salmon, eels and flounders.

along the Redbrook and Biggesweir sections. Redbrook is famous for its dace and, lower down, for big chub which are for the angler using bread-flake float tackle.

The Wye is tidal at Tintern Abbey and care should be taken along the banks. Day tickets can be bought from M. Jones, The Rock, Tintern, Chepstow, Gwent, for about 1½ miles of the water from Brockweir downstream. In between all of these famous places on the main river are many small tributaries like the Llynfi, Ithon, Monnow, Mithyl and Lugg. Fishing is available for the visiting angler at many places, while for the Lugg especially it would be wise to obtain a Birmingham AA associate card.

It seems hard to believe that the Wye, half a century ago, had deteriorated seriously due to over-netting, for it now produces more rod-caught salmon than any other English or Welsh river.

Bill Howes

Bill Howes

WATER AUTHORITY
Welsh National Water Development Authority, Wye River Division, Fisheries Officer, 4 St John St, Hereford. Tel 6313.
Licences: trout, freshwater fish and eels, season £3, juniors and OAPs £1.50, week £1.80, day 60p. Freshwater fish and eels only, season £1.80, juniors (under 16 at date of application) and OAPs 90p.
Close season: salmon September 30 to January 26 in the River Wye below Llanwrthwl Bridge, and from October 25 to January 26 in all other waters of the Wye and tributaries. Worms as bait are not allowed for salmon fishing between August 31 and April 15. Maggot bait not allowed between March 14 and October 26 on salmon fisheries on the River Wye, Ithon (and tributaries), Irfon (and tributaries), Duhonw, Marteg, Edw, Llnfi below Llangorse Eel Trap or Elan below Cabon Coch Dam. Natural or artificial prawn, shrimp or worm not allowed as bait for salmon in the Authority's area before April 15.
Size limits: salmon 12 in (31 cm), trout 7 in (18 cm), in the area above Rhayader Bridge, and 8 in (20 cm) in all other waters of the Wye and tributaries.

FISHERIES
Moccas Water: Apply A. T. Stockwell, Manager, Red Lion Hotel, Bredwardine, Hereford.
Clyro Court: Apply H. Brodie-Smith, Poolpardon Cottage, Clifford, Hay-on-Wye.

LOCAL CLUBS AND ASSOCIATIONS
Birmingham Anglers' Association, V. S. Hall, 40 Thorpe St, Birmingham 5BS 4AU.
Hay-on-Wye Fisherman's Association, B. Wiginton, Prospect House Antiques, Broad St, Hay-on-Wye, Hereford and Worcester.
Hereford and District Angling Association, P. H. Pountney, 8 Panson Place, Puston, Hereford and Worcester.

Llandrindod Wells Angling Association, C. Selwyn & Sons, Park Crescent, Llandrindod Wells, Powys.
Rhayader Angling Club, G. H. Roberts, Belmullet, Rhayader, Powys.
Ross Angling Club, V. R. Hepburn, 23 Claytons, Bridstow, Ross-on-Wye, Hereford and Worcester.
Worcester & District United Anglers Association, W. Meadows, 101 Bransford Rd, St Johns Rd, Worcester.

TACKLE DEALERS
A E Brookes, 958 Bristol Rd South, Birmingham B31 2PE.
Austin Clisset, 1801 Pershore Rd, Cotteridge, Birmingham.
Harold Greenway & Sons, main branch; 1010 Chester Rd, Pype Hayes, Birmingham 24. Tel 373 0057.
Roy Jarvis, 364 Shirley Rd, Acocks Green, Birmingham 27.
Clive Smith, 212 New Rd, Rubery, Birmingham.
W Powell & Son Ltd, 35–37 Carrs Lane, Birmingham.
Ray Hawkins, 73 Thornbridge Ave, Great Barr, Birmingham.
Stan Jones, 17 Raddle Rd, Selly Oak, Birmingham 29.
Simmonds & Priddey, Stratford Rd, Shirley, Birmingham.
Stan Lewis, 2 Severn Side South, Bewdley, Worcestershire.
I Parfitt, 5 Bank St, Chepstow, Gwynt.
Dan Caldwell, 45 Bristol Rd, Gloucester.
All Sports, 86 Barton Street, Gloucester.
H R Grant & Son, 6 Castle St, Hay-on-Wye.
F Perkins, Commercial Rd, Hereford.
H Hatton, St. Owen St, Hereford.
G B Sports, 19 High St, Ross-on-Wye.
G J Davis, Station Rd, Ross-on-Wye.
E R & D M Davies, West St, Rhayader, Powys.
H Keeling & Son, 48 Monnow St, Monmouth.
Mrs V Asbrey, 17 High St, Builth Wells.
M E Smith, Crescent Stores, Glasbury-on-Wye, Powys.
Layton & Davies, 7 Broad St, Leominster, Hereford.
J Wade Sports, 6 Corn St, Leominster, Hereford.

Kennet and its Canal

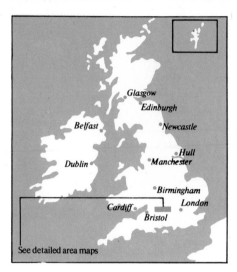

Acknowledged as one of the finest coarse and trout rivers in the South of England, the River Kennet rises near Avebury in Wiltshire and flows due east for 44 miles until it joins the River Thames at Reading. The river is often confused with the Kennet and Avon Canal because at most places along its length the canal flows close and parallel to it, sometimes mingling with it for long stretches, so that the two waters temporarily become one. Locals refer to such stretches as 'the river'.

From the source downstream through Marlborough to Hungerford, the water is principally a private trout and grayling fishery, controlled by various local riparian owners and the local Piscatorial Society. No day tickets or permits are issued. However, some limited coarse, trout and grayling fishing is available in the Hungerford area, on both river and canal, on a day or season-ticket basis. For further details enquire at Newton's (Newsagents), 6 High St, Hungerford, Berkshire. From Hungerford the river and canal flow to Kintbury where the waters are controlled for members only by the Kintbury Angling Club.

From Kintbury the waters flow to the tiny village of Hampstead Marshall, where $3\frac{1}{2}$ miles of river and canal are owned by the Craven Estate. This stretch was private for years, but was first opened to coarse anglers in October 1977. As in most parts of the Kennet, the coarse fishing here is excellent. It has so far yielded roach to $2\frac{1}{2}$lb, dace to 1lb 3oz (very near the British record), chub to 6lb, perch to $3\frac{1}{4}$lb and carp to 18lb, plus pike to 28lb.

The Craven Estate

The Craven Estate is now a day-ticket fishery costing £1.30 per day, and all enquiries should be directed to the Head Bailiff Bob Edwards whose lodge is situated on the riverbank just 100 yards downstream

Kennet and its Canal

(Below) A stretch of the Kennet's newest day-ticket water on the Craven Estate, near Hampstead Marshall.

Derrick Jones

From Hampstead Marshall the river flows through private estate fishing until it reaches Newbury. Here much of the water is controlled by various clubs and associations including the Newbury Angling Club where the fishing is for members only. There is a twelve-mile stretch of day-ticket water in Newbury and anglers should apply to the White House Inn.

Next, at Thatcham, the waters are controlled by the London Anglers' Association, Thatcham Angling Association, and various riparian owners. Neither of these Associations nor the riparian owners, unfortunately, issues day tickets.

Reading and District AA water

From Thatcham the river and canal flow to Woolhampton. This is the uppermost of all the stretches of the River Kennet controlled by the Reading and District Angling Association which controls much of the water from here down to Reading. Unfortunately, their waters are for members, associate members, and members' guests only. Associate membership costs approximately £11, but the waiting list is long.

(Below) The upper reaches of the Kennet, as here near Hungerford, are private, fly-only trout and grayling waters.

G. L. Carlisle

from Hampstead Marshall lock. It is the newest and longest day-ticket stretch of river and canal, totalling $3\frac{1}{2}$ miles. The estate's trout and coarse water runs past the lodge and downstream to a fine weirpool. After the weirpool comes a short stretch of the Kennet and Avon canal, with another weirpool nearby which marks the most downstream section of the fishery. Moving upstream from the lodge there are two miles of river incorporating several straights and bends, with Kintbury Lock at the halfway mark. A black railway bridge marks the most upstream end of this section, but there is more water to be fished above the railway bridge, and this is best reached from the lane which runs through the estate.

235

Kennet and its Canal

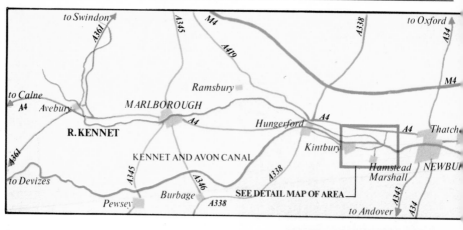

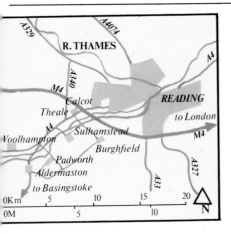

From Aldermaston, the waters flow to Padworth. Here is the noted Benyon Estate fishery, a 2-mile stretch held by the Reading and District Angling Association which also controls the adjoining East Towney and Padworth Mill fisheries. Remaining Padworth stretches are held by the Central Association of London and Provincial Angling Clubs, and are members-only waters.

Theale area

Both day and season-ticket fishing are available at Theale on a stretch known as the Back Water Stream. This is a Leisure Sport water, and permits are issued by Leisure Sport, RMC House, High St, Feltham, Middlesex. The stretch known as Cumbers Meadow is held by the Reading and District Angling Association, and a one-mile private syndicate stretch is controlled by Mike Stratton of T Turner & Sons, Whiteley St, Reading, Berks.

From Theale, the waters run to Calcot where the fishing is entirely controlled by the Reading and District Angling Association. After Calcot comes Sulhampstead. Here the Tyle Mill stretch is controlled by the British Waterways Board. This stretch includes river and canal, and day tickets can be

(Above) The Kennet and its attendant canal.
(Left) John Macklin trotting the weirpool on the Kennet at Thatcham.
(Below) In deep summer the Kennet must be among the most beautiful of English rivers.

Downstream from Woolhampton lies Aldermaston Mill pool which is famed for its barbel fishing. Some of the bank fishing in the area is controlled by Reading and District Angling Association and by the Feltham Piscatorial Society, but the mill pool is available on day ticket, with tickets issued at the Mill House.

P. H. Ward Natural Science Photos

Kennet and its Canal

obtained from Mrs A Bartlett, Canal Cottage, Sulhampstead, Berks.

From Sulhampstead, the river and canal flow to Burghfield. Some of the waters here are controlled by the Reading and District Angling Association, but day and season-ticket fishing on the river (including Burghfield weirpool) is also available from Leisure Sport in Feltham. Around Burghfield Island, bank fishing is controlled by the British Waterways Board.

Downstream from Burghfield, fishing in the Fobney area is controlled by the Reading and District Angling Association, and from Fobney the Kennet flows into Reading, where it eventually joins the Thames. Although the Reading and District Angling Association controls the fishing from Fobney downstream to County Weir, in Reading, fishing on the Kennet from County Weir downstream to the Thames is free, and apart from that which is granted by some riparian owners, it is the only free fishing on the River Kennet.

The Kennet's species

The river in general holds good stocks of specimen coarse fish including bleak, gudgeon, dace, roach, bream, chub, barbel, perch, pike, trout and grayling. There are

(Above) Watched by his dog, the angler is about to net a fat Kennet trout.
(Below) Detail of the Craven Estate water.

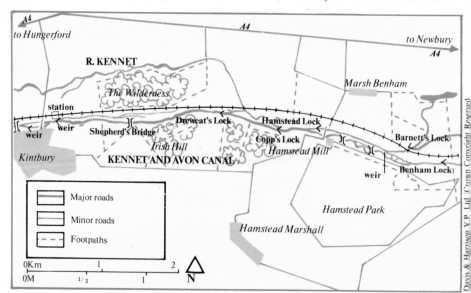

G. L. Carlisle

even a few big carp and tench. Barbel are not found above Thatcham, but from Thatcham downstream to Reading they are plentiful.

Trout and grayling are found in all parts of the river, but they are more prolific in the river above Newbury.

Kennet canal's fish

The canal holds all the above river species except barbel, trout and grayling. These are compensated for by carp and tench, which prefer the canal's slower pace.

The most reliable bait for the Kennet is the caster. It is a telling bait all through the season and most local anglers use hempseed as a backing-up groundbait. Tares are very good too, but they are most effective between June and September. Breadflake 'laid-on' with float tackle, or ledgered with an Arlesey Bomb will not always catch Kennet fish, but at times it will attract the really big roach, dace and chub.

The best method for the area, however, is trotting. Kennet fish are accustomed to taking their food 'on the run' in these fast-flowing waters. Ledgering is also effective.

INFORMATION

WATER AUTHORITY
Thames Water Authority, 2nd floor, Reading Bridge House, Reading, Berks. Tel 593333.
Thames Conservancy Division, 5th floor, Nugent House, Vastern Rd, Reading, Berks. Tel 583583.

LICENCES
Thames Water Authority fishing licence prices are reviewed yearly and run from 1 April, current licence costs are:
adult season £3, OAPs 50p, juniors under 16 no charge, 15 days 50p.
Close seasons: (Thames Conservancy Division) trout 14 October to 28 February; pike 15 March to 30 September; all other coarse fish including eels 15 March to 15 June. Between 1 April and 15 June only rod and line fishing may be allowed for trout with the aid of an artificial fly or spinning with artificial or preserved minnow or with live bait (which must be taken in a minnow trap, not by rod and line).
Bye-laws and size limits for this whole area were under review at the time of going to press. The Thames Water Authority recommend that you should contact them for new details (Tel: Reading 593333).

FISHERIES
Aldermaston Mill Pool, the Mill House, Aldermaston, near Reading, Berks.
Craven Estate, Head Bailiff, Craven Estate, Hampstead-Marshall, near Newbury, Berks. Tel Newbury 40505.
British Waterways Board, Melbury House, Melbury Terrace, London NW1.
Mrs A Bartlett, Canal Cottage, Sulhampstead, Berks.
Leisure Sport, RMC House, High St, Feltham, Middlesex.

LOCAL CLUBS AND ASSOCIATIONS
CALPAC (Central Association of London and Provincial Angling Clubs), F W Newman, 907a Oxford Rd, Reading, Berks.
Feltham Piscatorial Soc, R Sharman, 5 St Albans Ave, Hanworth, TW13 6RW.
Hungerford Canal Angling Assoc, W S Barnes, 2 Charnham St, Hungerford R3 1Y.
Kintbury Angling Club, J A Sykes, 30 Clarks Gardens, Hungerford, Berks.
London Anglers' Assoc, H J Wilson, 183 Hoe St, Walthamstow, London E17 3AP.
Marlborough and District Angling Assoc, J Stone, Fairview, Newbury, Berks.
Reading and District Angling Assoc, D Capon, 7 Blewbury Drive, Tilehurst, Reading, Berks.
Thatcham Angling Assoc, K G Roberts, 'Grovelands' 212 Benham Hill, Newbury, Berks.

TACKLE DEALERS
L N Nicholes, 85 Bedfont Lane, Feltham.
Tookes Fishing Tackle Store, 311 Ruislip Rd, East, Greenford, Middlesex.
The Pet Centre, 106 High St, Marlborough.
Leathercraft of Marlborough, 1 Hughendon Yard, off High St, Marlborough.
The Pet Shop, 53 Cheap St, Newbury.
Cording, 86 North Brook St, Newbury.
Reading Aquarist, 64 King's Rd, Reading.
Turner's, 21 Whitley St, Reading.
Wyres Bait and Tackle, 479 Oxford Rd, Reading.
Angling Centre, 165–6 Manchester Rd, Swindon.
The House of Angling, 60 Commercial Rd, Swindon.
Doric, 9 Crownmead, Bath Rd, Thatcham, nr Newbury. Newbury.

Hertfordshire

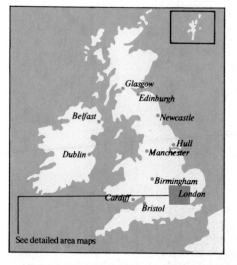

Hertfordshire includes the River Lee, reservoirs, lakes and gravel pits, and all species are to be caught including fish of specimen and near record size. The Lee is mainly a Londoner's river, and its popularity is quite evident at weekends when most stretches are visited by clubs and individual anglers.

The London Angling Association has several fisheries on the Lee, including a fine stretch at Ware, offering good fishing for roach, bream, dace and chub. Near the lock there is a short free stretch.

Association members also have two fine stretches of the Old River Lee at Hertford. The Upper Fishery runs from Folly Sluice, Hertford, to the confluence with the River Beane, while the lower section at Kings

See detailed area maps

(Above) A young angler seeks roach from the Grand Union Canal near Harefield. (Below left) Typical of the beauty of the Hertfordshire countryside is this mill beside the Rib at Standen.

Mead runs from Duckers Mill Pool to Ware Park Mill Point. Both fisheries are reached via the A10. There is also a section of free fishing along the towpath in Hertford.

At Wormley, both the Aqueduct Fishery and the Kings Weir Fishery include stretches of the main river and the diversion. The Kings Weir Fishery, extending from the Aqueduct Lock to the Waverley Club's water, is for members only but day-tickets are issued for the towpath section. These fisheries are reached via the A10, turning into Slipe Lane.

A wide variety of species are to be caught at St Margarets, where day tickets are issued along the bank. Then, at Stanstead Abbots, the Leisure Sport Angling Club has a single-bank length for season permit holders. More good swims are to be found in the Hoddesdon area where the London Anglers' Association has water. Bailiffs issue day tickets along the bank and the Association also has the Rye House Fishery, reached via the A10 to Hoddesdon.

The most noteworthy place is the Crown Fishery at Broxbourne, extending from Carthagena Lock to Broxbourne Bridge. It offers excellent fishing for chub, roach, dace and tench, and is also a noted match venue.

Leisure Sport Angling Club has the popular Fishers Green Fishery, noted especially for its barbel to 10lb, plus pike of 23lb and chub to over 5lb. This fishery includes a section of the river and the flood relief channel and is reached via the B194. Night fishing is not allowed.

At Waltham Abbey there is some free fishing, and another section where day tickets are issued. Then at Cheshunt there is a free stretch noted mainly for chub, with bleak, roach and gudgeon. It is reached via Windmill Lane, and there is a car park at the top of the lane.

The improving Lee

In the London area the River Lee has improved considerably, and the free fishing stretches at Stonebridge Lock, Ponders End, Edmonton and Tottenham, produce regular catches of roach, dace, chub, bleak, gudgeon and the occasional carp.

Day tickets and season permits are issued for fishing a section of the New River Loop at Enfield and one should apply to the Borough Treasurer, Civic Centre, Silver Street, Enfield.

The River Stort is a Lee tributary that holds chub, roach, dace, bream, bleak and pike. At Bishop's Stortford, the local club has a fine day-ticket stretch that extends into Harlow. Downstream, the towpath section

B. D'Abrera/Natural Science Photos

from Spellbrook to Iron Bridge is controlled by the London Anglers' Association, which also controls the Harlow Town Park fishery. Fishing is for members only but day tickets are issued to Harlow residents. The Association also has a stretch of water in the Burnt Mill area.

Another interesting river is the Rib. This has varying depths and holds trout, chub, roach and dace. Season permits are issued by the Leisure Sport Angling Club and the fishery is situated at Downfield Farm, Watton Road, near Ware, Herts—reached via the B158 and B1001.

Batchworth Lake

Rickmansworth Aquadrome boasts two popular lakes. Batchworth Lake, covering 80 acres, is well stocked with pike to 20lb, and bream over 6lb, plus some big carp. Day tickets are issued on the site, and there are boats for hire. The Aquadrome is reached from the A412 Uxbridge Road.

London Anglers' Association controls Springwell Lake at Rickmansworth, a large and established water reserved for members. The stock includes tench, bream, carp, roach and pike. Also included in this fishery is a short single-bank length of the River Colne which is reached via the A412, turning into Springwell Lane.

Four ex-gravel pit lakes known as Frogmore Pits, are situated about two miles south of St Albans, and are also controlled by the London Anglers' Association. They vary from 6-12ft in depth and yield good bream, tench, roach, carp and pike.

This fishery also includes a long stretch of the River Ver, which has plenty of roach and dace and is available on day ticket. It is reached from the A5, with the entrance at Hyde Lane.

Near Hitchin trout anglers have a natural lake of nearly two acres. The lake is fed by the small River Oughton, and owned by the Burford Trout Farm which issues day tickets

The waters of Hertfordshire offer every angler a varied range of fishing of the very highest quality.

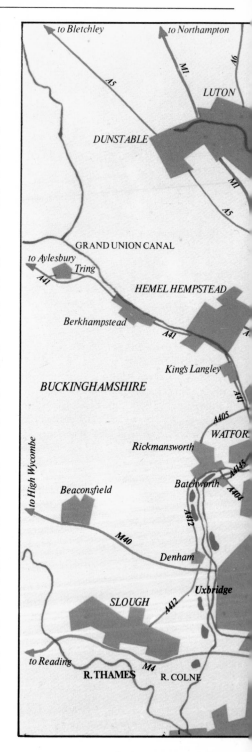

242

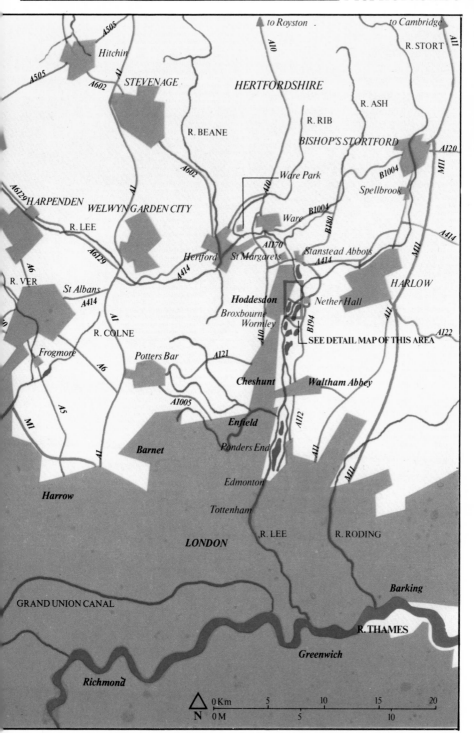

to Royston

to Cambridge

R. STORT

A11

A10

Hitchin

A505

A505

A602

A1

STEVENAGE

HERTFORDSHIRE

R. ASH

R. RIB

R. BEANE

A602

BISHOP'S STORTFORD

A120

B1004

Ware Park

A10

Spellbrook

MII

A6129

HARPENDEN

WELWYN GARDEN CITY

A1

B1004

Ware

A414

B180

R. LEE

A6129

Hertford

A170

St Margarets

Stanstead Abbots

MII

A6

A414

HARLOW

R. VER

St Albans

A1

A414

Hoddesdon

Nether Hall

A111

R. COLNE

Broxbourne

Wormley

B194

A122

Frogmore

A6

Potters Bar

A121

A10

SEE DETAIL MAP OF THIS AREA

A1005

Cheshunt

Waltham Abbey

A5

Enfield

A112

MI

Barnet

Ponders End

A11

MII

Harrow

Edmonton

Tottenham

R. LEE

R. RODING

LONDON

Barking

GRAND UNION CANAL

R. THAMES

Greenwich

Richmond

N

0 Km   5   10   15   20

0 M   5   10

243

and season tickets. Stocked with brown and rainbow trout, the fishing is by fly only, with a catch limit of four fish.

Another trout water is the Netherhall Fishery at Hoddesdon, which consists of a partly landscaped six-acre lake regularly stocked with rainbows. The top fish recorded weighed 6lb. Fishing is by fly only with a catch limit of four fish. There are no boats and wading is not allowed.

At the Crown Fishery, Carthagena Lock, Broxbourne, day tickets and season permits are issued. Access to the fishery is via Dobb's Weir Road.

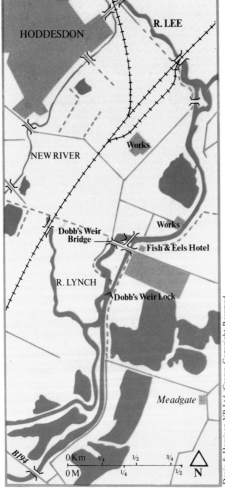

(Above) A famous venue for both experienced anglers and beginners— Dobb's Weir on the Lee.
(Left) Detail of Dobb's Weir, Hoddesdon.

The Broxbourne Fishery consists of three large lakes and a small pool all holding good fish. Among recorded specimens are pike of 26lb, carp of $21\frac{3}{4}$lb, bream of 8lb and roach of $2\frac{1}{2}$lb. Night fishing is allowed. Season tickets are issued by the Leisure Sport Angling Club. It is reached by the B194, entering by Meadgate Lane.

At Stanstead Abbots, and also controlled by the Leisure Sport Angling Club, is a group of ex-gravel pit lakes containing tench, bream, and carp to 18lb. This fishery also includes a single-bank length of the River Lee.

The fishery is reached by the A10 from London and the A414, with the entrance in Marsh Lane.

244

Frank Guttfield

Leisure Sport Angling Club also has two lakes and two stretches of the River Colne at Rickmansworth, known as No 1 and No 2 fisheries. Access to the No 1 fishery in Moor Lane is via the A412, A404 and A4145. The No 2 fishery is reached via the A412 into Colne Mead. Both fisheries are stocked with tench, bream, carp, roach, chub and dace, and are available on season permit.

Grand Union Canal

The length of the Grand Union Canal that cuts through Hertfordshire also offers ample fishing opportunities. One of the best lengths is a six-mile stretch from Batchworth Lock to Denham, Bucks. This length is controlled by the Blenheim Angling Society, and day tickets are issued along the bank.

A stretch of approximately 14 miles from King's Langley, through Berkhampstead and Tring, is noted for big roach, but is reserved for members of the London Anglers' Association. Another canal section, known as the Aylesbury Arm, also offers interesting fishing, and is controlled by the Tring Anglers, and by the Aylesbury and District Angling Association.

INFORMATION

WATER AUTHORITIES
Thames Water Authority, 2nd Floor, Reading Bridge House, Reading, Berks. Tel 593345.
Lee Division, The Grange, Crossbrook St, Waltham Cross, Herts. EN8 8LX. Tel 23611.
Thames Conservancy Division, 5th Floor, Nugent House, Vastern Rd, Berks. Tel 583583.

LICENCES
Thames Water Authority fishing licence prices are reviewed yearly and run from 1 April, current licence costs are:
adult season £3, OAPs 50p, juniors under 16 no charge, 15 days 50p. Weir permit £3.30.
Close seasons: (Lee Division) trout: 1 October to 28 February, coarse fish 15 March to 15 June. (Thames Conservancy Division) trout 14 October to 31 March, pike 15 March to 30 September, all other coarse fish including eels 15 March to 15 June. Between 1 April and 15 June only rod and line fishing may be used for trout with the aid of an artificial fly or spinning with artificial or preserved minnow or with live bait (which must be taken in a minnow trap, not by rod and line).
Size limits: (Lee Division) pike 24in (61cm), barbel 16in (40cm), chub, carp, tench, bream, trout and grayling 12in (31cm), perch 9in (23cm), rudd and roach 8in (20cm), dace 7in (18cm), gudgeon 5in (12cm), bleak 4in (10cm). (Thames Conservancy Division) pike 24in (61cm) barbel 16in (40cm), trout 14in (35cm), bream, carp and chub 12in (31cm), tench 10in (25cm), perch 9in (23cm), rudd 8in (20cm), dace, flounders and roach 7in (18cm), gudgeon 5in (12cm), bleak 4in (10cm).

FISHERIES
Abingdon Borough Council, The Council House, Abingdon,
Burford Trout Farm, Burford Lodge, Bedford Rd, Hitchin, Herts. Tel: Hitchin 52855.

LOCAL CLUBS AND ASSOCIATIONS
Aylesbury and District and Izaac Walton Angling Assoc, E Wheeler, 20 Verney Walk, Southcourt, Aylesbury, Bucks.
Blenheim Angling Soc, F W Lancaster, 20 Hilary Rd, Shepherds Bush, London W12.
Bishop's Stortford and District Angling Soc, C J Costema, 31 Thornbera Rd, Bishop's Stortford, Herts.
Central Assoc of London and Provincial Angling Clubs (CALPAC), F W Newman, 907a Oxford Rd, Reading.
Civil Service Angling Soc, W J Bayliss, 35 Limerston St, Chelsea, London SW10.
Leisure Sport Angling Club, Angling Manager, RMC House, High St, Feltham, Middx.
London Anglers' Assoc, H J Wilson, 183 Hoe St, Walthamstow, London E17.
Tring Anglers, J A Smith, 67 Lower Icknield Way, Marsworth, Tring, Herts.

TACKLE DEALERS
Simpsons of Turnford, Nunsbury Drive, Broxbourne.
Tamesis Tackle, 127 Crossbrook St, Cheshunt, Herts.
Don's of Edmonton, 239 Fore St, Edmonton, N18.
Queensway Angling & Pets, 52 Queensway, Hemel Hempstead, Herts.
Mecca Angling, 1-3 Parliament Square, Hertford.
Farrer's Tackle, 709 Seven Sisters Rd, South Tottenham, N15.
Leslie's Fishing Tackle, 14/16 Catherine St, St Albans.
Tackle Supply Yard, 405 Whippendall Rd, Watford, Herts.
Tackle Carrier, 157 St Albans Rd, Watford.

Upper Thames

See detailed area maps

No English river is more steeped in angling history than the Thames. Charles II was England's first serious fishing monarch and he often angled at Datchet. He was once accused by Lord Rochester of 'slaughtering gudgeons.' Once a royal river, the Thames has remained a truly national river and now provides sport for many thousands of fishermen from all over the country.

There are still arguments about the source of the Thames. Some think it is at Seven Springs near the Churn while others believe it to be at Thames Head near Cirencester. Either way John Burns was right when he called this willow-fringed meanderer from here down to the tide surge of the Nore 'liquid history.'

The Thames often misses the angling headlines leaving them to the more match-oriented waters of the Midlands or North, but it has yielded exceptional catches and individual specimens galore. Only recently, in October 1977, the English 5-hour match record was beaten at Pangbourne by a 175lb 3oz haul of bream—a catch only bettered on Denmark's Guden by 7lb. It has also yielded a 14lb 4oz barbel and at least half a dozen

others topping the 12½lb mark. The records show a best chub of 7lb 1oz; perch 4lb 5oz; bream 11¼lb; carp 30½lb; dace 1lb; pike 32lb; roach 3lb 9oz; and a trout caught near Reading which weighed 16lb 15oz—all truly great fish and all indicating the remarkable quality of the Thames.

The Thames Water Authority (TWA) issues permits allowing holders to fish any of 21 weir pools, Grafton, Radcot, Rushey, Shifford, Eynsham in the upper reaches and Sandford in Oxford where the barbel still grow big.

In the upper reaches above Cricklade trout and coarse species, like dace, grow well but much of this part of the river is preserved by individuals or is for members of controlling clubs only. The Isis Angling Club of Swindon controls two lengthy sections in this area, and has open membership.

No day-ticket water is available until Lechlade, where the Trout Inn issues tickets for about 2½ miles of bank from St John's lock upstream to the Roundhouse at Inglesham. The water has excellent fishing for most species including trout, and recently a barbel of 9lb was taken.

(Below) The River Thames downstream of Lechlade at Tadpole Bridge near Buckland. (Below right) The weir at Shifford, Oxon.

Buscot Weir is just downstream. The London Anglers' Association controls much of both banks from St John's bridge on the A417 to below Buscot Wharf, and day tickets are available along the bank at a modest price.

The famous Anchor Inn fishery controlled by Derek Liggins is at Eaton Hastings, off the A417. Day tickets are issued for this lengthy stretch which holds most species. Often a big shoal of bream can be caught feeding upstream near the spinney, good roach are often taken, and the downstream section on the bend is noted for its large chub. Most tactics are successful here.

Downstream is Grafton Weir where big trout and barbel are often caught; then at Radcot, the Radcot Angling Association controls a good stretch with day tickets available at the Swan Inn. Nearby, fishing at Radcot Weir is available for holders of

247

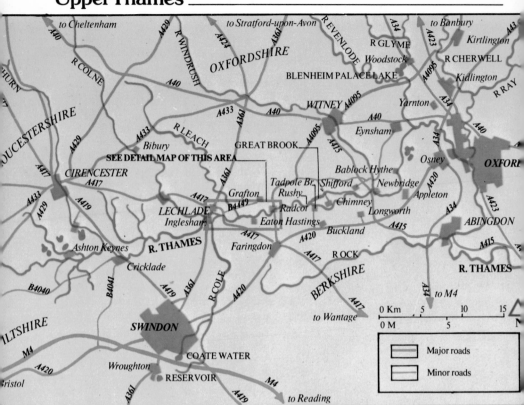

Thames Water Authority Access permits, as is Rushey Weir, downstream. From there to Tadpole bridge at Buckland, the Coventry and District Angling Association controls a very productive stretch with honorary cards available from Midland tackle dealers.

There is another Trout Inn near the bridge on the road from Buckland on the A420 and this controls a very good section of the Thames and issues day tickets. Here the river averages 5ft in depth and usually has a good stream running, making float fishing a joy.

Fine fishing water

Farther downstream at Newbridge on the A415, day tickets are available for two more stretches of fine fishing water. These are obtained from the Maybush Inn for about 1½ miles of fishing by the inn and for a stretch on the opposite bank by the Rose Revived Inn.

The Birmingham AA, which issues associate membership cards, controls water

from this point on the upstream right bank at Thames Side Farm near Longworth church, and a ½-mile stretch downstream at Appleton. Both sections have yielded some very big bream, and barbel to 9lb.

Near Chimney village off the B4449 is the Great Brook which holds very good chub and roach. Now controlled by clubs there are, however, some stretches still available by permission. It is difficult fishing in a confined and often weed-filled area, but most rewarding.

Below Newbridge there is very good fishing at Bablock Hythe off the A420, and day tickets are available from the Chequers Hotel and the Ferry Inn. The Oxford Alliance Angling Society has water here too, and their weekly and fortnightly permits can be bought at most Oxford tackle dealers.

At Yarnton on the A40 Oxford-Whitney road, the Birmingham AA controls 1 mile above King Weir, and a stretch on the right bank at Pixey where the approaches are from the A34 Oxford-Abingdon road. Just upstream the Oxford Alliance Angling Society controls the water at Eynsham.

Oxford-based clubs control most of the fishing in and around the city. Oxford Angling Association controls a very long length from Osney bridge, and they issue holiday permits for excellent fishing waters. Further information is always available from local tackle dealers.

Most Thames tributaries provide good fishing, though along most, like the Glyme, Evenlode and Windrush, it is strictly preserved. The River Colne has a high reputation for trout fishing akin to that of southern chalk streams. The Bull Hotel in Fairford on the A417 controls about 1½ miles of trout fishing and issues day tickets. Fishing is dry fly from April to 30

The Thames' tributaries offer good fishing although mainly preserved. Seen below, the River Windrush at Witney (left) and Burford (right).

Frank Guttfield

Richard Jemmett

Upper Thames

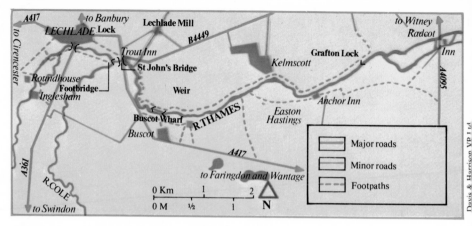

September. At Bibury on the A433 the Swan Hotel also has dry fly trout fishing for guests.

The River Cherwell is a fabulous water for those who take the trouble to learn its secrets. It holds a big head of most species including chub to 6lb, quality roach and big dace. The Birmingham AA and the Coventry and District Angling Association control stretches near Aynho on the A41 and at Kirtlington on the A4095. Farther downstream at Kidlington water is controlled by the Twickenham Angling Society and the Leighton Buzzard Angling Club.

There are also excellent stillwater fisheries. Chief among these are the lakes at Blenheim Palace near Woodstock. Fishing is from boats with the main species caught tench, roach, perch, and some really excellent pike fishing. Specimens over 20lb are taken.

Good gravel-pit fishing

There is some very good gravel-pit fishing at South Cerney in Gloucestershire with much of it available on day ticket. The Isis Angling Club controls a lot of pool and gravel-pit fishing and membership to this club is open. The South Cerney Angling Club controls rights to fishing at Ham Lane and Hills Lake pools, plus the Bradley Main Gravel pit. Weekly tickets are available. Nearby is the larger Ashton Keynes lake which is stocked with most stillwater species along with brown trout. Day tickets are obtainable from dispensing kiosks.

Near Swindon is Coate Water where day

tickets are available on the bank and where roach and bream abound along with tench and pike. Nearby is Wroughton Reservoir, a 2-acre trout fishery controlled by the Thames Water Authority. It is stocked with brown trout to 5lb and the number of rods per day is limited, so the angler is advised to book well in advance.

Tackle and tactics

Tackle and tactics suitable for Upper Thames fishing are very similar to that of fishing most Midlands waters. Maggots are the most popular hook baits, though excellent results are often achieved with seed baits, bread flakes or worms. Tares have recently become a popular and highly succesful bait in the Eaton Hastings and Buscot reaches, accounting for some big roach catches and some sizeable barbel.

In the Eaton Hastings section bream tend to run big and have fighting qualities greater than those from the slower waters in the east. A bream of 4lb will put up a remarkable fight akin to the bream of the lower Shannon in Co Limerick.

Big barbel have been tempted with most baits, often ledgered, ranging from worm to par-boiled potatoes. Like the bream, Thames barbel seem to be endowed with extra fighting capabilities.

Thames pike fishing has been underestimated. The river often yields pike in high double figures and many are taken with plugbaits.

The detail map shows a section of excellent day-ticket waters from Inglesham to Lechlade, St John's Bridge to Buscot Wharf, and the famous Anchor Inn fishery at Eaton Hastings. Most species are found here, with some large chub and big trout at Grafton Weir. Farther downstream is Blenheim Palace viewed across the lake (right) and then Oxford (below).

Richard Jemmett

Peter Stone

INFORMATION

WATER AUTHORITY

Thames Water Authority, 2nd Floor, Reading Bridge House, Reading, Berks. Tel 593333.
Thames Conservancy Division, 5th Floor, Nugent House, Vastern Rd, Reading, Berks. Tel 583583.

LICENCES

Annual £3.15, days 50p. Juniors under 16 years free, OAPs 50p. Weir permit £3.30.
31 December.
Close seasons: trout 14 October to 31 March; pike 15 March to 30 September; all other coarse fish including eels 15 March to 15 June. Between 1 April and 15 June only rod and line fishing may be used for trout with the aid of an artificial fly or spinning with artificial or preserved minnow or with live bait (which must be taken in a minnow trap, not by rod and line).
Size limits: pike 24in (61 cm), barbel 16in (40cm), trout 14in (35cm), bream, carp and chub 12in (31cm), tench 10in (25cm), perch 9in (23cm), rudd 8in (20cm), dace, flounder and roach 7in (18cm), gudgeon 5in (12cm), bleak 4in (10cm).

LOCAL CLUBS AND ASSOCIATIONS

Birmingham Anglers' Assoc, V S Hall, 40 Thorpe St, Birmingham 5B5 4AU.
Coventry and District Angling Assoc, E G Baxter, 15 Boswell Drive, Coventry, W Midlands.
Isis Angling Club, D A C Horsman, 9 Noredown Way, Wootton Bassett, Wilts.
Leighton Buzzard Angling Club, Fred Groom, 29 Albany Rd, Leighton Buzzard, Beds.

London Anglers' Assoc, H J Wilson, 183 Hoe St, Walthamstow, London E17 3AP.
Abingdon and Oxford Anglers' Alliance, A Goodchild, 44 New Cross Rd, Headington, Oxford.
Oxford and District Anglers' Assoc, F Jones, 20 Merlin Rd, Littlemore, Oxford.
Radcot Angling and Preservation Club, C R Neville, Clanville House, Bampton Rd, Clanfield, Oxon.
South Cerney Angling Club, H J Franklin, Sisters Farm, South Cerney, Cirencester, Glos.
Twickenham Piscatorial Soc, Mrs Nevill, 11 Carlton Close, Ember Lane, Esher, Surrey.

TACKLE DEALERS

I T Hayden, Fishing Tackle, 33 The Vineyard, Abingdon.
A B Beadle, 30 Ock St, Abingdon, Oxon.
J Sparkes and Son, Burford St, Lechlade, Glos.
Riverside Lechlade Ltd, Park End Wharf, Lechlade.
J Wilkins, 39a St James St, Cowley Rd, Oxford. Tel 43469.
Waltonian Tackle, 30a Observatory St, Oxford. Tel 57077.
G Williams, 115 London Rd, Headington, Oxford.
Arthur Smith, 95 Islip Rd, Oxford. Tel 56955.
Cookes Tackle Shop, 69 Northumberland Ave, Reading.
Thomas Turner, 21 Whiteley St, Reading, Berks.
Guilloud Ltd, 1 Old Crown, Slough, Berks, Tel 20437.
Slough Sports and Angling Centre, 245 Farnham Rd, Slough, Tel 21055.
House of Angling, 60 Commercial Rd, Swindon, Wilts.
Swindon Angling Centre Ltd, 175 Manchester Rd, Swindon. Tel 22701.
J Kent, 5–7 Mill St, Wantage, Oxon.
J M C Bunn, Maybush Inn, Newbridge, Witney, Oxon.
R F Bridgeman, 76 High St, Witney.

Middle Thames

See detailed area maps

Anglers have many opportunities for free and permit fishing along the middle reaches of England's major coarse fishing river—the Thames. From Oxford to Teddington, fishing is controlled by a number of clubs and includes the longest free-fishing stretch.

The London Anglers' Association has the biggest holding. Their waters are available to members of the many affiliated clubs, and for an associate membership fee of £5.50. Membership also gives admission to many other fisheries in and around London.

The middle reaches of the Thames hold large shoals of big bream, fine roach, dace, barbel and good chub. Trout, tench, perch, pike, bleak, gudgeon, eels, ruffe and, in several areas, carp are also found.

Much of the fishing from Oxford to Sandford is controlled by Oxford and District Association, and regular visitors enjoy excellent sport, often taking big catches of bream and roach. Visitors must have a permit. Below Sandford the fishing is held by the Oxford Alliance, and much of this extends through Radley and Pumney Farm, and is reserved for members of affiliated clubs.

One of the most popular permit fisheries is at Abingdon where the local Borough Council controls $2\frac{1}{2}$ miles from Nuneham Railway Bridge downstream to Culham footbridge. Known as the Corporate Fishery, it includes a fine weir pool that has produced barbel to 10lb. Residents living within three miles of Abingdon enjoy free fishing and the exclusive use of Abbey Meadow Island. Moreover, a resident's permit is overstamped by the Corporation so the holder does not need a TWA licence.

Permits for Abingdon

A 15p day permit, from the Council House at Abingdon, covers the fishery, and the visiting angler pays 5p for each consecutive day. An annual permit costs £1, and club parties and matches are bookable for a maximum of 30 anglers.

Downstream, the river sweeps round a sharp bend into the attractive Sutton Courtenay reach with its weirs and pools. It offers excellent fishing to members of Culham AA and can be reached from the

A415 and B4016. The LAA have double-bank fishing from the railway bridge at Appleford to Long Wittenham, plus a further section at Little Wittenham.

From Long Wittenham, Clifton Hampden PS, a member club of the Oxford Alliance, has the fishing along the north bank for about 1½ miles from the weir to Clifton Hampden weir. Then at Dorchester, the Dorchester AA controls the water. This is reached from the A423.

Warborough and Shillingford club members have a mile of water to Benson, and downstream the Jolly Angler AC has a stretch from Benson to below Wallingford, noted for shoals of big bream. Day and week tickets are available and the water is easily reached via the A423, A4130 and A329.

Bath Road PS holds the rights to the Mungewell Park Farm stretch where bream, chub, roach, dace and gudgeon figure chiefly in the catches—unfortunately for members only. Members of the Hanwell Prince of Wales AC then have the fishing at Little Stoke, the LAA from here to Goring.

The opposite bank, from Basildon to Pangbourne, is controlled by Ye Olde Thames AC and is noted for bream, with a world match record of 175lb 4½oz taken in 1977. Access is easy from the A329, but the water is reserved for members only.

Downstream there is some free fishing along Pangbourne Meadows, and in this area the National Trust has permit water along the Whitchurch meadows, reached from Pangbourne Village.

The next noted section is at Mapledurham where large pike are taken. The water is controlled to below the weirpool by the LAA and the Elthorne AA. The latter is for members only, but membership is available. The Chazey Farm fishery downstream is controlled by Englefield Green AA and offers chub, bream, roach and dace.

Tilehurst to Caversham Bridge

Popular with visiting anglers is the long stretch of free fishing on the opposite bank, extending from Tilehurst down through Caversham Reach, and offering fine mixed catches of roach, chub, dace and bream, plus fine pike in season. Reading Council controls King's Meadow and Christchurch Meadow along this bank, both easily reached from Caversham Bridge. Clubs can book the meadows for contests, and most weekdays anglers enjoy free fishing.

There is more free fishing on the towpath bank downstream of Caversham Weir and below Reading Bridge through the Dreadnought stretch to Sonning Bridge. On the opposite bank the LAA hold the rights to an exclusive fishery, and downstream the fishing is controlled by the Central Association of London and Provincial Angling Clubs (CALPAC).

At Shiplake, the Shiplake and Binfield Heath AC has a fishery for members, with fine bream, chub, roach and dace.

The next popular day-ticket stretch is at Remenham where the local club's water extends to Hambledon Lock and is easily reached from the A423.

Plenty of river traffic here in the summer, but the fishing on the Thames at Winsdor on this match stretch can produce some useful totals and the odd specimen.

Bill Howes

Middle Thames

The area of the Middle Thames—probably the greatest single complex of coarse fishing in the British Isles. Other areas may offer single, important species, but the Middle Thames has the greatest all-round range.

The LAA has another interesting fishery from Medmenham to Temple Ferry which has varied swims and holds most species. Part of this stretch is available on a 40p day ticket (juniors 20p).

Marlow is noted for excellent fishing, and the Marlow AC has water from Temple Lock downstream to near the road bridge, and then from Marlow Lock to a point opposite Wootton's boathouse. This includes the Marlow Race.

The adjoining Bourne End fishery, noted particularly for chub, with good shoals of roach and dace, is for LAA members only and tickets are now discontinued.

A long and exclusive fishery at Cookham is controlled by the local Cookham and District AC for members only, while downstream there are free and day-ticket stretches through to Boulter's Lock. Maidenhead AC bailiffs issue 35p day tickets along the bank from Monday to Friday.

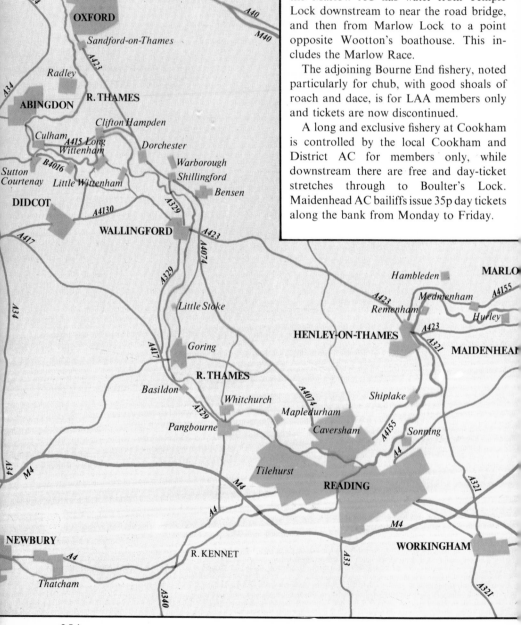

Free fishing is to be found down the river to Bray where a mile-long stretch is reserved for Boyer's Angling Scheme permit-holders.

One of the finest sections of the middle Thames is the Maidenhead AC-controlled Dorney Reach extending down to Boveney Church. Excellent catches of barbel and chub are to be made here, and 50p day tickets are issued from Monday to Friday. Fishing rights on the exclusive Racecourse Island at Windsor and on the opposite bank are held by the Civil Service AS which also has a fine stretch for members at Datchet.

Boveney Lock to Windsor

From Boveney Lock the LAA has fishing along the towpath to Cuckoo footbridge, and below this it is Salt Hill Club's water. The river here flows along Clewer Meadow, rounding Clewer Point and on towards Windsor Bridge. Day tickets are issued here and some big bream, chub and other species are to be taken.

Between the Salt Hill water and Windsor Bridge lies Brocas Meadow, overshadowed by Windsor Castle on the opposite side of the river. Fishing here is free, just a short walk from the council car park, and easily reached from Eton High Street.

The Romney weir and lock cut are controlled by the Old Windsor Angling Club, which issues day tickets for this, and for the single bank between Albert Bridge and Old Windsor Lock. Fishing is free, in this long lock cutting.

Downstream at Runnymede there is free fishing along the National Trust bank and from here, past Egham recreation ground with its large car park, to Staines road bridge. Fine barbel and carp are found here.

The towpath switches to the opposite bank below Staines bridge, and fishing is free along the remainder of the river through Penton Hook, Laleham, Chertsey and Shepperton, in Middlesex.

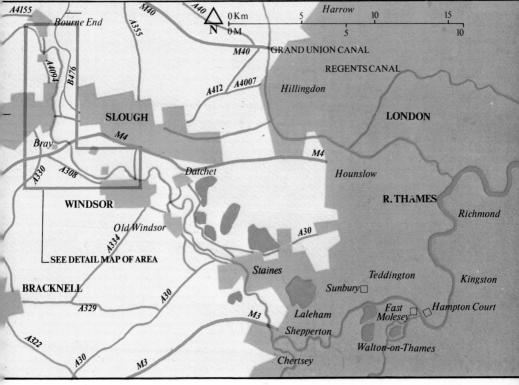

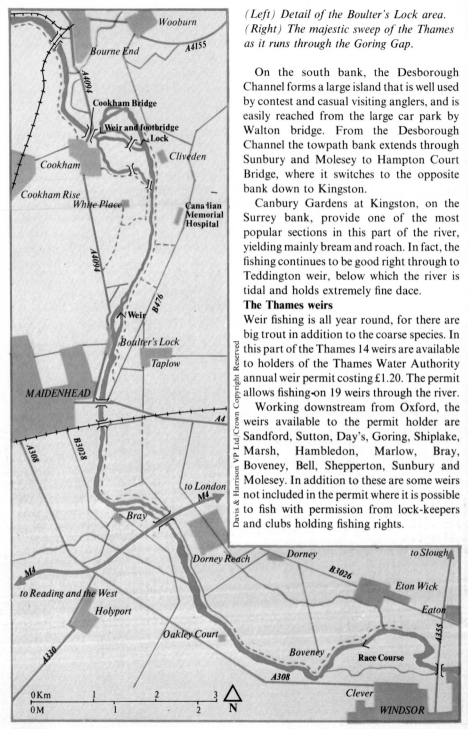

(Left) Detail of the Boulter's Lock area. (Right) The majestic sweep of the Thames as it runs through the Goring Gap.

On the south bank, the Desborough Channel forms a large island that is well used by contest and casual visiting anglers, and is easily reached from the large car park by Walton bridge. From the Desborough Channel the towpath bank extends through Sunbury and Molesey to Hampton Court Bridge, where it switches to the opposite bank down to Kingston.

Canbury Gardens at Kingston, on the Surrey bank, provide one of the most popular sections in this part of the river, yielding mainly bream and roach. In fact, the fishing continues to be good right through to Teddington weir, below which the river is tidal and holds extremely fine dace.

The Thames weirs

Weir fishing is all year round, for there are big trout in addition to the coarse species. In this part of the Thames 14 weirs are available to holders of the Thames Water Authority annual weir permit costing £1.20. The permit allows fishing on 19 weirs through the river.

Working downstream from Oxford, the weirs available to the permit holder are Sandford, Sutton, Day's, Goring, Shiplake, Marsh, Hambledon, Marlow, Bray, Boveney, Bell, Shepperton, Sunbury and Molesey. In addition to these are some weirs not included in the permit where it is possible to fish with permission from lock-keepers and clubs holding fishing rights.

G. L. Carlisle

INFORMATION

WATER AUTHORITY

Thames Water Authority, 2nd Floor, Reading Bridge House, Reading, Berks. Tel 593345.

Thames Conservancy Division, 5th Floor, Nugent House, Vastern Rd, Reading, Berks. Tel 583583.

LICENCES

Thames Water Authority fishing licence prices are reviewed yearly and run from 1 April, current licence costs are:

adult season £3, OAPs 50p, 15 days 50p. No charge for juniors under 16. Weir permit £3.30.

Close seasons: (Thames Conservancy Division) trout 14 October to 31 March, pike 15 March to 30 September, all other coarse fish including eels 15 March to 15 June. Between 1 April and 15 June only rod and line fishing may be used for trout with the aid of an artificial fly or spinning with artificial or preserved minnow or with live bait (which must be taken in a minnow trap, not by rod and line).

Size limits: (Thames Conservancy Division) pike 24in (66cm), barbel 16in (40cm), trout 14in (35cm), bream, carp and chub 12in (31cm), tench 10in (25cm), perch 9in (23cm), rudd 8in (20cm), dace, flounders and roach 7in (18cm), gudgeon 5in (12cm), bleak 4in (10cm).

FISHERIES

Abingdon Borough Council, The Council House, Abingdon, Oxon.

Reading Borough Council, The Council House, Reading.

LOCAL CLUBS AND ASSOCIATIONS

Abingdon and Oxford Anglers' Alliance, A Goodchild, 44 New Cross Rd, Headington, Oxford.

Bath Road Piscatorial Soc, C Gardner, 8 Lilac Gdns, Ealing, London W5.

Central Assoc of London and Provincial Angling Clubs (CALPAC), F W Newman, 907A Oxford Rd, Reading, Berks.

Civil Service Angling Soc, W J Bayliss, 35 Limerston St, Chelsea, London SW10.

Cookham and District Angling Club, R H Newton, 45 Guinions Rd, High Wycombe, HP13 7NT.

Culham Angling Assoc, R Wiblin, 33 Essex St, Oxford.

Clifton Hampden Piscatorial Soc, S Lavey, 64 Morrell Ave, Oxford.

Dorchester and District Angling Soc, R Bull, 15 Chiltern Gdns, Wattlington, Oxon.

Elthorne Angling Assoc, C Wilde, 9 Elmwood, Maidenhead Court Park, Maidenhead, Berks.

Englefield Green Angling Assoc, R Young, 65 Bond St, Egham, Surrey.

Jolly Angler Fishing Club, A Gray, Harcourt Lodge, St Lucians Lane, Wallington, Oxon.

London Anglers' Assoc, H J Wilson, 183 Hoe St, Walthamstow, London E17.

Maidenhead Angling Assoc, A Brocklebank, 39 Francis Way, Slough.

Marlow Angling Soc, G Owen, 15 Greenlands, Flackwell Heath, nr High Wycombe, Bucks.

Oxford and District Angling Assoc, J R Owen, 3 Southview Terr, Princes Rd, Cores End, Bourne End, Bucks.

Salt Hill AC, R. Ellis, 201 Chalvey Grove, Slough, Bucks.

Shiplake and Binfield Heath Angling Club, K Wilmott, 35 Albany Rd, Reading, Berks.

Twyford and District Angling Club, D Metcalf, Millwood, 10 Ambleside Close, Cowley, Oxford.

Warborough and Shillingford Angling Club, J Stopps, 5 Cholsey Close, Cowley, Oxford.

Ye Olde Thames Angling Club, G Hammond, Caversham, Reading, Berks.

TACKLE DEALERS

Thames Angling, 11 Feltham Rd, Ashford, Middlesex.

Patone Sports, 1 Woodthorpe Rd, Ashford.

Molesey Pets and Angling, 96 Walton Rd, East Molesey Surrey.

Dennis Tackle, 90 High St, Egham, Surrey.

R Gould, 104 Thorpe Lea Rd, Egham.

R Grief & Sons, 43 York Rd, Ilford.

Morgan's, 17 High St, Hampton Wick, Kingston, Surrey.

J Smith, 4 High St, Maidenhead, Berks.

Cookes, 69 Northumberland Ave, Reading.

Wyers, Oxford Rd, Reading.

Turners, 211 Whitley St, Reading.

Rulls Tackle, 258 Kentwood Hill, Tilehurst, Reading.

Edco Sports, 136 North St, Romford, Essex.

Keith's Tackle, 209-11 North St, Romford.

Metcalf & Son, High St, Tring, Herts.

Wallingford Tackle, 23 High St, Wallingford, Surrey.

Cycles and Tackle, 29 Bridge St, Walton, Surrey.

South East-Reservoirs

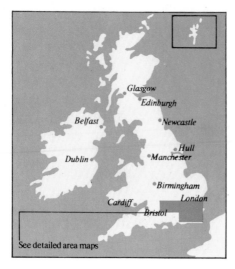

See detailed area maps

Anglers wishing to fish the reservoirs in London and the South-East must obtain a rod licence from one of three water authorities – the Thames, the Southern, or the Anglian.

The Thames Water Authority owns 15 reservoirs in Greater London with public day-ticket fishing – seven for trout and eight for coarse fishing.

Walthamstow Reservoirs

The Walthamstow Reservoirs in N17 include Reservoir 1 (19 acres), regularly stocked with carp and tench; Nos 2 and 3 (13 and 12 acres), with bream, pike, roach and carp; game fishing Reservoirs 4 and 5 (30 and 41 acres), with brown and rainbow trout; East Warwick (43 acres), with carp; West Warwick (38 acres), with pike and bream; High Maynard (38 acres), with perch, roach, carp, bream and rudd; and Low Maynard (25 acres), with bream, pike, roach and carp. Reservoir 9 is not for the public, and the very large Banbury Reservoir is controlled by the Civil Service AS.

Reservoir 4 is fly fishing only, and in 5 all methods of fishing using a rod and line are permitted except that the use of any form of live or deadbait or groundbait is prohibited. The reservoirs are about a mile from Tottenham and reached via the A10.

Barn Elms Reservoirs

In Barnes, SW13, the Barn Elms Reservoirs offer coarse and game fishing. Reservoirs 7 and 8 (23 and 18 acres) hold rainbow trout, No 6 (20 acres) bream, roach, carp, tench and perch; while No 5 (20 acres), newly opened on 5 April 1978, has fishing for rainbow trout from boats only. Reservoir 7 has fly fishing only.

Tickets for the Barn Elms Reservoirs and the Walthamstow Reservoirs are the same price—trout, day tickets £3 (part-day £3); coarse, day tickets 50p, season tickets £5.

The Queen Mother Reservoir (475 acres),

good for game fishing, is near Slough and Colnbrook and reached via the M4 and A4. It opened in 1976 and was stocked the year before with 46,000 rainbow and 40,000 brown trout. Constant restocking maintains an average density of 100 fish per acre and the reservoir now boasts some splendid fish of over 8lb in weight.

Fishing at this large reservoir is from boats only, with a catch limit of six fish, or four for part-day permit holders. Day tickets, including motorized boat hire, cost £8 for one angler, £12 for two and £16 for three anglers (£6, £9 and £12 respectively per half -day), and £6 for one angler, £10 for two and £14 for three anglers sharing a rowing boat (£4, £7 and £10 respectively per half-day). These charges increase at weekends and bank holidays. Juniors aged 8 to 16 are only entitled to a permit if fishing with an adult. Tickets can be obtained from the Thames

Water Authority or at the Recreation Centre in Horton Rd, Horton near Colnbrook.

Situated between Sunbury and Twickenham, Kempton Park West Reservoir (21 acres) is a rainbow trout game fishery with fish to over 7lb. Fishing is by fly only, from the bank, with a six-fish catch limit, or four fish for part-day permit holders. Day tickets cost the same as for Walthamstow and Barn Elms, and can be obtained from the Thames Water Authority (Metropolitan Water Division), New River Head, Rosebery Avenue, EC1.

All the TWA reservoirs are situated in and around London, except two. Wroughton

A sunny afternoon at Walthamstow. Numbers 4 and 5 are stocked with brown and rainbow trout, the remaining six hold the coarse species. There are 15 Thames Water Authority reservoirs available to anglers.

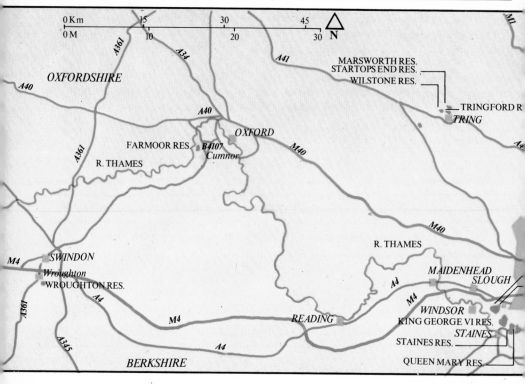

Reservoir (3 acres) is in Swindon, Wiltshire, and reached via the A361. It is stocked with brown and rainbow trout and for fly fishing only. Permits should be obtained in advance, from the TWA, Cotswold Division, 17 Bath Rd, Swindon.

Farmoor Reservoir (280 acres), the youngest TWA reservoir, is off the Cumnor Road, Farmoor, Oxford. It opened on 1 May 1978 and offers some good game fishing from the banks, being stocked with brown and rainbow trout. Fishing is by fly only. Permits are issued at the Reservoir, and charges are as for Walthamstow Reservoir.

For coarse and game close seasons on TWA reservoirs, check with the Authority.

Kempton Park West Reservoir. This is a 21-acre water stocked with rainbow trout. There are no boats, and fishing is confined to the banks from a series of steps placed at intervals round the perimeter. Limit is six fish on a day permit.

Bill Howes

260

ARDLEIGH RES.

COLCHESTER

Ardleigh

Layer-de-la-Haye

A12

ABBERTON RES.

B1026

A120

HERTFORDSHIRE

ESSEX

CHELMSFORD

A10

A1(M)

M11

A10

A130

A1(M)

KING GEORGE
RESERVOIRS

HANNINGFIELD RES.

A12

M11

Chingford

LONDON

South Hanningfield

WALTHAMSTOW RESERVOIRS

A127

—QUEEN MOTHER RES.

SOUTHEND-ON-SEA

—*Colnbrook*

R. THAMES

THAMES ESTUARY

—BARN ELMS RES.

——SEE DETAIL MAP OF AREA

M20

—KEMPTON PARK WEST RES.

East Molesey

M2

M2

—LAMBETH RESERVOIRS

M20

A22

A25

MAIDSTONE

A21

DORKING

Redhill

A25

BOUGH BEECH RES.

A20

Edenbridge

TONBRIDGE

KENT

ROYAL TUNBRIDGE WELLS

SURREY

M23

EAST GRINSTEAD

WEIR WOOD RES.

A20

A21

HYTH

SUSSEX

A22

B2026

New Romney

A23

A21

DARWELL RES.

POWDERMILL RES.

A26

Battle

A259

BARCOMBE LAKE RES.

LEWES

HASTINGS

A27

BRIGHTON

A27

WORTHING

to Eastbourne

South East-Reservoirs

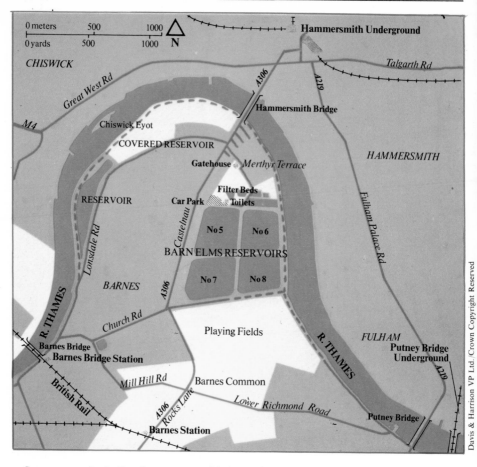

0 meters 500 1000   N

0 yards 500 1000

Hammersmith Underground

CHISWICK

Talgarth Rd

Great West Rd

A306

A219

M4

Chiswick Eyot

Hammersmith Bridge

COVERED RESERVOIR

Gatehouse   Merthyr Terrace

HAMMERSMITH

RESERVOIR

Car Park

Filter Beds

Toilets

Castelnau

Lonsdale Rd

No 5   No 6

BARN ELMS RESERVOIRS

Fulham Palace Rd

BARNES

A306

No 7   No 8

R. THAMES

Church Rd

Playing Fields

R. THAMES

FULHAM

Barnes Bridge

Barnes Bridge Station

Putney Bridge

Underground

A219

British Rail

Mill Hill Rd

Barnes Common

A306

Rocks Lane

Lower Richmond Road

Putney Bridge

Barnes Station

Some reservoirs in London are owned by the Thames Water Authority but controlled by the London AA. There are no day tickets but fishing is still available on an associate membership card which costs £5.50. Juniors under 14 years cannot enter or fish the reservoir—not even with an adult member. Associate members under 16 years may enter the reservoir (but not fish) if accompanied by an adult member.

Queen Mary and Staines North

Reservoirs in this group are the Queen Mary and the Staines North at Staines, two man-made reservoirs holding roach, bream and large pike; the King George Reservoirs, North and South, in Chingford, North-East London, both holding a variety of coarse fish; and Reservoir 4 in the Lambeth

(Above) The Barn Elms group of reservoirs. No 6 is stocked with coarse species, while 7 and 8 hold rainbow trout. (Right) Game anglers fishing Barn Elms.

Reservoir complex in East Molesey, Surrey. In the Lambeth Group, Reservoirs 2 and 3 are controlled by the Civil Service AS which also offers an associate member's card on application.

In Hertfordshire, fishing at the Tring Reservoirs—Startops End (26 acres), Wilstone (110 acres) and Marsworth (20 acres)—is available on a day ticket of 50p (except Sundays), and boat fishing (bookable in advance) costs £1. Evening tickets (after 5pm) are 30p, and for children under 14 years 25p.

The Anglian Water Authority issues rod licences for three reservoirs in Essex—two for game and one for coarse fishing.

Ardleigh Reservoir (146 acres), and Abberton Reservoir (1,210 acres), near Colchester, are available on a day ticket. The former is a landscaped water, noted for rainbows and brown trout to 9lb 11oz, with fishing from boats and bank and a catch limit of eight fish of 12in and over. Day tickets cost £2.80 (£2.20 after 5pm) or £3.60 at weekends and bank holidays – juniors £1.10, with boats an extra £4.50 per day (£2.80 per half-day). Tickets can be obtained from the Ardleigh Treatment Works in Colchester (Tel 230642) or at the reservoir fishing lodge. The reservoir is reached via the A137 Colchester to Manningtree road.

Abberton Reservoir

Abberton Reservoir is known for its quality coarse fishing and for the big bream which are often taken to stock other fisheries. Forty rods per day are allowed, and day tickets at 50p can be obtained at the reservoir, or in advance from the Essex

Water Company, Abberton Reservoir, Layer-de-la-Haye, Colchester.

Situated near Chelmsford, Hanningfield Reservoir (874 acres) is reached via the A130 to South Hanningfield. It is a landscaped reservoir offering roughly 560 acres of boat fishing and $2\frac{1}{2}$ miles of bank fishing. Fly fishing only is allowed, the reservoir being stocked annually with approximately 45,000 brown and rainbow trout. No day tickets are issued, but season permits at £120 plus VAT can be obtained from the Essex Water Company, Hanningfield Reservoir, South Hanningfield, Chelmsford (Tel 400381).

Reservoirs in Kent and Sussex require a Southern Water Authority rod licence. Darwell Reservoir near Battle and Powdermill Reservoir near Sedlescombe are available on a day ticket issued by the Hastings Fly Fishers' Club. The address is given at the end of the chapter.

Also in Sussex are Weir Wood and Barcombe Lake reservoirs. Weir Wood is situated near East Grinstead, 25 miles from London on the A22, and has nearly 250

acres, with brown and rainbow trout. An attractive reservoir with natural banks, it is regularly stocked, and offers bank and boat fishing with a catch limit of six fish. Tickets are issued by the Southern Water Authority, or may be reserved by telephoning Forest Row 2731.

Day tickets cost £2.70 (juniors and OAPs £1.30). Boat fishing costs £10 for a two-seater boat, £5.60 for a single boat – and for a half day, £7.40 for a two-seater boat, £4.30 for a single boat. Season tickets are £93, or £73 for a weekday season (juniors £60); a week season £17.

Barcombe Lake Reservoir

Barcombe Lake Reservoir (40 acres) near Lewes is a concrete reservoir for fly fishing only. It is controlled by the Ouse Angling Preservation Society which issues day tickets at £2 to its members only. The Society will consider applications for membership.

Near Edenbridge in Kent, Bough Beech Reservoir (275 acres) is an attractive landscaped reservoir offering fishing, by fly only, from bank and boat. No day tickets are issued, but the East Surrey Water Company, which controls it, issues season permits at £90 plus VAT, and Tuesday-to-Friday tickets at £65 plus VAT.

(Right) Hanningfield, near Chelmsford, has 560 acres of water for the boat angler and 2½ miles of bank in its 874 acres. There are no day tickets, but fishing is available on season permits costing £120 plus VAT. (Below) A cold and windy day on the famous Queen Mother Reservoir at Datchet. Its 475 acres can be covered by motorized or rowing boats. The reservoir is stocked annually with brown and rainbow trout.

Bill Howes

Richard Jemmett

INFORMATION

WATER AUTHORITIES
Anglian Water Authority, Diploma House, Grammar
School Walk, Huntingdon, PE18 6NZ. Tel 56181.
Southern Water Authority, Guildborne House, Chatsworth
Rd, Worthing. Tel 205252.
Thames Water Authority, 2nd Floor, Reading Bridge
House, Reading, Berks. Tel 593333.

LICENCES
Regional licence: adult £3.80, junior and OAPs £1.
Weekly tickets 75p all categories.
Divisional licence: £2, no concessions for OAPs and juniors.
The licences run from 1 January.

Thames Water Authority: course and game fishing £3,
OAPs 50p, 15 days 50p, no charge for juniors under 16.
Thames Water Authority: coarse and game fishing £2,
OAPs 50p, month 50p, day 25p. No charge for juniors
under 16.
Close seasons: see reservoirs individually for seasons.
Size limits: Anglian Water Authority: bream, carp, chub
and grayling 11.8in (30cm), tench 9.8in (25cm), perch 9in
(23cm), roach and rudd 7.8in (20cm), pike 23.6in (60cm),
trout 11.8in (30cm). Southern Water Authority: at most
reservoirs the size limit is 7in (17.8cm). Bag limits, vary,
however, and the angler should check this with the Water
Authority or the reservoir warden. Thames Water
Authority: pike 24in (61cm), trout 14in (35cm), bream,
carp and chub 12in (31cm), tench 10in (25cm), perch 9in
(23cm).

CONTROLLING BODIES
British Waterways Board, Melbury Hse, Melbury Terr,
London NW1. Tel (Fishing Dept.) Watford 2644.
East Surrey Water Co, London Rd, Redhill, Surrey. Tel
66333.
Essex Water Co, Abberton Reservoir, Layer-de-la-Haye,
Colchester, Essex. Tel 34356.

LOCAL CLUBS AND ASSOCIATIONS
Civil Service AS, N J Day, 74 Honor Oak Rd, SE23.

Hastings Fly Fishers' Club, D Clarke, 2 West Terr,
Eastbourne, E Sussex. Tel 25211.
London AA, H J Wilson, 183 Hoe St, Walthamstow,
London E17 3AP.
Ouse Angling Preservation Soc, Dr J L Cotton, Down
End, Kingston Rd, Lewes, E Sussex. Tel 4883.

TACKLE DEALERS
Brighton Fishing Tackle Shop, 72 Beaconsfield Rd,
Brighton, E Sussex.
Brighton Angler, 15 Church St, Brighton, E Sussex.
Reenes Fishing Tackle, 10 Buckhurst Place, Bexhill-on-Sea,
E Sussex. Tel 213565.
Brown's Tackle, 9 Holmesdale Rd, Bromley, Kent.
Dawson's Tackle, 1 Chatterton Rd, Bromley. Tel 460 7689.
Godfrey's Tackle, 52 Moulsham St, Chelmsford, Essex.
Ronnie Crow, Moulden Rd, Great Baddow, Chelmsford.
Home and Sport, 31a St Botolphs St, Colchester, Essex.
K D Radcliffe, High St, Colchester, Essex.
Kirkman Ltd, 40 The Broadway, Crawley, W Sussex.
Hastings Angling Centre, 33-35 The Bourne, Hastings.
T H Sowerbutts & Son, 151 Commercial Rd, London E1.
The Angling Kiosk, Hastings Pier, Hastings, E Sussex.
Rice Brothers, 1 High St, Lewes, E Sussex.
Don's of Edmonton, 239 Fore St, Edmonton, London
N18.
Johnson's, 1577 London Rd, Norbury, London SW16.
F Johnson, 167 Ferndale Rd, Clapham, London SW4.
Gerry's, 170 The Broadway, Wimbledon, London SW19.
Stabler's, 350 Garratt Lane, Earlsfield, London SW18.
Stanobs, 982 Harrow Rd, Kensal Rise, London NW10.
Specialist Tackle, 125 Dulwich Rd, Herne Hill, London
SE24.
Tooke's, 614 Fulham Rd, London SW6.
Benwood's, 60 Church St, Edgware Rd, London NW8.
Harding's, 239 High Rd, Willesden, London NW10.
Walthamstow Angling, 123 Fulbourne Rd, Walthamstow,
E17.
J Mitchell, 410 Kingsland Rd, Dalston, London E8.
Riley's, 322 High St North, Manor Park, London E12.

Essex and the Thames

See detailed area maps

improving, and restocking by the water authority has provided roach, perch, dace and plenty of pike.

The Blackwater is a small river with good dace fishing, and roach and chub. Most of it is controlled by the Kelvedon and District AA and is for members only. The same applies to the River Colne north of Colchester, which is controlled mainly by the Colchester APS.

The River Roding has very low levels in summer and floods quickly in winter. A large dredging scheme is planned for most of its length. It is a river for the lone angler who can cover a mile or more during the day, searching out the fish, and with just a few items of tackle in his shoulder bag or

Apart from the Thames on the southern edge of Essex, the county's rivers are small. Essex is also remarkably lacking in day-ticket fishing, Fishing is free on the tidal Thames, but on the other rivers there are probably only about 10 miles of day-ticket stretches, and to fish this county it pays to join a club. Apart from the Colchester AS, which takes members only from a 20-mile radius, and a few other clubs, membership is in the main available at tackle dealers.

The Chelmer

The River Chelmer has day-ticket fishing only below Colchester. Here the Marconi AS has about 4 miles from Great Baddow towards Little Baddow, and besides this stretch, the Chelmsford AA has nearly all the water from Chelmsford to Maldon—10 miles or so. Day tickets for both are available on the bank.

The most popular stretch here is probably the Hoe Mill stretch at Ulting, where access to the river is particularly good and the Chelmsford AA has a car park at the water.

Unfortunately, the Chelmer was badly polluted by cyanide for 10 years, which killed about 75 per cent of the fish. It is now

(Below) A quiet stretch of the Roding at Fyfield. Polluted downstream, it still gives good coarse sport in its upper reaches. (Right) The downstream entrance to the Teddington Lock, where, in recent years, the water has become considerably cleaner.

pockets. Good-sized dace and chub can often be seen, but catching them is a challenge. Perch are making a comeback, and big bream are had in the deeper parts.

Buckhurst

In Buckhurst, there is free fishing from Buckhurst Hill Bridge to Loughton Bridge, from Cascades Railway Bridge to Redbridge, and in a section at Woodford. Then, at Passingford Bridge, there are nearly two miles of day-ticket fishing with tickets available on the bank, and a further section at Stapleford Abbots, where tickets are obtainable from Arnold's Farm.

The lesser rivers, the Pant, Wid and Box will be enjoyed by the man who likes small stream trout fishing, but they are controlled by clubs for private fishing only. The Essex River Division of the Anglian Water Authority has some trout fishing on the Box, but it is often booked far in advance. The Pant is strictly private, controlled mainly by the Braintree and Bocking AS.

Perhaps the greatest asset in Essex is the pit fishing. The county is peppered with old gravel workings and chalk pits, and with numerous ponds in the area of Epping Forest which offer free fishing at present.

However, there is not room to cover all the Epping ponds in detail here. Among their number can be counted the Warren Pond and Connaught Waters in Chingford, The Hollow Ponds in Leytonstone, and the Eagle Ponds in Snaresbrook. Also with free fishing are the Wake Valley Ponds near Loughton, which produced a 26lb carp in 1977. They are situated alongside the A11 between the Robin Hood and the Wake Arms roundabouts.

Day ticket waters

Some of the better known waters available on day ticket are The Chase in Dagenham, Berwick Ponds in Rainham, the South Weald Lakes in Brentwood, Hainault Forest Lake in Redbridge (which has good access for disabled anglers), Corringham Ponds and Priory Park Lakes near Southend, Parrishes Lake in Langford, Bedfords Park Lake in Colliers Row, Romford, and The Warren in Stanford le Hope, which has good wild carp up to 12lb. Tickets are available on the site, and for all of them except Corringham Ponds, you require a licence from the Thames Water Authority. Corringham requires a licence from the AWA, Essex Rivers Division.

Bill Howes

Essex and the Thames

(Left) The tidal Thames at Orleans Gardens, Twickenham, a renowned hot-spot for the bream and roach hunter. (Below) Essex and the Thames, tidal up to Teddington Weir. The Roding, rising near Great Dunmow, joins the Thames at Barking Creek, while the Chelmer and Blackwater enter the sea near Maldon.

Stillwaters available to the public in north Essex include Gosfield Lake near Halstead, Thorpe Pits near Thorpe-le-Soken, Kelvedon, Mill Lake at Holbrook, and the well-known Layer Pits at Colchester. Then, by joining a local club to fish the rivers, you will also, in many cases have access to club lakes. Gosfield Lake has rods for hire, but check beforehand that there is no clash with a water-skiing event.

In recent years, the Thames from Teddington Lock to the estuary has seen a

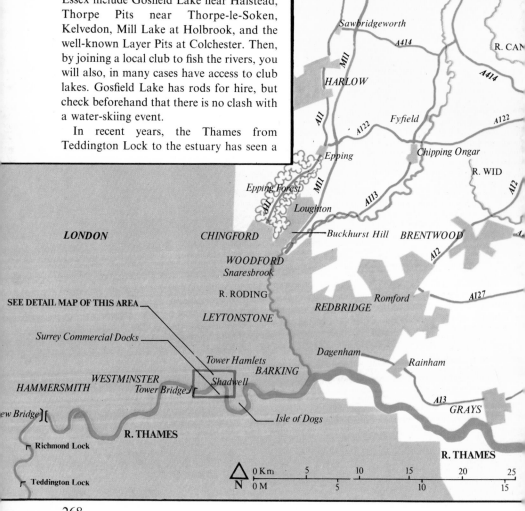

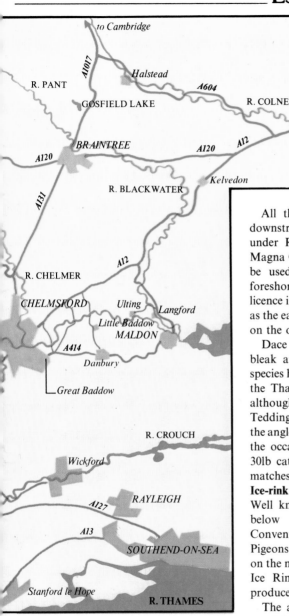

All the fishing from Teddington Lock downstream is classed as free, being granted under Royal Charters going back to the Magna Carta. Any lawful access points can be used and the angler can follow the foreshore once the tide is down. A TWA rod licence is still needed, however, to fish as far as the east of Southend and the isle of Grain on the opposite bank.

Dace and roach head the list of fish, with bleak and gudgeon following. Almost all species have been taken along this section of the Thames, including double figure carp, although these are a rarity. From Teddington to Richmond Half-Tide Lock, the angler can expect to find a few bream and the occasional barbel, and in recent times 30lb catches have been taken in five-hour matches at Richmond.

Ice-rink hot-spot

Well known hot-spots include the section below Teddington Lock opposite the Convent, the steps in front of the Three Pigeons Hotel at Richmond, and the section on the north bank in front of the Richmond Ice Rink. This stretch in particular will produce a few bream from time to time.

The area around Kew Bridge will yield roach and dace on long trotting methods, with the blockend feeder taking fish in winter. Generally, the angler has a good chance of taking fish wherever he can obtain access to the water, right down to Tower Bridge, where dace and bleak have been taken in the annual Thames Experiment held by the Thames Angling and Preservation

dramatic improvement in cleanness. More species of fish have returned to the river, and anglers can now make catches in areas where in the past they could not have stood the stench! The strong tidal flow has meant that fast-water fish like the dace have done very well.

Essex and the Thames

(Below) Teddington Weir, once famed for trout, but still offering coarse sport. Detail map shows London's Dockland, where several disused docks offer fishing for coarse species, and some trout.

Society. Below this point the angler can find small flounders, plaice, codling and eels.

London Docks

Many of London's docks hold very good quality fish, although the Port of London Authority does not allow fishing in any of its active docks. Some disused docks are controlled by clubs, however. In Tower Hamlets, fishing is currently available in Shadwell Basin and Western Dock (although this may soon close) through the Shadwell Basin Angling and Preservation Society, which welcomes new members, and will consider application for day tickets.

The Surrey Commercial Docks offer a variety of fishing at Canada and Albion Docks, and the large Greenland Dock. You can catch quality perch, roach and tench, double-figure carp, smelt, and some trout, which got into the Thames when floods carried them from Kempton Park West Reservoir where they had been introduced. There are also enormous eels. Access is easy, with an Underground station nearby, and ample car parking. The Southwark Fisheries and Preservation Society bailiffs the fishing and issues day tickets on the site.

The very deep water of the docks calls for sliding floats. The docks have produced most species of freshwater fish, and the angler who gets to know the waters will undoubtedly have good catches.

Further information about fishing the docks can be obtained from the clubs, or from one of the anglers instrumental in obtaining rights there, Dick Hodges, the Secretary of the Thames Angling and Preservation Society (TAPS).

If you fish tidal water you should be aware of the dangers. When wading, make sure you have a firm base on which to stand and be ready for the change of tide, which at times

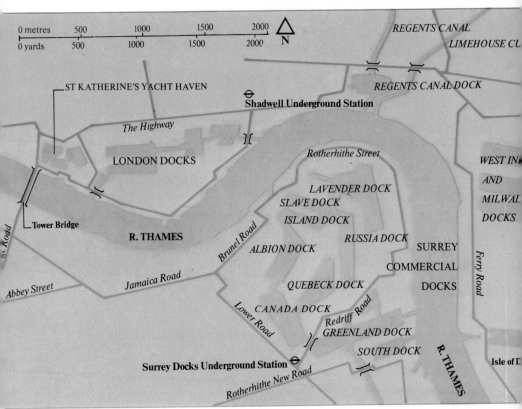

271

Essex and the Thames

can be very forceful. Watch out for the wash from passing boats. Then, if you follow the water down, don't get cut off by a fast-rising tide—a number of anglers have needed rescuing by helicopter. Remember—know your tides and venue, and tread carefully.

Tide tables can be obtained from some coastal tackle dealers, the angling press, or from the Port of London Authority (External Affairs Dept) for 74p including p & p (subject to increase). You can also buy a diary with tide tables for £1 (to non-members) from the National Federation of Sea Anglers.

Sea fish at Barking

Many species of sea fish are found from Barking Creek to the sea, and in recent years, good bags of codling and flounder have been taken. If you cannot obtain lug or ragworm, you can bait with common garden worms.

Access is again fairly easy, but watch out for mud banks.

A small boat is a benefit, but keep clear of the shipping lanes and make sure you have a qualified boat handler. Always carry two anchors and a spare set of oars in case the outboard motor packs up. Local knowledge pays in these areas, and a visit to the local tackle shop always helps.

Remember that there is a prize of £250, a salmon rod, and an annual silver trophy for the first rodcaught salmon from the Thames. Catches must be verified by a Port of London Authority Assistant River Keeper, however,—contactable through TAPS.

Alwyne Wheeler of the Natural History Museum in South Kensington has been carrying out research on the return of fish to the Thames and would like to hear from anglers who capture a strange fish.

INFORMATION

WATER AUTHORITIES
Anglian Water Authority, Diploma House, Grammar School Walk, Huntingdon PE18 6NZ. Tel 56181.
Essex River Division, Rivers House, 129 Springfield Rd, Chelmsford, Essex CM2 7NJ. Tel 647121.
Thames Water Authority, 2nd Floor, Reading Bridge House, Reading, Berks. Tel 593345.
Metropolitan Water Division, 173 Rosebery Ave, London EC1. Tel 837 3300.

LICENCES
Regional licence: adult £3.80, junior and OAPs £1. Weekly tickets 75p all categories.
Divisional licence: £2, no concessions for OAPs and juniors. Licences run from 1 January. No charge for children under 12. Thames Water Authority: whole area annual £3, OAPs 50p, 15 days 50p. No charge for juniors under 16.
Close seasons: Anglian Water Authority, coarse fish 15 March to 15 June inclusive; Thames Water Authority, coarse fish 15 March to 15 June inclusive, rainbow trout, no close season, brown trout 30 September to 1 March, sea trout 1 September to 31 March.
Size limits: Anglian Water Authority (Essex River Division): barbel 15.7in (40cm), bream carp, chub and grayling 11.8in (30cm), tench 9.8in (25cm), crucian carp, roach and rudd 7.8in (20cm), dace 7in (18cm), pike 23.7in (60cm), and trout 11.8in (30cm).

LOCAL CLUBS AND ASSOCIATIONS
Chelmsford AA, Mrs D Carter, 16 Pawle Close, Chelmsford, Essex.
Colchester APS, N F J Binks, 7 Churnwood Rd, Colchester, Essex.
Colchester PS, P Rogers, 3 Saxon Close, Colchester, Essex.
Essex Angling Consultative Assoc, B L G Wale, 4 Longmore Ave, Great Baddow, Chelmsford, Essex.
Kelvedon and District AA, J L Joyce, 32 Glebe Cres, Broomfield, Chelmsford, Essex.
Marconi AS, C J W Thompson, 109 Hillside Grove, Chelmsford, Essex.
National Federation of Sea Anglers, Bob Page, 26 Downsview Cres, Uckfield, Sussex TN22 1UB. Tel 3589.
Southwark Fisheries and PS, Peter King, 15 Coxson Place,

London SE1. Tel 403 0274.
Shadwell Basin APS, Hon Sec, Lansbury House, The Highway, London E1.
TAPS, Dick Hodges, The Pines, Tile Kiln Lane, Bexley, Kent. Tel 25575.

TACKLE DEALERS
Mike Norris Sports, Billericay, Essex.
E McDowell, 2 Rayne Rd, Braintree, Essex.
Morris, Kings Rd, Brentford, Essex.
Roblin, 114 High St, Brentford, Essex.
Godfrey's Tackle, 52 Moulsham St, Chelmsford, Essex. Tel 84562.
Ronnie Crowe, Mouldon Rd, Great Baddow, Chelmsford.
Home & Sport, 31a St Botolph's St, Colchester, Essex. Tel 5382.
K D Radcliffe, High St. Colchester, Essex.
L Bowler Fishing Tackle, Merry Fiddlers Roundabout, Dagenham, Essex. Tel 592 3273.
Rod & Line, 70 Loampit Vale, London SE13. Tel 852 1421
T H Sowerbutts & Son, 151 Commercial Rd, London E1. Tel 247 1724.
Don's of Edmonton, 239 Fore St, London N18. 807 5396.
East London Angling Centre, 205 Roman Rd, London E1. Tel 980 1488.
Walthamstow Angling, 123 Fulbourne Rd, London E17. Tel 527 1135.
J Mitchell, 410 Kingsland Rd, Dalston, E8. Tel 254 9333.
Robert's, 143 Leytonstone Rd, Stratford, E15. 555 9372.
Riley's, 322 High St North, Manor Park, E12. 472 4604.
Brown's, 682 Romfod Rd, Manor Park, E12. 478 0389.
Robertson's Fishing Tackle, 36 Prince Regent Lane, Plaistow, E13. Tel 476 3726.
Angler's Complete Tackle Ltd, 5 Tudor Parade, Well Hall Rd, SE9. Tel 859 2901.
Angler's Corner, 16a Swingate Lane, Plumstead, SE18. Tel 854 3221.
Ken's of Lewisham, 126 Loampit Vale, SE13. 692 2565.
Lee's Fishing Tackle, 397 Roman Rd, E3. Tel 980 1130.
Romford Angling Centre, 209 North St, Romford, Essex. Tel 63370.
The Yellow Shop, 30 Southchurch Rd, Southend-on-Sea, Essex. Tel 64038.
The Bait Box, 40 King St, Stanford le Hope. Tel 78821.

273

Kent and the Coast

Glasgow
Edinburgh
Belfast
Newcastle
Dublin
Hull
Manchester
Birmingham
Cardiff
London
Bristol

See detailed area maps

Although the whole of the River Medway was polluted several years ago, the fish have re-established themselves and the water is well-stocked with roach, chub, dace, bream, carp and bleak. Free fishing is found upstream of Allington Lock, through the centre of Maidstone, to Farleigh. The river at this point is approximately 100ft wide and 18ft deep in the middle, with little flow except when the lock gates are opened. Most fish are caught trotting with maggot and caster. Access is simple from the numerous roads that lead to the tow-path.

From Farleigh to Yalding the water is controlled by the Maidstone Victory Angling Club which issues day tickets at 50p (except Sundays) for a stretch on the north bank from Teston to Barming. Here one finds the fish already mentioned and a large head of gudgeon and ruffe. Access to Teston is from the A26 Maidstone to Tonbridge road. Then from Yalding to Ford Green Bridge the water is controlled by the Paddock Wood Angling Club and is for members only.

Tonbridge Angling Society controls the fishing area above Ford Green Bridge and all

the water through Tonbridge upstream to Ensfield Bridge. Much is reserved for their own members, but day tickets at 50p are issued for a stretch of nearly 3 miles from Eldridges Lock to Cannon Bridge on the west bank, and ½ mile on the east bank from Cannon Bridge to Works Lock. Access is from the A26 and several side roads. At this point the river has easy banks, with very little vegetation, slight flow, and an average depth of 8ft in the middle. All species already mentioned can be caught, and trotting is the best method. Other day-ticket water in the area is the recreation ground in the middle of Tonbridge and the shallows south of the town. Then the river up to Ensfield Bridge is for members only.

South of Tonbridge, the river shallows, the bank vegetation thickens and best fishing is for chub and dace. Ashurst Village on the B2210 is controlled by the Edenbridge Angling Club and is for members only. The Allington Lock to Yalding stretch is a productive one, but can have busy boat traffic on it during the summer months.

The River Rother

The River Rother acts as a drain for the water on Romney Marsh, taking it through Lock Gates and hence to the sea at Rye. There is little flow except after heavy rain when the lock gates are opened. Through its entire length it is approximately 50ft wide and 7ft deep and holds a very good head of chub, roach, bream, carp, and a few tench and pike. Shoals of mullet and sea trout are contacted on any bait; the rod-caught record thin-lipped mullet was taken from this water.

Much of the lower end of the river is controlled by the Rye and District Angling Club, its water stretching from Star Lock just outside Rye to Newbridge on the B2082, and then from Newbridge along the west bank for the first four fields upstream. Above this, the Rye and Clive Vale Angling Club controls the water as far as Blackwall Bridge,

274

Richard Jemmett

Wittisham Lane. Then there is free fishing on the west bank from Star Lock to Iden Lock and on the east bank from the first field above Newbridge. The Rother Fisheries control the next ½ mile on the east bank. Above this, the stretch to Blackwall Bridge belongs to the Rye and Clive Vale Angling Club and beyond this to the Clive Vale Angling Club.

Newenden on the A28 Hastings-Tenterden road is controlled both up and downstream by the Rother Fisheries, while upstream Sandhurst on the A268 Rye-Hawkhurst road is controlled by the Rye and District Angling Club. At Bodiam Bridge just off the A229 Hastings-Hawkhurst road, the Bodiam Angling Club has water up and downstream, and the Rother Fisheries control the water from Salehurst Village to Robertsbridge on the A21 Battle-Hurst Green road.

The only club on this water to issue day tickets is the Rye and District Angling Club who charge 50p per day or £1.50 per week for any of the waters they control. Tickets are obtainable from the cottage at Iden Lock or from the bailiff on the bank.

(Above) The River Medway at Aylesford. Nearby, there is free fishing upstream of Allington Lock and through Maidstone.

The River Stour
The Stour flows straight into the open sea at Pegwell Bay and is tidal as far as Fordwich. From Canterbury it flows through open marshlands, the banks lush with vegetation, but with very few trees and bushes. It is famous for its quality roach and large head of bream. Chub, barbel and grayling have recently been introduced, but most have gone upstream to the faster and shallower water. The water also contains large numbers of roach x bream hybrids. There is a run of sea trout which would be better if it were not for the pollution caused by the industries downstream of Sandwich. Mullet travel upstream well above Grove Ferry and there are occasional reports of salmon.

Fishing is free inside the town of Sandwich. Ledgering is the best method here as the tide ebbs and flows with a rise of about 12ft, and bread is the best bait because anything else will be attacked by small eels. The Sandwich and District Angling

275

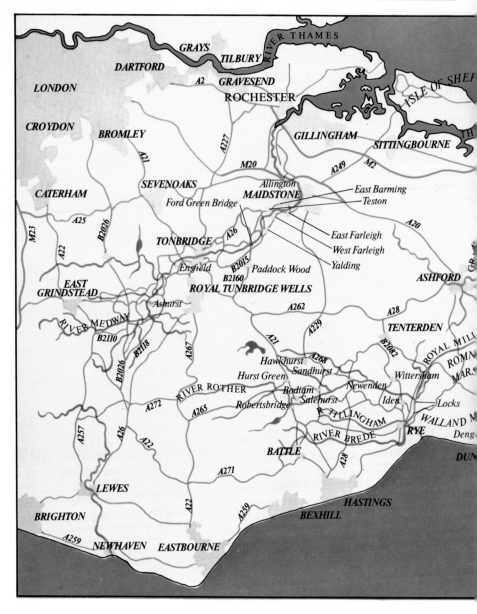

Association issues day tickets at 75p for water upstream of Sandwich to Richborough Castle. Betteshanger Colliery Welfare Angling Society has the fishing rights from here to Plucks Gutter on the B2048, and day tickets at 50p are obtainable on the bank. Access to this part of the river is difficult as it is mainly rough farm tracks.

From Plucks Gutter to above the Mill Pool in the village of Sturry the water is controlled by the Canterbury and District Angling Association. Access is by the A28 Canterbury to Margate road and then down to the river from Grove Ferry and Cut End.

SEE DETAIL MAP OF AREA

MARGATE SANDS

MARGATE

HERNE BAY

A299

Plucks Gutter

A256

WHITSTABLE

A28

A253

RIVER

RAMSGATE

Grove

STOUR

PEGWELL BAY

Sturry

Richborough

Fordwich

Castle

CANTERBURY

SANDWICH

West and East Stourmouth

A256

DEAL

B2068

LITTLE STOUR

A2

A258

A260

DOVER

FOLKESTONE

ANAL

HYTHE

A259

NEW ROMNEY

STRAITS OF DOVER

| 0 km | 5 | 10 | 15 |
| 0 M | 10 | 20 | 30 | N |

(Left) Map of the area showing the fine fishing in Kent's rivers Medway, Rother and Stour, and the principal sea fishing stations from Herne Bay to Dungeness.

From Grove Ferry to Fordwich is for club members only, and from Fordwich to Sturry is fly fishing for trout members only. At this point the river is about 40ft wide and 3ft deep, with a rather fast current over a gravel bottom and an abundance of streamer weed in the summer months. Fishing is excellent for chub, dace, roach, bream, with the occasional grayling and barbel. Upstream of Canterbury the river is either privately owned or syndicate-owned exclusively for fly fishing.

The Kent Coast

The Kent coast offers some of the finest sea angling in the British Isles. Many species are encountered with cod predominant, particularly during the autumn and winter. The great advantage of fishing this coastline is that excellent fishing can often be had only a mile or two beyond the embarkation point.

The North Sea, ebbing and flowing through the Straits of Dover, gives rather fierce tides, but the relatively shallow water compensates for this. Rarely is it over 14 fathoms deep, and is on average 7-10 fathoms. There is good fishing up the Thames as far as Gravesend and the Isle of Sheppey but this is estuary fishing. Open sea fishing begins at Whitstable.

Whitstable is reached directly from London via the M2 and A299. The sea around this town is shallow for the first five miles out, and on average less than three fathoms deep. Boat anglers can expect to find dabs, whiting and cod in winter, and flounders, eels and bass in summer. Shore anglers enjoy beachcasting for the same species from the gentle shelving beach east of the harbour.

Herne Bay lies 4 miles to the east of Whitstable still on the A299. Several available charter boats will take anglers to the famous Pansands for the excellent bass fishing in the summer, or to the broken

At Grove Ferry the river is approximately 60ft wide with the tides having an approximate nine-hour ebb and three-hour flood, the ebb tide giving the better sport. The rise and fall on a spring tide is about 3ft. Day tickets are available at 75p from the bailiff on the bank.

Kent and the Coast

Bill Howes

ground off Reculver for winter cod fishing.The town was famous for its tope fishing before the war, but this species seems to have declined since then. The average depth here is about 3 fathoms until one reaches the shipping lanes nearly 7 miles out. Most varieties of seafish are caught in the appropriate seasons with thornback ray and smooth-hounds especially prolific during the peeler crab season in April, May and June. For the shore angler, fishing from the Eastern Promenade can be very rewarding, particularly in the autumn and winter after dark. Unfortunately the $\frac{3}{4}$ mile long pier was closed as being unsafe in 1968.

Good fishing

The twin towers of the ruined church known as Reculver are 3 miles east of Herne Bay. The beach here shelves gently. and thornback and stingrays are caught during spring and summer and cod and whiting in autumn and winter. Shore angling is good for another 2 miles east of this landmark.

Several charter boats are on hire from the harbour at Margate. The water here is 5-6 fathoms deep and the bottom, except at Margate Sands, is of chalk and flints, unlike

(Above) Fishing for quality roach on the Kentish Stour near Canterbury, and (Right) detail map shows the sand banks and wrecks where fine cod and conger are fished.

the sand and gravel bottom at Herne Bay. Excellent bass and thornback ray are caught during spring and summer. The North Foreland Lighthouse is south-east of Margate, and the Elbow Buoy is approximately three miles out at sea from this point. Here one can expect the finest cod fishing to be had in the British Isles.

Many dinghy anglers favour the Longnose Buoy which is nearer, being a mile offshore, and where similar catches can be made. During the summer, bass fishing is good off the inshore chalk ledges and artificial lures are very successful. In the town there is a stone jetty and promenades from which most varieties can be taken depending on the season.

Broadstairs, on the A225 about 4 miles south-east of Margate, has a harbour where boats can be chartered to fish the same area as the Margate boats. Shore angling is possible from the harbour arm and from the

278

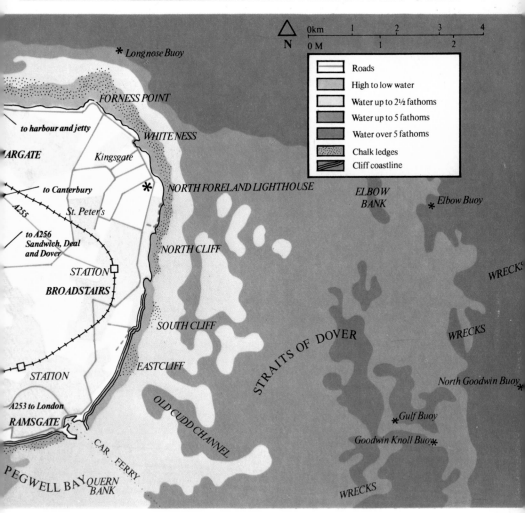

Roads
High to low water
Water up to 2½ fathoms
Water up to 5 fathoms
Water over 5 fathoms
Chalk ledges
Cliff coastline

chalk ledges north and south of the town.

Ramsgate, south of Broadstairs, is on a direct route from London via the M2, A222 and A253. With its very large harbour and excellent boat facilities, it accommodates both individual and charter anglers. The boats fish as far as the Elbow Buoy, particularly in winter for the cod, at North Goodwins for thornback ray during the summer months, and at Quern Bank for the good bass fishing. Pegwell Bay, which is a shallow water mark, is good for flatfish and whiting. Shore angling takes place from the harbour arms and a large variety of fish are

caught although the ground is rather snaggy from the western arm. Large shoals of mullet abound inside the harbour during the summer months and can be caught on freshwater tackle. Other shore stations include the Chines and Under-Cliffe.

Sand and shingle

Although Sandwich lies a mile inland from the coast there is a road through the sand dunes to the shore. The chalk of Ramsgate has now given way to sand and shingle and excellent sport can be had by the beach angler from this point. Big catches of cod are made during the autumn and winter,

279

Mike Prichard

and mainly flatfish, including soles, through the summer.

South of Ramsgate, and accessible via the M2, the A257 and the A258, Deal is the Mecca of sea angling. Large numbers of charter boats are launched from the steeply-shelving shingle beaches and just about every species of seafish has been caught at some time in these waters. A number of wrecks, particularly on the Goodwin Sands, provide good conger fishing, and in the summer tope and thornback are still caught in fair numbers over the sands. There is often good plaice fishing north of the town and south of Kingsdown, but the town's reputation is primarily for winter cod and whiting. Angling is allowed throughout the year from the modern pier and also night fishing at weekends.

Known as the gateway to England, Dover boasts a magnificent harbour with several angling charter boats. This is the narrowest part of the English Channel and the tides are therefore the strongest, but on neap tides the fishing is good, particularly for conger, cod and pollack found among the many wrecks. The water here is deeper than the rest of the

(Above) At Princes Parade Hythe, with good conditions, anglers can catch more cod than they can carry. Its steep shingle beach and deep waters make it ideal for beachcasting.

INFORMATION

WATER AUTHORITY
Southern Water Authority, Kent Area, 78 College Ave, Maidstone ME15 6SN. Tel 55211.
LICENCES
Salmon: season £13.50, 14 days £4.50, day ticket £2.25. **Migratory and non-migratory trout:** season £4, 14 days £1.15, junior season £1.15. **Freshwater fish and eels:** season £2.25, month £1.15, junior season 60p. Junior licences apply to anglers under 16.   Free licence available to OAPs for freshwater fish and eels. Possession of a licence permits an angler to use up to two rods at any one time. **Close seasons:** coarse fish March 15 to June 15 inclusive; salmon: October 3 to January 16 inclusive; migratory trout, brown and rainbow trout—seasons under review. Contact Fishery Officer for further information.
FISHERIES
Rother Fisheries, C. Foster, 4 The Green, Bodiam, Robertsbridge, E. Sussex.
LOCAL CLUBS AND ASSOCIATIONS
Betteshanger Colliery Welfare Angling Society, R Wilkinson, 4 South Goodwins Marina, Deal, Kent.
Broadstairs & St Peter's Angling Society, H Moor, 54 Stanley, Rd, Broadstairs.
Broadstairs Vikings, T Tatham, 8 St George's Ave, Broadstairs.
Canterbury & District Angling Association, N Stringer, Riversdale, Mill Rd, Sturry, Canterbury, CT2 0AF.
Cheriton & Morehall Angling Club, R Barnes, 301 Cheriton Rd, Folkestone.
Clive Vale Angling Society, R Glazier, 43 Rye Rd, Hastings, Sussex.

Kent and the Coast

Kent Coast and the bottom is very hard chalk with fissures. Varne Bank, lying nearly half-way across the Channel, can provide good cod fishing throughout the summer with brill and turbot often a bonus. For the shore angler, the large harbour gives plenty of opportunity, although the eastern arm was closed to anglers many years ago. The Southern Breakwater is only accessible by boat, but a ferry service will take anglers for a nominal charge. Admiralty Pier is free fishing and anglers will often be shoulder to shoulder feathering for the vast shoals of mackerel found here during the summer.

Folkestone

Folkestone Harbour, approximately 5 miles west of Dover, has charter boats which fish Varne Bank in summer and supply good inshore fishing in winter. Several of the inshore marks have 14 fathoms of water, and the sea bed is very rocky particularly off the Warren. Conger to 30lb are not uncommon near the British Rail Harbour Arm where anglers may fish for a small charge. West of Folkestone, the first mile of shingle beach runs off to snaggy ground, and further

westward gives way to sand. This beach extends for $4\frac{1}{2}$ miles, and the road at the top known as Princes Parade enables one virtually to fish from the car. Many species are caught here including bass, conger, plaice, cod and whiting. West of Hythe are the Military Ranges, where fishing is prohibited except on special occasions.

Dungeness is reached via the A259 to New Romney, then the B2071 out to the point. From Hythe to Dungeness the tide goes out so far that very little beachfishing is possible, but at Dungeness itself the steep shelving beach of shingle and the deep water make it ideal for the beach angler. Many years ago Leslie Moncrieff made this station famous for its cod fishing during the winter months. With the right conditions, anglers catch more cod than they can carry, and many of them are over 20lb. In summer Dungeness and Dengemarsh provide excellent sole fishing and quite often large shoals of mackerel come right to the water's edge. Nearly all species of seafish are contacted; at one time there was even a small thresher shark caught from the beach here.

Dover Sea Angling Association, J P Shearn, 9 Beechwood Close, Whitfield, near Dover, Kent.
Deal (1919) Angling Club, Beach St, Deal, Kent.
Deal and Walmer Angling Association, P Biddles, Pier Entrance, Deal.
Edenbridge Angling Society, J R Clyde, 3 Links Gardens, Norbury, London SW16.
Folkestone Sea Angling Association, T F O'Brien, 2 Weymouth Terrace, Cheriton, Folkestone, Kent.
Herne Bay Angling Association, T Randall, 6 Queen's Gardens, Herne Bay, Kent.
Heron Angling Society, J Baker, Spa Esplanade, Herne Bay.
Maidstone Victory Angling & Medway Preservation Society, B Hayman, 26 Sutton Rd, Maidstone, Kent.
Margate Old Centrals, B Bryant, 28 Alicia Ave, Garlinge, Margate, Kent.
Nayland Boat Sea Angling Society, A Burton, 9 Cornwallis Gdns, Broadstairs, Kent.
Paddock Wood Angling Society, G Haynes, 23 Bromley Gdns, Paddock Wood, Kent.
Ramsgate Beachcasters, R Teete, 31 Beachcroft Gdns, Ramsgate.
Royal Ramsgate Invicta Angling Association, Dennis Campbell, 91 High St, Ramsgate.
Rye and District Angling Club, J Fiddimore, Iden Boarding Kennels, Coldharbour Lane, Iden, Rye, Tel 384.
Sandwich and Distirict Angling Association, J Roe, 6 The Ridgeway, Cliftonville, Margate, Kent.
Sandgate Sea Angling Society, R Piddock, Corner Bungalow, West St, New Romney.
Seabrook Angling Club, R Munn, 8 Twiss Ave, Hythe, Kent.

Tonbridge & District Angling and Preservation Society, A S Wolfe, 59 Hunt Rd, Tonbridge, Kent.

TACKLE DEALERS
Medway Fishing Tackle, 103 Shipbourne Rd, Tonbridge.
Chas Williams, High St, Tonbridge.
Tackle Box, New Brunswick St, Maidstone.
Town's Tackle, Tonbridge Rd, Maidstone.
Sander's, Bank St, Maidstone.
Robin's, Landgate, Rye, Sussex.
H S Greenfield & Son, Bridge St, Canterbury.
Ron Edwards, 50–52 High St, Herne Bay.
F J Whitehead, 19 William St, Herne Bay.
Kingfisheries, 34 King St, Margate.
Geoff's, 36 Fort Hill, Margate.
Ramsgate Bait & Tackle Shop, 7 Westcliffe Arcade, Ramsgate.
Fisherman's Corner, 68 Harbour Parade, Ramsgate.
The Angler, 19 King St, Deal.
Channel Angling, Beach St, Deal.
Dinky Den, 67 Beach St, Deal.
Downs Tackle Centre, 29 The Strand, Walmer, Kent.
Foc'sle Fishing Tackle, 33 Beach St, Deal.
Heath, 19 King St, Deal.
Dover Tackle Shop, 120 Snagate St, Dover.
Bill's Bait & Tackle, 130 Snagate St, Dover.
Angler's Den, 162 Snargate St, Dover.
Gary's, 12 Fontine St, Folkestone.
J B Walker, 7 Marine Walk, Hythe.
Marnies Ltd, High St, New Romney, Tel 2172.
Grosvenor Marine and Sport, Coronation Buildings, Brougham Rd, East Worthing, Sussex, Tel 209146.

Sussex

See detailed area maps

Sussex, with its rolling Downs and wide, level Weald offers an abundance of sea fishing and plentiful coarse and game fishing in rivers, lakes and reservoirs.

The slow and stately south-flowing rivers give excellent summer fishing, and in the tidal reaches often offer mixed sea and freshwater fishing free of charge. The banks tend to be crowded in the holiday months, but in winter the angler can enjoy excellent sport with ample room.

The River Rother enters East Sussex before disappearing back into Kent and joining the Royal Military Canal. It was famed at one time for its big chub, which still present a challenge to the specimen-hunting angler. Fishing is available at Bodiam on a three-mile stretch both above and below the village, and day tickets are issued at the Bodiam Stores. In this region, a good mixed head of coarse fish includes roach, bream, chub, some tench, and the odd trout. Unfortunately, day tickets are not available when the water is block-booked for competitions at week-ends.

At Rye, the Rother cuts back into the county, and, together with the canal and two and a half miles of coarse fishing from Rye to Wittenham, is available on day ticket obtainable in advance from tackle shops in Rye, or at the Bedford Arms Inn. Below the town there is mullet and bass fishing in the estuary, with a run of sea trout that is considered by local anglers to be on the increase. The Rye and District Angling Society also issues day tickets for short stretches of the rivers Brede and Tillingham which run parallel with the major river and join it at Rye.

Pevensey Levels

To the west, lie the Pevensey Levels—marshland drained by innumerable wide ditches, or sluices, many of which hold fish. The large waters are leased by private angling clubs, but an enterprising angler could obtain permission to fish from local landowners. Fish in the Levels include eels, roach, chub, bream, perch and pike.

The Cuckmere River rises near Heathfield and joins the Channel at Exceat near Beachy Head. Most of the water is private and preserved for trout fishing in its upper

Arlington Reservoir, near Eastbourne, was formed when the Cuckmere was dammed.

Ken Whitehead

283

reaches, but one or two stretches are available. A most pleasant one is situated at Michelham Priory where the river flows round the buildings and forms part of the moat. Fishing is allowed on day ticket from the opening day of the season to the end of September only, and there is good general coarse fishing, especially for bream.

Alfriston

Above Alfriston, three and a half miles of coarse fishing are available on day ticket from the Compleat Angler Fishing Club, the tickets being sold from the Compleat Angler Tackle Shop or Eastbourne Tackle Shop. Below Alfriston Lock to the sea, there is excellent free estuary fishing for large mullet with the occasional bass and flounder.

The Sussex Ouse, rising at Horsham and flowing through Sheffield Park and Lewes to join the sea at Newhaven, is tidal to a point

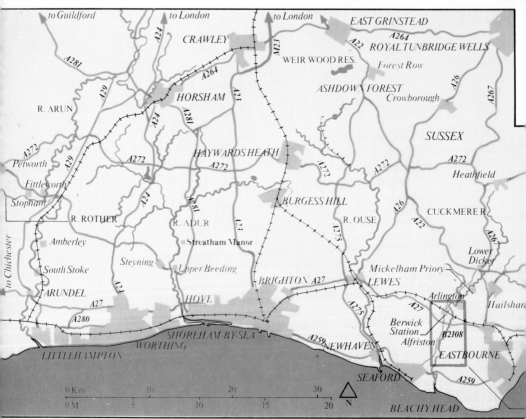

Spectrum Colour Library

(Above) Michelham Priory, near Eastbourne, where the Cuckmere River forms part of the moat. Day tickets are available.
(Below) Area map of Sussex, a county full of lakes and rivers and also possessing fine sea fishing marks.

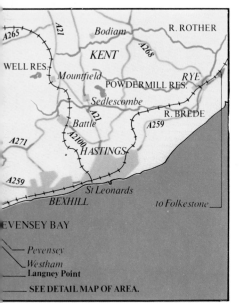

well above Lewes. It contains coarse fish, but is best known for its run of sea trout, some fish running into double figures. The run begins in May and is at its best during the summer months. The upper reaches are strictly private, but you can occasionally obtain permission to fish in the lower reaches from riparian owners.

Horsham to Shoreham

Another river rising near Horsham is the Adur, which runs coastwards to join the Channel at Shoreham. Although it is considered to be a coarse fishery offering roach, perch, chub, bream and a few dace, there is a run of sea trout that improves every year. The lower estuary reach is a favourite summer bass and mullet fishery that has its red-letter days.

Three-quarters of a mile of this river at Dial Post, upstream of the weir, is available on day ticket. These are available in advance at the tackle shop at Marine Place, Worthing; Lagoon Tackle at the Kingsway, Hove; or the Sports Shop in Worthing. There is also a three-mile day-ticket stretch at Steyning, from Beeding Bridge to Stretham Bridge on both banks, with tickets available at tackle shops in Steyning.

Before the last war, the River Arun and its big catches of bream from the Stopham area made headline news in the angling press. The river, flowing through the north of Sussex and joining the Channel at Littlehampton, is mostly private, with a few stretches available on day tickets, offering good coarse fishing with some bream and the occasional pike.

At Amberley, two miles of fishing on both banks are available by day tickets issued from the cafe at Amberley Bridge, while the tackle shop in Arundel sells day tickets for both banks of the river between South Stoke and Arundel Bridge—a stretch where the occasional sea trout is taken by spinning. Then from Arundel Bridge to Littlehampton there are five miles of free fishing on the right bank, with fair sport, especially for bass and mullet in the lower reaches.

The Western Rother

The Western Rother, a tributary of the Arun joining it at Stopham, offers fishing for barbel, which were placed there from the River Severn several years ago and have thrived. Sea trout and brown trout are present, the latter through the stocking and restocking efforts of various local clubs. Fittleworth General Stores issue day tickets (Monday to Friday only) for a two-mile stretch between Stopham and Fittleworth Bridge. Four miles of fishing are then available from Coulteshaw Mill, where barbel were introduced, to Fittleworth, with tickets issued at the Red Lion Inn at Petworth.

Several lakes can be enjoyed in Sussex, the largest complex of which is the Southern Leisure Centre of Chichester. Here, Peckham's Copse Trout Fishery has two trout lakes of 20 acres each, and there are five lakes for coarse fishing, containing bream, carp, perch, pike, roach, rudd and tench. Trout tickets cost £8 per day from April to May and £7.50 thereafter, with boats £2.50 per day. Day tickets for coarse fishing cost £1 (juniors 50p) and season tickets £6.60 (juniors and OAPs £3.30). The lakes are situated at North Munham, south of the A27 Chichester bypass. There is also a bar, café and heated outdoor swimming pool.

Near Petworth, Burton Mill Pond has fishing controlled by the West Sussex County Council and is available on day tickets obtainable at the site. Also in the Chichester area, the Chichester Canal can be fished on a 30p day ticket obtainable from the Chichester Canal Angling Association or from Dunnaways Stores in Hunston Village south of Chichester on the B2145.

Reservoir anglers are well catered for. The famous Weir Wood Reservoir, 25 miles from London along the A22 road, has nearly 250 acres containing brown and rainbow trout, and is set in the ancient Ashdown Forest. Since its first stocking in 1955, the reservoir has been carefully controlled, and under Ken Sinfoil, the head bailiff until January 1978, has gone from strength to strength. Boats and tickets may be reserved by telephoning Forest Row 2731.

Arlington Reservoir, near Eastbourne, was formed five years ago by damming the Cuckmere River to form a 150-acre basin.

Framed along its south bank by the Downs, it offers trout fishing on day tickets, with boat hire optional. The water is well stocked and this very comfortable fishery is run by bailiff Bryn Evans and his wife Kate.

Fishing is permitted from 7 am to dusk, and anglers should remember that there is a size 10 hook limit on the water. Reservations must be made by telephoning Alfriston 870815. The water can be reached by train from Victoria, by booking to Berwick Station which is ten minutes from the reservoir bank, or via the A22 Eastbourne road, turning onto the B2108 Seaford road at Lower Dicker.

Two reservoirs on the eastern side of the county contain trout and issue day tickets.

(Right) Detail map showing the Cuckmere near Alfriston and Arlington Reservoir. (Below) As it nears the sea, the Cuckmere, now tidal, meanders gracefully through a peaceful Sussex countryside.

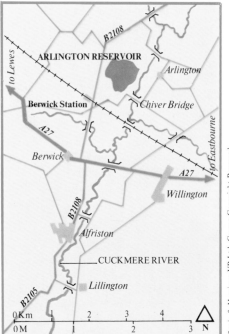

They are especially useful for the holiday angler staying in the Hastings area. Darwell Reservoir (155 acres) at Mountfield, and Powdermill Reservoir (54 acres) at Sedlescombe lie off the A21 just a few minutes outside Hastings. They are leased by the Hastings Flyfishers' Club, which re-stocks the water regularly and allows fishing from boats and banks. Reservations should be made by telephoning Robertsbridge 880407 for Darwell, and Sedlescombe 248 between 9am and 10am daily for the Powdermill Reservoir.

Hastings reservoirs

Hastings also has three reservoirs in the town controlled by the Hastings, Bexhill and District Freshwater Angling Association. Wishingtree Reservoir is a tench and carp fishery with a ban on keepnets and only ten day tickets issued per day, while Buckshole and Hamers Pond are general coarse fisheries. A day ticket costing 50p (juniors 10p, OAPs and the registered disabled free) covers both Buckshole and Hamers Pond

and is available on the site. For Wishingtree Reservoir, tickets at 50p (juniors and OAPs 25p) must be purchased in advance by sending s.a.e. to T Barton, 51 St Helen's Park Rd, Hastings.

There are just three areas of free fishing in Sussex; a part of the River Arun at Arundel on the right bank to the Ford Railway Bridge, with tickets obtainable from the South West Water Authority, and Piltdown Pond near Uckfield. The third, and very popular place, is the large Heath Pond on the south-eastern edge of Petersfield—a good fishery which offers roach and perch with some double-figure carp.

Sussex sea marks

For the sea angler, there are a succession of marks and shore stations along the coastline that can, even at this present time of lean sea sport, give a good day's fishing. At Hastings, anglers fishing off the beach between the Harbour Arm and East Groyne catch species that include bass, cod, conger and dogfish in season.

(Left) Anglers fishing the Arun, with Arundel Castle in the background.
(Below) Wintry fishing from Worthing Pier as the tide rips through.

G L Carlisle

Eastbourne offers varied sport, ranging from fishing for flatfish in the Pevensey Bay area, to bass and cod fishing from the beach at Langney Point. Catches off the pier include red and black bream and mullet, while further along the coast at Beachy Head, the shore angler may meet with conger and bass, depending on the state of the tide. Offshore marks—especially around the Royal Sovereign Light—provide angler fish, bass (especially towards Beachy Head) cod, conger, dogfish, tope, sole and the occasional turbot.

Newhaven is a boating centre although there is some fishing available in the harbour. Most boats are equipped for reaching deep sea marks, and are fitted with echosounders, two-way radio, and all possible comforts. They get to grips with the offshore wrecks some 15-20 miles out, and are noted for their catches of big Channel cod.

Fishing from Brighton's Banjo, Medina and Russell Street beaches, and from the pier and Worthing pier, offer sport with bass, conger, cod mullet, plaice and whiting, with similar species coming to the boat on offshore marks. Littlehampton is naturally renowned for its catches of black bream, which are taken several miles out in boats that also find bull huss, bass, conger, dogfish, gurnard and ling.

INFORMATION
WATER AUTHORITY
Southern Water Authority, Guildbourne House, Chatsworth Rd, Worthing, Sussex. Tel 205252.
LICENCES
Salmon: season £13.50, 14 days £4.50, day ticket £2.25.
Migratory and non-migratory trout: season £4, 14 days £1.15, junior season £1.15. **Freshwater fish and eels:** season £2.25, month £1.15, junior season 60p. Junior licences apply to anglers under 16.

Close seasons: coarse fish 15 March to 15 June inclusive; salmon 3 October to 16 January inclusive; migratory trout, brown and rainbow trout—seasons under review.
Size limits: coarse none; migratory trout 15in (38cm); non-migratory trout 10in (25cm).
FISHERIES
Southern Leisure Centre, M Gates, Manager, Vinnetrow Rd, Chichester. Tel 87715.
LOCAL CLUBS AND ASSOCIATIONS
Chichester and District Angling Soc, Mrs M Stimson, 17 Willowbed Drive, Chichester, W Sussex.
Chichester Canal Angling Assoc, D S Richardson, 117 Rose Green Rd, Bognor Regis, W Sussex.
Clive Vale Angling Club, Barry Sergeant, 11 Linley Close, Hastings, E Sussex. Tel 435804.
Compleat Angler Fishing Club, V Honeyball, The Cottage, Parkland School, Brassey Ave, Eastbourne, E Sussex.
Crawley Angling Club, D J Coles, 42 Darby Dale, Southgate West, Crawley, W Sussex.
Hailsham Angling Assoc, A W Bates, Analan, Sandy Cross, Heathfield, E Sussex.
Hampshire and Sussex Anglers Alliance, I L Savage, 13 Grosvenor Gdns, Aldwick, Bognor Regis, W Sussex.
Hastings, Bexhill and District Freshwater Angling Assoc, J Gutsell, 14 Jameson Cres, St Leonards-on-Sea, E Sussex.
Hastings Flyfishers' Club, D Clarke, 2 West Terr, Eastbourne, E Sussex. Tel 25211.
Haywards Heath and District Angling Soc, S F Whetstone, 2 West View Cottages, Lindfield, Haywards Heath.
Petersfield and District Angling Club, G A McKee, 25 North Lane, Buriton, Petersfield, W Sussex.
Petworth Angling Club, D A Pugh, 3 Cherry Tree Walk, Petworth, E Sussex.
Rye and District Angling Soc, J Fiddimore, Keeper's Cottage, Coldharbour Lane, Rye, E Sussex.
Steyning and District Angling Club, Brian Miller, School Rd, Upper Beeding, W Sussex.
Worthing and District Piscatorial Soc, Mr Hay, 85 Overhill, Southwick, W Sussex.
TACKLE DEALERS
G & A Shepherd, 10 High St, Arundel, W Sussex.
Brighton Fishing Tackle Shop, 72 Beaconsfield Rd, Brighton, E Sussex.
Brighton Angler, 15 Church St, Brighton, E Sussex.
Burgess Hill Angling Centre, 143 Church Rd, Burgess Hill.
Reenes Fishing Tackle, 10 Buckhurst Place, Bexhill-on-Sea, E Sussex. Tel 213565.
Kirkman Ltd, 40 The Broadway, Crawley, W Sussex.
Compleat Angler, 22 Pevensey Rd, Eastbourne, E Sussex. Tel 24740.
Eastbourne Tackle Shop, 183b Langney Rd, Eastbourne.
Hastings Angling Centre, 33-35, The Bourne, Hastings.
The Angling Kiosk, Hastings Pier, Hastings, E Sussex.
Angling Specialists, (Horsham), 27 Queen St, Horsham, W Sussex.
Clarkes Sports, 11 East St, Horsham, W Sussex.
Lagoon Bait and Tackle Shop, 327 Kingsway, Hove.
Rice Brothers, 1 High St, Lewes, E Sussex.
J D Moore, 45 Beaconsfield Rd, Littlehampton, W Sussex.
Harbour Tackle Shop, 107 Fort Rd, Newhaven, E Sussex.
C A Robins, 22 Lordgate, Rye, E Sussex.
Sports Shop, 191 Tarring Rd, Worthing, W Sussex.
Ken Dunman Ltd, 2 Marine Place, Worthing, W Sussex.

Bill Howes

Bill Howes

Somerset and the Avon

See detailed area maps

The rich farming counties of Avon and Somerset encompass many fishing waters to match. Some, like the Bristol Avon, are long recognized by the travelling match anglers of the Midlands, as well as by the home-bred matchmen of Bristol and the South-West.

The middle and lower reaches of the Avon have encountered spasmodic pollution problems, but the 1972 National Championship fostered a wider interest and showed the river's potential to a far larger audience. Since then, although it has been through another 'low' period, it once more yields first-class sport. The initial contest breakthrough happened in fact just before the 1972 National, when Chris Summers of Droitwich, Worcestershire, tapped a huge shoal of bream cruising in the Sutton area and made the scales groan with a weight of nearly 56lb. This pioneer catch was then beaten by a remarkable 78lb 9oz bream catch made at Ladydown.

Chew and Blagdon

The Bristol Avon attracts most of the angling headlines, but is not the only quality water. The world-renowned Chew and Blagdon trout waters are in this area, and other first-rate stillwater coarse fishing is found south beyond the Mendips. There are also the man-made land reclamation waterways, such as the King's Sedgemoor Drain. Nearby is the broad River Huntspill, and through the flat, rich alluvial plain between the Mendips and Quantocks run rivers such as the Parrett and its tributaries the roach-famous Tone, the Yeo, the Brue and the Axe. A short distance north into Gloucestershire is the large ship-carrying Sharpness Canal which follows the line of the A38. They all provide good fishing for thousands of local and long-distance anglers each week, and constitute an added bonus each year for anglers holidaying at nearby Weston-super-Mare, Burnham and Minehead.

Wiltshire Avon

The Bristol, or Wiltshire Avon rises high on the Cotswolds above Tetbury and soon becomes the home for some excellent trout fishing. In these sparkling, clear waters it also holds superb-quality green-backed roach. In 1969 a batch was netted there at random to help out the Severn which had a period of disappointing sport. Close on a thousand were taken in one netting—most of them topping the 1lb mark, dozens over 2lb and the best near 3lb in weight.

The Avon near Conham, on the outskirts of Bristol. Still a medium-sized river.

Richard Jemmett

291

The river in these areas, where it loops through lush pastures, is preserved. Indeed, there is little day-ticket fishing anywhere along the Avon. Fortunately, from Malmesbury downstream, much is controlled by local associations which either have open membership or issue annual honorary permits. These can be obtained in advance from secretaries or local tackle dealers.

Bristol and District AA waters

Near Malmesbury, the Bristol and District Amalgamated Anglers control a one-mile length with good roach, dace and chub fishing. They also control a stretch downstream near Christian Malford. At Sutton Benger the Isis Angling Club has water, an open membership, and other good fishing grounds on the upper Thames not too far away to the north-east.

This is an area which has yielded match catches to 50lb, bream to 4–5lb and some very good pike. The largest Avon pike the author recorded was caught by Ken Lansbury in 1959 near Newbridge below Bath and weighed 33lb 4oz.

Notable among other Avon fish are the 15¾lb carp caught at Staverton in 1967 by J Davies, a chub of 5lb 7oz caught in 1963, and a bream of 8½lb caught in 1965. An experimental stocking with barbel was carried out was carried out some years ago by the River Authority of the time. Although not flourishing as they have along the Severn, the largest authenticated barbel is 9lb 11oz.

Chippenham and Laycock

Below the weir near Chippenham is a small stretch of free fishing. The river then begins to slow and steady itself. The Chippenham Angling Club controls a fair stretch with day tickets available at the local tackle dealer, while just below Lacock, the Bristol and District Amalgamated Anglers have extensive holdings, as they have at Pewsham. Melksham and District Amalgamated Anglers (members of the Bristol DAA) and the Portcullis Angling Club also have waters in the area. At Staverton the Ushers Angling Club controls a very good section below the

milk factory where the water is steady, averaging 6ft in depth. One peg, which is just into the water and clearly defined by a bankside tree, has very good margin fishing for roach and bream under the rod tip; while just downstream on the wide left-hand bend, Lloyd Davies won his 1972 National section by float fishing the far bank.

Bradford on Avon Angling Association issues day tickets for their excellent Tythe Barn Fishery, while downstream the Bristol and District Amalgamated Anglers control water at Freshford and sections at Limpley Stoke and Farleigh. Here the Bath Anglers' Association have extensive holdings including the weir where the big barbel were caught. They also have very good waters downstream at Claverton and at Manor Park at Bathampton. At the latter the Bristol and District Amalgamated Anglers have more fishing at Meadow Farm.

The Bath area

There is some free fishing at Bath, but most bank space is naturally controlled by the Bath Anglers' Association which also has

The large area of Somerset and Avon offers the angler rewarding and varied sport.

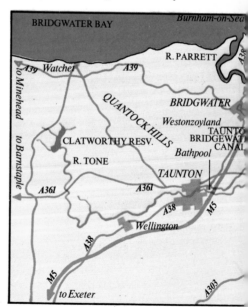

292

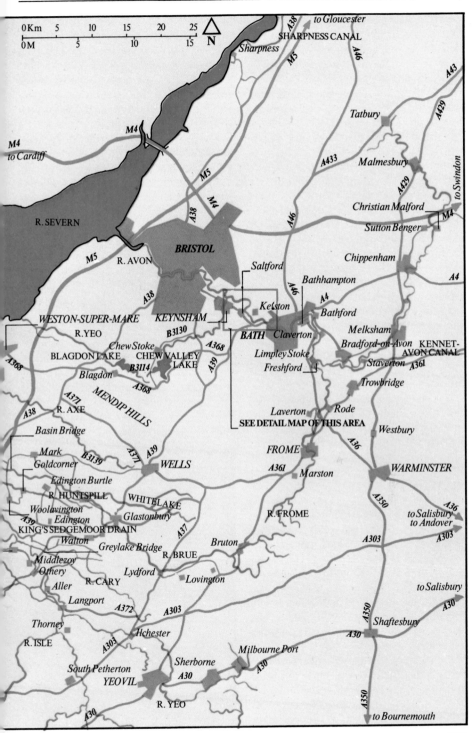

SHARPNESS CANAL
to Gloucester
Sharpness
A38
A46
M5
A43
Tatbury
A433
Malmesbury
A429
M4
M4
to Cardiff
M5
A38
M4
Christian Malford
A429
to Swindon
M4
Sutton Benger
R. SEVERN
BRISTOL
Chippenham
M5
R. AVON
Saltford
A46
Bathhampton
A4
Kelston
A4
Bathford
WESTON-SUPER-MARE
KEYNSHAM
BATH
Claverton
Melksham
R.YEO
B3130
Bradford-on-Avon
KENNET-
Chew Stoke
A368
Limpley Stoke
AVON CANAL
BLAGDON LAKE
CHEW VALLEY
Freshford
Staverton
A361
B3114
LAKE
A39
Blagdon
A368
Trowbridge
MENDIP HILLS
A371
Laverton
Rode
R. AXE
A38
SEE DETAIL MAP OF THIS AREA
Westbury
Basin Bridge
FROME
A36
Mark
B3139
A39
WELLS
A361
WARMINSTER
Goldcorner
Marston
Edington Burtle
R.HUNTSPILL
A350
to Salisbury
Woolavington
WHITELAKE
R. FROME
A36
to Andover
Edington
Glastonbury
A303
A303
KING'S SEDGEMOOR DRAIN
A37
Walton
Bruton
A303
Greylake Bridge
R. BRUE
Middlezoy
Lydford
Lovington
to Salisbury
Othery
R. CARY
Aller
A350
Langport
A372
Shaftesbury
A30
Thorney
A303
Ilchester
A30
R. ISLE
A303
Milbourne Port
South Petherton
Sherborne
A30
YEOVIL
A30
A350
R. YEO
A30
to Bournemouth

waters at Bathford and Batheaston. At the latter, Bristol and District Amalgamated Anglers have a lengthy stretch with access at the horse showground. Bathampton Angling Association control good roach and bream waters here, and have water at Kelston where catches to 50lb have been recorded.

Start of the match scene

At this point the match country begins. There is a good stretch from Kelston to Saltford controlled by the Bristol and West of England Federation, with good access at Sheppards boathouse. They also control long sections at Swinford below and above Willisbridge. These are stretches of good, easy float water, with roach making up most of the catches, and bream from the 'skimmer' size to plump fish of 2lb.

The best-known Avon fishing venues are perhaps at Keynsham. The sport here is very even and many contests take place. Most of the water is controlled by the Bristol and West Federation, or by the Keynsham Angling Association or the Ridgway and District Anglers' Association. Day tickets are available from local tackle shops.

The Avon is best known as a float water. Stick-float fishing in its various forms is the most popular, though the waggler float also finds its place. Like the Warwickshire Avon, however, small swimfeeder fishing is now showing excellent results.

The Frome

Of the Avon tributaries the Frome is the major. A shallowish, winding stream, it has good small trout fishing as well as coarse fishing. Day ticket fishing is available for about seven miles from Lower Marston to Shawford and at Rode and Stapleton the Bristol and District Amalgamated Anglers control waters from the weir downstream, and downstream of Blackberry Hill bridge. This water produces chub to 4lb and most other allied species.

On the River Marden the Calne Angling Association has large sections of mixed fishing with the accent on trout.

The Somerset Plain lies to the south, and sports a network of natural and man-made waterways. Most important of the former is the River Parrett system, which, although troubled by pollution from its long tidal reach, somehow manages to recover quickly. It is a good early trout water in the upper reaches, and the March Brown and similar patterns, fished wet, usually meet with success. Season permits for the trout fishing can be obtained from the Half Moon Hotel in South Petherton, as they can be for about eight miles of good coarse fishing.

At Langport, day tickets can be obtained from the local tackle dealer for a five-six mile stretch controlled by the Wessex Federation of Anglers which also has water at Thorney Mill. The Parrett bream and pike are good. The best bream caught by the author neared $6\frac{1}{2}$lb and a pike taken on a large copper spoon, fished deep and slow, weighed 18lb though most are about 8lb.

Fast-flowing Tone

A major Parrett tributary is the fast-flowing River Tone which rises high in the Quantock Hills, soon to feed Clatworthy Reservoir before flowing to Taunton. The trout fishing is excellent, though mostly preserved in the upper sections. Then from Wellington it deepens, slows and becomes the home of some super-quality roach.

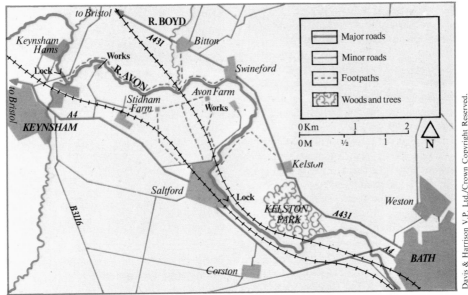

The Tone made the angling news with some prodigious catches of roach in the 1969–70 season. Since then sport has dropped back but many big fish are still to be caught. Permits are available in Taunton tackle shops for stretches at Bathpool and Wellington and downstream to the confluence. The same tackle dealers also sell day

Detail map shows the Bath-Keynsham area of the prolific Bristol Avon.
(Below left) Bridgwater-Taunton Canal.

tickets for the Taunton-Bridgwater Canal which has large tench and carp. They mostly come to worm bait, but the canal water is very clear and the fish are hard to tempt.

The River Yeo meanders for 25 miles across Somerset from Milborne Port to join the Parrett near Langport. Around Sherborne there is excellent trout fishing. Coarse species start to show in the Yeovil area where day tickets can be obtained to fish the Westland Sports Angling Club water, and at Ilchester downstream where Ilchester Angling Club controls several miles of water.

The Brue's fine coarse fishing

From a scar in the Mendip Hills the top-quality River Brue flows to the sea at Burnham. Along the way it develops into a fine coarse fishery. Membership to the Bristol and District Amalgamated Anglers is more than useful to fish at West Lydford, Lovington, Meare, Edington (where the roach are good) and Bason Bridge. At Bason Bridge they always seem fatter, and are joined by black-backed, slab-sided bream

Mike Millman

Somerset and the Avon

which fight as well as Shannon bream.

The man-made waters of Somerset are famed in fishing circles, having yielded massive catches of bream and roach, pike over 20lb, and even tench and carp. In some seasons very heavy weed growth makes the choice of swim a difficult one, but somehow the bream are always ready to feed.

The Huntspill

The Bridgwater Angling Association holds fishing rights to most of these waters, the widest of which is the River Huntspill famed for its recent match catches. The current popular section is the left bank below Woolavington Bridge and on to Withy Grove—the section where Coventry angler Joe Cramp set a new match catch record of 74lb 6oz in 1973. Anglers also enjoy fair success upstream on the same bank near the first fence and at the top end near Gold Corner when the breeze is from the southwest. The River Cripps joins the Huntspill here to link it with the River Brue. Many good bream catches are made along this short waterway, although weed is a problem during the summer months.

Another connecting waterway is the Glastonbury Canal (South Drain). Like the River Cripps, it holds a big head of bream,

roach and perch, as well as providing the chance of contacting a good tench or the odd large carp. The North Drain follows the course of the Brue, and a good access point is at the village of Mark. Bream is the most likely species to be found, and bread and worm cocktail baits are very successful if a feeding shoal is located.

King's Sedgemoor Drain

In the past, the King's Sedgemoor Drain has been a favourite water. Its eight miles of water to Greylake Bridge are good on their

---

INFORMATION
WATER AUTHORITY
Wessex Water Authority, Techno House, Redcliffe Way, Bristol BS1 6NY. Tel 25491 or 290611.
Avon and Dorset Division, 2 Nuffield Rd, Poole, Dorset BH17 7RL. Tel. 5021.
Bristol Avon Division, PO Box 95, Broad Quay, Bath. Tel 316906.
Somerset Division, PO Box 9, King Square, Bridgwater, Somerset. Tel 57333.
LICENCES
Salmon: season £15.50, week £7.75, day £2.60. **Trout:** season £4.00, month £2.00, day £1.00. **Freshwater fish:** season £2.60, month £1.30, day 50p. Juniors, OAPs and the registered disabled at half price unless otherwise indicated.
Close season: salmon, Rivers Avon and Stour 30 Sept to 1 Feb; all other parts of the Avon and Dorset Division 30 Sept to 1 March. Non-migratory trout (including rainbow trout), River Avon and its tributaries above the Mill Dam at Bicton Mill (except the part of the River Nadder which lies above the road bridge at Barford St Martin), 15 Oct to 15 April; in all other parts of the division 15 Oct to 1 April. Migratory trout 31 Oct to 15 April. Freshwater fish and eels 14 March to 16 June.
Bristol Avon Division, non-migratory trout (including rainbow trout) 15 Oct to 1 April.
Somerset Division; salmon 30 Sept to 1 Feb. Migratory trout 31 Oct to 15 April. Freshwater fish and eels 14

March to 16 June.
Size limits: Avon and Dorset Division: trout 9.8in (25cm) On the River Stour (excluding tributaries) and the River Avon below Town Bridge, Fordingbridge—grayling 11.8in (30cm). No prawn, shrimp. worm or plug allowed when fishing for salmon or migratory trout before 15 May.
Bristol Avon Division: trout 10in (25cm). No person shall take more than two non-migratory trout in any day. No barbel shall be taken, no more than two freshwater fish (excluding eels).
Somerset Division: in all waters to the west of a line drawn from Stolford to Wellington—trout 7in (18cm), in all other waters 9.8in (25cm). No prawn, shrimp, worm or plug allowed when fishing for salmon before 15 May. In all divisions, during the close season for freshwater fish, the use of any maggot, silkweed or cereal bait is prohibited.
A reservoir licence is not required to fish a reservoir in the Somerset Division as they are covered by a general licence. For reservoir close seasons, apply to the Somerset Division of the Wessex Water Authority.
LOCAL CLUBS AND ASSOCIATIONS
Bath Anglers' Assoc, A J Smith, 14 Hampton Hse, Grosvenor Bridge Rd, Bath. Tel 29000
Bathampton Angling Club, A Adams, 38 Beech Ave, Combe Down, Shepton Mallet, Somerset. Tel: Shepton Mallet 3021
Bradford-on-Avon Angling Club, B Parsons, 26 Cloford Close, Trowbridge. Tel 63773

Mike Millman

day, but can be disappointing. Access points are not frequent, and more often than not a long walk is necessary though the bream invariably make their mark visually. Good sport can be had at the end of the first meadow below Parchey Bridge and catches have included quality roach and bream, occasionally tench and carp, and even dace. Weston Zoyland was the scene of Dave Burr's 1965 National Championship catch record—more than 76lb.

The Langacre Rhyme joins the King's

Local clubs control the good fishing to be found on the Avon at Bathampton weir.

Sedgemoor Drain near Middlezoy, the Eighteen Foot Rhyme runs from Walton, and the most recent is the Aller Moor Relief Channel which drains from Othery and Langport and joins it near Greylake. Roach and small rudd are the predominant fish in these smaller peaty waters and maggot is the best bait for them. Bream are on the increase, and for them bread is the favourite.

Bridgwater Angling Assoc, B Valentine-Slack, 6 Toll Hse Rd, Cannington, Somerset. Tel: Combwich 652044
Bristol and District Amalgamated Anglers, J S Parker, 16 Lansdown View, Kingswood, Bristol BS15 4AW
Bristol and West of England Federation, V Tyrrell, 16 Falcon Close, Westbury-on-Trym, Bristol. Tel 500165
Calne Angling Assoc, R J Reeves, 16 Wessex Close, Calne, Wilts. Tel 814516
Chippenham Angling Club, A Giles, 104 Eastern Ave, Monkton Park, Chippenham
Illchester and District Angling Assoc, R Hughes, 32 St Cleer's Orchard, Somerton, Somerset.
Isis Angling Club, D A C Horsman, 9 Noredown Way, Wootton Bassett, Wilts. Tel: Wootton Bassett 2718.
Keynsham Angling Assoc, B Veale, 117 Wellsway, Keynsham, Bristol. Tel: Keynsham 2919.
Melksham and District Angling Assoc, V Abbott, 34 West End Rd, Melksham, Wilts.
Portcullis Angling Club, G Rees, 21 North St, Downend, Bristol. Tel: 652897.
Ridgeway and District Angling Assoc, R J Walker, 17 Birch Court, Keynsham. Tel Keynsham 5228.
Ushers Angling Club, R W Rudd, 29 Kingsdown Rd, Trowbridge, Wilts. Tel 63755.
Wessex Federation of Anglers, J J Mathrick, 25 Ashwell Lane, Glastonbury, Somerset. Tel 28133.
Westland Freshwater Angling Club, B Swain, 108 Beechwood, Yeovil, Somerset. Tel 28133.

TACKLE DEALERS
M D Roberts, 30 Brock St, Bath.
R Smith and Ford Sports, 2A The Shambles, Bradford-on-Avon.
Bridge Sports Ltd, 42 Eastover, Bridgwater.
R Perrett, 31 Westernzoyland Rd, Bridgwater.
Martakies Sports, 20 Gloucester Rd North, Filton Park, Bristol.
J B Sports, 31A Sandy Park, Brislington, Bristol.
K Davies, 410 Wells Rd, Red Lion Hill, Bristol.
C Newman, 20 High St, Chippenham.
D & J Sport, 71 Cricklade St, Cirencester.
M E Veater, Sports Shop, Cooks Hill, Clutton, Bristol.
Mrs Higgins, Cam Pet Supplies, Market Place, Castle Cam.
Watersport, 17A High St, Keynsham.
A W Rule, 8 Perrett Close, Langport.
E & O Brown, Kit Box, 38 Gloucester St, Malmesbury.
Sport & Leisure, 36 High St, Malmesbury.
Hobbies Centre, 39 High St, Melksham.
Batemans Sports Ltd, Kendrick St, Stroud, Glos.
The House of Angling, 60 Commercial Rd, Swindon.
G Hinton & Sons, 62 Bridge St, Taunton, Somerset.
The Tackle Shop, 32 Roundstone St, Trowbridge.
R W G Thatcher, 18 Queen St, Wells.
H Leeming, River View, Breadon, Weston-Super-Mare.
W G Ball, Pet Food Stores, 47A High St, Wincanton.
E & H Doney, 5 Band St, Yeovil.
Hagas Ltd, 12 Silver St, Yeovil.

Hampshire Basin

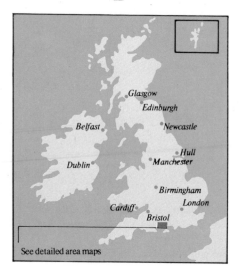

Glasgow
Edinburgh
Belfast
Newcastle
Hull
Dublin
Manchester
Birmingham
London
Cardiff
Bristol

See detailed area maps

The Hampshire Basin, drained by the rivers Stour and Avon, provides some of the best coarse fishing in the British Isles. Both rivers produce quality fish in large numbers, despite reports of disease, pollution, water abstraction, and the adverse effect of weed-cutting. At Christchurch, the Royalty Fishery is probably England's most famous day-ticket water, providing anglers with first-class mixed fishing through summer and winter.

Day tickets

Much of the Avon's coarse fishing is available only to members of local clubs, and day tickets are rarely offered, but pubs along the rivers often issue tickets at reasonable prices for their stretches. Good fishing can be had at the Bull and the White Horse at Downton, both inns controlling beautiful stretches of water. The Throop Fishery on the Dorset Stour, north of the A3060 four miles out of Christchurch, is also a first-class day ticket venue. It has barbel, chub, roach, dace and, surprisingly, tench and carp as well.

The Avon and Stour are basically summer fisheries, although winter fishing is excellent.

These rivers hold roach, chub, dace, and numbers of big pike. Particularly good for pike is the Avon and the area below the by-pass bridge on the Royalty Fishery which has produced many pike over 20 lb. Access to the Royalty is by the A35 Christchurch ring-road and along the Hurn road for about a mile. The Royalty no longer produces huge barbel since maggots were banned a few years ago, but the water still holds large chub, roach and dace.

Stillwater fishing

Stillwater fishing in the Hampshire Basin is limited, but what fisheries there are hold extensive stocks of specimen and coarse fish. Hatchett Pond (a 25-acre lake) a mile outside Beaulieu on the B3054 Lymington road, is typical of these waters. It is mostly shallow, but contains one or two deep gullies up to 10ft deep. Basically spring-fed, it has clear water with extensive growths of dense bottom weed. In recent years Hatchett Pond has produced many large tench, and bream up to 11lb have been caught. Heavier fish are known to exist, and this water probably holds the British record for common bream. There are also roach, perch, rudd, eels, and numerous pike. Coarse fishing is by permit only, and tickets are obtainable at the Forestry Commission, Queens House, Lyndhurst.

Mixed fishing at Broadlands Lake

Broadlands Lake near Romsey is a recent addition to the available waters. It is reached by the A3057 out of Romsey and 300 yards on the right the road is signposted to Rowham. Situated on the Broadlands Estate (home of the Mountbatten family), the lake was originally excavated to provide ballast for the M27 motorway. It was then filled with water from the River Test, weeds were planted, banks landscaped, and stock fish introduced. The object was to provide a good mixed fishery, readily available by purchasing day tickets. The stocking cam-

298

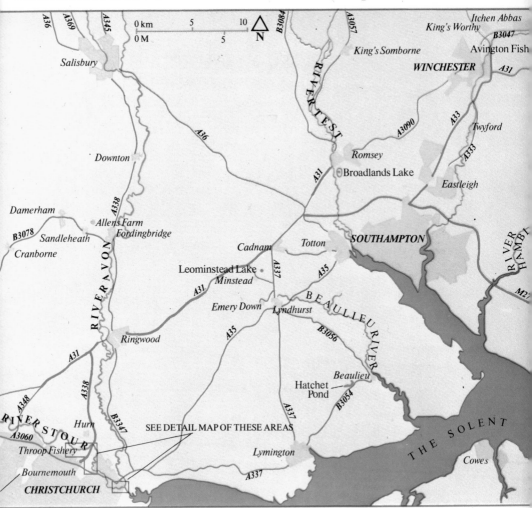

paign was carefully carried out using only large tench to 6lb, rudd to 4½lb, carp to 15lb and grayling to 3lb. Heavyweight perch were recently added, and although the lake was only opened early in 1977 many good bags of big fish have already been taken.

Trout fishing throughout the area is good. At Winchester, the now famous Avington Park Fishery has produced a succession of world record fly-caught rainbow trout to a fraction under 20lb. The fishery is situated south of Itchen Abbas three miles along the B3047 from Kings Worthy, north of Winchester.

At Lyndhurst, Leominstead trout lake provides first-class fishing in New Forest surroundings. It is one of the most beautiful and tranquil waters in the Hampshire Basin.

Damerham trout lakes

Access is by the A337 to Romsey and Minstead, turning left to Emery Down a few miles out of Lyndhurst. Farther west, at Damerham near Fordingbridge on the B3078, the man-made Damerham trout lakes provide over three miles of actual bank space to visiting anglers. Near Allens Farm at Sandleheath is a much smaller but highly popular fishery.

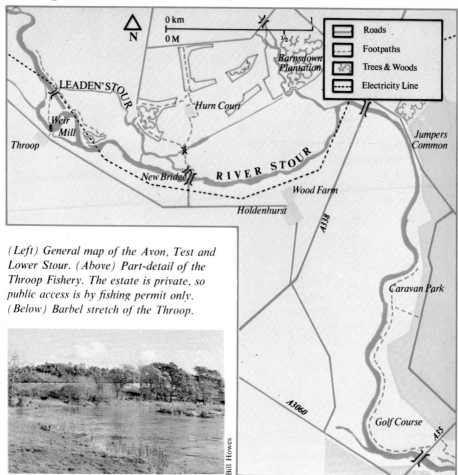

(*Left*) *General map of the Avon, Test and Lower Stour. (Above) Part-detail of the Throop Fishery. The estate is private, so public access is by fishing permit only. (Below) Barbel stretch of the Throop.*

Bill Howes

Most of these trout lakes are stocked with fish which average over 2lb in weight—and Avington holds fish over 25lb. All these fisheries operate on a day-ticket basis with a one-fly-only rule. Recommended flies for the area include the whisky fly, muddler minnow, corixa, leaded shrimp, Avington nymph, and black and peacock spider. But the angler must experiment all the time with varied patterns.

The New Forest is full of tiny rivers most of which hold good stocks of brown trout for the angler who prefers to fish for wild 'brownies'. During the autumn many of these attractive forest streams have a run of sea trout.

Individual trout up to 17lb have been caught from tiny brooks it is almost possible to jump across. Sea trout between 6 and 8lb are relatively common. Most of these fish are caught on fly tackle or artificial lures. Tickets to fish the forest streams are obtainable from the Forestry Commission, Queens House, Lyndhurst, Hants.

World-famous trout rivers

The rivers Test and Itchen are spring-fed and flow over chalk. They are world-renowned for trout fishing waters and in their lower reaches give a fine annual catch of about 1,000 salmon. But the major part of these waters is privately owned. For certain stretches of both rivers, however, day rods

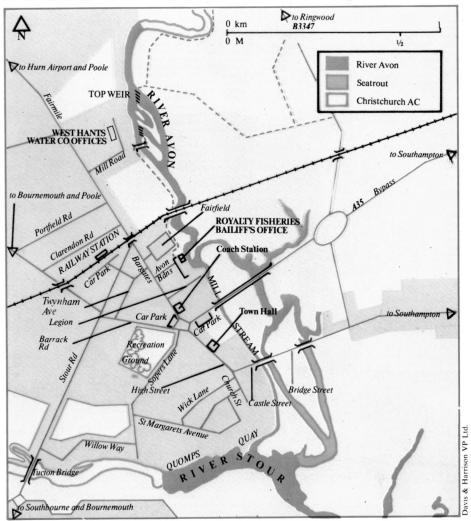

0 km

0 M   ½

to Ringwood
B3347

	River Avon
	Seatrout
	Christchurch AC

N

to Hurn Airport and Poole

Fairmile

TOP WEIR

RIVER AVON

WEST HANTS
WATER CO OFFICES

Mill Road

to Southampton

to Bournemouth and Poole

Portfield Rd

Clarendon Rd

RAILWAY STATION

Car Park

Bargates

Avon
Bdns

Fairfield

ROYALTY FISHERIES
BAILIFF'S OFFICE

Coach Station

A35 Bypass

Twynham
Ave
Legion

Barrack
Rd

Stour Rd

Car Park

Recreation
Ground

Sopers Lane

MILL

Car Park

Town Hall

STREAM

to Southampton

High Street

Wick Lane

Church St

Castle Street

Bridge Street

St Margarets Avenue

Willow Way

Tucton Bridge

QUOMPS

QUAY

RIVER STOUR

to Southbourne and Bournemouth

Davis & Harrison VP Ltd.

are available at a cost of £8.50 to £35 per rod per day. The Test tends to be more expensive than the Itchen as the trout are bigger and more waters are keepered. Colonel Eric Hay (Tel: Twyford 713458) operates a 24-hour answering service, and after personally vetting applicants, will issue day rods on both rivers. We have been asked not to publish details of these stretches. A trout licence from the Southern Water Authority is necessary before fishing on the Itchen and Test.

There is very little free fishing in the area.

In Hampshire, there is a stretch on the river Itchen by the Weirs in Winchester, owned by the Winchester City Council. In Southampton, the owner of the Woodmill-Mansbridge fishery does not object to anyone fishing from the left bank for coarse fish. For these free waters, rod licences are obtainable from the Southern Water Authority. In Bournemouth, there is a very small section of the Stour owned by the Bournemouth Corporation below the sewage outfall. For this stretch rod licences are available from the Wessex Water Authority.

301

Hampshire Basin

(Left) Detail map showing access roads to one of Britain's greatest and most famous coarse fisheries, the renowned Royalty. Many specimen roach, chub, dace and barbel have come from this water. But to catch these fish requires a high standard of technique by the fisherman. (Right) Winter angling on the Avon. This stretch offers good chub fishing.

Robin Fletcher

WATER AUTHORITIES

Wessex Water Authority, 2 Nuffield Rd, Poole, Dorset. Tel: 5021. Controls the Avon and Stour, Damerham Lakes, Throop and Royalty Fisheries.

Southern Water Authority, 2 Market St, Eastleigh, Hants. Tel: 614662. Controls the Test and Itchen. Allens Farm and Avington Fisheries. Hatchett Pond. Broadlands and Leominstead Lakes.

LICENCES

Wessex Water Authority

Salmon: season ticket (st) £12, week ticket (wt) £4.50, day ticket (dt) £3. **Trout:** st £3, monthly ticket (mt) £1.50, dt 75p, junior day 35p. **Freshwater fish:** st £2, mt £1, dt 50p. Juniors, OAPs and registered disabled half price unless otherwise indicated. Single rod and line. Price revision January 1978.

Close seasons: Salmon, Rivers Avon and Stour, September 30 to February 1. Non-migratory trout (including rainbow trout), River Avon and tributaries above the Mill Dam at Bickton Mill (except the part of the River Nadder which lies above the road bridge at Barford St Martin) October 15 to April 15. Migratory trout, October 31 to April 15. Freshwater fish and eels, March 14 to June 16. Size limits: trout 9.8 in (25 cm). On the River Stour (excluding tributaries) and the River Avon below Town Bridge Fordingbridge, grayling 11.8 in (30 cm). No prawn, shrimp, worm or plug allowed when fishing for salmon or migratory trout before May 15. During the coarse close season no maggot, silk-weed or cereal.

Southern Water Authority

One scale of rod licences covers whole region. **Salmon:** st £9, fortnight ticket (ft) £3, dt £1.50. **Migratory and non-migratory trout:** st £3, ft 75p, junior season 75p. **Freshwater fish and eels:** st £1.50, mt 75p, junior season 40p. Junior licences apply to anglers under 16 on day of issue. A free fishing licence available to OAPs for freshwater fish and eels. A licence allows two rods. **Close season:** As Wessex (coarse fish); salmon, October 3 to January 31 inclusive. Migratory trout, brown and rainbow trout seasons under review.

FISHERIES

Royalty Fishery, Christchurch

Owned by the West Hants Water Company. Permits for coarse fishing from Davis Tackle, Christchurch (Tel: 5169) or from Bailiff. **Close season:** As Wessex. **Charges:** dt 75p, wt £3, ft £5, mt £8, st £25. Pike fishing permitted November 1 to March 14 at no extra charge (no spinning). Charges do not include rod licence. Limited coarse fishing permits for Stour and Christchurch Harbour obtainable from Christchurch AC, or Chub Keynes at Christchurch Quay: dt 40p. Royalty salmon fishing let by the season (February 1 to June 30) to a limited number of rods, with daily lettings in July only (£10 day). Daily permits for sea fishing (Bridge Pool) £7.50 day. Parlour (from August 1) £3.10 day. Upper main river £2.10 day (from August 1). Permits from bailiff at Avon Bdgs, Christchurch.

Tel: 5262, no advance bookings. For other salmon and sea trout fishing apply early in writing to the Royalty Fishery Manager, West Hants Water Co, Mill Rd, Christchurch.

Throop Fishery, Hants

Christchurch Station 2½ miles. Salmon, trout, sea trout, and coarse fishing. Salmon and trout fishing rates on application. Coarse fishing: st £15, ½ st £9, wt £4.50 ft £6.50, dt £1.50 (reduced rates for OAPs and juveniles, special rates for clubs, booking essential). Enquiries to Ernest Leah, South Lodge, Holdenhurst, Bournemouth BH8 0EF (Tel: 35532). Coarse tickets, licences and information from Taylor's Christchurch.

Allens Farm, Sandleheath

Four lakes and chalk stream near Sandleheath, Fordingbridge. Fly fishing for rainbow. Enquiries, J P & M Read, Allens Farm (Tel: Rockbourne 313).

Damerham Trout Lakes

Fordingbridge 3 miles. Six lakes. Rainbow and brown trout. Open April 2 to October 31. Day permit always available. For: Colin Harms, Rockbourne 446. Hotel: Compasses Inn (Tel: 231); dt £7.56, st £180 or £270.

Avington Park Lakes, Winchester

For rod apply Avington Park Fisheries. Tel: Itchen Abbas 312 dt £8.50.

Broadlands Lake, Romsey

Opened June 16 1977. Apply Broadlands Estate Office, or to fish hut, bailiff in attendance 8 a.m.-8 p.m.: dt £1 juniors, OAPs 50p, st £25, clubs £20.

Hatchett Pond, Lymington

Coarse fishing for bream, carp, tench and pike. Permits from the Forestry Commission, Queens House, Lyndhurst (Tel: 2801); or the Information Centre, Lyndhurst: dt 32p, wt 86p. Also at Smith's Sports, Lymington, and tackle shops in Christchurch.

The Forestry Commission manage various waters in the New Forest; Hatchett Pond, Cadman's Pool at Stoney Cross, and Whitten Pond, Burley. Free fishing, for juniors at Round Hill Pond, Brockenhurst, Slufters Pond, Linwood, Janesmoor Pond, Stoney Cross. With few exceptions permits are available for fly fishing on all streams through Crown land in the New Forest, between May 1 and September 30.

Leominstead Lake, Lyndhurst.

Privately owned. Apply Leo Jarmel. Tel: Lyndhurst 2610; dt £7, st £140.

TACKLE DEALERS

Smith's Sports Shop, 25 Queen St, Lymington.
M Davis, Fishing Tackles, Christchurch. Tel: 5169.
Taylors, Barracks Rd, Christchurch. Tel: 4518.
Custom Tackle, Columbia Rd, Ensbury Pk, Bournemouth.
Swallows, 5 The Bridges, West St, Ringwood.
Sea Anglers' Supply, Milbrook, Southampton.
The Rod Box, St George's St, Winchester. Tel: 61561.

Bill Howes

Isle of Wight

Glasgow
Edinburgh
Belfast
Newcastle
Hull
Dublin
Manchester
Birmingham
Cardiff
London
Bristol

See detailed area maps

Separating the Isle of Wight from the Hampshire mainland, the Solent offers a wide variety of mixed sea angling. A superabundance of food, comparatively shallow water, and savage tides attract many kinds of fish providing first-class fishing for beach and boat anglers alike. Big tope are often encountered in the Sowley area and fish to 50lb have been caught from Park Shore by beach fishermen.

Smooth-hounds in huge packs

Farther west, where the shore line is comprised of mud and salt grass, big sting ray also fall to beachcasting tackle, and fish of 40lb or more are caught during most summer seasons. Good-sized smooth-hounds roam the Solent in huge packs, and anglers using ragworm or de-shelled hermit crabs often catch large numbers of prime specimens. Thornback ray and bass are also common in Solent waters.

Solent bass anglers usually fish Stone Point on the eastern side of Lepe Beach, or Sowley Boom or Hampstead Ledge on the island side of the Solent. These areas are best fished with natural baits, and strips of locally caught cuttlefish are the most favoured lure.

Beyond Hurst Castle a long submerged shingle bank provides a feeding ground for vast shoals of small to medium-sized bass, and most of these can be caught by trolling a red-gill sandeel behind a moving boat.

Fishing inside the Solent is good but seldom easy. Strong tides and drifting weed make for difficult conditions. Persevering anglers, however, often catch exceptional specimens. Quite apart from bass, tope, sting ray, smooth-hounds, skate and a host of smaller fish, the Solent is capable of producing the occasional big conger or monster monkfish. A 62lb monkfish was caught recently a few hundred yards off Sowley beach by a boat angler, while a young angler beachcasting into deep water at Hurst Castle brought in a 49lb conger eel.

Facing out into the channel, the south and south-western side of the Isle of Wight is noted for its good fishing. Beach anglers who fish such marks as Rocken End, Chale, Atherfield and Brook Beach regularly catch large conger, skate and monkfish from the shore. Anglers in this area who specialize in bass also catch plenty of good-sized fish up to and well into double figures. The offshore marks round the island provide even more scope; tope, turbot, skate, ray, conger, pollack and heavyweight cod are all caught during the course of a normal season.

All round the coast of the island there is good fishing from beaches and from some piers. Sandown, a sheltered resort, has ideal fishing conditions all year round with boats available along the shore, and lugworm and king rag plentiful locally. Here, conger, dogfish, dabs, skate and mackerel can be fished from deep water, with plaice, flounder, bass and sole inshore.

Sandown and Totland also have good beach and pier fishing with boats available. At Sandown there is bass all year round with the largest in early autumn, and plaice, sole, turbot, mackerel, garfish, and large skate,

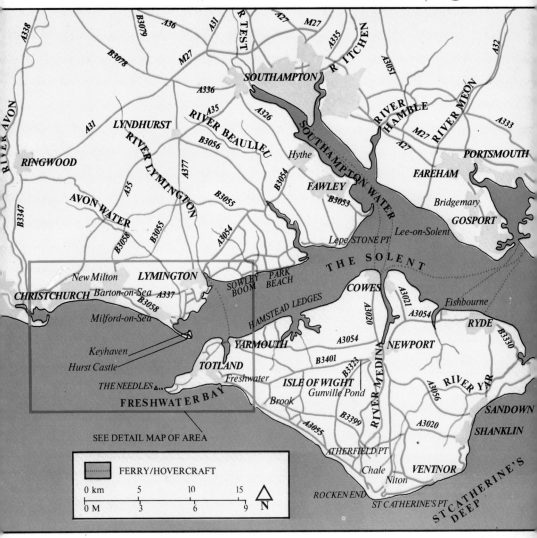

(*Above*) *Fishing areas of Southampton Water, Solent and the Isle of Wight.*

ray and conger in late summer and early autumn. In Totland, bass can be caught off the shingle bank from a boat, and bass and conger from the shore. In Cowes there is good fishing for whiting in the harbour, with bass, mullet and pollack off the Parade, and pouting and bass in the Solent.

Excellent shark fishing

Off St Catherine's Point, vicious tide-rips and very deep water combine to provide unique opportunities for shark fishing enthusiasts. In past years this area produced

a seemingly endless stream of heavyweight porbeagle sharks including one fish which for a while held the record for the species. A combination of overfishing and a decrease in mackerel shoals has led to a general decline in numbers of the porbeagle shark, but the St Catherine's area is still one of the best places in the British Isles to try for a high-leaping thresher shark. Fish of record-breaking

305

Barnabys Picture Library

(Above) Freshwater Bay, Isle of Wight, holds common skate of over 100lb.

proportions are regularly sighted off the corner of the island. Numerous 200lb-plus specimens have been caught by shark boats drifting in St Catherine's Deep, and fish of twice this weight have broken anglers' tackle, often after several hours of hard fighting.

Quite apart from porbeagle and thresher sharks, the St Catherine's area has also produced a strange silver-coloured shark covered in dark spots and blotches. When this particular shark was caught by the author, the Natural History Museum in London was notified and it was thought that it could be one of a new species as yet

unrecorded. Unfortunately, this shark was caught on a day when porbeagle shark were extremely plentiful, and the angler, by the time he had landed the fish, was too tired to realize he had a potential record-breaking new species on his hands. In consequence, when the fish had been weighed and photographed, it was then cut up and sent to a local mink farmer to be used as fodder. Since this strange and very beautiful fish was caught, many anglers have fished the Isle of Wight in the hope of catching a similar specimen. But no one has yet made contact with one of these 'unknown' sharks.

Winter fishing is often very good round the Island. Big cod are fairly common and fish of 20-25lb are regarded as good but not exceptional catches. Fish of up to 40lb are taken during most winter seasons, and a record-breaker could be caught at any time.

Other than good sea fishing, the Isle of Wight also provides limited coarse fishing facilities. Most of the river and lake fishing on the Island is controlled by the Isle of Wight Freshwater Angling Association which lets some fishing on a day ticket basis for 50p. Annual membership costs £4 (juniors £1, OAPs 50p) with a 50p entrance to the club, but a temporary membership is offered at £2 per week.

Gunnville Pond

The River Yar holds a mixed head of coarse fish including roach, dace and pike, with brown trout at Alverstone and trout only above Newchurch. The IoW Freshwater Angling Association controls most of the water along the river through Alvestone and Sandown to the Old Cement Mills at Brading. There is some excellent carp fishing at Gunnville Pond. Carisbrooke (which is for members only), and carp, tench, roach, perch and bream at Somerton Reservoirs, Cowes. Day tickets are available for the Cement Mills Pond at Newport which holds carp, tench and rudd. There is little trout fishing on the island. A few private waters are stocked, and one or two streams hold some wild brown trout, but they are of little more than fingerling size.

St Catherine's Point, Isle of Wight, is a paradise for shark enthusiasts. (Above) A porbeagle shark being landed.

Visiting anglers will be well advised to visit Scott's Fishing Tackle shop in Newport where up-to-date information on day tickets and fish stocking is always available. Boat trips can be arranged either through this shop or on the quayside at Yarmouth. Local charter boats are usually heavily booked, so to avoid disappointment it pays to book a place on the boat in advance.

For fishing either the Solent or the South West side of the island, ports such as Lymington and Keyhaven provide ample charter boat facilities. Again advance bookings are advisable. Local shops such as Smith's Sports Shop in Lymington, Sea Angler's Supplies at Southampton, Taylor's in Christchurch, and Avon Sales in New Milton can usually arrange boat trips or provide telephone numbers of qualified charter boat skippers.

Sea marks off the Isle of Wight provide reasonable fishing on a year-round basis. There is plenty of good coarse fishing on the mainland and also some on the Island itself. All anglers are well catered for, irrespective of which style of angling they prefer. Big fish, small fish, the area has something for everyone.

Ventnor on the south side of the island offers varied fishing.

307

Isle of Wight

Detail map shows fishing in The Solent and the western point (The Needles) of the Isle of Wight.

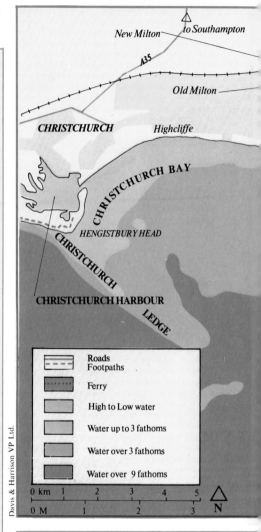

INFORMATION

WATER AUTHORITY

Southern Water Authority, Hampshire and Isle of Wight Area, Eastleigh House, 2 Market St, Eastleigh, Hants SO5 5WA. Tel: Southampton 614622.

LICENCES

Migratory and non-migratory trout: season £4.50, 14 days £1.15, junior season £1.15. **Freshwater fish and eels:** season £2.25, month £1.15. Junior season 60p. Junior licences apply to anglers under the age of 16 on day of issue. OAPs may fish free.

Close seasons: coarse fishing March 15 to June 15 inclusive; migratory trout, brown and rainbow trout October 30 to March 31.

Size limits: there are no official size limited for coarse fish in the Southern Region, although local rules may be enforced by some clubs and fishery owners. Size limits for trout are as follows: sea trout 15in (37.5cm), brown and rainbow trout 10in (25cm).

FERRIES TO THE ISLE OF WIGHT

There are three ferry services operating between the Hampshire mainland and the Isle of Wight.

The Lymington Ferry (Tel 73301) has a service to Yarmouth (IOW) operating on the hour from 6am to 8pm. On Sundays the last boat returning to the mainland is at 9.40 (summer season). For children under 14 the fare is half the adult fare.

The Southampton Hovercraft (Tel 21249) runs a service to Cowes (IOW), every hour on the hour, from 8am to 8pm. The last return hovercraft is at 7.30pm (summer season). Different fares for a day return and a period return, with a partial reduction for children. On Saturdays and Sundays, a child travelling with an adult may travel free of charge.

The Portsmouth British Rail Ferry (Tel 27744) runs a service to Ryde (IOW) operating every hour (every half hour on Saturdays) from 6am to 11.35pm. The last return ferry is at 11.45pm. Children travel half-price. There is a special cheap-day return for travel after 12 noon (children half-price). For passenger and car travel it is advisable to book in advance. Details of ferry times are correct at time of going to press.

On the Hampshire mainland:

R A Stride, The Watch House, Coastguards Way, Mudeford, Hants.

R Keynes, The Quay, Christchurch, Hants.

On the Isle of Wight:

Harry Simmonds Tel Yarmouth 392.

H Attrill & Sons, The Duver, St Helens, IOW.

W Souter, Arctic Rd, Cowes, IOW.

E Williams, Arctic Rd, Cowes, IOW.

E & W Clark, Clarence Rd, East Cowes, IOW.

(for shark and general boat fishing) 9 Priory Rd, Carisbrooke, IOW.

Sea-Tac, 4–6 Wilkes Rd, Sandown, IOW.

Mr Newell, High St, Seaview, IOW.

C J Bolland, Heathfield Villas, Totland, IOW.

LOCAL CLUBS AND ASSOCIATIONS

Hampshire Anglers' Consultative Association, Mrs P Baring, Well House, Malshanger Green, Oakley, Basingstoke, Hants.

Isle of Wight Angling Society, R Watts, Bouldnor Battery Bungalow, Yarmouth, IOW.

Isle of Wight Freshwater Angling Association, W Kingswell, 12 Manor Rd, Lake, Seadown, IOW.

Sandown and Lake Angling Society, Mrs V Withers, 74 Station Ave, Sandown, IOW.

Shanklin Angling Society, T Heath, 17 Hope Rd, Shanklin, IOW.

Vectis Boating and Fishing Club, J C Williams, 101 Newnham Rd, Ryde, IOW.

Ventnor Angling Club, Mrs E Morris, Fernhill, Kent Rd, Ventnor, IOW.

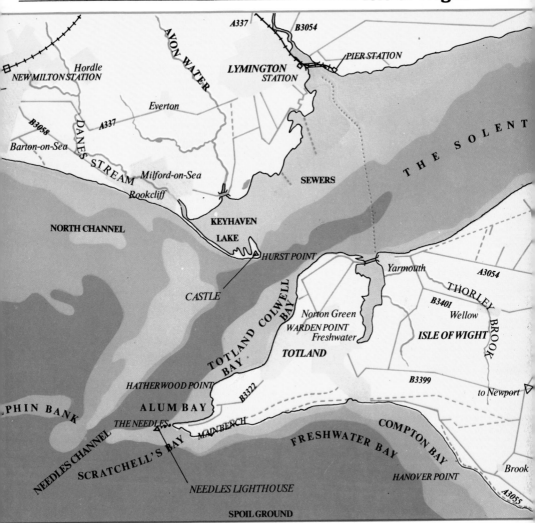

The map shows locations including: NEW MILTON STATION, Hordle, AVON WATER, A337, B3054, LYMINGTON STATION, PIER STATION, Everton, A337, B3058, Barton-on-Sea, DANES STREAM, Milford-on-Sea, Rookcliff, SEWERS, THE SOLENT, NORTH CHANNEL, KEYHAVEN, LAKE, HURST POINT, Yarmouth, A3054, CASTLE, THORLEY BROOK, COLWELL BAY, Norton Green, B3401, Wellow, WARDEN POINT, Freshwater, ISLE OF WIGHT, TOTLAND BAY, TOTLAND, HATHERWOOD POINT, B3322, B3399, to Newport, PHIN BANK, ALUM BAY, THE NEEDLES, MAIN BENCH, SCRATCHELL'S BAY, NEEDLES CHANNEL, FRESHWATER BAY, COMPTON BAY, Brook, HANOVER POINT, A3055, NEEDLES LIGHTHOUSE, SPOIL GROUND

NATIONAL ANGLING CLUBS

The Shark Angling Club of Great Britain, B. Tudor The Quay, East Looe, Cornwall.

The National Shore Casting Association, G W Wilson, 71 McNamara Rd, Rosehill, Wallsend.

TACKLE DEALERS

Davids Foodmarket, Lane End, Bembridge, IOW.

Bruces, 3 Clarence Rd, East Cowes, IOW.

Sports and Pastimes, 140 High St, Newport, IOW.

Don's Sports, 14 Cross St, Ryde, IOW.

The Tackle Box, 73 High St, Ryde, IOW.

Sea-Tac, 4–6 Wilkes Rd, Sandown, IOW.

Mr Dobson, Pier Rd, Seaview, IOW.

Alvera's, High St, Seaview, IOW.

The Sports Shop, 74 Regent St, Shanklin, IOW.

Plumbley & Sons, The Broadway, Totland, IOW.

Bates & Son, 5 Spring Hill, Ventnor, IOW.

Patstone & Cox Ltd., 25 High St, Southampton, Hants.

Smith's Sports Shop, 25 Queen St, Lymington, Hants.

M Davis, Fishing Tackles, Christchurch, Hants.

Taylor's, Barrack Rd, Christchurch, Hants.

Sea Anglers' Supply, Milbrook, Southampton, Hants.

Handicraft Shop, Gore Rd, New Milton, Hants.

Waterhouse & Connings, Woolston, Southampton, Hants.

The Fo'csle, Woolston, Southampton, Hants.

Holt & Haskell, High St, Shirley, Southampton, Hants.

Connor & Mitchell, St Mary's, Southampton, Hants.

West Country-Sea

See detailed area maps

The British record (rod-caught) list for sea fish shows how productive the waters off Dorset, Devon and Cornwall are. No fewer than 52 boat and shore records have been set and the figure is constantly growing. The area could well be described as the 'coast of wrecks' as the sea from Portland Bill to Land's End is littered with the rusting remains of ships sunk during two World Wars. These provide homes for vast numbers of fish and, despite concentrated fishing from charter boats, continue to give large catches.

Lyme Bay

Weymouth and other ports in Dorset have boats that frequently make the run to marks in Lyme Bay. The liner *Empress of India,* among others, is inhabited by fine conger, while off the Devon coast, Lyme Bay and Start Bay are the hunting grounds of Brixham charter skippers. Brixham's skippers started fishing wrecks in the 1960s and its famous boat *Our Unity* is seldom out of the angling news. Their biggest haul was 5,000lb of ling, conger and pollack, made by eight anglers in about six hours fishing.

Tides run swiftly in both bays, and good

wrecking is restricted to neap tide periods. If you are thinking of tangling with an 80lb conger make sure that you bear the tides in mind when making a booking. Anglers who forget this are naturally disappointed when their big day turns out to be fished on less productive ground, in more sheltered waters.

Plymouth

Thirty miles down the coast is the great seaport of Plymouth, now regarded as Britain's number one sea angling centre. Approximately 25 fully equipped and licensed boats are available for charter, and an unending stream of outsize fish find their way to the scales at the end of each day. Records set at Plymouth include conger 109lb 3oz, pollack 25lb, coal-fish 30lb 12oz and turbot 32lb 4oz. Wreck fishing is a speciality, but the great reefs of Eddystone, West Rutts and Hands Deeps are also popular. These lie in deep water, but can be reached in a couple of hours.

Inshore boat fishing is also productive. The whiting grounds four miles south of Rame's Head are famous for big fish, and specimens of 3-5lb are no surprise. The area's shore fishing can also be recom-

Big pollack roam close to Start Point (left) and go for float-fished sandeel. (Right) West Bay near Bridport.

Ron Sutherby

mended, and you can take your pick of rock, storm beach and quiet sandy estuaries. The main species are the colourful ballan wrasse, which reach 7lb in the deep kelp-strewn gullies, pollack and bass.

Looe

Looe is perhaps the shark fishing capital of the world. Each day throughout summer, 25 boats go beyond the Eddystone, where 'blues' provide plenty of excitement. They mostly weigh around 50lb and at the end of each week there are at least six fish in the 80-110lb class. Unfortunately, too many small sharks are unnecessarily killed by holiday anglers eager to show off their catch at the end of the day. To qualify for membership of the Shark Angling Club of Great Britain the minimum weight caught is 75lb, and it would probably be advisable for sharks below this weight to be returned unharmed to the sea. Other shark species found off Looe are the

A. F. Kersting

311

West Country-Sea

Mike Millman

Map of the Devon and Cornish coastline
noted for its remarkable sea fishing.
Here is the shark fishing capital of
the world, and excellent sport with
conger, pollack and turbot.
(*Above*) Rusty Anchor at Plymouth Sound.

ILFRACOMBE

BRISTOL CHANNEL

BARNSTAPLE BAY

Appledore

HARTLAND POINT

A39

Bideford

A388

R. TAMAR

A39

A39

Crackington Haven

A388

B3263

LAUNCESTON

A30

B3266

A30

A388

DEVON

TREVOSE HEAD

R. FOWEY

PADSTOW

TAVISTOCK

B3276

A30

BODMIN

A38

PLYMOUTH

TOWAN HEAD

A30

A390

A388

NEWQUAY

A39

A30

Bodinnick Ferry

A38 A38

Golant

FOWEY

A387

A374

A390

Llansallos

LOOE

A390

A390

ST GEORGE'S ISLAND

TRURO

A39

A540

Mevagissey

HATT ROCK

PENCARROW HEAD

WEST RUTT

A39

A3048

OLD SAWMILLS REACH

St Ives

Mylor Bridge

CANNIS ROCK

GRIBBIN HEAD

PHILLIPS ROCKS

HANDS DEEP

B3306

A3074

Ferry

CORNWALL

A394

TREFUSIS POINT

PENZANCE

Marazion

Mawnan Smith

FALMOUTH

ROSEMULLION HEAD

EDDYSTONE LIGHTHOUSE

A30

A394

HELFORD RIVER

SEE DETAIL MAP FOR THIS AREA

Lamorna

B3293

MANACLE POINT

LAND'S END

A3083

ENGLISH CHANNEL

KYNANCE COVE

Coverack

Lizard

LIZARD POINT

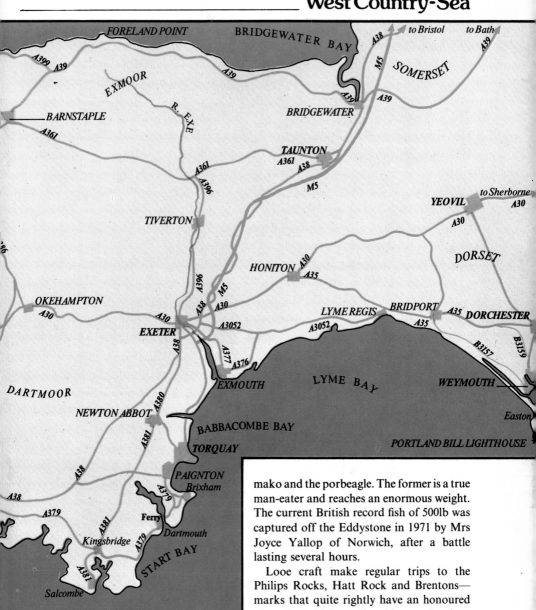

FORELAND POINT

BRIDGEWATER BAY

to Bristol   to Bath

A38

A39

M5

SOMERSET

A399 A39

EXMOOR

R. EXE

A39

A39

A39

BARNSTAPLE

A361

A361

BRIDGEWATER

TAUNTON

A361 A38

M5

YEOVIL

to Sherborne
A30

A30

TIVERTON

A396

HONITON A30

A35

DORSET

OKEHAMPTON

A396

M5

A30

A30

A3052

LYME REGIS BRIDPORT

A3052

A35 DORCHESTER

A35

B3157 B3159

A30

A38

EXETER

A377 A376

EXMOUTH

LYME BAY

WEYMOUTH

DARTMOOR

A380

BABBACOMBE BAY

Easton

NEWTON ABBOT

A381

TORQUAY

PORTLAND BILL LIGHTHOUSE

A38

PAIGNTON
Brixham

A379

A379

A38

Ferry

A381

Dartmouth

Kingsbridge

A379

START BAY

A381

Salcombe

0 km   10   20
0 M   5   10   15   N

Major roads

Minor roads

mako and the porbeagle. The former is a true man-eater and reaches an enormous weight. The current British record fish of 500lb was captured off the Eddystone in 1971 by Mrs Joyce Yallop of Norwich, after a battle lasting several hours.

Looe craft make regular trips to the Philips Rocks, Hatt Rock and Brentons—marks that quite rightly have an honoured place in British angling history. In these places the pollack is king. It is a hefty green and gold fish whose power-dive for the bottom after it has taken a bait, is something one never forgets. Pollack of 10lb are common, and tackle-busting fish up to 20lb are never far away.

These reefs are also fished by skippers from Fowey, but their main quarry is bass on

Mike Millman

the inshore grounds. Most of them make for the Cannis Rock, due south of Gribben Head, where fish averaging 6lb are taken on live sandeel. Many species find their way into Fowey Harbour, and near the Bodinnick Ferry, where the water is very deep, conger fishing is particularly good at night. Eels up to 75lb have been taken on squid and mackerel, and stories of gigantic conger breaking up tackle and gaffs do have some truth in them. A little farther upstream is Old Sawmills Reach where fine flounder and bass are caught on the making tide. Spoons tipped with worms are much favoured locally and account for big flatties.

Fowey

Shore fishing at Fowey is especially good during the autumn. From the harbour mouth to the tidal limits there are dozens of spots where you can catch big wrasse, bass, pollack and flounder. Golant, renowned for its flounder, produced the record fish of 5lb 11oz. The fish tend to lie behind sandbanks running across the river, and a moderate cast from the railway siding will put crab or worm bait in the right place.

Outside the harbour to the east, between Pencarrow Head and Llansallos, the water is reached by a very steep path. The effort can be worthwhile, as monster wrasse shelter under rocky overhangs and provide plenty of

rod-bending sport. One recent catch gave 27 fish over 4lb, and three over 6lb, which is specimen weight for the species.

Pollack fishing can also be rewarding along this wild stretch of coast. Most are taken by spinning with artificial or natural sandeels. Sliding float fishing with crab, king rag, or ragworm is also successful. Conger roam the gloomy canyons after dark and more than one 40lb fish has come writhing out of the depths after taking a juicy strip of

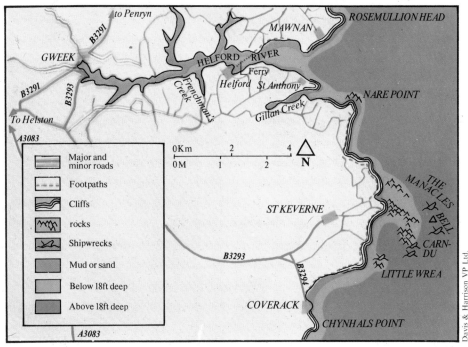

Our detail map shows the notorious Manacles Reef, superb for bass, pollack and conger fishing.
(Left) Golant in Cornwall and (below) Kynance looking towards the Lizard.

squid or mackerel offered on an 8/0 hook to a wire trace. Take a word of warning however; congering from desolate rocks at night is no game for the lone angler. Always have a friend along, and be fully equipped with lights, 20ft of rope and a first-aid kit.

Mevagissey

The small port of Mevagissey is another sea angling centre. Each day charter boats bring shark, ling, conger, coalfish, and pollack ashore, while wreck fishing is a speciality for skipper Bernard Hunkin who has found the British record ling and angler fish. Inshore wrecks off the Dodman Point have also produced record fish—a red bream weighing an incredible 9½lb and an electric ray only fractionally short of 100lb.

The shoreline within 30 miles of Mevagissey is perfect for shore fishing. There are dozens of spots providing all the popular species, while Falmouth, with its huge harbour and miles of tidal rivers cutting deep inland, is a paradise for shore and dinghy anglers. Most species are present throughout the year, but autumn is the best period. Soft

Towan Head near Newquay is a popular mark for rock fishing—hard-fighting tope to 50lb are caught, and record gurnard, whiting and turbot.

back and peeler crab offered on bottom or float gear will be quickly snapped up by flounder, plaice, dabs, wrasse, pollack or bass. Spinning from rocks with artificial or natural baits—from Zone Point, Trefusis Point, or Pendennis Point, produces mackerel, garfish, bass and pollack.

Manacles Reef

A few miles away is the notorious Manacles Reef, a superb spot for bass, pollack and conger fishing. The reef lies directly across the southern approach to Falmouth, and its outer edge is marked by a large red buoy, chained to the sea-bed 200ft below. Many ships have gone to the bottom in the past, and modern wrecks like the *Cape Finisterre* are fished with excellent results.

Over the reef itself is bass country. Fish of 7–10lb are common, with a percentage weighing !3lb. These are caught by drift-line methods or by trolling with artificial eels. Pollack fall to the same methods, but during daylight the fish lie deep so it is essential to work the bait close to the bottom. At dawn and dusk when pollack rise high in the water, one trolls just a few feet below the surface.

Strong tides

Manacle gullies hold big turbot and many fish over 25lb have been caught on ledgered mackerel and squid strip. Tides run fairly strongly in the area, so springs should be avoided if possible. It also pays to remember that any wind stronger than Force Three brings in a heavy ground swell making fishing almost impossible. Self-drive boats are available at a few places nearby. John Badger (Tel Mawnan Smith 250 675) has 18 footers, while Cliff Howes (Tel Penryn 74204 summer, 74069 winter) hires three 17ft motor boats and four sailing boats.

The coastline from the Manacles to Land's End is very rugged and picturesque, providing places for abundant shore fishing. Coverack, Lizard Point, Kynance Cove,

Marazion and Lamorna Cove are just a few places close to the water. You can take your choice of fish, although most bags are made of wrasse, bass and mackerel. However, the tip of England is dangerous and for experts only. For this reason local anglers who fish from precipitous rock ledges are known as 'mountain men'.

North Cornish coast

Cornwall's north coast is very different from the southern. The open Atlantic Ocean pounds the shore, and more than one fisherman has lost his life when an unexpected 20ft wave plucked him from a seemingly safe perch.

Among the most famous marks for rock fishing are Towan Head at Newquay and Trevose Head near Padstow. Both produce outstanding catches, but the latter, with its hard-fighting tope, is more popular. Fish up to 50lb come within casting range and fight hard after taking mackerel or squid strip suspended from balloon floats.

Boat fishing for the normal species is largely unexploited on the north coast, although a fair number of charter boats operate from Newquay, mostly on a half-day

316

Mike Millman

INFORMATION
ANGLING CHARTER BOATS
Our Unity, E Passmore, 25 Bella Vista, Brixham, Devon.
Fowey Sea Angling Centre, 20 Fore St, Mevagissey, Cornwall (for deep sea and bass fishing).
Colin Tabb, 2 Fore St, Golant, Fowey, Cornwall.
Looe Shark Fleet, Frank Hoskin, The Quay, East Looe, Cornwall (25 craft for charter).
Eileen, Bernard and Les Huskin, 36 Kiln Close, Mevagissey, Cornwall.
Mevagissey Shark Angling Centre, West Wharf, Mevagissey (14 boats for charter).
Tackle Box, Dick Johnson, 13 Fore St, Mevagissey (approximately 12 boats for charter).
H Winter-Taylor, Harbour View, North Quay, Padstow, Cornwall.
John Watts, Rock, near Padstow.
Fred Williams, 10 Custom House Quay, Penzance.
Plymouth Angling Boatmen's Assoc, Graham Andrews, 30 South View Park, Plympton (approx 25 craft for charter).
Michael Digby, Battery Lane, Polruan, Cornwall.
John Poynter, 20 Enner Close, Old Town, St Mary's, Isles of Scilly.
Girl Alison, Dave Lang, The Harbour Kiosk, Torquay.
CLUBS AND ASSOCIATIONS
Shark Angling Club of Great Britain, Brian Tudor, The Quay, East Looe, Cornwall.
Appledore Shark Angling Club, W D Hutchings, The Royal George, Appledore, N Devon.
British Conger Club, R H J Quest, 5 Hill Crest, Mannamead, Plymouth. (Comp Sec) S Bealing, 4 Hillsborough Ave, Exeter.
Axminster Sea Angling Club, L Brown, 14 Bonners Glen, Axminster.
Barnstaple and District Angling Assoc, R Gotts, Elm Cottage, Park Rd, Braunton, N Devon.
Bridport and West Bay Sea Angling Club, Mrs Pettett, Home Farm View, Bothampton, Bridport.
Brixham Sea Angling Assoc, G Walton, 85 New Rd, Brixham.
Callington Sea Angling Club, R Nay, Greenhadges, Stoke Rd, Callington, Cornwall.
Tope Angling Assoc of Great Britain, R Paradise, Trelawney Rd, Camborne.
Dartmouth and District Angling Club, E Curl, 105 Britannia Ave, Townstall, Dartmouth.
Falmouth Docks Angling Club, M Miners, 7 Berkely Hill, Falmouth.
Fowey Angling Club, Mrs P Shelley, Chaswin, Trevarrick, St Austell, Cornwall.
Plymouth Sea Angling Club, J White, 41 Baring St, Greenbank, Plymouth.
Tor Bay Sea Angling Assoc, Mrs S Rowe, 59 Kenwyn Rd, Torquay.
Weymouth Sea Angling Club, J Churchouse, Rishon, Longfield Rd, Weymouth.
TACKLE DEALERS
The Tackle Shop, West Bay, Bridport, Dorset.
Anglers' Den, 13 Bolton St, Brixham.
Camborne's Sports, 28 Cross St, Camborne.
The Sportman's Rendezvous, 16 Fairfax Place, Dartmouth.
Bill's Tackle Box, 34 Arwenack St, Falmouth.
Fowey Sea Angling Centre, 20 Fore St, Fowey.
Frank Hoskin, The Quay, East Looe.
The Tackle Box, 13 Fore St, Mevagissey.
Central Sports, Central Square, Newquay.
Radford's, Duke St, Padstow.
Lanxon Bros, 18 Causeway Head, Penzance.
Osborne and Cragg, Bretonside, Plymouth.
The Tackle Box, Exeter St, Plymouth.
N J Lander, Fore St, St Ives.
Anglers' Corner, 15 Duke St, St Austell.
Treweeks Fishing Tackle, 18 East Hill, St Austell.
John Langdon, 20 Mary St, Truro.
Gilbert Sports, 4 St Albans St, Weymouth.

basis. Padstow is now the centre of the porbeagle and shark boom. Massive fish up to 465lb have been taken within a few hundred yards of the shore off Crackington Haven and much larger fish to 650lb have been lost.

Appledore in North Devon is another porbeagle shark port, but tidal conditions make fishing difficult on occasions. On certain low water springs it is necessary to leave harbour at 5.30 am.

In the Bude area, several secluded bays offer good beach fishing, although this can be spoilt by heavy rollers and surf. Thousands of elvers make their way up the River Strat in the spring and are followed by large bass. Spinning from the harbour wall can be productive.

Further north, the coastline becomes more exposed to winds from the Atlantic and there are few charter boat facilities. If a boat can be arranged, conger, skate and pollack are to be found, with some good bass around Appledore and Bideford.

Ilfracombe, Cheyne Beach, Capstone Point and Lee Bay offer good bass, pollack, wrasse, pouting, conger and dogfish.

Index